W9-DEU-123

Religions in

NORTH AMERICA

REV. DWAYNE THOMAN
& ROBERT SANTOS

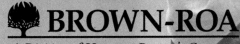
BROWN-ROA

A Division of Harcourt Brace & Company

Dubuque, Iowa

Consultants
Rabbi Norman M. Cohen—Judaism
Rev. Dennis Colter—Christianity
Henry Fawcett—Native American religion
Dr. Muzammil H. Siddiqi—Islam/Bahá'í
Dr. Jonathan Silk—Buddhism/Hinduism/Sikhism
Dr. Ted J. Solomon—Judaism
Jane Stembridge—Protestantism

Statistical information is from *The World Almanac and Book of Facts*, 1996;
World Almanac Books—an imprint of Funk and Wagnals; One
International Boulevard, Suite 444, Mahwah, NJ 07495-0017.
Christian scriptural quotations are from the New Revised Standard
Version—The New Oxford Annotated Bible with the
Apocryphal/Deuterocanonical Books, 1991; edited by Bruce M. Metzger
and Roland E. Murphy; New York: Oxford University Press, 200
Madison Avenue, New York, NY 10016.

Photo Credits
Nancy Anne Dawe—cover (lower middle) 150, 154, 163, 178, 189,
                197, 221
Mimi Forsyth—cover (top left), 2–3, 24, 30, 36, 277, 285
Robert Fried—100, 240, 260, 266, 289
Richard B. Levine—cover (lower right, top center), 67, 138, 230, 236, 250,
                272
Mary Messenger—225
Gene Plaisted, OSC—cover (middle right), 63, 79, 82, 92, 103, 108, 111,
                115, 119, 126, 142–43, 202
Frances M. Roberts—212
Robert Roethig—55, 87, 182, 297, 307
James L. Shaffer—7, 19, 50–51, 72, 134, 167, 171, 244, 256
Skjold Photography—cover (lower left), 43, 46–47
D. Jeanene Tiner—13, 22, 146–47, 311

Printed in the United States of America.

ISBN 0-697-17794-7

10   9   8   7   6   5   4   3   2   1

Contents

Chapter 1

Seek the Lord while he may be found, call upon him while he is near.

—*Isaiah 55:6*

After reading this chapter, you will be able to

- Write a definition of religion
- Describe several practical reasons for studying religion
- Explain how the study of religion can enhance your success in life
- Evaluate your own readiness to examine your worldview

Introduction to

RELIGION

Introduction

Rev. Roberts,

This is ex-Beatle, John Lennon. I've been wanting to write you but I guess I didn't want to face reality. I never do this, this is why I take drugs. Reality frightens me and paranoids me. True, I have a lot of money, being a Beatle, been all around the world, but basically I'm afraid to face the problems of life. Let me begin to say, I regret that I said the Beatles were more popular than Jesus. I don't even like myself anymore, guilt. My cousin, Marilyn McCabe has tried to help me. She told me you were praying for me. Here's my life . . . . Born in Liverpool, my mom died when I was little. My father left me at three. It was rough because just my aunt raised me. I never really liked her. I had an unhappy childhood, depressed a lot. Always missing my mom. Maybe if I'd had a father like you, I would have been a better person. My own father I hate with a passion because he left my mom and me, came to me after we found "A Hard Day's Night" and asked for some money. It made me so mad, Paul had to hold me down. I was going to kill him. I was under the influence of pills at that time. Married Cynthia, had a son John. I had to marry her, I really never loved her. She always embarrassed me walking around pregnant, not married, so I married her. Only one regret, John has had to suffer a lot because recently she's been married again. He and me never get to see each other because Paul and me never got along anymore and that's how the four ended . . . . As the song we wrote, Paul and me, "Money Can't Buy Me Love," it's true. The point is this, I want happiness. I don't want to keep up with drugs. Paul told me once, "you made fun of me for not taking drugs, but you will regret it in the end." . . . Explain to me what Christianity can do for me. Is it phony? Can He love me? I want out of hell . . . .

Sincerely, John

P.S. I am, I hate to say, under the influence of pills now. I can't stop. I only wish I could thank you for caring.

—David Edwin Harrell, Jr., Oral Roberts: An American Life (Bloomington, IN: Indiana University Press, 1985), 310.

John Lennon's sadness—caused by the turmoil of an unhappy childhood, the accumulation of wealth, and the lure of drugs—may very well be symptomatic of this age. Many people seek happiness in things that do not truly bring human happiness. Many times we discover that our priorities and values are misplaced; the material things of this world cannot buy those priorities and values that are most important and most satisfying. It is religion that tries to help human beings form a clear vision about life and find priorities and values that bring lasting happiness.

Tilling the Soil

People of every culture in every time have sought answers to questions which deal with more than the ordinary concerns of everyday life. Ordinary concerns include obtaining an adequate food supply, providing protection from the elements and from enemies, and taking care of one's health. Other concerns, not quite as basic, relate to the structure of social relationships, an adequate system of government, and a scientific understanding of the universe.

Forming a Worldview

More than these, people have sought—and continue to seek—answers to questions about the very experience of life. These are called "**ultimate questions.**" Ultimate questions are those which address concerns about the mysteries of life and ethics.

- Is there a God?
- Is there more than one God?
- If God exists, what is God like?
- Does God care for or relate to people in any way? If so, how?
- How did God come to exist?
- What does God "do"?
- How can people relate to God?
- How did all the parts of the universe come into existence?
- Will the universe exist forever, or will it come to an end?
- What is life?
- What is human life?
- Is there a purpose for human existence? If so, what?
- How do I find happiness in life?
- What is a human being?
- What will make my life successful?
- What is death?
- What, if anything, happens after death?
- Why is there so much suffering in the world?
- Does this suffering have a purpose?
- Can anything be done about it?
- How are human beings to relate to one another?
- How are we to relate to the universe?

These are ultimate questions. One's responses to these questions form a person's **worldview**. A *worldview* is an overall perspective about the meaning of existence.

ultimate questions
questions which address essential mysteries of life and ethical concerns. For example, "Does God exist?"

worldview
from the German *weltanschauungen*, it is an individual's or group's response to ultimate questions

Religions deal with worldviews. In fact, the word *religion* comes from a Latin word (*religare*), which means "to bind or tie up, to fasten together." Thus religions attempt to bind together responses to ultimate questions to form a certain worldview. Religious systems seek to articulate a worldview which helps the members of a specific religion make sense of life and its meaning.

In this course you will be introduced to the worldview of many different religions. These views will range from ones which are very familiar to you to those which may seem very different from your own perspective. All of them will help you in the formation of your own worldview as you seek your own answers to life's ultimate questions. Emphasis will be placed upon religions in North America.

Planting the Seed

Common Roots

Religion and humanity are thoroughly interrelated. They share the same root. As a result, it is virtually impossible to separate the origin or history of one from the other. For example, if one studies the lives of ancient human beings, one will inevitably encounter traces of ancient religion.

Europe

On the continent of Europe, evidence of ancient religion exists in prehistoric cave paintings. In cave paintings found throughout modern-day France and Spain, one comes face to face with the very influences that shaped the lives of early humankind. We call these influences *religion*.

The paintings, many of which are more than twenty thousand years old, are among the oldest known artwork. The Niaux cave of Ariege, France, is noteworthy for its Bison with Superposed Arrows (15,000–13,000 B.C.E.). This cave painting has deep gouges in it, which quite possibly were made by spears. The purpose of the gouges is unknown. What was the influence that resulted in this behavior?

It has been theorized that the artist who created the bison image looked upon it as a real bison. In the artist's mind, control exerted over the bison image translated into control over a real-life bison. It is believed that prehistoric hunters threw spears at these images to guarantee a bountiful hunt the next day.

North America

On the continent of North America, evidence of ancient religion exists in the form of ground-up red hematite. Nearly eight thousand years ago, the ancestors of modern-day Native Americans began to depend less on hunting and more on gathering and foraging. Large bands of migratory hunters broke into smaller groups, such as the Red Paint People of the Northeast.

The Red Paint People are noteworthy for lining the graves of their dead with ground-up red hematite. The purpose of the ground-up red hematite is unknown. What was the influence that resulted in this behavior?

It has been theorized that the redness of the hematite represented life-sustaining blood, which enabled the body to live on. Ground-up red hematite was used continuously for nearly 2,500 years.

Defining Religion

It would be helpful at this time to develop a definition of religion. What is religion? You may be surprised to learn that this question is very difficult to answer. Religion has been defined and redefined countless times.

Some Definitions

These are just a few of the more well-known definitions of religion. They have been offered by individuals who, in many cases, spent a lifetime studying religion and thinking about its role in human affairs. According to these individuals, religion is:

An Amish woman goes about her daily work.

- *a set of symbolic forms and acts which relate [people] to the ultimate conditions of [their] existence* (Robert Bellah)

- *a unified system of beliefs and practices relative to sacred things, that is to say, things set apart* (Emile Durkheim)

- *the relation of [a person] to himself [or herself]* (Ludwig Feuerbach)

- *a system of symbols which acts to establish powerful, pervasive, and long-lasting moods and motivations in [people]* (Clifford Geertz)

- *the sigh of the oppressed creature, the heart of a heartless world . . . the soul of soulless conditions . . . the opium of the people* (Karl Marx)

- *a set of beliefs, practices, and institutions which [people] have evolved in various societies* (Talcott Parsons)

- *ultimate concern* (Paul Tillich)

- *a set of rituals, rationalized by myth, which mobilizes supernatural powers for the purpose of achieving or preventing transformations of state in [human beings] or nature* (Anthony Wallace)

- *a system of beliefs and practices by means of which a group of people struggles with [the] ultimate problems of human life* (J. Milton Yinger)

All of these definitions of religion are thought-provoking—even the shortest of them. On the one hand they are possessed of depth, and on the other they barely scratch the surface of what we call *religion*. It is often said that "religion binds people together." Though this assertion is correct in some instances, it does not amount to a definition of religion that can be used in all circumstances by all peoples. For, as evidenced in society, religion sometimes is a source of division among people.

Followers of various Middle Eastern religions, or religions that originated in the Middle East (Judaism, Zarathustrianism, Christianity, Islam, Baha'i), tend to think of religion as the sacred part of life. They separate the sacred from the secular. From their perspective, what is set apart for religious purposes or uses is sacred, and what is left over is secular. The synagogue, the temple, the church, the mosque, or the house of worship reinforces the idea of a clear and distinct separation between the sacred and the secular.

Those who follow various Asian religions (Hinduism, Buddhism, Sikhism) as well as followers of the Native American religions of North America espouse a different view. From their perspective, religion is not just the sacred part of life. For them, all of life is sacred. In sum, religion is part of the sacred, not merely the sacred part.

In light of such differing perspectives, care must be taken when attempting to define religion. Specific, far-reaching definitions of religion are not useful; they do not stand the test of time. Within a short period, these definitions are replaced. For this reason, this book has adopted a very basic definition of religion, which hopefully will not exclude, offend, or be rendered obsolete.

Religion is often described as a major religious group with a belief system and a set of religious practices. We might add to that description: Religion includes "a collection of specific influences that affects or alters behavior."

Understanding Distinctions

Understanding the following distinctions will assist your study. These terms will be used in the sense described in this textbook.

Distinguish religion and denomination. Although we tend to use these terms rather loosely, it is better to contain their definitions somewhat. It is more correct to think of religion as the broad religious branch and a **denomination** as a specific group within it. For example, Christianity is the religion and Lutheranism is a denomination. Judaism is the religion, but it has several branches within it.

Distinguish belief and practice. Beliefs refer to those central concepts which a religion holds to be most important. These are basic to the religion and generally change very little throughout history or from one group to another within the same religious family. **Practices** flow from these beliefs. Practices may change considerably from time to time and group to group. For example, all Jews believe in the importance of the Torah or the Law, but the ways in which Jews have lived it out has varied throughout history and varies today from one branch to another.

religion

a major religious group with a belief system and a set of religious practices; includes a collection of specific influences that affects or alters behavior

denomination

a subset of a religion, a group within a larger religious branch

beliefs

those central concepts which a religion holds to be most important

practices

actions and prayers which flow from a religion's beliefs

Distinguish religion and ethics. A common perception, particularly in the West, is that religion deals primarily with ethics, that is, with do's and don'ts, how one should act. Actually, religions deal more with responses to those fundamental questions about the mysteries of life. Ethical concerns then flow from those responses. The extent to which religions respond to ethical questions varies from one group to the next.

ethics

how one should act; in a religion, determined by the response to fundamental questions dealing with the mysteries of life

Celebrating Religious Identity and Diversity

In 1893, a group calling itself the World's Parliament of Religion met at Chicago, Illinois. For seventeen days, representatives of the world's religions explored their differences and similarities. Unknown to them, the parliament set into motion the academic study of religion as well as the interfaith movement. In the United States, it ignited interest in the religions of Asia, particularly Hinduism.

One hundred years later, the World's Parliament of Religion once again converged on Chicago. For eight days, 6,500 participants from fifty-six countries gathered at the Palmer House to celebrate religious identity and diversity. Native Americans, Jews, Zarathustrians, Christians, Muslims, Baha'is, Hindus, Buddhists, Sikhs, and many others came together for the occasion. An observer of the event wrote: "The Palmer House and the streets of Chicago were filled with . . . costumes, languages and accents, ritual smells and sounds, and . . . goodwill."

Participants did more than celebrate. They focused their attention on a host of environmental problems. Speakers asserted that the world's religions could solve environmental problems, termed "matters of the human heart and will."

The Parliament issued the document *Toward a Global Ethic*, which many saw as the highlight of the eight-day meeting. The document drew upon the "core values in all the major religious and spiritual traditions." *Toward a Global Ethic* underscores the need of religions to cooperate in order to solve problems. The document's language is rooted in "humanity's common wisdom" as opposed to the scriptures of any one religion. It represents a common approach to the cultural and environmental problems now confronting humankind.

The parliament's work is now being carried on by the Council for a Parliament of the World's Religions (CPWR), which helped to organize the gathering. The council has established the (Chicago) Metropolitan Interreligious Initiative, which brings people of different faiths together. The council has conducted discussions aimed at establishing a permanent, international interreligious body. *United Religions* has been suggested as a name for the organization. Talk has also been devoted to the creation of a World Interreligious Academy, which would serve as a center for interreligious study, dialogue, and cooperation.

Let's Talk about It . . .

1. What do you consider to be "matters of the human heart and will"?
2. What do you think are some of the "core values in all the major religious and spiritual traditions"?
3. Do you think it would be helpful to have a center for interreligious study, dialogue, and cooperation? Why?

Taking Root

The Influences of Religions

Influences can be classified or categorized. Historical events, beliefs, practices, and observances can be considered influences, providing that they change behavior. People must accept, or recognize, these influences if the influences are to have any power in their lives. Once again, in very broad terms, a religion includes a collection of specific influences (historical events, beliefs, practices, and observances) that affects or alters peoples' behavior (thoughts, words, deeds).

Let's see if this definition is useful, or applicable. To accomplish this task, we will focus on an historical event, a belief, a practice, and an observance taken from religions native to North America, the Middle East, and Asia.

Historical Event as Influence

The Washani religion is a Native American religion which originated in North America. Over the centuries it has assumed three different forms: aboriginal, Christian, and revived.

The prophet Smohalla revived the Washani religion. *Washani* is a Shahaptian word meaning "dancers." Smohalla was influenced by the Paiute prophet Wovoka, originator of the Ghost Dance. Both taught their followers that non-stop dancing would enable them to regain control of their land, and cause them to be carried up into the sky on feathers. A number of Native American tribes believed that the Ghost Dance, which sometimes went on for several days, would end the power of whites and usher in a period of prosperity.

The historical event: In 1890, at Wounded Knee, South Dakota, a U.S. 7th Cavalry regiment met a group of Native Americans en route to a Ghost Dance. Three hundred fifty Native Americans were massacred. The widespread Ghost Dance came to an abrupt end. (In the early twentieth century, the U.S. government moved against another Native American dance. It outlawed the Sun Dance of the Plains tribes in 1910.)

This historical event (U.S. troops killing participants of a Ghost Dance) altered, and continues to alter, the behavior of those who belong to the Washani religion. This historical event is one of the influences important to the Washani religion.

Historical event changes behavior: Followers of the Washani religion are reluctant to share details of their religion, especially of the dances, with outsiders.

Belief as Influence

Christianity was expressed in a number of ways in the first centuries, but there was an overall sense of continuity. Disagreements existed and were dealt with, although harshly at times. While different philosophies and theologies dominated at different times, the church's divisions were not, in the end, overwhelming. However, in 431 C.E., a serious rupture occurred and was followed by a series of other ruptures in 451, 1054, and 1534. As a result of these ruptures, several separate and distinct varieties of Christianity came into existence: Eastern, Roman Catholic, Orthodox, and Anglican. Each of these groups parted ways with the others partially because of differences in belief. After the separation, more differences in belief usually developed, and more divisions took place. On the other hand, the Churches of Eastern, Roman Catholic, Orthodox, and Anglican Christianity hold several beliefs in common—and have held them without wavering.

Belief: One of these beliefs has to do with the bread and wine blessed at the main worship service of each group. Members in these churches share bread and wine, as Jesus and his closest disciples shared bread and wine at the Last Supper. The Churches of Eastern, Roman Catholic, Orthodox, Anglican, and Lutheran Christianity understand this sharing in the same way. According to their belief, at a certain point the bread and wine become the body and blood of Jesus. The members of these churches believe that Jesus is truly present in the blessed bread and wine.

Belief changes behavior: Eastern, Roman Catholic, Orthodox, and Anglican Christians bow, genuflect, and, at times, kneel before the bread and wine after it has been consecrated (changed into the body and blood of Jesus). They are careful to avoid dropping a crumb or spilling a drop.

Practice as Influence

Islam is another religion that originated in the Middle East. The followers of Islam, or Muslims, are called upon to fulfill the Five Pillars of Islam: shahadah (profession of faith), salat (prayer or worship), zakat (almsgiving or charity), sawm (fasting), and hajj (pilgrimage).

Practice: Muslims fulfill salat (prayer and worship) by turning toward Makkah (Mecca) and praying. They do this five times a day.

Practice changes behavior: At dawn, noon, mid-afternoon, sunset, and evening, Muslims simply stop what they are doing, turn toward the holy city of Makkah, and offer prayers. Sometimes these prayers are offered in public places, which may be non-Muslim.

Observance as Influence

Hinduism is a religion that originated in Asia. Most of the world's Hindus live in India, which each year is the scene of very colorful festivals.

Observance: One of the most popular festivals is Holi, which takes place in the spring. It is an occasion for Hindus to recall the life of Krishna, an incarnation of the god Vishnu. The celebration reminds Hindus that divinity will ultimately triumph over demonic forces.

Observance changes behavior: On Holi, class barriers descend, and people mix freely. Hindus throw gulal (colored powder) on people. Sometimes the colored powder is added to water and sprayed. Participants also make a large bonfire, which symbolizes enlightenment.

Why Study Religion?

At first glance, it might seem that the study of religion in such a pluralistic society as ours would be a waste of time. To some people, religion doesn't seem to be as important as it once was in history. A closer look, however, will reveal that there might very well be some quite practical reasons for studying religion, even if one is not particularly religious or interested in forming a worldview.

First of all, anyone expecting to be successful in life needs to know about the world in which he or she lives. Just as one needs to know about the course of human history, the principles of science, great works of art and literature, the basics of mathematics, business practices, and the structure of government, so too one needs to know about religion. Religion has been and continues to be an integral part of human life. Whether we like it not, religion is a fact. Religion and religious views have had and continue to have a determining influence upon human activity. Wars have been—and continue to be—fought for religious reasons. Many people have been abused in the name of religion, but religion has also uplifted and helped many people. Knowledge in the field of religion, as well as in all the other areas of academic study, will help you understand the perspective of other people. It will help you understand why people do the things they do. Even a basic, general knowledge in this area can help you understanding the world in which you live.

Second, your knowledge of religion will help you relate more successfully with other people. As explained earlier, religion has a determining influence upon people's worldviews. You may very well discover, for example, that your knowledge in religion will help you in the area of dating. Having a general knowledge of a religious perspective may help you better understand your dating partner. At least it will give you a starting point. Sometimes in the world of business, especially on the international level, it is necessary to know the religious perspective of another culture. Your knowledge of a particular religion could very well prevent a major *faux pas*. Even if you are not religious yourself, your knowledge of religion will help you in the area of relationship skills.

Third, and probably most important, the study of religion can dramatically enhance your character in many ways. It will help you to set aside stereotypes and thus deepen your respect for all people. Surely respect for all people is a necessary quality for successful living in our global village. Your study of religion will open you to fresh and new ways of looking at responses to those ultimate questions. It will broaden your perspective. In a world often broken by division, the study of religion will help you recognize the unity that binds the human family together.

Forming Your Worldview

More than this, the study of religion will help you in the formation of your own worldview. No one knows what the future holds for us. Western culture since the sixteenth century has seen increasing diversity and change. Our present experience tells us that change will happen at an ever increasing rate. Just consider the rate of change in technology in your own lifetime, especially in computers. Your ability to adapt to change will directly affect your level of success in the future. At the same time, human beings need stability. A person's worldview can be that element of stability. A worldview is like a lens through which we look at life; it guides the present and directs us into the future. Your worldview, thoughtfully formed and deeply rooted, will serve you well in the twenty-first century.

It would be wise to guard against **syncretism.** Syncretism is the collection of many different beliefs. It would be similar to shopping for an outfit without regard to how all the items fit together. Studying various religions is not like going shopping. A mismatched outfit you put together for "clash day" at school may serve you for the purpose of the day, but it will not serve you if you going to a party, attending church, or participating in the prom. A syncretistic worldview may serve you for a short span of life, but it will not hold up under the stress of many different life situations and changes in the future. A worldview is not like clothing worn on the outside; it comes from the inside and must be deeply rooted. A worldview should serve you in dealing with many situations of life.

Incorporating practices from other religions need not result in syncretism.

syncretism

a collection; in religion, a collection of various beliefs not especially related to each other

The formation of a worldview does not mean that one abandons one's own religious perspective. On the contrary, it would be more helpful to consider your own religion as "home base." This is your worldview at the present. Allow your study of other religions to first uncover the richness of your own. Perhaps there is a particular belief or practice that already exists in your own religious tradition, but you are unaware of it. The discovery of this tradition will enhance your appreciation of your own religion. Allow your study of other religions to enhance the beliefs and practices you already have. Perhaps you discover in another religion a belief that affirms that which you already believe. Or perhaps you discover a belief which is directly contrary to yours. In either case, your own belief can be strengthened.

A worldview need not be rigid and inflexible. It might change slightly or dramatically. You may very well discover that your life experience will lead you to amend your worldview. Over the course of a lifetime, you may expand, broaden, deepen your worldview many times. But this change in worldview happens best if you have the foundation of a solid home base. You should not change for the sake of change. Any change you make should help you develop a worldview that will serve you well.

Religious Tolerance

Huston Smith, author of *The World's Religions*, provides another insightful and succinct answer to the question of why we should study religions. He writes: "The surest way to the heart of a people is through their religion." In other words, the study of religion fosters understanding of the other; it helps people relate to different kinds of people. In a society such as our own, which is multiracial, multiethnic, and multireligious, the study of religion can produce enormous benefits.

By studying religion, people recognize what unites them; they come to recognize the similarity of their histories, beliefs, practices, and observances. The Hindu teacher Sri Ramakrishna was one of countless individuals to notice the similarities among religions. On one occasion, he spoke about these similarities: "With sincerity and earnestness one can realize God through all religions. The Vaishnavas will realize God, and so will the Shaktas, the Vedantists, and the Brahmos. The Mussalmans and Christians will realize Him too. All will certainly realize God if they are earnest and sincere."

What is your level of religious tolerance? Most of us believe that we are tolerant of other religions, or would be tolerant if confronted by a person belonging to a religion or religious tradition other than our own. Until one is tested, one does not know the degree of one's religious tolerance. The best test occurs in the midst of a real-life situation involving real people. Though the following test does not meet this criterion, it should give you at least an idea of how you would behave when meeting people who belong to a religion other than yours.

The following test was modeled on the Test for Tolerance designed by the Ontario Centre for Religious Tolerance.

Test for Tolerance

Test Instructions

This test assumes that you are not a Jew, Muslim, or Hindu. If you belong to one of these religions, you can still take the test, but please inform your teacher so that he or she can make the necessary adjustments.

This test has six steps:

Step One: Write down the word *Jew* on a sheet of paper. Read the eight options listed below. Upon learning that a follower of Judaism had moved into the house or apartment next door, what would you do? Choose the option that best describes your probable reaction.

Step Two: Skim over chapter 3. Repeat the test.

Step Three: Repeat the test, assuming that the person is a Muslim. In your mind Islam is a Middle Eastern religion whose followers participate in jihad, which, according to the media, means "holy war."

Step Four: Skim over chapter 8. Repeat the test.

Step Five: Repeat the test, assuming that the person is a Hindu. You once noticed a woman with a dot on her forehead knocking at the person's front door. And you have seen people doing unusual stretching exercises in the backyard.

Step Six: Skim over chapter nine. Repeat the test.

The Test

Imagine that a person who follows a religion other than your own moves into the house or apartment next door. What would you do? Actually, there are a number of options.

Option One: Ask the person to describe his or her religion; offer a description of your faith, if the person is interested. Ask the person whether you can accompany him or her to worship; extend an invitation to your place of worship, if he or she is interested.

Option Two: Ask the person to describe his or her religion, and offer to reciprocate.

Option Three: Treat the person in the same way that you treat other neighbors; simply ignore the issue of religion.

Option Four: Suggest to the person that he or she consider converting to your religion. Do not express any interest in learning about his or her religion.

Option Five: Tell the person that he or she should convert to your religion; repeat this often. Do not express any interest in learning about his or her religion.

Option Six: Say to the person, "This is a Christian neighborhood and a Christian country." Tell him or her to move away.

Option Seven: Encourage your neighbors to make life miserable for the person so that he or she will move away.

Option Eight: Spray-paint a message on the front of the person's house or apartment; break one of his or her car windows; leave a dead rat on his or her front door, and so on.

Test Interpretation

The test provides an indication of your level of religious tolerance. Options One and Two actively promote religious tolerance. Option Three passively promotes religious tolerance. Option Four expresses religious intolerance. Option Five expresses annoying religious intolerance. Option Six represents serious religious intolerance and harassment. Option Seven represents very serious religious intolerance and harassment. Option Eight constitutes extreme religious intolerance and criminal harassment.

Did your level of religious tolerance increase upon learning more about the person's religion?

Raise Your Level of Religious Tolerance

These are just a few ways that you can raise the level of your religious tolerance:

One: Make a conscious effort to attain a higher level of religious tolerance. In other words, move to a lower number on the list of options.

Two: Telephone a place of worship, such as a synagogue, temple, mosque, or church, and ask to be given a tour.

Three: Ask someone who follows a religion or religious tradition other than your own if you can accompany him or her to worship.

Four: Ask this person to join you the next time you worship.

Five: Read about other religions and religious traditions at libraries, World Wide Web sites, and so on.

Growing and Blooming

A cursory look at the listing of churches in the yellow pages may be a mind-boggling experience. With such a variety of religions, it may seem impossible to gain a good grasp of all these religious views. Your study of religions will help you to break down the complexity and recognize how these groups share common roots.

How to Study Religions

First of all, it is helpful to distinguish between the eastern and western religious perspective. Study the accompanying Chart 1. Universally, human beings perceive a fundamental and common human "problem." That problem might be defined as "separation" from ultimate reality—whether one defines ultimate reality as a personal God or an impersonal force. The East and West have different ways of responding to this common problem. Each explains the cause, consequences, and solution in different ways. Carefully consider the response of each. Also study Chart 2. This chart shows how eastern and western people think differently concerning God, time, importance of the individual, and attitude toward the world.

Chart 1
Fundamental Human Problem: Separation

West

Cause: sin

Consequences: overcome sin, find forgiveness, need redemption

Source of revelation: a personal God who speaks to individuals and to the group God cares about the message; calls for a decision

Salvation from: sin: pride, disobedience, rebellion

Means of salvation: God saves; requires a personal act of the will

Redemption: at the end of time as part of a group

East

Cause: a type of ignorance

Consequences: overcome ignorance, find the truth, put aside ignorance

Source of revelation: an impersonal abstract being or reality; the divine is removed from human-like care: free response

Salvation from: state of being in ignorance

Means of salvation: actualize oneself

Redemption: attain oneness with ultimate being

—*Adapted from Ward J. Fellows,* Religions East and West *(New York: Holt, Rinehart and Winston, 1979), 433–36.*

Chart 2
East–West Differences in Thinking

West

God

A personal being who thinks and loves

God is immanent (everywhere) yet . . .

God is transcendent (beyond)

Time: Linear

The individual: Important

Attitude toward world: Transform, change, make it better

East

God

An absolute and unknowable, impersonal "that"

Monism: everything is part of one God and/or polytheism— many gods

Remote, transcendental force

Time: Cyclical

The individual: Lose identity (as a drop of water in the ocean)

Attitude toward world: Non-interest, accept things as they are

Second, try to get a grasp of a religion's basic concepts. The worldview of any religion will have certain core beliefs from which flow other beliefs and practices. It is simply not possible—nor does it make sense—to try to learn all the details about a particular religion. Use a good reference to answer specific questions. Gaining a grasp of the religion's core concepts (which are usually simple and straightforward) will help you understand the sense of the whole. Groups of religious bodies within a specific religion—for example, Christianity—will share many common beliefs. However, each group may emphasize a specific belief more than the others. Look for these similarities and differences.

Third, gain a grasp of the historical development of religions. Religions are important to the events of human history and to one another. Consider how a particular religion relates to other events of history with which you are already familiar. One church body may flow out of another. Often, a specific church body develops as a response to another. For example, in the East, Buddhism developed as a reaction to Hinduism. In the West, Protestant Christianity developed as a reaction to Catholicism. Also look for similarities of religious emphases. For example, a desire to simplify, emphasis on the intellectual, or emphasis on the affective are patterns which repeat themselves in history and in religions. Consult maps for areas, countries, and cities. Draw diagrams and charts which help your understanding.

Reaping the Fruit

Some Words of Caution

Don't expect religions to be perfect. Don't expect that any specific religious worldview will be totally consistent. Often a religious system is highly consistent within itself, but it does not appear to be so from an outsider's point of view. Be patient with your perception of a religion as your understanding grows.

Don't expect individuals who are members of a specific religion to be perfect. Not all Jews place God first in their life; not all Moslems submit to Allah; and Christians are still trying to master the fine art of loving their neighbor. In a sense, when it comes to the practice of religious belief, everyone is a hypocrite. After all, that is one function of religion: to call individuals to a more integrated worldview and a higher level of morality.

Don't judge a specific religion as "stupid." You may disagree with certain beliefs and practices, and you may be sure you could never accept a certain religion as your own. Recognize the difference in worldview, but also try to be tolerant of the other. Sometimes it helps to gain a deeper understanding of the cultural background of a specific religion. Finally, don't stereotype individuals who belong to a specific religion. They have a right to be understood and accepted as the individuals they are and appreciated for the religious background from which they come.

Problems

Do bad religions exist? The labels *good* and *bad* can be applied to anything, including religions. What matters is who does the labeling. This book does not use these labels, yet it acknowledges that good and bad religions do exist. What we know of "bad religion" comes from people who once belonged to a religion, or religious tradition, which they now consider to be bad. As these people look back, they judge as bad the influences that comprise the religion or religious tradition. A definition of bad religion is based on their descriptions. Often a bad religion, or religious tradition, is known as a **cult.** Two points must be made about cults: (1) a cult is not always a small group, (2) a cult is not always trying to extort money from a person.

What is a cult? In short, a cult is an organization characterized by mind control, charismatic leadership, deception, exclusivity, alienation, exploitation, and a totalitarian worldview.

Mind control: The group subjects people to coercive persuasion or behavior modification techniques.

Charismatic leadership: The group's leader, surrounded by a handful of close associates, claims to be divine or to possess special knowledge. He or she possesses absolute power and privilege, and demands total obedience.

Deception: The group's recruiting and fund-raising activities contain hidden objectives. Front groups are sometimes used.

Exclusivity: Members of the group are secretive or vague about their activities and beliefs.

Alienation: Group members are separated from their family, friends, and society at large. Members begin to look upon the group as their family, and adopt the group's values. Subtle or abrupt personality changes often accompany alienation.

cult
an organization characterized by mind control, charismatic leadership, deception, exclusivity, alienation, exploitation, and a totalitarian worldview

Cults can use even the most modern of methods to reach possible new recruits.

Exploitation: Group members are pressured into donating to special projects, taking expensive courses, purchasing literature, or participating in inappropriate sexual activities, including child molestation.

Totalitarian worldview: The leader's goals, which are known as "group goals," come first; they are more important than members' goals or even society's goals. The totalitarian worldview includes the "we/they syndrome." The group resorts to unethical behavior to achieve the leader's goals.

Separation of Church and State

Why is the separation between church and state important? Each year, the religious fabric of United States society becomes more complex, more diverse, more elaborate, and more intricate; above all it grows steadily more beautiful. It has been estimated that the United States is home to nearly two thousand religions.

Three hundred years ago, the number of religious buildings on present-day U.S. soil was very small. Period records show that there were 75 Congregationalist churches, 41 Anglican churches, 13 Dutch Reformed churches, 12 Roman Catholic churches, 5 Presbyterian churches, 4 Baptist churches, 4 Lutheran churches, and 1 Jewish synagogue.

The vast number of flourishing religions in the United States stems from this country's historic separation of church and state. A society in which only one religion exists, or a society whose members follow one religion, does not have to maintain a strict separation between church and state. The United States has never been such a society.

The first amendment to the United States Constitution embodies the principle of church-state separation. That amendment reads: "Congress shall make no law respecting an establishment of religion, or prohibiting the free exercise thereof; or abridging the freedom of speech, or of the press; or the right of the people peaceably to assemble, and to petition the government for a redress of grievances."

The survival of a pluralistic democracy, especially one that is multiracial, multi-ethnic, and multi-religious, depends on the enforcement of such an amendment. To explain this point, a high school history teacher gave this example:

Let's say that most people belong to "Religion V." They are strict vegetarians; they eat neither fish nor fowl. Most legislators belong to Religion V, and they decide that it is wrong for restaurants to serve meat. Restaurants should offer only vegetarian cuisine. Their view becomes law. Is there a separation between church and state in this society? The private religious practice of not eating meat has become a public law, which has made eating meat illegal. Do you think that those who belong to Religion V will have a problem with this law? The answer is no.

If they don't, who will? Not everyone belongs to Religion V. A fair num-
ber of people belong to "Religion M." Those who belong to Religion M
are not vegetarians; they are meat-eaters. From their perspective, this law
violates the first amendment. Congress has blurred the distinction
between church and state. It has made a "law respecting the establish-
ment of religion"—Religion V.

The first amendment's establishment clause was designed to prevent this from occurring. The clause reads: "Congress shall make no law respecting an establishment of religion . . . ." This clause has been used by the U.S. Supreme Court to settle a number of legal disputes, many of which involved public schools, public office holders, and public buildings. Essentially, the establishment clause of the first amendment requires government to remain "neutral toward religion." This means that government "cannot authorize a church, cannot pass laws that aid or favor one religion over another, cannot pass laws that favor religious belief over nonbelief, cannot force a person to profess a belief."

The following are among the cases involving religion that the Supreme Court has used the establishment clause to settle.

- In *Engel v. Vitale* (1962), the Court found school prayer to be un-constitutional. In *Abington School District v. Schempp* (1963), the Court found Bible reading over the school intercom to be unconsti-tutional.

- In *Stone v. Graham* (1980), the Court found posting the Ten Commandments in schools to be unconstitutional.

- In *Wallace v. Jaffree* (1985), the Court found that state laws enforcing a moment of silence in schools have a religious purpose and are therefore unconstitutional.

- In *Edwards v. Aquillard* (1987), the Court found a state law requiring equal treatment for creationism to have a religious purpose and to be therefore unconstitutional.

- In *Torcaso v. Watkins* (1961), the Court held that Maryland could not require applicants for public office to swear that they believed in the existence of God.

- In *Allegheny County v. the ACLU [American Civil Liberties Union]* (1989), the Court ruled that nativity scenes could not be displayed inside of government buildings.

While many people feel the Court, in these decisions, has taken the establishment clause seriously, others believe the Court has gone well beyond the intent of the law to not favor one religion over another. The debate continues. Whatever the outcome, it is obvious that there exists in the United States a far stronger tolerance for religions than is seen in many other countries today.

Conclusion

> *If the thought comes to you that everything that you have thought about God is mistaken and that there is no God, do not be dismayed. It happens to many people. But do not think that the source of your unbelief is that there is not God. If you no longer believe in the God in whom you believed before, this comes from the fact that there was something wrong with your belief, and you must strive to grasp better that which you call God. When a savage ceases to believe in his wooden God, this does not mean that there is no God, but only that the true God is not made of wood.*
>
> *— Leo Tolstoy*

The study of religions can be very objective, and it can be very personal. You may find yourself wrestling with ultimate questions. You may wrestle with your response. It may feel a bit frightening at first to face ultimate questions. It may feel more comfortable not to bother with these "deep" questions of life. (Indeed, it *is* more comfortable!) But avoiding these questions means passing up an opportunity to deal with questions which recur throughout the course of one's life. You won't always find the answer to a question, but your honest attention to the ultimate questions addressed in this course will enrich you, deepen your appreciation for life, and enhance your success in the twenty-first century.

"Faith is a kind of climbing instinct, which draws us upward and onward."
—William Ralph Inge

Discovering

1. Be sure that you can define each of the vocabulary words.

2. What do the various definitions of religion in this chapter have in common? How do you define religion?

3. State and explain the influences of religions.

4. Name some practical reasons for studying religion.

5. Name and explain some study skills which will assist you in your study of religion.

Exploring

1. Identify four to six reasons for studying religion. Explain how they can help you personally to be more successful in life.

2. Discuss in a small group the positive effects of building a worldview from a specific religious home base.

3. In a small group discussion, compare the relative merits of a syncretistic worldview with one which is a more integrated system. Which will serve your long-term success better? Why?

Integrating

1. What are some stereotypes about specific religions or individuals you need to deal with before embarking on an honest study of religion?

2. Assess your worldview right now. How much have you wrestled with the ultimate questions posed in the text? List those you feel you have a good response to. List those you need to deal with more. Keep these handy for reference as you study various religions.

3. What other ultimate questions do you think should be part of a worldview?

4. How does the quote from Tolstoy on page 22 relate to the formation of a religious worldview?

5. Discuss in a small group how the study of religion could improve human relations in your own community.

Words to Know

beliefs	religion
cult	syncretism
denomination	worldview
ethics	ultimate questions
practices	

Chapter 2

After reading this chapter, you will be able to

- Identify elements of the Native American worldview
- Explain common characteristics of Native American religions
- Assess the value of aspects of Native American religions for life today

NATIVE AMERICAN

Religions

Introduction

Jay Cody, an eighteen-year-old member of the Seneca nation, is proud of his heritage and is glad that Native American contributions are finally beginning to be appreciated. He explains his feelings below.

> *Throughout most of my education in school, I have learned only of the so-called primitive and barbaric lifestyles of the early Native Americans. If it weren't for my parents' memories and stories about our heritage, I would never have grown to appreciate my own roots and history. Recently, I was really excited to hear my high school teacher talk about Native Americans in a positive way. I was so proud to hear that Iroquois ideals inspired the United States Constitution.*

The Iroquois Influence

The Handsome Lake religion is a Native American religion, which originated in North America. Followers can be found among six tribes, or nations: the Mohawk (People Who Possess the Flint), the Onondaga (People on the Hills), the Seneca (Great Hill People), the Oneida (Granite People), the Cayuga (People at the Mucky Land), and the Tuscarora (Shirt Wearing People). The Seneca prophet Handsome Lake founded the religion, which combined many Native American and Christian beliefs. Essentially, Handsome Lake revitalized the efforts of Deganawidah, who unified the tribes and formed the Iroquois Confederacy.

The Iroquois Confederacy has been described as "the world's first federal-style government, in which internal affairs were left to each nation, while overriding issues of 'national security' . . . were decided by a Grand Council." The confederacy governed itself according to a fifteenth-century constitution. The Constitution of the Iroquois Nation directly influenced the United States Constitution, especially the Bill of Rights. The Iroquois constitution passed from one generation to the next by word of mouth, until it was finally written down. It is both a religious and a political document.

Paragraph twenty-six refers to Iroquois leaders as "mentors and spiritual guides of their people." It directs them to say: "Hearken, that peace may continue unto future days! Always listen to the words of the Great Creator, for he has spoken. United people, let not evil find lodging in your minds." And Paragraph Nine appears to have inspired the American legislative process. It reads: "First the question shall be passed upon by the Mohawk and Seneca Lords, then it shall be discussed and passed by the Oneida and Cayuga Lords. Their decisions shall then be referred to the Onondaga Lords (Fire Keepers) for final judgment."

The ideals embedded in the Iroquois constitution eventually entered the colonial mainstream. In 1754, King George II of Great Britain sent Benjamin Franklin to New York to form an alliance with the Iroquois Confederacy. Franklin's observations of the Iroquois system inspired his plan to unite the colonies in the face of a French threat. He called for "one general government to be formed in America . . . within and under which Government, each Colony [would] retain its present Constitution." Such Iroquois ideals were later resurrected by those who framed the Articles of Confederation and the United States Constitution.

Tilling the Soil

The term *Native American religion* refers to hundreds of Native American religions that developed and evolved on the continents of North and South America over the last fifty thousand years. This chapter deals with nine Native American religions from North America which continue to endure: Bole-Maru religion, Chinigchinix religion, Drum religion, Handsome Lake religion, Indian Shaker religion, Kuksu religion, Prophet Dance religion, Washani religion, and the Native American Church.

To facilitate the study of Native American religion, scholars have typically divided the continent of **North America** into **culture areas**: Eastern Woodlands (Northeast and Southeast), Southwest, Great Plains, Great Basin, Plateau, California (Intermountain and Peninsula), Northwest Coast, Far North (Subarctic), Arctic, Mesoamerica (or Middle American), and Circum-Caribbean. Because the Mesoamerica and Circum-Caribbean culture areas fall completely outside of United States boundaries, they will not receive coverage here.

The study of Native American religion overlaps with the study of Native Americans, the people among whom these religions took root.

Native American culture areas
divisions of Native Americans, primarily based on geography

Planting the Seed

The study of Native American history can be divided into two broad periods: before the time of contact (before contact with Europeans) and after the time of contact (after contact with Europeans). The first period includes the arrival of Paleo-Siberians and Aleuts/Inuits; the shift from hunting to gathering; and the emergence of the Adena, Hopewell, Mississippian, Mongollon, Hohokam, and Anasazi cultures of the Formative Period. The second period includes the arrival of Europeans; Spanish, English, and American interactions with Native Americans; and the suppression of Native American religion.

Before the Time of Contact

Native Americans descend from two racially different groups: Paleo-Siberian and Aleut/Inuit.

The Paleo-Siberians

It is believed that the first Native Americans were descendants of Paleo-Siberians. This ancient people inhabited what is today Siberia, an arctic region spanning the continents of Europe and Asia. The Paleo-Siberians set out from Asia for North America by walking across a thousand-mile-wide stretch of tundra. Known as the Bering Strait land bridge, or Beringia, this stretch of tundra once connected Asia and North America. Between 50,000 and 10,000 B.C.E., small groups of Paleo-Siberians streamed into North America and pushed southward at a rate of four miles a year.

The Aleut/Inuit

Between 3000 and 1000 B.C.E., after the stretch of tundra had disappeared, the Aleut and Inuit (Eskimo) began making their way from northern Asia to North America by boat or canoe. The Aleut and Inuit, who survive to this day, share many genetic characteristics. They do not have the same genetic makeup as most modern-day Native Americans, who are the descendants of Paleo-Siberians.

Taking Root

Hunters and Gatherers

The first Native Americans were **migratory hunters**. They pursued big game, such as big-horn bison, saber-toothed tigers, and woolly mammoths. By 6000 B.C.E., the glaciers, which had once covered the northern part of North America, had retreated (melted). Many large land animals had become extinct. These developments brought dramatic change to the lives of Native Americans. To a great degree, the once large, roaming bands of migratory hunters were replaced by smaller, region-based groups of sedentary gatherers.

Around 1000 B.C.E., the smaller, region-based groups began to fragment. Native Americans were entering the **Formative Period**, or Classic Indian Period. The Formative Period was characterized by the development of agriculture, domestication of animals, construction of houses and villages, production of pottery and woven baskets, and greater formulation of religious beliefs and practices. Religion was not a separate entity in the life of Native Americans; rather, it permeated the whole of life. This is true to this day. Many of the beliefs of Native Americans are expressed in mythological language, and the tellers of the story move in and out of the **myths**, needing no transitions.

---

migratory hunters

Native American hunters in the period before European contact who pursued big game such as big-horn bison and woolly mammoths

Formative Period

the time of development, characterized by agriculture, domestication of animals, construction of houses and villages, production of pottery and woven baskets, and greater formulation of religious beliefs and practices

The Adena and the Hopewell of the Northeast; the Mississippian of the Southeast; and the Mogollon, Hohokam, and Anasazi of the Southwest were the most important peoples of the Formative Period. They were the forerunners of the tribes, or nations, that European explorers would encounter upon arriving in North America.

The Adena and Hopewell

The Adena and the Hopewell of the Northeast left behind lasting traces of their religious beliefs and practices. They were **mound builders**. Atop the graves of their dead, they built up mounds of earth. The mounds contained scores of objects, such as beads, figurines, masks, mirrors, and pipes. The Adena placed their dead in log-lined tombs, and then constructed over the tombs animal-shaped mounds, such as the Great Serpent Mound in Peebles, Ohio.

The Hopewell generally built up larger, more elaborate mounds than the Adena. Some mounds were fifty feet high and two hundred feet wide. The Hopewell mounds in Newark, Ohio, once covered four square miles. The Hopewell were prolific traders. Excavations of their mounds have uncovered obsidian from the Rocky Mountains, copper from the Great Lakes, shells from the Pacific coast, silver from Canada, and alligator teeth from Florida. The Hopewell culture lasted five hundred years longer than that of the Adena.

The Mississippian

The Mississippian of the Southeast constructed huge earthen mounds, commonly referred to as temple mounds. An entire mound complex of Mississippian origin exists at Cahokia, Illinois. The complex, or village, covers six square miles along the Illinois River. It consists of eighty-five mounds. Monk's Mound, the largest of the earthen mounds, is more than one thousand feet long, seven hundred feet wide, and one hundred feet high.

Unlike the Adena and the Hopewell who preceded them, the Mississippian built up mounds for more than one purpose. Some mounds honored the dead, others functioned as platforms on which ceremonies took place, still others served as foundations for houses and public buildings.

Artifacts discovered in and around Adena, Hopewell, and Mississippian mounds reveal something about the religious beliefs and practices of these peoples. For example, stylized skulls, bones, and weeping eyes frequently appear on copper sheets, pottery, and sculpture. This points to an interest in death and its lingering effects on the community.

Some scholars have associated the mounds with cleansing rituals. It has been suggested that structures built atop the mounds were deliberately burnt. The burning cleansed (purified) an individual, a family, or perhaps an entire community.

myth
a traditional story which unfolds a part of a people's worldview, a story with layers of meaning

mound builders
Native Americans who built huge burial and temple mounds, often in the shape of animals

A cliff dwelling in Mesa Verde, Colorado

The Mongollon, Hohokam, and Anasazi

The Mongollon, the Hohokam, and the Anasazi of the Southwest made considerable strides in agriculture. They cultivated beans, corn, cotton, squash, and tobacco. And they had time to create intricate jewelry and pottery designs. In addition, the Mongollon were known for their innovative pit houses, the Hohokam designed elaborate irrigation systems, and the Anasazi perfected the design of pueblos.

Between 1500 and 1200 C.E., the Mongollon, the Hohokam, and the Anasazi cultures came to an end. The Mongollon were, more than likely, absorbed by the Anasazi; the Hohokam, which, in the Pima language, means "vanished ones," and the Anasazi ("the ancient ones") appear to have abandoned their settlements.

By the time the Europeans arrived in the New World, there were numerous nations of Native Americans in each of the cultural areas. Confederacies were well developed.

After the Time of Contact

Native American relations with the Dutch, English, French, Norse, Portuguese, Russians, Spanish, and other Europeans followed a familiar pattern: the Europeans used force against Native Americans and/or kidnapped them. Critics loudly denounced such actions, and Native Americans fought back by engaging in counter-offensives and preemptive attacks.

The Spanish, the English, and later the Americans made systematic efforts to suppress Native American religion. At the time, authorities argued that Native Americans would constitute less of a threat if they were prevented from observing and partaking in long-held religious beliefs and practices. These attempts to suppress Native American religion are recounted below.

Suppression

Spanish suppression of Native American religion

Under Spanish auspices, Roman Catholic religious communities established schools for Native American children. In these schools, the children were taught, among other subjects, the fundamentals of the Christian religion. These children already had a religion, which their ancestors had practiced for thousands of years. The forced abandonment of those religions caused the children to experience social isolation. In 1661, the Spanish carried out an overt attack on the religion of the Pueblo tribes. They invaded the **kivas** (ceremonial structures) and destroyed hundreds of **kachina** (ancestral spirit) masks.

English suppression of Native American religion

In many ways, the English behaved much like the Spanish. One notable missionary, John Eliot (1604–1690), translated the Bible into a Native American dialect. Eliot converted many Native Americans living in the Northeast to Christianity. Among the Algonquian, the new Christians were known as "**Praying Indians**." The sudden emergence of a Christian minority within the Northeast tribes wreaked much internal havoc.

American suppression of Native American religion

In 1805, Chief Red Jacket of the Seneca people responded in the following way to a missionary from the Evangelical Missionary Society of Massachusetts, a missionary whom we know only as *Cram:*

Since [the Great Spirit] has made so great a difference between us in other things, why may we not conclude that He has given us a different religion, according to our understanding?

The Great Spirit does right. He knows what is best for His children. We are satisfied.

Brother, we do not wish to destroy your religion, or to take it from you. We only want to enjoy our own.

But the attempts at conversion of the Native Americans continued. In the late nineteenth century, Richard Pratt founded the Carlisle Indian School in Pennsylvania (1879). Its expressed purpose was to assimilate Native Americans into the dominant culture. Similar schools gradually became common on reservations throughout North America.

Around this time, Edwin Eells, an agent of the United States government, sought to suppress the Indian Shaker religion, or Indian Shaker Church. He denounced its incorporation of Native American religious practices. In 1892, members of the Indian Shaker religion, after having secured legal assistance, affirmed their freedom to worship and to conduct services on Northwest Coast reservations.

In the same century, the United States government confronted the spread of the **Ghost Dance**, a creation of the Paiute prophet Wovoka. A number of Native American nations believed that the dance, which sometimes went on for several days, would end the power of whites and usher in a period of prosperity. In 1890, at Wounded Knee, South Dakota, United States troops met a group of Native Americans en route to a Ghost Dance. A skirmish followed, and 350 Native Americans were massacred. In the early twentieth century, the United States government moved against another Native American dance; it outlawed the **Sun Dance** of the Plains nation in 1910.

kiva
ceremonial structure

kachina
ancestral spirit mask; masked impersonator; "messenger of the god"

"Praying Indians"
Native Americans among the Algonquians who were converted to Christianity

Ghost Dance
a Native American dance that lasted several days; performed to end the power of the whites and provide a period of prosperity

Sun Dance
chief ceremony of the Plains nations; performed to gain supernatural power to fulfill a vow

I Wonder If the Ground Has Anything to Say

The occasion for the speech was an Indian council in the Valley of Walla Walla in 1855. Young Chief of the Cayuse gave this speech before being forced to sign away the land.

I wonder if the ground has anything to say? I wonder if the ground is listening to what is said? I wonder if the ground will come alive . . .? I hear what the ground says. The ground says, it is the Great Spirit that placed me here. The Great Spirit tells me to take care of the Indians, to feed them aright. The Great Spirit appointed the roots to feed the Indians. The water says the same thing. The Great Spirit directs me. Feed the Indians well. The grass says the same thing, feed the Indians well. The ground, water, and grass say, the Great Spirit has given us our names. We have these names and hold these names. The ground says, the Great Spirit has given us our names. We have these names and hold these names. The ground says, the Great Spirit has placed me here to produce all that grows on me, trees and fruits. . . . The ground says, it was from me human beings were made. The Great Spirit, in placing people on the earth, desired them to take good care of the ground and to do each other no harm . . .

—Janet Schaffran and Pat Kozak, More than Words *(Yorktown Heights, NY: Meyer-Stone Books, a division of Meyer, Stone, and Company, Inc., 1986).*

Let's Talk about It . . .

1. What does the ground say?
2. What point does the Chief make? How does he use the ground and the Great Spirit to support his claim?
3. How does this speech relate to the "American Suppression of Native American Religion?"

Growing and Blooming

Before the first Europeans arrived, the Adena, Hopewell, Mississippian, Mongollon, Hohokam, and Anasazi cultures had given birth to more than three hundred tribes, or nations. These tribes had a combined population of nearly one million.

The nations demonstrated great cultural diversity. For example, nearly every nation had its own language. It is estimated that Native Americans relied on 2,200 languages to communicate.

Such diversity characterized virtually every aspect of tribal life. Architecture and transportation are just two examples. In addition to Mongollon pit houses and Anasazi pueblos, there were lean-tos, long-houses, wigwams, teepees, igloos, earthlodges, and wickiups. In the area of water transportation, there were Haida dugouts, Algonquian birchbark canoes, Mandan bullboats, Inuit umiaks, and Paiute tule canoe-rafts.

In the area of religion, Native American nations demonstrated the same diversity. Nearly every nation had its own distinct religion. Descriptions of nine living Native American religions are given below.

Bole-Maru Religion

The Bole-Maru religion exists in (north-central) California, though not exclusively. The religion takes its name from the Patwin word *bole* and the Pomo word *maru*, which are the names of dances. Followers of the Bole-Maru religion can be found among the Maidu, Patwin, and Pomo nations.

An instrumental shaper of the Bole-Maru religion was the Hill Patwin prophet Lame Bill. He was a dreamer, or prophet-innovator. To this day, the leaders of the religion are known as dreamers. Their dreams or dream revelations shape Bole-Maru ceremonies, such as the Bole-Hesi Dance, the Bole or Maru Dance, and the Ball Dance. During the Ball Dance, dancers toss cloth balls to their partners. They have precise patterns for tossing the balls, patterns that are based on dream revelations.

Banners, flag poles, and ceremonial dress form a part of the religion. Adherents of the Bole-Maru religion believe in a supreme being and in an afterlife. They stress a simple lifestyle, which does not include the use of alcohol.

"When we Indians kill meat, we eat it all up. When we dig roots, we make little holes. When we build houses, we make little holes. When we burn grass for grasshoppers, we don't ruin things. We shake down acorns and pine nuts.

We don't chop down the trees. We only use dead wood. But the White people plow up the ground, pull down the trees, kill everything. . . . The White people pay no attention. . . . How can the spirit of the earth like the White [people]? . . . Everywhere the White [people] has touched it, it is sore."

—*The reflections of a nineteenth-century Wintu woman. The Wintu, the Nomlaki, the Hill Patwin, and the River Patwin speak derivatives of the Wintun language. Lame Bill, the founder of the Bole-Maru religion, belonged to the Hill Patwin tribe.*

Chinigchinix Religion

The Chinigchinix religion exists in (southern) California. It is practiced by the San Luiseno Band of Mission Indians and the Pauma Band of Mission Indians, who live on the Rincon and Pauma-Yuima reservations.

Geronimo Boscana, an early nineteenth-century Catholic missionary, claimed that the religion centered on the teachings of the prophet Chinigchinix. According to the Chinigchinix religion, after Chinigchinix died, he ascended into heaven. It is believed that he constantly watches his followers. He also punishes them for disobeying his teachings.

The Chinigchinix religion is known for its elaborate rituals. The Ceremony of the Bird, or Eagle Ceremony, is a very popular ritual. Followers of the Chinigchinix religion observe rites of passage for both boys and girls, mourning ceremonies, a dance in honor of the prophet whenever there is an eclipse, dream quests, and cremation. They also make use of **sand paintings**.

Religious laws promote endurance, obedience, and self-sacrifice. The Chinigchinix religion is sometimes referred to as an "indigenous missionary movement" because its followers spread Chinigchinix's teachings.

sand painting
a painting made with colored sand, often used in religious ceremonies, especially with healing rites

> *One day, Sun-God willed the Luisenos to move eastward and settle in the land of the rising-sun. Many boats were made by the young braves, and the Luiseno tribe began their voyage to find a new home. Uu-yot led the fleet eastward through heavy mist and fog up the San Luis River. . . .*
>
> *Later and without warning, a period of darkness and storms descended upon the area, with sharp lightning flashes and roaring crashes of thunder.*
>
> *Torrential rains fell upon the land. The river overflowed, creating a dangerous situation for the tribe. Uu-yot led his people to higher ground and all were saved. They prayed to the Great Spirit to quiet the forces of nature that again they might live in peace and safety.*
>
> *—Taken from the Luiseno story "Before This Land." The San Luiseno Band of Mission Indians of the Rincon reservation are among those who follow the Chinigchinix religion.*

Drum Religion

The Drum religion, sometimes called the Dream Dance, has followers among the Ojibwa, Menominee, Patawatomi, Kickapoo, Mesquakie, and Winnebago nations of the Northeast. A Dakota woman by the name of Tailfeather founded the religion, which revolves around the sacred **Dance Drum.**

Dance Drum
drum used in the Drum religion; considered a living being

In the midst of a skirmish between Dakota warriors and United States forces, Tailfeather hid herself beneath the lily pads of a lake. While hiding, Tailfeather received teachings from the Great Spirit. She was told to share these teachings with other nations. As instructed, the Dakota constructed a Dance Drum, which Tailfeather had seen in her vision. They gave it to the Ojibwa, who, in turn, copied it and gave it to another nation.

Followers of the Drum religion regard the Dance Drum as a living being. They take special care of the drum: they do not allow it to touch the ground, they cover it, they keep a light burning near it, and they monitor their behavior when near it. Followers believe that all Dance Drums descend from the original Dance Drum.

Do not abuse your wife. Women are sacred. If you make your wife suffer, you will die in a short time. Our grandmother, Earth, is a woman, and in abusing your wife you are abusing her. By thus abusing our grandmother who takes care of us, by your action you will be practically killing yourself.

—"A Winnebago Father's Precepts." Followers of the Drum religion can be found among the Winnebago.

Handsome Lake Religion

The Handsome Lake religion is practiced by the Iroquois Confederacy, which is made up of the Cayuga, Mohawk, Oneida, Onondaga, Seneca, and Tuscarora nations of the Northeast. The Seneca prophet Handsome Lake founded the religion, which combines Native American and Christian elements.

The "good word," or the Code of Handsome Lake, is the heart of the religion. The code spells out proper behavior, such as avoiding alcohol and keeping observances that honor the Creator. Preachers representing the ten historic longhouses recite the Code of Handsome Lake. This takes place each autumn at the Six Nations Meeting. The Handsome Lake religion is headquartered at Tonawanda, New York, where the **wampum strings** of Handsome Lake are kept.

wampum strings
beads strung together, often as a belt, and used as currency or as a means of keeping records or recording treaties

The Good Spirit created many things which he placed upon the earth. The Evil Spirit tried to undo the work of his brother by creating evil. The Good Spirit made tall and beautiful trees such as the pine and hemlock. The Evil Spirit stunted some trees. In others he put knots and gnarls. He covered some with thorns, and placed poison fruit on them. The Good Spirit made animals such as the deer and the bear. The Evil Spirit made poisonous animals, lizards and serpents, to destroy the animals of the Good Spirit's creation. The Good Spirit made springs and streams of good, pure water. The Evil Spirit breathed poison into many of the springs. He put snakes into others. . . . Everything that the Good Spirit made, his wicked brother tried to destroy.

—From an untitled Mohawk story. The Mohawk are one of six nations belonging to the Iroquois Confederacy. The Handsome Lake religion is practiced throughout the confederacy.

Indian Shaker Religion

The Indian Shaker religion of the Northwest Coast was founded by John and Mary Slocum. In 1881, John Slocum became ill, died, and came back to life. He told his wife and others that he had returned to help Native Americans improve their lives.

Slocum set out to preach his message and make plans for the construction of a church, but again fell ill. As his wife, Mary, approached his sickbed, she began to tremble uncontrollably, which resulted in his miraculous recovery.

The trembling, or shaking, was looked upon as a manifestation of divine power. Slocum recovered and his popularity soared.

"Shaking" became an important part of the movement's worship. The Indian Shaker religion, like the Handsome Lake religion, combined Native American and Christian elements. The first churches were replete with crucifixes, candles, bells, and pictures. The Indian Shaker religion calls on its followers to respect the ways of their ancestors, such as living off of the land.

> *We call upon the forests, the great trees reaching strongly to the sky with earth in their roots and the heavens in their branches, the fir and the pine and the cedar, and we ask them to: Teach us, and show us the way.*
>
> *—Taken from the* Chinook Psalter. *The Chinook were one of the nations influenced by the Indian Shaker religion.*

Kuksu Religion

The Kuksu religion can be found among the Cahto, Coast Miwok, Costanoan, Esselen, Konkow, Maidu, Nisenan, Patwin, Pomo, Salinan, Wintu, and Yuki peoples of (northern) California. The religion is practiced only by males, who are inducted into the Kuksu Society and given instruction from age eight to sixteen.

Society members meet in large, circular, earth-covered dance houses. Dance plays an important role in the life of the society. Members impersonate spirits and dance to bring rain, to nourish the earth, and to produce good crops.

Common are "big head" headdresses from which sticks radiate. Overall, the Kuksu dances are believed to renew the world and promote environmental abundance. Followers of the Kuksu religion, which is a secret society, are usually reluctant to discuss their religious beliefs and practices.

> *Hundreds of years ago, in the shelter of this valley, lived Tu-tok-a-nu-la and his tribe. He was a wise chief, trusted and loved by his people, always setting a good example by saving crops and game for winter.*
>
> *While he was hunting one day, he saw the lovely guardian spirit of the valley for the first time. His people called her Ti-sa-yak. He thought her beautiful beyond his imagination. Her skin was white, her hair was golden, and her eyes were like heaven. Her voice, as sweet as the song of a thrush, led him to her. But when he stretched his arms toward her, she rose, lighter than a bird, and soon vanished in the sky.*
>
> *—Taken from the Miwokan story "Bridal Veil Fall." Many male members of the Miwok nation follow the Kuksu religion.*

Prophet Dance Religion

The Prophet Dance religion of the Northwest Coast and Plateau revolves around a prophet, or dreamer. Most often, this individual has had a near-death experience, during which he or she received special knowledge and powers.

Many prophets possess the ability to make predictions. These predictions are based on interpretations of natural phenomena, such as earthquakes, falling stars, and volcanic eruptions. A number of prophets predicted the arrival of Europeans, and their subsequent exploitation of Native American peoples.

A prophet typically gathers his or her followers together for a circle dance. At some point during the meeting, the prophet delivers a message and all present, including the prophet, confess their sins. Adherents of the Prophet Dance religion also perform a marriage dance, which is more or less a marriage ceremony.

The earth was once a human being; Old One made her out of a woman. "You will be the Mother of all people," he said. Earth is alive yet, but she has changed. The soil is her flesh, the rocks are her bones, the wind is her breath, the trees and grass her hair. She lives spread out, and we live on her. When she moves we have an earthquake.

—Okanogan creation story. The Okanagan were one of the nations influenced by the Prophet Dance religion. Modern-day Okanagan, or Okanogan, live in British Columbia.

Circle dances are common religious expressions in Native American culture.

Washani Religion

Followers of the Washani religion are found among the Cayuse, Klickitat, Nez Perce, Northern Paiute, Palouse, Sinkiuse, Tenino, Umatilla, Wallawalla, Wanapam, Wishram, and Yakima nations of the Northwest Coast and Plateau. *Washani* is a Shahaptian word that means "dancers" or "worship." The Washani religion was revived by the prophet Smohalla.

Smohalla instructed his followers to return to the traditions of their youth and to cease living like the intruding Europeans. The ceremonies over which Smohalla presided were colorful, routinely making use of bells and flags. He taught that Native American peoples would regain control of their land and would be carried up into the sky on feathers.

Smohalla attached great significance to the number seven. A seven-pointed star appeared on his shirt, and seven people were selected to prepare and serve dishes at the Feast of the New Food.

Modern-day Washani worship consists of dances, feasts, memorials, naming ceremonies, and weddings. Many Washani ceremonies take place in a longhouse, which has led some to describe the Washani religion as the *Longhouse religion*. Other names include the *Seven-Drum religion* and the *Indian religion*.

> *Someday the Great Chief Above will overturn the mountains and the rocks. Then the spirits that once lived in the bones buried there will go back into them. At present those spirits live in the tops of the mountains, watching their children on earth and waiting for the great change which is to come. The voices of these spirits can be heard in the mountains at all times.*
>
> —Untitled Yakima story. Followers of the Washani religion can be found among the Yakima.

Native American Church

The Native American Church began in the Great Plains in the year 1918. Its founders sought to preserve Native American religious practices, particularly the use of peyote, common to the Cheyenne, Otoe, Ponca, and other nations. They modeled themselves on a mainline Christian church, hoping that such a structure would enable them to survive.

The church's articles of incorporation, which were signed on October 10, 1918, reflect something of its purpose. According to this document, the Native American Church was founded "to foster and promote the religious belief of the several tribes of Indians in the State of Oklahoma, in the Christian religion with the practice of the Peyote Sacrament as commonly understood and used among the adherents of this religion in the several tribes of Indians in the State of Oklahoma, and to teach the Christian religion with morality, sobriety, industry, kindly charity and right living and to cultivate a spirit of self-respect and brotherly union among the members of the Native Race of Indians. . . ."

Today, branches of the church exist in seventeen states, including California, Idaho, Iowa, Montana, Nebraska, Nevada, New Mexico, South Dakota, Utah, and Wisconsin. Adherents can also be found in at least two provinces of Canada, Alberta and Saskatchewan.

It should be pointed out that the use of **peyote**, a small, spineless cactus that grows in Texas and Mexico, is sacramental, not recreational. Those who ingest (eat) peyote, like those who fast, seek a greater awareness of the divine. Peyote allows them to receive instructions from the Great Spirit, communicate with dead loved ones, and experience healing.

Canadian members of the church once invited a team of medical professionals to attend peyote ceremonies so that they could help to dispel misconceptions surrounding peyote. According to newspaper accounts, these professionals described the peyote ceremony as beautiful and unusual. They later concluded that peyote was not harmful. Despite these and other findings, the United States Supreme Court has given individual states the right to restrict peyote use (1990).

peyote
a small, spineless cactus that grows in Texas and Mexico; has a sacramental use among some Native American groups

The solid sky, the cloudy sky, the good sky, the straight sky.

The earth produces herbs. The herbs cause us to live. They cause long life. They cause us to be happy.

The good life, may it prevail with the air. May it increase. May it be straight to the end.

Sweet Medicine's earth is good. Sweet Medicine's earth is completed. Sweet Medicine's earth follows the eternal ways. Sweet Medicine's earth is washed and flows.

—An untitled Cheyenne song. Some of the first members of the Native American Church belonged to the Cheyenne nation. In part, the church came into existence to preserve Cheyenne customs.

A Living Testimony—Douglas Long

I'm a full-blooded Winnebago Indian from the state of Wisconsin. I've been an active member of the Native American Church since I was nine years old. In 1982 we had our national conference up in Red Pheasant, Saskatchewan, and I was elected president of the Native American Church of North America. I am full-time clergy here in the state of Wisconsin. We have been able to have some of our leaders ordained by the Lutheran, Catholic, or Episcopalian Churches. I had been trained ever since I was a young boy. We do send some of our people to Cook Christian Training School in Arizona, where they get certificates of graduation and can be recognized by the councils of churches in various states. I might add that the Native American Church of Wisconsin is a member of the Wisconsin Council of Churches.

The purpose of this church is to foster and promote religious beliefs in Almighty God and in the customs of Native American tribes throughout North America; to promote morality, sobriety, industry, charity, and right-living; to cultivate a spirit of self-respect and brotherly love and unity among the church's members throughout North America; and to maintain the right to own property for the purpose of conducting church business and services. As a people, we place explicit faith, hope, and belief in Almighty God and declare full, confident, everlasting faith in our church, through which we worship God. Furthermore, we pledge ourselves to work for the protection of the sacramental use of peyote.

In the beginning, the Native American Church was not fully Christian. For the past six thousand years, the Aztec and Mayan Indians of South America were known to use peyote. Around 1600, with the influence of Christianity, the elders realized that many of the teachings of the Native American Church coincided with the teachings of Christianity. For instance, name-giving really coincides with baptism, giving you everlasting life. It means that the Great Spirit will call your name on Judgment Day, as in the Book of Revelation. That is why elders way back in the 1600s, 1700s, and 1800s began to adapt Christianity to Native American Church ways.

It is known among many church members that peyotism began in the Southwest, moved through the southern plains into the Midwest and upward through the northern plains into the Northwest. The Native American Church of the United States was organized in 1950 in order to protect the use of our sacrament peyote in a bona fide religious ceremony. The use of our sacrament peyote corresponds to the use of bread and wine in the Christian Church.

The sacrament peyote and other ceremonies typically take place in a tepee. A tepee, in the past, was made of buffalo robes or bark from a tree, but we now use regular canvas. The tepee is put up with a tripod of three poles signifying the triune God—Father, Son and Holy Spirit. Those first three poles are tied together and then nine other poles are put up around the original three. These, along with the poles outside which hold the draft flaps on the tepee, represent Jesus Christ and his disciples. Inside is the fireplace. This has variations among various tribes throughout the United States and Canada. Some use a crescent, a half moon, which faces the east.

Usually the conductor, the leader of the prayer service, sits on the west side of the tepee. He has a helper because we use a drum and a staff, also a gourd, a drumstick, and a feather. On his left is an incense burner, called a *cedar man* because most tribes throughout the U.S. burn cedar for incense. Incense is burned after a prayer has been said, after a special blessing or after administration of the sacrament—maybe to a sick person, for a birthday, a funeral service, a wedding, Christmas, Thanksgiving, Easter or Palm Sunday. Palm Sunday is the day that we usually have our baptisms, but sometimes we have them on the person's birthday.

During these times, various rituals are performed throughout the night. The cedar man burns the cedar in the fireplace. Then they use an eagle feather to pass some of this cedar smoke, this incense, upon the person who is being prayed for in the belief that the burning of the cedar is just like the incense in the Old Testament and that the prayer will be taken to God above. To take care of the fireplace—since our services are conducted from dusk until dawn—there is a fire man, and he sits on the north side of the doorway. The doorway always faces east.

At the beginning of the ceremony, the leader offers a prayer outside the tepee door. Then he leads the congregation, and they line up from the east of the doorway towards the east, completely around the tepee. The leader enters from the north side of the tepee through the doorway, leading the rest of the people. Then they all take their seats.

At midnight, water is offered. It is brought into the tepee, and a special prayer is offered over it. Then the fireplace is prepared. Water is sacred; it is used with prayers because it sustains all life on this planet. After the ceremony of the water, one of the elders may speak about the reason for the meeting. Then the singing and the drum continue.

From the beginning of the evening, the staff and the gourd, the drumstick and the drum are passed to all male members who are seated around the fireplace. They sing praises to God—thanksgiving, honor, and glory to God and his son Jesus Christ and the Holy Spirit. Under the direction of the prayer leader, prayers are offered by various people.

At 3 a.m. another special stop is made, signifying Jesus Christ going into the Garden of Gethsemane and asking his disciples to stay awake and watch. At that time the cedar man prays for the whole congregation and the beneficiaries of this prayer service. Singing is then continued until just before daybreak. Water is called again, and soon after that the prayer service is concluded. Everyone comes out of the tepee, breakfast is served, and then fellowship is enjoyed by everyone until as late as they want to stay during the day.

—*Adapted from Remmelt and Kathleen Hummelon, editors,* Stories of Survival *(New York: Friendship Press, 1985).*

Let's Talk about It . . .

1. What natural symbols are used in the worship of the Native American Church? What is the meaning of each natural symbol?

2. How has the Native American Church combined Native American religious practices and Christianity?

Growing and Blooming

Native American religions that originated both before and after the time of contact share a number of central beliefs and practices.

Supreme Being

Tribal religions of North America share an almost universal belief in the existence of a supreme being, or ultimate spiritual reality. Though various tribes have endowed this being, or reality, with human characteristics, they do not believe it is human.

Some religions refer to the supreme being as **Great Spirit** or Great Mystery. Others call the supreme being by a specific name. For example, the Pawnee of Nebraska address the supreme being as Tirawa.

Spirit World

Native American religions believe in the existence of a **spirit world.** This world is as real as the human world. Both worlds exist on earth, as well as beyond it. The spirit and human worlds overlap. They are on top of each other, or inside of each other. The relationship of one to the

Great Spirit
Great Mystery, the supreme being

spirit world
the all-pervading world of the spirits which overlaps with the non-spirit, human world

other can be thought of as a circle within a circle, or one circle, which is actually two circles perfectly aligned. It is in this sense that the spirit world can be described as all-pervading.

As a rule, Native American religions are very attuned to occurrences in the spirit world. The spirit and nonspirit (human) worlds are thoroughly interrelated—what happens in the spirit world directly affects the course of events in the human world. Some Native American religions view nature as a manifestation of the spirit world. **Nature**, then, is a visible extension of the spirit world.

Spiritual Beings

Native American religions devote a great deal of attention to the activities of **spiritual beings**. In most cases, these beings are distinguished by their abode, or place of residence. They include sky beings, atmospheric spirits, earth spirits, and guardian spirits.

Sky beings

Sky beings include the sun, the moon, and the stars. Very often, the sun is closely associated with the supreme being. Some tribes look upon it as a manifestation of the supreme being. The moon is intimately connected with the cycles of vegetation.

Atmospheric spirits

Personified **atmospheric spirits** include the Four Winds, the Whirlwinds, the Rain Spirits, and the Thunderbirds. The Thunderbird is a terrific, giant eagle-like creature that causes storms. Its blinking eyes are the source of lightning, and its flapping wings are the source of thunder. Some modern-day peoples of Siberia also believe in the existence of such a creature. Quite possibly, the concept of the Thunderbird was brought to North America by the Paleo-Siberians, which would make it thousands of years old.

Earth spirits

Spirits of the earth, or spirits of the biosphere, also abound. These spirits perpetuate animal and plant life. An **earth spirit** determines whether an animal or plant thrives. Buffalo Spirit, Caribou Spirit, and Maize Spirit are most frequently mentioned. Earth spirits are also associated with natural places, such as lakes, mountains, rivers, swamps, and streams. Even certain kinds of stones, however small, are thought to be under the sway of a spirit.

Nature lives to the extent that these spirits manifest themselves. Many Native Americans believe that the Earth itself is animated by a spirit, whom they call Mother Earth.

Guardian spirits

Guardian spirits have played a role in nearly every tribal religion. They are typically animal spirits, such as Buffalo Spirit, or spirits merely disguised as animals. Those who belong to tribes of the Northeast, Great Plains, Great Basin, and Plateau undertake vision quests to acquire guardian spirits. A **vision quest** usually takes place in a remote setting. People desiring a vision of their guardian spirit seclude themselves, and submit to a regimen of fasting and meditation.

nature
for Native Americans, a visible extension of the spirit world

spiritual beings
several types of noncorporeal beings

sky beings
the sun (often closely associated with the supreme being), the moon, and the stars

atmospheric spirits
personified forces of nature

earth spirits
spirits who perpetuate animal life or inhabit natural places or inanimate objects

guardian spirits
typically animal spirits (or spirits disguised as animals) partial to a group or an individual

vision quest
a regimen of fasting and meditation undertaken by Native Americans as preparation for a vision of the guardian spirit; usually takes place in a remote setting

If successful, people receive medicine (supernatural power) from their guardian spirit. In addition, they are given a rhythm or song and instructions for making a **medicine bundle**. This bundle contains articles associated with the vision quest, and typically remains within the family. In other words, the guardian spirit, the source of the medicine, stays with the family. Inherited guardian spirits are referred to as **totems**.

Totems are especially important to tribes of the Northwest. For centuries, these tribes created totem poles. Totem poles are made from trees and anchored vertically in the ground. The image of one or more totems (guardian spirits) are carved onto each pole and then painted. Beavers and eagles are very common. Often a series of images communicates a family legend or a clan story.

Hero Figure

Some Native American religions make reference to a **hero figure**, or cultural figure. Most often, this being unleashes creative energies, or forces, which improve people's lives.

Occasionally, the hero figure brings human beings forbidden knowledge, or knowledge that the supreme being is not ready to share. In this capacity the hero figure assumes the role of a trickster. Tricksters frequently assume animal shapes, which vary according to culture area. Tricksters take on the form of white hares in the Northeast; coyotes in the Great Plains, the Great Basin, the Plateau, and California; and ravens in the Northwest.

Medicine People

Medicine people, or shamans, perform a variety of functions. They are visionaries; it is their responsibility, their duty, to steer the tribe toward or away from a particular course of action. Very often, they play the role of innovators, challenging their people to devise new methods of doing things. A number of eighteenth- and nineteenth-century religious movements were started by individuals resembling medicine people. Handsome Lake, founder of the modern-day Handsome Lake religion of the Iroquois, is one example.

The medicine people were and are also responsible for the healing of physical illnesses of people. They are knowledgeable of herbs and other treatments for many diseases, and they set bones as well.

medicine bundle
bundle with articles associated with the supernatural power received from a guardian spirit

totems
inherited guardian spirits among Native Americans

hero figure
cultural figure which unleashes creative energies, or forces, which improve people's lives; sometimes a trickster

medicine people
shamans, visionaries, spiritual guides, and physical healers

Mystery and the sacredness of life surround Native American religions.

Rituals

Rituals promote harmony between the spirit and human worlds. Dancing, throwing tobacco, and returning game to the earth are well-known Native American rituals.

Dancing

Among Native American dances, the Sun Dance is the most popular. The Arapaho, Arikara, Assiniboine, Blackfeet, Cheyenne, Comanche, Crow, Gros Ventre, Hidatsa, Kiowa, Lakota/Dakota, Mandan, Pawnee, Plains, Plains Cree, Plains Ojibwa, Ponca, Sarsi, and Ute tribes all perform a ritual known as the Sun Dance. This dance is performed to gain supernatural power or to fulfill a vow made to a spirit in exchange for special assistance.

The Buffalo Dance was performed to ensure success in hunting buffalo. Agricultural groups gave rise to the Rain Dance, the Green Corn Dance, and the Hopi Snake Dance (in honor of the rain god). Among Pueblo groups, the dancers are often members of the Kachina Society.

The Ghost Dance, noted earlier, gave hope to people who were losing their hunting grounds and starving on the infertile reservations. Ghost dancers circled round, holding hands and singing ghost dance songs. On their shirts were painted stars, the moon, the sun, and magpies, which were thought to make the dancers' shirts bulletproof. Dancers often fell into a trance in which they visited a land covered with buffalo and met their dead ancestors. The dance was seen as a way to return the land to the way it was before the white men came.

The dance patterns are usually simple, although many Plains groups have complicated patterns. The dances are often accompanied by music made with drums, rattles, clappers, flutes, whistles, and panpipes. In general, everything associated with the dance is sacred.

The Sweat Lodge

sweat lodge
a ritual structure for the sweat bath, a purifying religious ceremony

The sweat bath is an important religious ceremony. There is even spiritual value in constructing the **sweat lodge**, and threatened punishments for any lack of reverence or any abuse. The structure faces a body of water and is built around birch or willow arches. The arches are covered with blankets or skins, or, if permanent, bark, soil, and grass. Heated sweating stones are placed in the lodge, and water is sprinkled on them. The participant sprinkles water on himself and chants prayers, including prayers for purification, strength, and good fortune. Finally, the participant bathes in the nearby water.

The Origin of Guardian Spirits and of Sweat Lodge

Sweat Lodge was a chief long, long ago; but he wasn't called Sweat Lodge then. He was just called chief. He decided to create all the animals and all the birds. So he created them and named them all. He named each animal and each bird. Then he told each one of them: "In times to come, when people have been created, they will send their children out, during the day or during the night, and you will talk with them and tell them what they will be able to do when they grow up. You will tell the boys that they are to get things easily, are to be good hunters, good fishermen, good gamblers, and so on. You will tell the girls that they will be able to get things easily. At that time I will be Sweat Lodge, myself."

Then he spoke to them again: "I'll have no body, no head, nor will I be able to see. Whoever desires to construct me will have the right to do so. The one who builds me may pray to me for good looks, or whatever he may wish—the one that made me. I'll take pity on him, and I'll give him what he requests—the one that made me. People may approach me thus: If anyone is injured, or if he is sick, or if he is poisoned, he may come to me for help and I'll give it to him. Also, when anyone is dying, he may come to me, and I'll help him then also. I'll help him to see the next world. So in this world I am Sweat Lodge, for the help of human beings."

—Told to Verne F. Ray in 1930 by Chief Jim James of the Sanpoil.
Ella E. Clark, Indian Legends of the Pacific Northwest
(Berkeley, CA: University of California Press, 1953), 183.

Let's Talk about It . . .

1. What is the purpose of the sweat lodge?
2. Why do you think the sweat lodge is personified in this story?

Other Rituals

The use of tobacco has a long and rich history among Native Americans. Often tobacco was thrown into a fire before eating, or a tobacco-filled pouch was thrown on the ground before a person entered a dangerous place or undertook a perilous journey. To this day, tribal powwows do not get under way unless participants pass a tobacco pipe. It is believed that partaking of the tobacco pipe brings cooperation and understanding to the proceedings.

In some tribes, after an animal has been killed and eaten, the animal's bones are reassembled and then returned to the earth (buried). By respecting game in this way, hunters believe that they are protecting their food supply, or ensuring a plentiful supply of food for the future.

A Calendar

Winter

Winter Solstice (December 20, 21, or 22). The season of winter begins on this day. This is the darkest, or shortest, day of the year.

Iroquois Midwinter Ceremony (observed in January or February). The nations of the Iroquois Confederacy gather to recite the Code of Handsome Lake. They do this to ensure continued prosperity. They look upon the code as having revised their ancestors' fortunes.

Spring

Vernal Equinox (March 20, 21, or 22). The season of spring begins on this day. Light and dark are in balance.

Earth Day (April 22). On this day, people everywhere reverence Mother Earth.

Summer

Summer Solstice (June 20, 21, or 22). The season of summer begins on this day. This is the brightest, or longest, day of the year.

Throughout the year, significant dances draw Native American groups together.

Sun Dance Festival (observed in June, July, or August). The Arapaho, Cheyenne, Shoshone, and Sioux, all of the Great Plains, observe this four-day festival by reflecting on their shortcomings and helping others. The festival includes special dances and prayers.

Green Corn Ceremony (observed in June, July, or August). For the Seminole of the Eastern Woodlands as well as other tribes, this ceremony begins a period of renewal. Native Americans spend this time fasting, dancing, playing sacred ball, praying, and meditating in sweat lodges.

Autumn

Autumnal Equinox (September 20, 21, or 22). The season of autumn begins on this day. Light and dark are in balance.

Iroquois Green Corn Ceremony (observed in August or September). The nations of the Iroquois Confederacy gather once again to recite the Code of Handsome Lake. The length of the code requires it to be recited on more than one occasion. Games play a big role in this celebration, because of the nearing winter.

Maidu Indian Day (observed in October). On this day, members of the Maidu nation express thanks for their gifts and talents. They mark the day by cooking acorns, making baskets, knapping flint, and telling stories. Many Maidu follow the Bole-Maru and Kuksu religions.

Discovering

1. Be able to explain each of the words in the vocabulary list.
2. Name and briefly explain the two broad periods of Native American history.
3. Discuss in a small group Native American life before contact with Europeans.
4. Why did the Spanish, English, and Americans suppress Native American religions? Do you agree with their reasoning? Explain.
5. What shapes Bole-Maru ceremonies?
6. What significance does the Dance Drum have to the Drum religion?
7. How did the Indian Shaker religion originate?
8. What do Native Americans believe the sun is associated with? The moon?
9. How do Native Americans personify the thunderbird?
10. Why are those of the Native American religion interested in acquiring guardian spirits?
11. What role does the hero figure assume in Native American religion?
12. What is the responsibility of the medicine people in Native American religion?
13. Explore the mound builders:
    - What were the functions of the earthen mounds?
    - What do they reveal to us about early Native American religious beliefs and practices?
    - How do the Mississippian earthen mounds differ from those of the Adena and the Hopewell?

Exploring

1. Gather with two or three classmates and review the sections on Beliefs and Practices. Then identify and list the ultimate questions Native American religions seem to deal with. Then discuss how Native American religions respond to these questions.
2. Choose one of the United in Nature sections and show how the beliefs and practices of that tradition are present in that writing. Identify a common theme of the United in Nature sections.
3. Choose one of the observances to research and write about in some detail. In your writing, place yourself at the observance as a member of that particular community and describe what is happening. Be as specific as you can (for example: colors, people present, music, food, etc.). Be sure to include the thoughts and feelings you experience while you are participating in the observance.

Integrating

1. What insights about Native American religions have you gained from this chapter? Be able to explain two or three aspects which were most insightful.

2. Evaluate the merits of Native American religions. In a small group, list and discuss those aspects which seem most applicable to life today. State a specific example of how you would apply these beliefs or practices.

Words to Know

atmospheric spirits

Dance Drum

earth spirits

Formative Period

Ghost Dance

Great Spirit

guardian spirits

hero figure

kachina

kiva

medicine bundle

medicine people

migratory hunters

mound builders

myth

Native American culture areas

nature

peyote

"Praying Indians"

sand painting

sky beings

spirit world

spiritual beings

Sun Dance

sweat lodge

totems

vision quest

wampum strings

Chapter 3

After reading this chapter, you will be able to

- Identify the meaning of words associated with Judaism
- Compare aspects of the Jewish worldview with your own
- Appraise the influence of Judaism on western civilization

JUDAISM

An Introduction

Rachel and Kevin, both Christians, stood at the entrance of the sanctuary in the synagogue. Hesitation must have registered on their faces. The Jewish man who welcomed them handed the visitors a prayer book and said, "That's okay. You can come in. There's nothing here that contradicts your faith."

Indeed, there is much in the Jewish faith with which any Christian or Muslim would be comfortable. Modern Judaism, Christianity, and Islam all derive from ancient Judaism; in other words, ancient Judaism is a kind of "parent" to these religions. While nature religions derive their "truths" from observations of nature, these three religions are called "revealed" religions because adherents to these faiths believe that "the truth" is revealed to them by God. God reveals what it is that people need to know about God, themselves, and their world through the events of history and people. Thus these three religions share the same basic perspective on revelation which is a fundamental aspect of western religions. In many other areas beyond this, western people owe a great deal of gratitude for the ways in which the Judaic heritage has shaped their civilization and religious faith.

Modern Jews, numbering about thirteen and one-half million in the world, descend from a line of people extending back into the ancient Middle Eastern world. They come from a grouping of wandering peoples who originated in what is modern-day Iraq. It is remarkable that this small group has even survived the ravages of time. Yet they have not only survived but have significantly shaped western civilization through their leadership in such fields as science, medicine, entertainment, business, industry, and sports.

Albert Einstein brought the world to the atomic era. Jonas Salk developed a vaccine to immunize against polio. In the later years of the twentieth century, he set out to develop a vaccine against AIDS. Bob Dylan, Benny Goodman, Leonard Bernstein, George Gershwin, Aaron Copland, and Barbra Streisand have been musical greats. Jewish comedians include Jerry Lewis, Groucho Marx, Woody Allen, George Burns, Bette Midler, and Jerry Seinfeld. Henry Kissinger has been a leading statesman in the United States. Jerry Sigel and Joe Shuster gave the world the comic-book hero Superman. Sandy Koufax was a famous pitcher for the Los Angeles Dodgers. Steven Spielberg has produced such great movies as *E.T.*, *Jurassic Park*, *Indiana Jones and the Temple of Doom*, *Empire of the Sun*, and *Schindler's List*. Finally, name a modern teen who has not worn blue jeans—an article of clothing developed by Levi Strauss.

But the influence of Judaism goes far beyond individuals who have had a formative influence upon generations of westerners. The very worldview of western peoples: the way we think of God, the dignity of people, and our role in the world come essentially from our common Jewish heritage. It is probably fair to say that every westerner carries within himself or herself some aspect of a Jewish worldview.

Tilling the Soil

"Hear, O Israel! The Lord is our God, the Lord alone. You shall love the Lord your God with all your heart and with all your soul and with all your might. Take to heart these instructions with which I charge you this day. Impress them upon your children. Recite them when you stay at home and when you are away, when you lie down and when you get up. Bind them as a sign on your hand and let them serve as a symbol on your forehead; inscribe them on the doorposts of your house and on your gates."

—*Deuteronomy 6:4–9*, Tanakh—The Holy Scriptures, *The New Jewish Publication Society Translation According to the Traditional Hebrew Text.*

This is the **Shema**, a statement of belief that best expresses the essence of Jewish faith. Jews recite it frequently, both in public worship and privately. Jewish people typically do not agree on many fine points of theology, but they do agree on this single statement: "Hear, O Israel: The Lord is our God, the Lord alone."

The Jewish view is that God's self and God's will have been revealed through the events of history. From the very beginning, God began to form a people, beginning with an individual and his family and eventually forming a entire nation as God's own. This is the **covenant** relationship which God nurtured over the course of many centuries. Thus, in order to understand Judaism, it is necessary to have a clear understanding of the Jewish experience through history.

Biblical History

Every religion or religious tradition has a beginning. In most cases, the story of that beginning has been preserved. The early history of Judaism and the Jewish people can be found in the Hebrew Bible. The events it describes exerted a lasting influence on the lives of Jews throughout the centuries. Often, the most heated debates among the different movements of Judaism—Conservative, Orthodox, Reform, and Reconstructionist—center on their interpretation of biblical events and the overall weight that they give to scripture.

The words *Judaism* and *Jew* derive ultimately from the name *Judah*. Judah was one of Jacob's twelve sons and the ancestor of the tribe of Judah. According to the Hebrew Bible, the history of Judaism and that of the Jewish people began with Abraham. Tradition regards Abraham as the first Jew.

From Abraham to Moses: A Family

It all began with Abram, the leader of one of the Habiru tribes who originated in ancient Iraq. He and his wife Sarai lived sometime between 1850 and 1700 B.C.E. They lived in a culture in which the people believed in many gods. In contrast, Abram followed only one god, known to him as *El Shaddai*. Abram heard the voice of this god call him to leave Ur, his native city, and move to a new land.

Shema
the Judaic confession of faith: "Hear, O Israel: The Lord is our God, the Lord alone." (Deuteronomy 6:4)

covenant
a sacred agreement, contract, testament between two parties

> *"Go from your native land and from your father's house to the land*
> *that I will show you.*
>
> *I will make of you a great nation,*
>
> *And I will bless you;*
>
> *I will make your name great,*
>
> *And you shall be a blessing.*
>
> *I will bless those who bless you*
>
> *And curse him that curses you;*
>
> *And all the families of the earth*
>
> *Shall bless themselves by you."*
>
> —*Genesis 12:1–3*, Tanakh—The Holy Scriptures.

Abram listened to this voice and moved to the land of Canaan. His belief in this one god alone is the root of **monotheism** in the West. His belief in the promises of this god is the beginning of the covenant between God and the Jewish people.

For Abram and Sarai, this covenant deepened through many difficult times in their lives. They sought relief from famine by going to Egypt for a time. Upon returning to Canaan, they became prosperous "in cattle, silver, and gold," but remained childless. This was considered a curse because people of the time believed they lived on through their children.

Eventually Abram had a son, Ishmael, with his wife's slave girl, Hagar. Even though Abram and Sarai remained childless, God renewed the promise that one day they would have a son. Because of their fidelity, God changed their names to *Abraham* and *Sarah*. Abram had himself and all the males of his household circumcised as a sign of the covenant with God. Then one day three messengers visited Abram and Sarai and promised them a son. Within a year, the birth of Isaac fulfilled the promise.

The greatest test of Abraham's faith came when God asked him to sacrifice his son Isaac. Remaining true, Abraham sought to carry out God's request. An angel of the Lord stopped him at the last moment. Abraham demonstrated remarkable faith in this one god, El Shaddai. Because of his example, Jews, Christians, and Moslems call Abraham their *father in faith*. He is a model for believing and trusting in God, especially through the difficult times of life.

The story of the covenant continues through Isaac's descendants. Jacob was his son; later God changed Jacob's name to *Israel*. Altogether, Abraham, Isaac, and Jacob are the **patriarchs** of the Jewish faith.

The famous twelve tribes of Israel traced their ancestry to Jacob's sons and grandsons: Reuben, Simeon, Judah, Issachar, Zebulun, Benjamin, Dan, Naphtali, Gad, Asher, Ephraim, and Manasseh. The first ten were Jacob's sons by his four wives Leah, Rachel, Zilpah, and Bilhah. The last two were his grandsons—the sons of Joseph, blessed by Jacob and given an inheritance through Joseph. Levi is regarded as the thirteenth tribe, but this group did not possess tribal lands. The priesthood was its inheritance.

monotheism

a belief in one God; religion based on that belief

patriarchs

male ancestors in the faith, the originators or founders of a religion; for Jews, Abraham, Issac, and Jacob especially

From Moses to Exile: A Nation

Eventually, famine or a series of crop failures drove the sons of Jacob to the neighboring country of Egypt. There they found a source of food for themselves and their livestock. Through the influence of Joseph, who had preceded his brothers to Egypt, this family migrated to Egypt. There the family grew into a great people. In the beginning, the pharaoh and the Egyptians welcomed the Hebrew people, as they were known. When they grew in numbers, the Egyptians eventually turned against them and forced them to become slaves.

Around 1290 B.C.E., a great leader, Moses, rose up among the people. Moses and his brother Aaron tried to convince the pharaoh to set the Hebrews free. Pharaoh's stubbornness caused the God of the Jews to send plagues upon the Egyptians. The last plague, which resulted in the death of every firstborn in Egypt, led the pharaoh to finally free the troublesome people. Not long after the Jews had left Egypt, the pharaoh pursued them. They were at the edge of the Sea of Reeds (Red Sea), and were more or less cornered. According to the Hebrew Bible, God thwarted the pharaoh's pursuit and saved the Jews. The story is recorded in Exodus 13:17–17:16.

As Pharaoh drew near, the Israelites caught sight of the Egyptians advancing upon them. Greatly frightened, the Israelites cried out to the LORD . . . . Then the LORD said to Moses, "Why do you cry out to Me? Tell the Israelites to go forward. And you lift up your rod and hold out your arm over the sea and split it, so that the Israelites may march into the sea on dry ground." . . . Then Moses held out his arm over the sea and the LORD drove back the sea with a strong east wind all that night, and turned the sea into dry ground. The waters were split, and the Israelites went into the sea on dry ground, the waters forming a wall for them on their right and on their left. The Egyptians came in pursuit after them into the sea, all of Pharaoh's horses, chariots, and horsemen . . . . The waters turned back and covered the chariots and the horsemen— Pharaoh's entire army that followed them into the sea; not one of them remained.

—*Exodus 14:10, 15–16, 21–23, 28,* Tanakh—The Holy Scriptures.

"It is the beginning of wisdom to be amazed at the fact of our being free."

—*Abraham Joshua Heschel*

So Moses led the people out of Egypt to freedom. This remarkable escape of the Hebrew slaves from a powerful nation is the called the **Exodus**. Just as a nation's Independence Day is a foundational event for a nation, so is the Exodus a foundational story for Judaism. It is an event that helped to forge a new nation and new identity.

The Exodus is the primordial freedom story. It has become an inspiration for oppressed people throughout history. Moses' famous demand, "Let my people go!" is a rallying cry for people seeking freedom. Surely it has been an inspiring image for people in the civil rights movement in the United States.

Abram's belief in El Shaddai probably began as a notion of a clan god. Moses may have had the same idea. But when he encountered the divine presence in a burning bush and asked who it was that sent him, the response was, "I AM WHO I AM." In Hebrew this is YHWH. At this point, monotheism evolved to a new level as Abraham's notion of a clan god evolved to the idea of a national god.

YHWH

Each of these four letters stands for a Hebrew character: YHWH, or JHVH. This is the holiest name of God in Judaism. This name is known as the tetragrammaton.

Because the Hebrew language does not contain any vowels, the exact pronunciation of this name is not known. The names Yahweh *and* Jehovah *represent non-Jewish attempts to pronounce this name; the first is considered more authentic. Throughout the centuries, Jews have been forbidden to pronounce the tetragrammaton. Only the Jewish high priest could utter it. Once a year, the priest entered an area of the Jerusalem temple known as the* Holy of Holies. *There, he called upon God by name, asking the Lord to forgive the sins of the Jewish people.*

Let's Talk about It . . .

1. Why do you think the Jewish faith forbids Jews from pronouncing the tetragrammaton?
2. How do other religious groups show respect for the name of God?

The Exodus gave birth to a new nation, now called the *Israelites*. This new nation now faced forty years (a number which also means "a generation" or "a long time") of wandering in the desert before returning to their homeland. During this time, they learned reliance upon this god who provided them with water and manna in the desert. The covenant with God evolved into a national covenant when the people agreed to the **Decalogue**, the Ten Commandments, at Mt. Sinai. This momentous event, together with the Exodus, synthesizes Jewish history and forms for Jews the paradigm of redemption.

Chapter 3

Weeks after leaving Egypt, Moses led the Jews through the wilderness to the foot of Mount Sinai. There, the Jews encountered God, and Moses received the Torah, or Law. Included in the Torah are the Ten Commandments (Exodus 20:2–14 and Deuteronomy 5:6–18 in the Jewish scriptures). Exodus 19:16–20 records God's appearance atop Mount Sinai:

> *On the third day, as morning dawned, there was thunder, and lightning, and a dense cloud upon the mountain, and a very loud blast of the horn; and all the people who were in the camp trembled. Moses led the people out of the camp toward God, and they took their places at the foot of the mountain.*
>
> *Now Mount Sinai was all in smoke, for the LORD had come down upon it in fire; the smoke rose like the smoke of a kiln. . . . As Moses spoke, God answered him in thunder. The LORD came down upon Mount Sinai . . . and the LORD called Moses to the top of the mountain . . . .*
>
> *—Exodus 19:16–20*, Tanakh—The Holy Scriptures.

Shortly after the theophany (God's appearance), Moses receives the Ten Commandments, which, as mentioned earlier, are listed in the Tanakh in Exodus 20:2–14 and Deuteronomy 5:6–18. In Judaism, the Ten Commandments are numbered differently from some Christian versions. (In the Christian Bible, see Exodus 20:2–17 and Deuteronomy 5:6–21.)

> 1. *I the LORD am your God who brought you out of the land of Egypt, the house of bondage: you shall have no other gods besides me.*
> 2. *You shall not make for yourself a sculptured image. . . .*
> 3. *You shall not swear falsely by the name of the LORD your God. . . .*
> 4. *Remember the sabbath day and keep it holy. . . .*
> 5. *Honor your father and your mother. . . .*
> 6. *You shall not murder.*
> 7. *You shall not commit adultery.*
> 8. *You shall not steal.*
> 9. *You shall not bear false witness against your neighbor.*
> 10. *You shall not covet your neighbor's house: you shall not covet your neighbor's wife, or his male or female slave, or his ox or his ass, or anything that is your neighbor's.*
>
> *—Exodus 20:2–14*, Tanakh—The Holy Scriptures.

After the people of Israel were presented with the Law, they continued to journey through the wilderness. Forty years later, they reached the Promised Land, their homeland. These nomadic people settled into an agricultural-based economy. A system of judges arbitrated disputes for members of each tribe. Eventually the tribes organized themselves into a loose confederation.

But, wanting to be like their neighbors who had more centralized governments and rulers, they formed a new kingdom, the kingdom of Israel, in 1020 B.C.E. As a unified nation, they had only three kings: Saul, David, and Solomon. It was Solomon who built the magnificent temple in Jerusalem, known as the First Temple. For centuries, the temple served as the focal point for Jewish life and religion, symbolizing God's presence and the covenant between God and the Jewish people.

The kingdom split in 922 B.C.E., after Solomon's death. The northern kingdom, called *Israel*, consisted of ten tribes. the southern kingdom, called *Judah*, consisted of two tribes (the tribe of Judah and the tribe of Benjamin). Assyria conquered Israel in 721 B.C.E., and the ten tribes gradually faded from view. The ten tribes of Israel were either destroyed or assimilated, perhaps through slavery, into Assyria; historically they are known as the **ten lost tribes of Israel**.

In 587 B.C.E., Judah met a similar fate. The Babylonians conquered Judah, and many of the people were deported to Babylonia. For seventy years, the Jewish leaders lived in Babylon. The era of the great prophets who constantly reminded the people to worship only YHWH included this time of exile.

This was a dark period in Jewish history. The people felt that their troubles were their own fault. They had been unfaithful to God and thus this destruction and **Exile** were their own doing. It was a time of much soul searching. The people began to reflect upon their past. This was a formative time for their scriptures: much writing and editing was done.

From Exile to Dispersion: A Chosen People

In 539 B.C.E., Cyrus of Persia (who had conquered the Babylonians) allowed the refugees to go back home. Many did return to rebuild their nation, their religion, and their lives. Since many others did not return home, this date can be identified as the beginning of the **Diaspora** or **Dispersion.** This means the Jewish people "scattered" to many communities outside their native land. By the year 515 B.C.E., those who returned had rebuilt the temple in Jerusalem. That structure became known as the Second Temple. From this point on, these people became known as the *Jews*, since they were the survivors of the tribe of Judah.

Prophets were prominent at the time of the establishment of the kingdom. These prophets pointed out the folly of making alliances with foreign powers over their allegiance to the one God. They railed against idol worship and pointed out injustice wherever they saw it.

Historically the Jewish people were a minority jostled about by their more powerful neighbors. They had known famine, homelessness, war, injustice, and exile. In short, they were the underdogs. Yet hope for better days always lived on in their hearts and national consciousness.

As the period of the prophets waned in about the fifth century B.C.E., for some groups in Judaism hope became expressed in the concept of a **messiah.** The meaning of *messiah* has varied in history depending upon the political and religious situation of the Jewish people, as well as on

---

ten lost tribes of Israel

the ten tribes of Israel destroyed or assimilated, perhaps through slavery, into Assyria, following 721 B.C.E.

Exile

the seventy years during which Jewish leaders were sent to and remained in Babylon, following the conquest of Judah in 587 B.C.E.

Diaspora or **Dispersion**

collective term for the dispersal of Jews to areas outside of Israel and for those Jews living outside of Israel

messiah

a person who brings about a national triumph over enemies and resulting importance of the nation in world affairs, or a spiritual renewal of the Jewish people (a messianic age of a new moral order)

the groups or movements within Judaism. Sometimes it has meant an anointed (appointed by God) person who would save or redeem the people—lead the nation to triumph over enemies and to hold a place of importance in world affairs. This individual was thought to be a descendant of King David.

More often, the messiah has meant a spiritual renewal of the Jewish people. This spiritual renewal would likely begin with the Jewish people and extend outwards to embrace the entire human family and create a transformed world. Whether the messiah is seen as an individual to bring about the new order or as a messianic age of a new moral order, the concept of messiah always embodies the notion of hope for a better life.

From the very beginning the notion that the Hebrews were a **"chosen people"** developed. This notion is not meant to convey the message that the Jews considered themselves privileged above other people. Rather, they saw themselves as chosen by God for a special mission in history. Their mission has been to bring God's word to the entire world.

When we remember that Judaism gave birth to both Christianity and Islam, we should also be aware that these two religions account for almost three billion of the world's population. Further, when we consider the effect Judaism has had on western civilization, we recognize the influence this tiny group of people has had out of all proportion to their numbers. Perhaps it is in these ways that the mission of the Jewish people, as a chosen people, is being fulfilled.

chosen people
the Jewish people with a sense of a special mission in history: to bring God's word to the entire world

Post-Biblical History

Rabbinical Judaism

Upon returning to their homeland after the Exile, the Jews set about the task of rebuilding their lives, as well as their temple. Yet from this time on, the Jewish people were dominated by one power after another. At first they were a district in the Persian Empire. The Greeks took over the area in 332 B.C.E., giving us the term *Judaea* or *Judea* for the land around Jerusalem. A short period of independence (167–63 B.C.E.) followed until the Roman conquest of 63 B.C.E.

The Romans destroyed the temple in 70 C.E., and renamed Jerusalem *Aelia Capitolina*. Sixty-five years later, Roman armies eliminated the last traces of Judea, and the tribes of Judah and Benjamin were scattered. The area which included Judea became known as *Palestine*, a Greek form of the Hebrew word for the Philistines, who once lived along the coastal areas. The dispersion of the Jews that began at the time of the Exile now became total. This Galut, or Golah (exile), lasted until the emergence of modern-day Israel.

It was the task of the Jews in dispersion to find a way to preserve their faith. Since it was no longer possible to practice animal sacrifice in the temple, the Jews began to gather in synagogues in the cities in which they lived. A **synagogue** is not necessarily a building, but rather an "assembly." Thus any Jewish home can be a synagogue as long as the required ten Jewish adult males are present and they have a copy of the **Torah**. A rabbi, one schooled in the teachings of the scriptures, normally conducts the service.

What Is Torah?

What is Torah? It is what God has revealed to us, and what we have come to understand about God. It is the ideas and ideals, the laws and commandments, that make up our religious heritage. It is the experience of Abraham, the legislation of Moses, the vision of the Prophets, the commentary of the Rabbis, the insight of the Mystics. It is the questions we ask, and the answers we receive, when we seek to understand God, the world, and ourselves.

It is the way of life; the path to self-fulfillment; the design for a better world.

—Chaim Stern, ed., Gates of Prayer *(New York: Central Conference of American Rabbis, 1975), 696.*

Let's Talk about It . . .

1. Why is the Torah so important to the Jewish people?
2. What is the importance of the Torah for Christians and Muslims?

In the time following 70 C.E., without priests, temple, or sacrifice, Judaism emphasized scripture study, prayer, charity, the synagogue, and the scholars and rabbis. The decision regarding which of the collected writings were truly the word of God and thus to be included in the Jewish scripture resulted in the Hebrew Bible as it is known today. The Jewish scriptures are divided into three sections: the Law (Torah), the Prophets, and the Writings. Of these, the Torah has the highest importance.

The Torah, or Law, is the collection of the first five books of the Bible: Genesis, Exodus, Leviticus, Numbers, and Deuteronomy. These books contain the central ritual and ethical laws that govern Jewish life. The word *Torah* can also refer to the whole Hebrew Bible or to the entire collection of Jewish teachings. The term **written Torah** refers to the whole Hebrew Bible, or **Tanakh**. These terms are synonyms for Jewish scriptures. The letters *t*, *n*, and *k* in the word *Tanakh* stand for *Torah*, *Nevi'im*, and *Kethuvim*—the three divisions of the Hebrew Bible. The Hebrew Bible consists of thirty-nine books (*Tanakh—The Holy Scriptures*, Jewish Publication Society).

Tanakh

Torah (The Five Books of Moses)—The Hebrew names are based on the first words in each book:

- *Genesis—Bereshit ("In the beginning . . .")*
- *Exodus—Shemot ("The names . . .")*
- *Leviticus—Vayikra ("And He called . . .")*
- *Numbers—Bemidbar ("In the wilderness . . .")*
- *Deuteronomy—Devarim ("The words . . .")*

Nevi'im (The Prophets): *Joshua, Judges, I Samuel, II Samuel, I Kings, II Kings, Isaiah, Jeremiah, Ezekiel, Hosea, Joel, Amos, Obadiah, Jonah, Micah, Nahum, Habakkuk, Zephaniah, Haggai, Zechariah, Malachi*

Kethuvim (The Writings): *Psalms, Proverbs, Job, The Song of Songs, Ruth, Lamentations, Ecclesiastes, Esther, Daniel, Ezra, Nehemiah, I Chronicles, II Chronicles*

Over the course of a year, the entire Torah is read aloud. Each week, Jews read a passage from the Torah (The Five Books of Moses). This Torah passage, or Torah portion, is known as a parshah, or sidra. There are fifty-four parshahs. The first parshah is called Bereshit (Genesis 1:1–6:8), which is also the name of the Bible's first book. The last parshah is Vezot Ha'berachah (Deuteronomy 33:1–34:12). It is read on Simchas Torah. The festival Simchas Torah means "Rejoicing in the Law." On Simchas Torah, Jews read the last Torah passage and then proceed to read the very first. This shows that the Torah never ends.

Let's Talk about It . . .

1. Which books of the Jewish Bible did you recognize?
2. Share what you know about some of the books of the Jewish Bible.

The Hebrew word **mitzvot** means "commandments." The Torah contains 613 commandments. There are 248 positive commandments and 365 negative commandments. A positive commandment spells out what a person should do, and a negative commandment spells out what a person should not do. The commandments cover virtually every aspect of daily life.

Today every synagogue or temple contains at least one copy of the Torah handwritten in the original Hebrew on a decorated parchment scroll of the Torah. The scrolls are covered with fabric, and adorned with a silver breastplate. The handles of the scrolls are topped with silver crowns. Sometimes tiny bells are attached to these crowns. The scrolls are kept in a cabinet called an **ark**, from the term *ark of the covenant*. The Torah is read from a special lectern, and a lamp burns perpetually, symbolizing the light of the word. Jews never touch the parchment, which shows respect for the Torah. When reading from the scrolls, they use a yad (hand-shaped pointer) to keep their place.

mitzvot
Hebrew word meaning "commandments"

ark
the cabinet where the Torah scrolls are kept

Mishnah

the oral Torah of a legal nature, which was gathered together and written down

Gemara

comments and rulings about the Mishnah which were collected and recorded

Talmud

the Mishnah and Gemara, a commentary on the Jewish scriptures

oral Torah

the Talmud (the Mishnah and the Gemara); explains the written Torah

The oral Torah helps to explain the written Torah. Significant interpretations of the Law developed over the next several centuries following the destruction of Jerusalem. Around the third century C.E., the prohibition against writing down the oral Law was lifted. The oral Torah of a legal nature was gathered together and written down; this document was called the **Mishnah**. Over succeeding centuries, comments about the Mishnah were also collected and recorded. This document was given the name **Gemara**.

By the fifth century C.E., the Mishnah and the Gemara had been combined into one collection known as the **Talmud.** The Talmud is a commentary on the Jewish scriptures by various rabbis in these centuries. It includes various interpretations of the scriptures and applications to everyday life. The Talmud is second to the Torah as a source of guidance for the Jewish faith. One Talmud was produced in Babylon and another in Palestine. The *Babylonian Talmud* is the most comprehensive; the *Palestinian*, or *Jerusalem*, *Talmud* is smaller and of lesser importance.

For the most part, the term **oral Torah** generally refers to the Mishnah and the Gemara (the Talmud). At one time, the teachings embodied in these works were transmitted by word of mouth (orally).

From the Babylonian Talmud

Study of Torah leads to precision, precision to zeal, zeal to cleanliness, cleanliness to restraint, restraint to purity, purity to holiness, holiness to meekness, meekness to fear of sin, fear of sin to saintliness, saintliness to the holy spirit, and the holy spirit to eternal life.

—*A passage from the tractate (division) Aboda Zara (20b) of the Babylonian Talmud.*

Let's Talk about It . . .

1. What is the message of this sacred writing?
2. How is this writing's message evidenced in the beliefs and practices of the Jewish faith?
3. How can this message be applied to other faiths?

Rabbinical Judaism developed over the centuries to include an emphasis on work and the proper use of God's gifts. Traditionally rabbis were required to have a trade by which to earn their living. The writings and studies that came into being helped the Jewish people find ways to adapt their laws to new conditions. Work and study led to a methodical way of living out one's calling; applied to the business world, the standard problem-solving techniques guaranteed a higher-than-average rate of success.

European History: In Search of a Homeland

The Jewish people in dispersion have nevertheless had a precarious existence. At times, persecution forced the Jews to migrate; at other times, they enjoyed relative peace and prosperity. Roman laws governing their status, prohibiting ownership of land, and limiting their occupations had a formative influence on their life well beyond the end of the Roman Empire in 475 C.E.

Islam exploded out of the Arabian peninsula in the seventh century. It fanned out into the Middle East, advanced across northern Africa, entered Spain, and reached Tours in France by 732, a century after Mohammed's death. Officially, laws against Jews were harsh under Islam. Practically speaking, the laws were frequently ignored and the Jews shared in the prosperity of Islam. This was especially true in Babylonia from 750–847. Overall, Jews fared better under Islam than under Christianity.

In the West, Judaism had survived in Spain since the first century. After the Moslem conquest the Jews there also enjoyed a golden age of freedom, and important scholars of this time were counted among them. When persecution in Babylonia and Spain increased, the Jews moved into Christian Europe.

In Christian Europe, Jews were forced to live in special sections of cities called **ghettos.** The ghettos were usually crowded and in the worst parts of the cities. Still, by the tenth century, Europe became a major center of Jewish life. But often when the Christians of Europe faced serious problems, Jews become the **scapegoats** for the ills of society. They were blamed for everything from the economic woes of the society to the plagues. **Anti-semitism** is a plague itself that has followed the Jews throughout their history, the length of Europe and far beyond.

ghetto
a section of a city where Jews (or another minority group) were required to live

scapegoat
a goat upon whose head was symbolically placed the sins of the people, after which the goat was sent to the wilderness; one who bears the blame for the sins or faults of another

anti-semitism
hostility toward or discrimination against Jews as a racial or ethnic group or as a religion

Auschwitz Concentration Camp, Poland

Zionist movement

search for and control of a homeland for the Jewish people, brought to reality in the mid-twentieth century

In the late nineteenth century, the innate search for a homeland found expression in the **Zionist movement**. Theodore Herzel (1860–1904), who wrote *The Jewish State (Der Judenstaat)*, provided the impetus for modern Zionism. The movement met with opposition from both within the Jewish community and outside of it. In the 1890s, Jews began to resettle parts of their native land after centuries of absence. After WW I, the British, who controlled the area, were persuaded to support this movement. Gradually support for Zionism increased. It was not until after WW II and the Holocaust that the establishment of the State of Israel in 1948 realized the goal of Zionism. The Jews have defended their new nation from numerous attacks by their Arab neighbors, some of whom were displaced during the resettlement. Today Zionism works to maintain and support the State of Israel. Some Jews today see the existence of modern-day Israel as the messianic era so long hoped for.

Planting the Seed

Individual Jews follow various traditions within Judaism. Jews may be Orthodox, Reform, Conservative, or Reconstructionist. According to Orthodox and Conservative Judaism, a Jew is one born of a Jewish mother or one who undergoes formal conversion. In the view of Reform and Reconstructionist Judaism, a Jew is one born of a Jewish parent and reared as a Jew or one who undergoes formal conversion. Thus being a Jew is not necessarily a matter of religious faith—there are non-religious Jews and practicing Jews.

Modern-Day Judaism

The various movements listed here are all varieties of Judaism, or traditions within Judaism. In general, they differ in their interpretation and application of Jewish law.

Orthodox Judaism is the oldest tradition within Judaism. The Orthodox movement believes that God gave Moses both the written and the oral Torah atop Mount Sinai. In their view, the Torah has remained intact and unchanged, and contains 613 commandments, which all Jews must follow. The commandments of Jewish law are considered absolutely binding. Members observe the letter of the Law concerning the Sabbath; they do not work, travel, write, conduct business, carry money, or light fires. They observe the dietary laws to the most minute detail. Men and women sit separately in the synagogue. They use only Hebrew in their prayers and ceremonies. The men wear a **yarmulke** in the synagogue and frequently at all times. New York City has a large population of Orthodox Jews.

Hasidic Judaism is a mystically-oriented group within Orthodox Judaism. Hasidic Jews react against philosophical and theological means of finding God and seek God in a direct, mystical way. This more simple, heartfelt approach to God commonly occurs in the world's religions. Many Hasidic Jews live in Eastern Europe. In the United States, they most commonly live in and near New York City.

The **Reform movement** within Judaism originated in Germany in the eighteenth century, but reached its full expression in the United States. The first explicitly Reform congregation was Temple Har Sinai, organized in Baltimore in 1842. Reform Judaism has moved away from the strictness of Orthodox Judaism. Early Reform leaders placed greater emphasis on belief than on law. Faithfully practicing Judaism meant responding to God rather than keeping all the laws.

Reform Jews observe the high standards of morality set forth in the Torah, but do not follow practices that are incompatible with modern civilization. Members sit by family groups in the synagogue; the vernacular is often used rather than Hebrew, and instrumental music is allowed. Reform Judaism might be defined as a religious philosophy that tries to harmonize Judaic tradition and the demands of today's culture.

Conservative Judaism is a term used in the United States for Jewish worship that modifies the Law to meet modern needs while avoiding the more drastic changes of the Reform movement. It seeks a path between Orthodox and Reform Judaism. For the most part, Conservative Jews accept the binding nature of Jewish law, but maintain that it must change over time to reflect prevailing social realities. When considering whether to permit or to forbid something, a Conservative rabbi might ask: Is it grounded in the history and wording of the Law itself? Will it result in the enhancement of the Torah as a whole?

Orthodox Judaism
oldest tradition within Judaism; believes that God gave Moses both the written and the oral Torah atop Mount Sinai; keeps strict laws, including dietary laws

yarmulke
skullcap worn by Jewish men to show respect for God

Hasidic Judaism
devout form of Judaism with a strong mystical element

Reform movement
Jewish worship that modifies the Law to meet modern conditions

Conservative Judaism
a term used in the United States for Jewish worship that modifies the law to meet modern needs while avoiding the more drastic changes of the Reform movement

A high degree of theological diversity characterizes the Conservative movement. Members follow the pattern of traditional Judaism but seek to adapt it to particular times and places. They observe the Sabbath and the high holy days and may use both Hebrew and the vernacular in worship. They observe most of the dietary laws. Men wear the yarmulke only during the religious service.

Taking Root

Even though Jews were present in North America as early as Columbus (whose ships carried converted Jews), Jewish religious history officially begins in the United States in 1654. In that year, a group of refugees from Recife in Brazil came to New Amsterdam (New York). The Jewish presence was tolerated in New York. In time, the Jews in the city gained approval for public worship (sometime between 1685 and 1695) and formed the Congregation Shearith Israel. By 1729, they had grown sufficiently to build a house of worship.

Gradually more Jewish families came to North America. Small communities of Jews settled in Newport, Charleston, Savannah, Richmond, and Philadelphia. In 1773, the largest community in the United States consisted of 500 Jews who lived in Charleston. Until the American Revolution, no rabbis were present among the congregations. A highly literate laity preserved the teachings of Judaism.

All of the early Jews to North America were refugees from Spain and Portugal. In the nineteenth century, they were joined by Jews emigrating from Germany and Poland. After 1836, entire groups of Jews from Europe came to the United States. In 1840, there were about 15,000 Jews in the United States; by 1850, 50,000; by 1860, 160,000; and by 1880, 250,000.

Immigration increased dramatically between 1881 and 1921. In these years, the Russians conducted a series of persecutions among Jewish communities in Russia and parts of Poland under their control. These sporadic persecutions are called **pogroms.** Most of those who survived these persecutions immigrated to the United States. Almost two million Jews came to the United States during these years. The 270 synagogues in existence in the United States in 1880 grew to 1,902 in 1916. Further immigrations of Jews occurred in the years immediately preceding and following WW II. Today about 4.3 million Jews live in the United States; 350,000 live in Canada. Few Jews live in predominantly Christian Mexico.

One cannot begin to understand the feelings of contemporary Jews without an appreciation of the significance of the **Holocaust.** With Hitler's rise to power in Germany, millions of Jews were trapped in Germany, Poland, Hungary, and Czechoslovakia. The Holocaust was nothing less than the extermination of an entire race of people. It is believed that six million Jews, one-third of the entire world population of Jews, were killed. Anti-semitism gave birth to an unspeakable horror. Gentiles can begin to gain a better grasp on today's Jewish perspective by extensive reading, visits to museums such as the Holocaust Museum in Washington, DC, and by viewing movies of these tragic days, such as *Schindler's List.*

pogroms

sporadic persecutions of the Jews, especially those in Russia and Poland

Holocaust

the name given by Jews to the attempt by Nazi Germany under Hitler to exterminate the entire Jewish race; six million Jews were killed

Growing and Blooming

Earlier in the chapter we stated that the western view of God, the dignity of people, and the human role in the world comes essentially from our common Jewish heritage. So what do you believe about these aspects of a worldview? For example:

- What do you believe about God? Is God good?
- Does God care for you? For all people?
- What, if anything, does God expect of us?
- From God's point of view, do all people have the same basic rights?
- Is it legitimate to advocate for social change?
- Do you have a right to expect that you will have a fulfilling, happy life?

Your answers to these questions may very well derive from the western Judaic heritage. Pause for a moment to consider your responses before continuing to read.

Beliefs

On God

God is one.

"Hear, O Israel, the Lord our God, the Lord is one."

Monotheism is the radical new concept of God given to the western world by Judaism. To westerners, it is hardly noticeable as radical, but it contrasts sharply with the polytheistic concept of most earlier groups of people whom the Jews met. Gradually over time, from Abraham to the prophets, the Judaic concept of monotheism became more focused. For Abraham, El Shaddai was one of any number of clan gods. For the prophets, YHWH was the one and only God. Belief in one God became expressed in the Shema. As monotheism became more clear, so too did the people's understanding of God's nature.

The blowing of the shofar is part of the Rosh Ha-Shanah celebration.

God is personal.

With the ever deepening relationship of the covenant, Judaic faith began to affirm that God is personal. Unlike other gods who were often distant and aloof, YHWH drew close to people and cared deeply for them. People are always in God's presence, and God is involved in their lives.

God is saving.

In fact, God cared so much for the people that God was always seeking to save them from one form of harm after another. Jews could look back on their history and cite innumerable examples of how God was a saving God. God watched over Abraham, Isaac, and Jacob and their families. It was God who raised up Moses as a great leader. The prime example of God's saving action was the Exodus-Sinai event, in which God saved the people from the slavery of the Egyptians, gave them the Law, and eventually brought them to their own land, a land "flowing with milk and honey."

God is faithful.

Human relationships are troubled by minor, and sometimes very serious, violations of infidelity. The God-human relationship, on the other hand, is never violated with infidelity on the part of God. While people may turn against God and even sometimes deserve separation from God, God is never unfaithful. For the Jews, this loyalty on the part of God is an awesome truth. It constantly challenges people to be more faithful in their relations with God and with one another.

God is above all.

"For my plans are not your plans,
nor are My ways your ways
—declares the Lord.
But as the heavens are high above the earth,
so are my ways high above your ways
and my plans above your plans."
—Isaiah 55:8–9, Tanakh—The Holy Scriptures.

Sometimes people believe that their prayers or actions or sacrifices can coerce God to do certain things for them. Jews believe that God cannot be manipulated by any means whatsoever. While among people and involved, God is still beyond. God is Absolutely Other. Instead of seeking to control God, people should seek to know God's plan and God's will for them. Constantly people should seek to see things from God's perspective and seek always to fulfill God's will.

On People

Recall that central to the Jewish worldview is the covenant relationship with God. This is a personal relationship of love, trust, and fidelity between God and people. Just as their concept of God became more refined over time, so their understanding of who they are in this relationship likewise became more clear.

Human dignity

Relatively speaking, westerners affirm the importance of human beings. We are concerned with individual human rights and freedoms. Laws are written to ensure the protection of these rights and freedoms. Such concern for the dignity of human beings finds its roots in the Jewish worldview.

Human beings are created good and in the image and likeness of God. "And God created man in his image, in the image of God he created him; male and female he created them" (Genesis 1:27). "And God saw all that he had made, and found it very good" (Genesis 1:31a). In fact, all of creation is good.

Social justice

Since human beings are created in the image and likeness of God, they are all children of God—brothers and sisters to one another. From this it follows that they have certain responsibilities to one another. And since all of creation is good, every individual should be enabled to enjoy the goods of creation.

The prophets especially emphasized social responsibilities people have to one another. In the time of King Jeroboam II (786–746 B.C.E.) of the northern kingdom, Israel, Amos brought to light the transgressions of Israel:

> *Thus said the LORD:*
> *"For three transgressions of Israel,*
> *For four, I will not revoke it:*
> *Because they have sold for silver*
> *Those whose cause was just,*
> *And the needy for a pair of sandals.*
> *[Ah,] you who trample the heads of the poor*
> *Into the dust of the ground,*
> *And make the humble walk a twisted course!"*
> —*Amos 2:6–7*, Tanakh—The Holy Scriptures.

Amos sharply criticized merchants who fixed their scales for cheating, who bought the poor for silver, the needy for a pair of sandals (8:5–6). Isaiah proclaimed the kind of actions God expects of people:

> *"No, this is the fast that I desire:*
> *To unlock fetters of wickedness,*
> *And untie the cords of the yoke*
> *to let the oppressed go free;*
> *To break off every yoke.*
> *It is to share your bread with the hungry,*
> *and to take the wretched poor into your home;*
> *when you see the naked, to cover him,*
> *and not to ignore your own kin."*
> —*Isaiah 58:6–7*, Tanakh—The Holy Scriptures.

The Dawn

The Teacher sat around a blazing fire with a small number of students late at night. Their meandering conversation was broken by periods of silence when they all gazed at the stars and the moon. Following one of these periods when no one spoke, the Teacher asked a question. "How can we know when the night has ended and the day has begun?"

Eagerly one young man answered, "You know the night is over and the day has begun when you can look off in the distance and determine which animal is your dog and which is the sheep. Is that the right answer, Teacher?"

"It is a good answer," the Teacher said slowly, "but it is not the answer I would give."

After several minutes of discussion a second student ventured a guess on behalf of the whole group, "You know the night is over and the day has begun when light falls on the leaves and you can tell whether it is a palm tree or a fig tree."

Once again the Teacher shook his head. "That was a fine answer, but it is not the answer I seek," he said gently.

Immediately the students began to argue with one another. Finally one of them begged the Teacher, "Answer your own question, Teacher, for we cannot think of another response."

The Teacher looked intently at the eager young faces before he began to speak. "When you look into the eyes of a human being and see a brother or sister you know that it is morning. If you cannot see a sister or brother you will know that it will always be night."

—William R. White, Stories for the Journey (Minneapolis: Augsburg Publishing House, 1988), 97–98.

Let's Talk about It . . .

1. How would you have answered the question?
2. What is your reaction to the Teacher's answer?

Morality

Human beings are to care for one another. Rules in society help to ensure that people do in fact exercise their responsibilities toward one another. Such rules help to provide for the harmonious functioning of society.

According to rabbinical Judaism, 613 commandments comprise the Law. These relate both to ritualistic and ethical behavior. Ten of these have become the moral foundation of the western world. They are called the Ten Commandments. The Ten Commandments do not answer every question concerning moral behavior. They are not intended to cover every kind of moral situation. But they do provide the fundamental moral basis from which other moral prescriptions can be developed.

In the Jewish view, people are to live up to their fullest potential. They are to be individually faithful to the covenant. They are to seek to know and fulfill God's will. They are to live as responsible, caring members of society. To do less is to **sin**. The Hebrew word *chet* means "missing the mark." It is like an archer who shoots the arrow and doesn't quite hit the bull's eye. To fail to be our best self is to "miss the mark."

To "miss the mark," to sin, does not mean there is no hope for becoming a better person. In Jewish understanding, God is always faithful to the covenant, even when people are not. Thus God stands always ready to invite people back. God seeks to forgive people and welcome them into his embrace. It is up to people to respond to God's invitation.

sin
in Judaism, "missing the mark"; a failure to live as a responsible, caring member of society

On Progress

Recall Jewish history. They were a minority people jostled about by more powerful forces. Characteristically they played the role of the underdog. Thus a people in such a situation would naturally look to a better day. They would hope and seek greater prosperity, peace, and security. An oppressed and persecuted people would naturally seek change.

The covenant relationship with God revealed a new social order. The affirmation of life, the image of a bountiful banquet, a lush mountain, a time of justice, a beautiful city are all themes which thread their way through Jewish scripture.

> *The Lord of hosts will make on this mount*
> *For all the peoples*
> *A banquet of rich viands [food],*
> *A banquet of choice wines—*
> *Of rich viands seasoned with marrow,*
> *Of choice wines well refined.*
> *And he will destroy on this mount the shroud*
> *That is drawn over the faces of all peoples*
> *And the covering that is spread*
> *Over all nations:*
> *He will destroy death forever.*
>
> —Isaiah 25:6–7, Tanakh—The Holy Scriptures.

This Jewish perspective lays the groundwork in western nations for the notion of social transformation. The status quo is never acceptable.

Practices

Contemporary Jewish life is characterized by cycles of various practices and festivals. These cycles give Jews a structure which enables them to express their faith.

Judaism has taught Christians and Moslems alike a great love for the word of God. Jews spend a great deal of time and effort studying the word. As stated earlier, the Torah is of highest importance for Jewish faith. Its teachings range from such commands as the Ten Commandments to regulations concerning food preparation.

The more traditional the group, the more likely they will be to abide by the laws regarding food. These laws are known as *Kashrut*, which comes from the word *kashur* (**kosher**) meaning "proper" or "pure." For example, there is a prohibition against eating pork (because pigs do not chew their cud), a prohibition against eating shrimp (because shellfish do not have fins and scales), a prohibition against mixing meat and milk while cooking or eating (because this amounts to killing an animal it its mother's milk). Stipulations concerning proper food preparation are also listed.

Jewish faith is formed in the family. Here is the center of both Jewish practices and festivals. The events may be celebrated at the synagogue or temple as well, but the focus remains the home. Central to these celebrations is the Sabbath. It is remembered both in the home and synagogue. The whole of the Jewish week revolves around the Sabbath.

Special celebrations include circumcision and bar- or bat-mitzvah. Following the custom of Abraham, boys are circumcised when they are eight days old. Circumcision is a sign of the covenant and has been practiced by Jews from ancient times. The boy is officially named at this time.

Bar- or bat-mitzvah marks the passage from childhood to adulthood. A boy becomes **bar-mitzvah** the day after his thirteenth birthday and a girl becomes **bat-mitzvah** a day after her twelfth birthday. The terms literally mean son or daughter of the commandment. A boy or girl must study the Torah for an extended period of time and must learn to read Hebrew. On the day of bar- or bat-mitzvah, the boy or girl publicly reads from the Torah for the first time in the midst of the community. At a typical ceremony, the young person reads that day's Torah passage in Hebrew and then comments on it. From then on, the young man or woman takes on adult responsibilities in the Jewish faith.

kosher

"proper" or "pure"; in Judaism, refers to the proper observance of stipulations regarding food

bar-mitzvah

initiation of thirteen-year-old Jewish boy into the community

bat-mitzvah

initiation of a twelve-year-old Jewish girl into the community

An Orthodox bar-mitzvah

Reaping the Fruit

The annual festivals of Judaism extend the structure for enabling Jews to celebrate and express their faith. These festivals are celebrated in the home as much as they are in the temple or synagogue. In fact, the celebration of these festivals is essentially family oriented.

Shabbat or Sabbath

In contrast to other religions which may nominate one day out of the entire year as the most important celebration (for example, the Easter celebration of the resurrection of Jesus for Christians), Jews would name the worship service which happens on a weekly basis—the **Shabbat** or **Sabbath** is considered the most important observance above all others. Keeping Shabbat is one of the most important mitzvot; it is the only mitzvah mentioned in the Decalogue.

Jews remember and observe Shabbat. Jews remember Shabbat by emphasizing its roots as recorded in scripture: (1) after creating, God rested on Shabbat (Exodus 20:11); (2) after being freed from a life of slavery in Egypt, the Jews rested on Shabbat (Deuteronomy 5:15). Indeed, the moments of quiet and opportunity for recreation at the end of a busy week are a welcome experience for contemporary westerners.

Jews take the regulations and rules of Shabbat seriously. To understand Shabbat restrictions, one must grasp the meaning of **melachah**. The word *melachah* refers to work of a creative nature; it is work that controls one's environment. Thirty-nine types of this work are forbidden on Shabbat.

Sabbath preparations in the home are completed before sundown on Friday. Shortly before sunset, the mother lights two candles (symbolizing the need to remember and observe) and prays a blessing. After readings and prayer, the family and guests gather for the evening meal. A special hymn is sung and each of the children is blessed by the parents. The wine and the day are blessed. Then two loaves of braided, egg-rich bread, the *challah*, are blessed. The meal follows and concludes with songs, teachings, and prayers. There may also be a service in the synagogue on Friday evening.

The Sabbath day is joyful and festive. The day often begins with a morning synagogue service. On Saturday afternoon, Jews gather for another festive, leisurely meal. Once again, prayers and blessings are recited. After eating, people study Torah, play a board game, or take a walk. Traditionally, Jews eat a light meal in the late afternoon, which is the third and last meal of Shabbat.

On Saturday evening (about forty minutes after sunset, or when three stars are visible), Jews perform Havdalah (a ritual of division, or separation). One person recites blessings over wine, spices, and candles, expressing hope for Shabbat's return. The blessings that follow signal the end of Shabbat; they emphasize the division of Shabbat from the coming week.

Shabbat or **Sabbath**
in Judaism, the weekly celebration from dusk on Friday until darkness on Saturday

melachah
work of creative nature, work that controls one's environment

A Jewish Calendar

Autumn Festivals

Year one of the Jewish calendar symbolically represents the first year of the world's existence. The year 2000 C.E. is the Jewish year 5760, until the new year begins in the fall. Jews follow a lunar calendar for setting the dates of their festivals. Thus the celebration of these festivals varies somewhat in relation to the secular calendar.

The first of the festivals is **Rosh Ha-Shanah.** For Jews, Rosh Ha-Shanah is the birthday of the world and the beginning of the new year. This festival usually takes place during the month of September. The blowing of the *shofar*, a ram's horn, opens the celebration. It is the beginning of ten *Days of Awe* (or *High Holy Days* or *Ten Days of Repentence*) in which people are encouraged to examine their lives in relationship to the Law. It is believed that the books of heaven are open at this time and Jews are to seek forgiveness of their sins from each other.

These ten days of repentance conclude with **Yom Kippur**, the Day of Atonement. This is considered a most solemn day of fasting and the holiest day of the year. Jews may not work, eat, drink, engage in sexual activity, bathe, anoint the body, or wear leather shoes on this day. The day is devoted to prayer and reflection, as each individual makes his or her confession to God. The worship service for this day includes corporate confession of sins, prayers for pardon, and a prayer asking God for absolution of sins. Also included is a memorial for those who have died. The service concludes with the blowing of the shofar.

In the same month of the Jewish calendar (Tishri), the harvest festival of **Sukkot** is celebrated. It is also called the *Feast of Booths* or *Festival of Tabernacles*. It recalls the wilderness travels of the people of Israel in the desert. Since no permanent buildings could be built, booths or tents were used. Thus one may see similar booths or tents in the yards of synagogues and homes. These booths may be decorated with fall fruits, vegetables, flowers, and branches.

A celebration called **Simchat Torah** (meaning "Rejoicing in the Law" or "Joy in the Torah") closes the Sukkot festival. It marks the end of the yearly reading of the Torah. The last verses of the Torah are read, the scroll is rewound, and the first words of the Jewish scriptures are read.

Winter Festivals

Hanukkah, also called the *Feast of Dedication* or *Festival of Lights*, commemorates the rededication of the temple in 164 B.C.E. The temple had been desecrated by worship and statues initiated by the Greeks, but purged after the revolt led by Judas Maccabee. A *hanukiah*, or *menorah*, an eight-branched candelabra, is a central feature of this festival. When the temple was to be dedicated, only enough oil for one day was found for the lamp. The miracle celebrated on this feast is that the oil lasted until more oil could be obtained, a period of eight days. One more candle is lit each day of Hanukkah.

Rosh Ha-Shanah
Jewish new year holy days, the ten "Days of Awe"

Yom Kippur
the Day of Atonement which concludes the ten days of Rosh Ha-Shanah

Sukkot
The Feast of Booths or Festival of Tabernacles, which recalls the wilderness travels of the people of Israel in the desert

Simchat Torah
the last day of the Sukkot festival which marks the end of the yearly reading of the Torah

Hanukkah
the feast commemorating the victory of the Maccabees over the oppressors of the Jewish people

It is customary to eat fried and sweet foods during this festival. Children are customarily given a gift each day of Hanukkah. Because of its proximity to Christmas, Christians sometimes think of this as a "Jewish Christmas." This is an incorrect association, as the celebration of Hanukkah has nothing to do with the Christian celebration of Christmas.

Another fun-filled and joyous festival is **Purim** or the *Feast of Lots* which takes place in late winter. It recalls the biblical story of Queen Esther who foiled a plot to massacre all the Jews in the Persian Empire. The book of Esther is read and the children boo the villain and cheer the heroine. Special pastries and an exchange of gifts are part of the celebration.

Spring Festivals

A central spring festival is **Pesah**, or **Passover**. Originally a celebration of the spring wheat and barley harvest in Israel, this eight-day festival commemorates the last plague in Egypt and celebrates the Jewish people's liberation from slavery in Egypt. On the first two nights of Pesah, Jewish families gather for the *seder*, an elaborate ritual meal celebrated in the home. Special foods, such as *matzah*, unseasoned horseradish, chopped apples mixed with nuts, cinnamon, a roasted egg, parsley or radish, and salt water are used in the meal. Each of these carries a symbolic meaning. At the seder, the *haggadah* (story of liberation, or Exodus) is told.

A new festival, **Yom Hasho'ah**, or *Holocaust Day of Remembrance* was added to the calendar by Israel shortly after it became a state in 1968. It is a day to recall the totality of the Holocaust and to honor the six million Jews who died under Hitler and the Nazis. Special tribute is made to those who participated in the Warsaw ghetto uprising.

Fifty days after Pesah, the Jews celebrate **Shavu'ot**, also known as *Feast of Weeks* or *Pentecost*. This Jewish festival celebrates the harvesting of spring crops and God's giving the Torah to the Jews atop Mount Sinai—for this reason, it is considered the birthday of the Jewish religion. In Reform Judaism, Shavu'ot is the day for confirmation ceremonies.

Purim
the *Feast of Lots* commemorating deliverance of the Persian Jews by Esther

Pesah or **Passover**
the eight-day Jewish festival commemorating the Exodus

Yom Hasho'ah
the Holocaust Day of Remembrance

Shavu'ot
the Feast of Weeks or Pentecost; the birthday of the Jewish religion

Conclusion

The synagogue service was now drawing to a close. It didn't seem that the service had really lasted almost ninety minutes. Rachel and Kevin had witnessed the great respect the Jews hold for the Torah as they processed through the congregation with the Torah. They noticed the care with which the Rabbi had unrolled the scroll, and they listened attentively to his message. Kevin welcomed the quiet moments for reflection after a busy week of school and track practice. Rachel decided it was time that she pay more attention to her own faith and of how she could be more respectful of it.

Both decided that this optional assignment to attend the synagogue service on a Friday evening wasn't so bad after all.

Discovering

1. Be sure you are able to explain each of the terms in the vocabulary list.

2. Meet with two classmates. Each person is to take one of the sections under biblical history: family, nation, or chosen people. Then explain to each other the experience of the Jewish people during that time period.

3. Discuss in a small group the post-biblical history of Judaism. What are the principle themes of this period?

4. What do Jews believe about God, people, and human progress?

5. Explain the meaning of each of the Jewish festivals and how they are celebrated.

Exploring

1. Compare Jewish history with Jewish beliefs. Show how Jewish beliefs derive from Jewish experience.

2. List the Jewish festivals and state the central meaning of each festival. Then create a parallel list of secular or religious celebrations with the same meaning. For example, Passover which celebrates freedom is similar to a nation's independence day.

3. Discuss in a small group contemporary examples of how the Jewish worldview is evident in your culture.

4. A friend has been having some difficult times. What attitudes, values, or virtues from the Jewish experience can you use to help your friend?

5. Talk to a Jew about his or her experience of being a Jew. If you are Jewish, explain to a friend who is not Jewish how your Jewish faith affects your life.

6. In a small group of people with whom you feel free to share on a personal level, discuss these questions:

   • Do you think it is important to designate one day of the week to rest?

   • Do you think that a day of rest would have or has had a significant effect on your faith life?

1. What if Judaism had never existed? How would your life be different?

2. Attend a synagogue service in your community. What aspects of Judaism related in this chapter are evident in the service? Afterwards, visit with members of the congregation to learn more about your experience.

3. Identify four or five aspects of your worldview that are similar to the worldview of Judaism and perhaps come from Judaism.

4. Formulate a list of attitudes and practical activities you can personally implement to combat anti-semitism.

5. What lessons does the Jewish experience of suffering teach you about dealing with suffering in a constructive manner?

Words to Know

anti-semitism	kosher	Shabbat or Sabbath
ark	melachah	Shavu'ot
bar-/bat-mitzvah	messiah	Shema
chosen people	Mishnah	Simchat Torah
Conservative Judaism	mitzvot	sin
covenant	monotheism	synagogue
Decalogue	oral Torah	Sukkot
Diaspora or Dispersion	Orthodox Judaism	ten lost tribes of Israel
Exile	patriarchs	Talmud
Exodus	Pesah or Passover	Tanakh
Gemara	pogroms	Torah
ghetto	Purim	written Torah
Hanukkah	Reform movement	yarmulke
Hasidic Judaism	Rosh Ha-Shanah	Yom Hasho'ah
Holocaust	scapegoat	Yom Kippur
		Zionist movement

Chapter 4

After reading this chapter, you will be able to

- Explain the beliefs and practices that are the heritage of all Christians
- Show how Eastern Christians have been faithful to these early beliefs and practices
- Share your appreciation and understanding of Eastern Christianity

Introduction to
CHRISTIANITY

Introduction

Who Is Jesus?

Jesus Christ is not only my closest and most intimate friend, but he is manifested almost daily, forcefully (and beautifully) in the people with whom I come in contact. "Ordinary" days are made extraordinary by chance encounters, by human encounter that moves the heart or lifts the Spirit or is shaped like laughter.

—Maureen Cannon, poet

He came to enlighten my early years with the radiation of his power, like a dawning sun; he whispered to me the kind words that make a destiny: "Come, and follow me!" Little by little I discovered and verified anew the lightning truth of Jesus' words, "Whoever sees me sees the Father."

—Cardinal Leo Joseph Suenens

I am a musician: for me the meaning of Jesus in my life is tied to all the struggles and hard work the life of an artist demands. Through my music, I try to communicate to others what is in my heart: the Lord's grace, his gifts and love.

—Karen Olsen

Christ Jesus is everything.

—Pope Damasus I

Jesus is our Savior and once lived as one of us. Now, I believe he lives inside each of us and we pray to him each and every day to help us live a life similar to the one he did, one of love and service.

—Amy, high school senior

"You are the Messiah, the Son of the Living God."

—Simon Peter of Capernaum (Matthew 16:16, New Revised Standard Version)

Tilling the Soil

Responses to the question *Who is Jesus?* have taken on various expressions through the centuries. Sometimes the responses about who **Jesus** was or the effects of Jesus on humankind were so varied that new denominations developed within **Christianity**. Millions of Christians though agree with Simon Peter: "You are the Messiah, the Son of the Living God."

Judaism of the first century C.E. had a different response to Jesus. Even though the sufferings and scattering of the Jewish people had led them to nourish a hope for a messiah, most did not identify Jesus of Nazareth as that messiah. Jews today would affirm that Jesus was

Jesus
The man born in Bethlehem about 6 to 4 B.C.E. who Christians believe is the Son of God become human and the messiah

Christianity
The religion founded on belief in Jesus, many denominations of which exist today

thoroughly Jewish. His teachings reflect many themes already contained in the Torah and the prophets. Jesus seems to have had an extraordinary gift for allegory and a remarkable skill for making clear and precise points in his teaching. Jews would affirm that Jesus was an exceptionally compassionate man. He had a deep concern for people who were marginalized: the poor, women, children, strangers, and even Gentiles. Nevertheless, justice on behalf of the disadvantaged is already a strong theme in the Hebrew Scriptures. Jews may affirm that Jesus was a good Jew, an insightful teacher, a holy man, and even perhaps a prophet, but not the messiah, and certainly not divine.

In order to understand more clearly the various responses to the question *Who is Jesus?* it is helpful to distinguish between the **Jesus of History** and the **Christ of Faith**. The term *Jesus of History* refers to the historical human, Jesus of Nazareth. It describes what we know, or can learn about, the human Jesus. The term *Christ of Faith* refers to what people believe about the Jesus of History. It refers to Christians' affirmations about Jesus as the Son of God become human and as the messiah, and his effect on their lives.

Jesus of History
the historical human, Jesus of Nazareth

Christ of Faith
Christians' affirmations about Jesus as the Son of God become human and as the messiah, and his effect on their lives

One Solitary Life

He was born in an obscure village, the child of a peasant woman.
He grew up in an obscure village.
He worked in a carpenter shop until he was thirty, and then for three years he was an itinerant preacher.
He never wrote a book. He never held an office.
He never owned a house. He never had a family. He never went to college.
He never traveled, except in his infancy, more than two hundred miles from the place where he was born.
He never did one of the things that usually accompany greatness.
He had no credentials but himself.
While he was still a young man, the tide of public opinion turned against him.
His friends ran away. One of them denied him.
He was turned over to his enemies. He went through the mockery of a trial.
He was nailed to a cross between two thieves.
His executioners gambled for the only property he had on earth, his seamless robe.
When he was dead, he was taken down from the cross and laid in a borrowed grave
    through the pity of a friend.
. . . centuries have come and gone, and today he is the central-piece of the human race and the leader of
    human progress.
I am well within the mark when I say that
  all the armies that ever marched,
  all the navies that ever sailed,
  all the parliaments that ever sat, all the kings that ever reigned,
  put together,
  have not affected the life of man on earth as powerfully
  as that One Solitary Life.

—*James A. Francis*

The Jesus of History

We know strikingly little about the Jesus of History. He was born sometime around 6 to 4 B.C.E. in Bethlehem, a small town about five miles south of Jerusalem. (Because of an error in calculating the calendar, historical scholars estimate that Jesus was born not in what became—in the Christian calendar—the year "1," but a few years before that.) His mother was Mary and his foster-father, Joseph of the house of David. On the eighth day, according to Jewish custom, Jesus was circumcised. Shortly after, the family fled to Egypt because of a threat against Jesus' life. When they returned, they settled in their hometown of Nazareth, in Galilee, a region in northern Palestine. Here Jesus presumably learned the carpentry trade of his father and was schooled in the Torah.

This stained-glass window presents the twelve apostles going forth with Jesus' message.

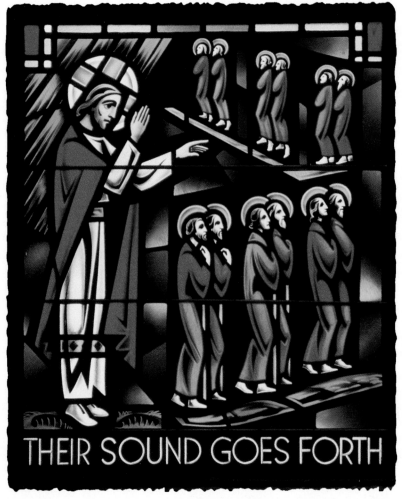

THEIR SOUND GOES FORTH

apostle
one of twelve members of Jesus' inner circle of followers

Several years later, as an adult, Jesus was baptized by his cousin, John the Baptist. He then began his own teaching ministry, traveling throughout Palestine, especially Galilee and Judea, talking to people about God's loving care for them; about people's need to show love and compassion for each other and especially for those who are poor, sick, disabled, sorrowful, and alienated from society; and about the need for conversion.

In a very short time, Jesus built a reputation for wisdom and goodness. He cured the sick and the crippled, worked with the poor, and showed extraordinary understanding and concern for those in trouble. He attracted a small group of disciples. From among these disciples, Jesus chose an inner circle of twelve whom we call **apostles**. His teachings eventually led to conflicts with some of the Jewish and Roman authorities. These conflicts became so intense that Jesus may have eventually been brought before the Jewish high court, the Sanhedrin. He was charged with blasphemy and turned over to the Roman rulers of Palestine. The Roman governor, Pontius Pilate, condemned Jesus to death by crucifixion. Jesus was executed on a cross at the hands of the Romans and was buried in an admirer's tomb.

Getting a Closer Look . . .

The sentences and scripture references below outline the events of Jesus' life as recorded in the Gospels of the Christian Scriptures. Use a Bible to look up five of the scripture references and briefly summarize the content of each passage. Be prepared to discuss your findings in class.

Jesus' birth was preceded by that of his cousin John, later known as John the Baptist, or the Baptizer (Luke 1:5–25).

The angel Gabriel told Mary that she would give birth to the Son of God, who would be called Jesus (Luke 1:26–38).

Elizabeth, the mother of John the Baptist, is visited by her cousin Mary, Jesus' mother (Luke 1:39–56).

While in Bethlehem for a census, Mary and Joseph could not find lodging and were forced to take refuge in an animal shelter, where Jesus was born (Matthew 1:18–25 and Luke 2:1–7).

Mary and Joseph brought him to the temple in Jerusalem to be circumcised and named (Luke 2:21–38).

John the Baptist told people that a great man would come after him (Matthew 3:11–12, Mark 1:7–8, Luke 3:15–17, and John 1:24–28).

John the Baptist baptized Jesus in the Jordan River; this event inaugurated Jesus' three-year ministry (Matthew 3:13–17, Mark 1:9–11, Luke 3:21–22, and John 1:29–34).

Satan, the New Testament personification of evil, tempted Jesus to forsake his mission, or purpose (Matthew 4:1–11, Mark 1:12–13, and Luke 4:1–13).

Jesus gathered his first followers (John 1:35–51).

Jesus chose twelve companions—the twelve apostles (Matthew 10:1–4, Mark 3:13–19, and Luke 6:12–16).

Jesus explained to his disciples how to pray to God; his words became known as the Lord's Prayer (Matthew 6:7–15 and Luke 11:2–4).

In the presence of Peter, James, and John, Jesus was transfigured (Matthew 17:1–9, Mark 9:2–13, and Luke 9:29–36).

Jesus journeyed to Jerusalem for the last time (Matthew 21:1–10, Mark 11:1–10, Luke 19:28–40, and John 12:12–19).

One of the twelve apostles, Judas Iscariot, conspired with Jesus' enemies (Matthew 26:14–16, Mark 14:10–11, and Luke 22:3–6).

The last meal that Jesus ate with his closest followers, a meal celebrating Passover, came to be known as the Last Supper, or the Lord's Supper, and is observed by most Christian churches in one form or another. (Matthew 26:26–29, Mark 14:22–26, Luke 22:14–23).

With his disciples in the Garden of Gethsemane, the scene of his arrest, Jesus prayed to fulfill his mission. (Matthew 26:36–46, Mark 14:32–42, Luke 22:39–46, and John 18:1).

The Roman authority in Palestine, Pontius Pilate, condemned Jesus to death following the crowd's demands (Matthew 27:24–26, Mark 15:15, Luke 23:25, and John 19:16).

Jesus was crucified. (Matthew 27:32–44, Mark 15:21–32, Luke 23:26–43, and John 19:16b–27). Crucifixion was a form of capital punishment to which non-Romans were subjected.

Jesus died, and his body was placed in a tomb guarded by Roman soldiers (Matthew 27:57–61, Mark 15:42–47, Luke 23:50–56, and John 19:38–42).

After three days Jesus rose from the dead and appeared to his followers (Matthew 28:1–10, Mark 16:1–14, Luke 24:1–43, John 20:1–29, 21:1–14).

Jesus instructed the disciples to spread his message (build his church), and then ascended into heaven (Mark 16:15–19 and Luke 24:44–53).

The Christ of Faith

The first followers of Jesus saw a lot more than these details about Jesus of Nazareth. They witnessed his miracles of feeding the hungry, healing the sick, and raising the dead. The intensity, cleverness, and challenge of his teachings captivated them.

Miracles

According to the Gospels in the Christian Scriptures, Jesus performed his first miracle at Cana in Galilee—changing water into wine at a wedding celebration (John 2:1–11). More than forty miracles are attributed to Jesus, including:

- Calming a storm (Matthew 8:23–27, Mark 4:36–40, and Luke 8:22–25)

- Walking on water (Matthew 14:22–23, Mark 6:45–52, and John 6:16–21)

- Curing Peter's sick mother-in-law (Matthew 8:14–15, Mark 1:29–31, and Luke 4:38–39)

- Giving sight to two blind men (Matthew 9:27–31)

- Driving demons out of people at Gerasene (Matthew 8:28–34, Mark 5:1–15, and Luke 8:26–35)

- Bringing back to life his friend Lazarus (John 11:1–4), Jairus's daughter (Matthew 9:18–26, Mark 5:21–43, and Luke 8:40–56), and the widow of Naim's son (Luke 7:11–17)

Parables

parable

a short story that highlights an attitude or principle; used by Jesus in his teaching

Jesus used **parables** in his teachings. A parable is a short story that highlights an attitude or principle. Nearly three dozen parables of Jesus are recorded in the Gospels, including:

- The House Built on Rock (Matthew 7:24–27 and Luke 6:47–49)

- The Sower (Matthew 13:1–23, Mark 4:1–20, Luke 8:1–15)

- The Good Samaritan (Luke 10:25–37)

- The Rich Fool (Luke 12:16–21)
- The Lost Sheep (Luke 15:3–7)
- The Prodigal Son (Luke 15:11–32)
- The Rich Man and Lazarus (Luke 16:19–31)
- The Gold Pieces (Luke 19:11–27)

The Prodigal Son

There was a man who had two sons. The younger of them said to his father, "Father, give me the share of the property that will belong to me." So he divided his property between them. A few days later the younger son gathered all he had and traveled to a distant country, and there he squandered all his property in dissolute living. When he had spent everything, a severe famine took place throughout that country, and he began to be in need. So he went and hired himself out to one of the citizens of that country, who sent him to his fields to feed the pigs. He would gladly have filled himself with the pods that the pigs were eating; and no one gave him anything. But when he came to himself he said, "How many of my father's hired hands have bread enough and to spare, but here I am dying of hunger! I will get up and go to my father, and I will say to him, 'Father, I have sinned against heaven and before you; I am no longer worthy to be called your son; treat me like one of your hired hands.'" So he set off and went to his father. But while he was still far off, his father saw him and was filled with compassion; he ran and put his arms around him and kissed him. Then the son said to him, "Father, I have sinned against heaven and before you; I am no longer worthy to be called your son." But the father said to his slaves, "Quickly, bring out a robe—the best one—and put it on him; put a ring on his finger and sandals on his feet. And get the fatted calf and kill it, and let us eat and celebrate; for this son of mine was dead and is alive again; he was lost and is found." And they began to celebrate.

Now his elder brother was in the field; and when he came and approached the house, he heard music and dancing. He called one of the slaves and asked what was going on. He replied, "Your brother has come, and your father has killed the fatted calf, because he has got him back safe and sound." Then he became angry and refused to go in. His father came out and began to plead with him. But he answered his father, "Listen! For all these years I have been working like a slave for you, and I have never disobeyed your command; yet you have never given me even a young goat so that I might celebrate with my friends. But when this son of yours came back, who has devoured your property with prostitutes, you killed the fatted calf for him!" Then the father said to him, "Son, you are always with me, and all that is mine is yours. But we had to celebrate and rejoice, because this brother of yours was dead and has come to life; he was lost and has been found."

—Luke 15:11–31, NRSV

Let's Talk about It . . .

1. What is the moral of this parable?
2. Does someone need to be Christian to appreciate the moral of this parable? Why or why not?
3. Is this parable appropriate for life in society today? Why or why not?

Discourses and Other Teachings

Some of Jesus' teachings, known as discourses, were not communicated in the form of a parable. Nearly thirty discourses are recorded in the Gospels, including:

- The Sermon on the Mount (Matthew 5:1–7:29 and Luke 6:20–49), which includes

  — the Beatitudes (Matthew 5:3–12 and Luke 6:20–23)

  — The Lord's Prayer (Matthew 6:9–13)

  — The Golden Rule (Matthew 7:12 and Luke 6:31)

- The Great Commandment (Matthew 22:34–40 and Mark 12:28–34)

The Gospels record some thirty short statements that Jesus made during the course of his public ministry. Some of these are particularly rich in meaning and are commonly quoted:

- The lamp under a basket (Matthew 5:14–15, Mark 4:21, and Luke 8:16–18, 11:33–36)

- The physician and the sick (Matthew 9:12–13, Mark 2:17, and Luke 5: 31–32)

- The divided kingdom (Matthew 12:25–26, Mark 3:23–26, and Luke 11:7–18)

- The good shepherd (John 10:1–18)

 # Planting the Seed

Shortly after the death of Jesus, his followers declared he was raised from the dead. Some claimed that they had seen him alive. They said that three days after his death he rose from the dead, came among them from time to time, talked with them, and shared meals with them. They said that he had commissioned them to "make disciples of all nations, baptizing them in the name of the Father and of the Son and of the Holy Spirit." Teach them, Jesus said, "to obey everything that I have commanded you. And remember, I am with you always, to the end of the age" (Matthew 28:19–20).

So powerful was the first disciples' belief in these events that they took the message of Jesus to the four corners of their world. By the end of the first century, Christians had established communities in the western regions of modern-day Turkey, in Greece, and as far west and north as Rome. Christianity continued up the Italian peninsula in the second century. By the end of the third century, Christians had established themselves in communities across northern Africa, throughout Spain and France, and into Germany west of the Rhine. By the end of the fourth century, Christianity had crossed the English channel into Britain. Today two billion people worldwide respond to the question *Who is Jesus?* and call themselves Christian.

In this chapter we will introduce the history of Christianity, explain common beliefs of Christians, and consider the beliefs and practices of Eastern Christianity. Chapter 5 discusses Roman Catholicism, and

Chapter 6 treats the Churches of the Reformation. Chapter 7 will discuss other Christian experiences in North America from the nineteenth and twentieth centuries.

Pentecost to Peace: The Birth of a New Religion (30 C.E.–313 C.E.)

Even though Christianity is rooted in the person of Jesus of Nazareth, it is more correct to say that the religion itself begins with **Pentecost**. The word *Pentecost* comes from the Greek *he pentekoste*, which means "the fiftieth day." In Judaism, Pentecost—Shavu'ot or the Feast of Weeks—is celebrated fifty days after Passover. It marks God's giving of the Torah to Moses at Mount Sinai. In Christianity, Pentecost is celebrated fifty days after Easter. It marks the descent of the Holy Spirit upon the followers of Jesus.

According to the Christian Scriptures, the beliefs of the first disciples concerning Jesus became more focused as a result of this event. After the death and resurrection of Jesus, his disciples were gathered together. They were filled with the Holy Spirit who gave them the courage to proclaim their beliefs about Jesus. The Acts of the Apostles, the fourth book of the New Testament, describes the event:

And suddenly from heaven there came a sound like the rush of a violent wind, and it filled the entire house where they were sitting. Divided tongues, as of fire, appeared among them, and a tongue rested on each of them. All of them were filled with the Holy Spirit and began to speak in other languages, as the Spirit gave them ability.

—Acts 2:2–3, NRSV

Pentecost
for Christians, the religious feast recalling the descent of the Holy Spirit upon the followers of Jesus fifty days after Easter

The Christian Pentecost recalls the gift of the Holy Spirit to the Church.

Peter's First Sermon

But Peter, standing with the eleven, raised his voice and addressed them, "Men of Judea and all who live in Jerusalem, let this be known to you, and listen to what I say. . . . You that are Israelites, listen to what I have to say. Jesus of Nazareth, a man attested to you by God with deeds of power, wonders, and signs that God did through him among you, as you yourselves know—this man, handed over to you according to the definite plan and foreknowledge of God, you crucified and killed by the hands of those outside the law. But God raised him up, having freed him from death, because it was impossible for him to be held in its power. For David says concerning him,

> *'I saw the Lord always before me,*
>
> *for he is at my right hand so that I will not be shaken;*
>
> *therefore my heart was glad, and my tongue rejoiced;*
>
> *moreover my flesh will live in hope.*
>
> *For you will not abandon my soul to Hades,*
>
> *or let your Holy One experience corruption.*
>
> *You have made known to me the ways of life;*
>
> *you will make me full of gladness with your presence.'*

"Fellow Israelites, I may say to you confidently of our ancestor David that he both died and was buried, and his tomb is with us to this day. Since he was a prophet, he knew that God had sworn with an oath to him that he would put one of his descendants on his throne. Foreseeing this, David spoke of the resurrection of the Messiah, saying,

> *'He was not abandoned to Hades,*
>
> *nor did his flesh experience corruption.'*

"This Jesus God raised up, and of that all of us are witnesses. Being therefore exalted at the right hand of God, and having received from the Father the promise of the Holy Spirit, he has poured out this that you both see and hear. For David did not ascend into the heavens, but he himself says,

> *'The Lord said to my Lord,*
>
> *"Sit at my right hand,*
>
> *until I make your enemies your footstool."'*

"Therefore let the entire house of Israel know with certainty that God has made him both Lord and Messiah, this Jesus whom you crucified."

—Acts 2:14, 22–36

Let's Talk about It . . .

1. What claims did Peter make regarding Jesus?
2. For what purpose did he quote King David?

Taking Root

The power of Pentecost caused these first disciples to reflect back upon their experiences of Jesus. Gradually an outline of basic Christian **doctrines** took shape. The articulation of these doctrines resulted from the discussions and writings of the leading thinkers as well as the influence of the events of the time.

Initially, Christians were a tiny **sect** within Judaism; they were Jews who affirmed that Jesus of Nazareth was the Messiah. Thus one task, as it were, was to define themselves in relationship to Judaism. Eventually this led to the separation of Christianity from Judaism and its establishment as a separate religion. Another task for these first Christians was to define themselves in relationship to Rome. The Christians were a religious sect not well liked by the Romans because of their refusal to participate in the state religion. Sporadic persecutions lasted from the time of Roman emperor Nero (54–68) to 313 when Roman emperor Constantine declared the **Edict of Milan**. The Edict of Milan granted freedom of religion within the Roman Empire. This event is known as the "peace of the church." These events, as well as dialogues among the Christians themselves, helped to shape the central beliefs and practices of Christianity.

doctrine
basic religious beliefs

sect
a group adhering to a distinctive doctrine or to a leader; a small group of people within a given religion who hold beliefs or practices which are considered unconventional

Edict of Milan
the decree of Constantine in 313 granting religious freedom in the Roman Empire

Christian Scriptures

The *Scriptures*, or *Scripture*, is another name for the Bible. The word *scripture* comes from the Latin *scriptus*, which means the "process of writing." And the word *Bible* comes from the Greek *Byblos*, the name of an ancient Phoenician city renowned for the production of papyrus.

The Bible of Christianity is a collection of books, not a single book. It is divided into two major parts, the Old Testament and the New Testament. A **testament** is a covenant (contract) between God and humankind.

From the Christian perspective, there are two historic covenants. Both have redeeming value and remain in effect. The first was entered into by God and the people of Israel. And the second was entered into by Jesus on behalf of the whole human race.

The history of the first covenant is told in the Hebrew Scriptures or Old Testament, and the history of the second covenant is told in the Christian Scriptures or New Testament. It has become increasingly popular among Bible scholars to refer to the Old Testament as the First Testament (a record of the first covenant, or testament), and to refer to the New Testament as the Second Testament (a record of the second covenant, or testament).

testament
a covenant between God and humankind

Old Testament

Old Testament

the name given to the Hebrew Bible by Christians; thirty-nine books sacred to Judaism and accepted by all Christians

The **Old Testament** is the Hebrew Bible, a body of writings sacred to Judaism. There are thirty-nine books in the Hebrew Bible, which Jews call the *Tanakh*. More background was given on this scripture in the previous chapter on Judaism. All Christians accept these thirty-nine books. Not all Christians, however, refer to the thirty-nine books of the Old Testament by the same names or place them in the same order.

The Books of the Hebrew Bible

- Genesis, Exodus, Leviticus, Numbers, Deuteronomy
- Joshua, Judges, Ruth, 1 Samuel, 2 Samuel, 1 Kings, 2 Kings, 1 Chronicles, 2 Chronicles, Ezra, Nehemiah, Esther
- Isaiah, Jeremiah, Ezekiel
- Hosea, Joel, Amos, Obadiah, Jonah, Micah, Nahum, Habakkuk, Zephaniah, Haggai, Zechariah, Malachi
- Psalms, Proverbs, Job, The Song of Songs, Lamentations, Ecclesiastes, Daniel

God said, "See, I have given you every plant yielding seed that is upon the face of all the earth, and every tree with seed in its fruit; you shall have them for food. And to every beast of the earth, and to every bird of the air, and to everything that creeps on the earth, everything that has the breath of life, I have given every green plant for food."

—*Genesis 1:29–30, NRSV*

Apocrypha

Apocrypha

fifteen books or parts of the Old Testament considered canonical by some Christian groups and noncanonical by others

Over the centuries, fifteen books were added to the Old Testament. These books are commonly known as the **Apocrypha**. The Greek word *apocrypha* means "things that are hidden." These fifteen books, and additions to a few of the thirty-nine, were not included in the Hebrew canon of Scripture in Palestine. They were, however, with the exception of the Second Book of Esdras, included in the canon of the Greek-speaking Jews of Egypt, the canon known as the *Septuagint*.

For some Christians, these fifteen books carry the same weight as the original thirty-nine. They use the term *Deuterocanonical*, which means "second canon," to describe these books. Some Christian groups insert these books (where appropriate) among the original thirty-nine. Orthodox Christians and Roman and Eastern Catholics use the Septuagint as the source for the Old Testament.

For other Christians, the fifteen books of the Apocrypha are important but not as important as the original thirty-nine. They often group these books together and place them at the end of the Old Testament or after the New Testament. Not all Christians refer to the fifteen books of the Apocrypha by the same names or place them in the same order. In general, Protestant Bibles keep the Apocrypha separate from the thirty-nine books of the Old Testament.

The Books of the Apocrypha

- 1 Esdras, 2 Esdras, Tobit, Judith
- Additions to the Book of Esther
- Wisdom of Solomon, Ecclesiasticus, Baruch
- Letter of Jeremiah; Prayer of Azariah and the Song of the Three Young Men; Daniel and Susanna; Daniel, Bel, and the Snake, Prayer of Manasseh
- 1 Maccabees, 2 Maccabees

New Testament

The **New Testament** is the second major part of the Christian Bible; it is sometimes referred to as the Christian Scriptures. The New Testament includes accounts of Jesus' life and teachings and recounts the history of the early church. All Christians accept the twenty-seven books of the New Testament. They refer to these books by the same names and place them in the same order. The New Testament contains twenty-seven books:

The Books of the New Testament

- The Gospels according to Matthew, Mark, Luke, and John
- The Acts of the Apostles
- The Letters—Romans, 1 Corinthians, 2 Corinthians, Galatians, Ephesians, Philippians, Colossians, 1 Thessalonians, 2 Thessalonians, 1 Timothy, 2 Timothy, Titus, Philemon, Hebrews, James, 1 Peter, 2 Peter, 1 John, 2 John, 3 John, Jude
- The Book of Revelation

New Testament
the Christian Scriptures; accounts of Jesus' life and teachings and the beginning of the Christian Church, letters from early church leaders, and an **apocalyptic** book

apocalyptic
a kind of writing which uses many symbols and images to talk about the endtime, and often a present or coming event

An Apocalyptic Reading

. . . I saw four angels standing at the four corners of the earth, holding back the four winds of the earth. . . . I saw another angel ascending from the rising of the sun, having the seal of the living God, and he called with a loud voice to the four angels . . . saying, "Do not damage the earth or the sea or the trees. . . ."

—*Revelation 7:1–3, NRSV*

Christian Beliefs

Christian Creeds

The reflections and discussions of the first centuries of Christians led to the formulation of several creeds. A **creed** is a statement of a community's essential beliefs. Some of the early Christian creeds are the Apostles' Creed, the Athanasian Creed, and the Nicene Creed. The Apostles' Creed is one of the earliest. For this reason, it has been called "an ecumenical symbol of faith." Some believe that the apostles themselves wrote the creed; others believe that the creed reflects their teachings but dates from the second century C.E. The Athanasian Creed is a summary of Christian belief attributed to Saint Athanasius (293–373).

The creed that has become commonly used by Christians is the Nicene Creed, which was formulated by the first two ecumenical councils (325 and 381). Note the structure of this creed. It consists of four parts. The first three parts deal with what Christians believe about God as Father, Son, and Holy Spirit. The fourth part deals with what Christians believe about the church, baptism, and the afterlife. The doctrines stated in the creeds are shared by nearly all Christians. Each specific denomination has further beliefs which are elaborations upon these basic beliefs and which may be unique to that denomination.

creed

a statement of a community's essential beliefs; some Christian churches have creeds, while some are non-creedal

This icon of "Jesus, Lord" is in St. Stanislaus Church, Winona, Minnesota.

Jesus, the Christ and Son of God

First among these basic beliefs is that Jesus was the messiah, the Christ. The first Christian Jews looked back over their long Jewish experience and saw Jesus as the fullest expression of God's promised one. But the early Christians concluded that Jesus was even more than the messiah expected by some groups within Judaism. God, who had so carefully and deliberately formed a people in a covenant relationship, now showed the greatest concern possible by becoming human. No longer did God simply manifest himself through burning bushes, the power of plagues, the parting of seas, and pillars of fire and cloud, or through people such as Abraham and Sarah, Moses and Isaiah; now God chose the most radical manifestation possible—by becoming human. In this way, God showed the ultimate in love and care for human beings.

Christians then had to explain what they meant by this. Was Jesus God merely acting like a human being? In other words, was Jesus just going through the motions, as it were, pretending that he was human? Or was Jesus a human raised to the status of a god? Indeed, this would not have been an unusual conclusion, since kings, for example the Roman emperors, were often perceived as divine. In the end, Christians affirmed that Jesus was fully God and fully human. Jesus really was God, and Jesus really experienced the fullness of being human. Jesus was seen, in a sense, as a bridge connecting God with humanity.

Paul's View of Jesus

In his Letter to the Philippians, Paul included what was possibly an early Christian hymn about Jesus:

> Let the same mind be in you that was in Christ Jesus,
> who, though he was in the form of God,
>> did not regard equality with God
>> as something to be exploited,
> but emptied himself,
>> taking the form of a slave,
>> being born in human likeness.
> And being found in human form,
>> he humbled himself,
>> and became obedient to the point of death—
>> even death on a cross.
> Therefore God also highly exalted him
>> and gave him the name
>> that is above every name,
> so that at the name of Jesus,
>> every knee should bend,
>> in heaven and on earth and under the earth,
> and every tongue should confess
>> that Jesus Christ is Lord,
>> to the glory of God the Father.
>
> *—Philippians 2:5–11, NRSV*

Let's Talk about It . . .

1. According to the reading, what is Jesus' relationship to God?
2. What are Christians claiming about Jesus in this hymn?

What exactly was the meaning of Jesus? Why did God become human? In the first chapter, we discussed the universal human sense that somehow people are separate from something Other. Recall that East and West explain the cause of this separation differently. In Western thinking, the cause of this separation is human sin. Human sin is overcome by God's redeeming act on behalf of humanity. For Christians, God became human in the person of Jesus to atone or make up for human sin. In Christian thinking, the sin of the first humans against God was so great that there was nothing human beings could do to bridge the separation. Only God could atone for the sin. The title *Christ* tells us that the Christians saw Jesus as having this messianic mission.

The word *Christ* means "he who was anointed." Christians believe that God had a Son and that the Son of God became a human being whose name was Jesus. The word *incarnation* comes from the Latin *caro*, which means "flesh." The incarnation alludes, therefore, to the Son being-made-flesh. Christians believe that Jesus of Nazareth was both divine and human, and will remain so forever. "For God so loved the world that he gave his only Son, so that everyone who believes in him may not perish but may have eternal life" (John 3:16). Thus Jesus, through his death and resurrection, restored human beings to their original dignity and won for them salvation.

incarnation

the divine "takes on flesh," the divine becomes human; in Christianity, the second person of the Trinity became human in the person of Jesus of Nazareth

God as Trinity

The early Christians' deepening understanding of the meaning of Jesus and especially their experience of communal life after the resurrection and ascension (return to heaven) of Jesus led to a new understanding of God. The belief which emerged from these early experiences became known as the **Trinity**. According to the Christian Scriptures, the disciples gathered at Pentecost "were filled with the Holy Spirit and began to speak in other languages, as the Spirit gave them ability." This experience of the "Spirit" continued in the daily experiences of the disciples and in their teaching and ministry. In some way, God's presence continued with them after the ascension of Jesus. This presence was God the Holy Spirit. Thus Christians perceived God as God the Father, God the Son, and God the Holy Spirit.

Trinity

the belief held by most Christians that God is one in essence but three in person— Father, Son, and Holy Spirit

Most groups of Christians today understand God's self-revelation as a trinity of persons; each person in God is seen as distinct and equal to the other two. Like the Jews, Christians believe that God is one, but they also believe that God is three persons in one God. Jews and Moslems often assert that this means Christians have three gods, but Christians steadfastly maintain their monotheistic belief. Christians declare that God is one, but can be understood and related to as Father, Son, and Holy Spirit, while admitting that this belief is not completely understood and never explained satisfactorily. The Athanasian Creed refers to the Trinity in these words: "The Father is God, the Son is God, and the Holy Spirit is God, and yet there are not three gods but one God."

The Nicene Creed

We believe in one God, the Father, the Almighty,
maker of heaven and earth, of all that is, seen and unseen.
We believe in one Lord, Jesus Christ,
the only Son of God, eternally begotten of the Father,
God from God, Light from Light, true God from true God,
begotten, not made, one in Being with the Father.
Through him all things were made.
For us and for our salvation he came down from heaven:
by the power of the Holy Spirit he was born of the Virgin Mary, and became man.
For our sake he was crucified under Pontius Pilate;
he suffered, died, and was buried.
On the third day he rose again in fulfillment of the Scriptures;
he ascended into heaven and is seated at the right hand of the Father.
He will come in glory to judge the living and the dead,
and his kingdom will have no end.
We believe in the Holy Spirit, the Lord, the giver of life,
who proceeds from the Father and the Son.
With the Father and the Son he is worshiped and glorified.
He has spoken through the prophets.
We believe in one holy catholic and apostolic Church.
We acknowledge one baptism for the forgiveness of sins.
We look for the resurrection of the dead, and the life of the world to come.
Amen.

Virgin Birth

Christians believe that a young Jewish virgin by the name of Mary gave birth to Jesus. They regard the Father (the first person of the Trinity) as Jesus' father. In their eyes, the Holy Spirit (the third person of the Trinity) made it possible for Mary to become pregnant and give birth to Jesus. Christians look upon Joseph, who was Mary's Jewish husband, as the (earthly) father figure in Jesus' life. Christians do not agree on whether Mary remained a virgin throughout her life.

Resurrection

The single most important event for Christianity is the resurrection of Jesus of Nazareth. According to the Gospels of Matthew, Mark, Luke, and John, after Jesus had died, his body was placed in a cave-like tomb. On the morning of the third day after his death, a group of women went to the tomb and discovered that it was empty. A short while later, Jesus appeared to them, as well as to many of his other followers.

While some Christian groups see the resurrection in symbolic terms, most Christians believe that God raised Jesus from the dead and gave him a new glorified life, with a body that could be seen and touched (Luke 24:39–40, John 20:20). They do not believe that this was a mere resuscitation of the dead body of Jesus, but rather that it was a resurrection into a new dimension of existence in which Jesus is not limited by time and space. Christians see this as a promise of their own (and everyone's) resurrection at the end of time, when Christ will judge all. Paul's First Letter to the Corinthians is often quoted to show the importance of belief in Christ's resurrection:

> If Christ has not been raised, your faith is futile and you are still in your sins. Then those also who have died in Christ have perished. If for this life only we have hoped in Christ, we are of all people most to be pitied.
>
> —1 Corinthians 15:17–19, NRSV

Salvation

The word salvation comes from the Latin *salvare*, which means "to save." Christians believe that Jesus saved the human race from an eternity without God by ending the separation that had existed since the time of the first humans. In reference to the salvation brought by Jesus, Saint Athanasius wrote, "the Son of God became man so that we might become God."

Most Christians see Jesus' death on the cross as the sacrifice that brought about this salvation. The Letter to the Hebrews says: "But as it is, [Christ] has appeared once for all at the end of the age to remove sin by the sacrifice of himself" (Hebrews 9:26). And then, "For by a single offering [Christ] has perfected for all time those who are sanctified" (Hebrews 10:14).

Living as a Christian

Christian ethics

Because of their Judaic heritage, Christians share with Jews their reliance on the Ten Commandments. These commandments are considered basic, fundamental teachings of the moral life. They provide a basic and essential order to the proper functioning of society. Sometimes the Ten Commandments are divided into two parts: those that deal with love of God and those that deal with love of neighbor.

Christian ethical life, however, is based on the Christian Scriptures (New Testament), as well as the Hebrew Scriptures (Old Testament). In addition to the Ten Commandments, Christians also look to the **Beatitudes** as guides for the moral life. The Beatitudes are part of Jesus' teachings about what makes people blessed and close to God.

Beatitudes
a list of attitudes and actions that Jesus taught as good; part of Jesus' Sermon on the Mount (Matthew 5, see also Luke 6) which serve as guidelines for Christian living; a kind of "prescription for happiness"

The Beatitudes

Blessed are the poor in spirit, for theirs is the kingdom of heaven.

Blessed are those who mourn, for they will be comforted.

Blessed are those who hunger and thirst for righteousness, for they will be filled.

Blessed are the merciful, for they will receive mercy.

Blessed are the pure in heart, for they will see God.

Blessed are the peacemakers, for they will be called children of God.

Blessed are those who are persecuted for righteousness' sake, for theirs is the kingdom of heaven.

Blessed are you when people revile you and persecute you and utter all kinds of evil against you falsely on my account.

Rejoice and be glad, for your reward is great in heaven.

—Matthew 5:3–12a

The Beatitudes are a kind of prescription for happiness. They build upon a natural desire for happiness in ways which are often surprising and seemingly contradictory to human ways of finding happiness. Happiness is not ultimately found in earthly desires but in the attitudes which lead to the very reign of God.

Essentially, the teachings of Jesus can be summarized in his command to love, which in turn is a summary of the Law of Moses. In fact, his very statement of the law of love includes two commands found in the Torah (Deuteronomy 6:4–5 and Leviticus 19:18).

One of the scribes came near and . . . asked him, "Which commandment is the first of all?" Jesus answered, "The first is, 'Hear, O Israel: the Lord our God, the Lord is one; you shall love the Lord your God with all your heart, and with all your soul, and with all your mind, and with all your strength.' The second is this, 'You shall love your neighbor as yourself.' There is no other commandment greater than these."

—Mark 12:28–31

Fundamentally, Christian moral teachings derive from this two-fold command to love God and neighbor. It is often referred to as the *Great Commandment.*

Christian practices

The Lord's Supper: Communion

Certain practices evolved from these early Christian beliefs. First and central among these was the commemoration of the Lord's Supper (Jesus' last supper with his friends before he died). "They devoted themselves to the apostles' teaching and fellowship, to the breaking of bread and the prayers" (Acts 2:42). Apparently the first Christians continued to practice the regular Jewish prayer rituals, but they added to this a regular Sunday gathering in someone's home where they read from Christian writings or listened to the apostles and then "broke bread." This blessing, breaking, and sharing of bread and the blessing and sharing of wine commemorated the action of Jesus at his last supper with his friends before he died. The sharing of the blessed bread and wine (or grape juice) in many Christian communities today has evolved from this practice.

Several descriptions of the Last Supper can be found in the New Testament. According to Matthew 26:26–28:

> *While they were eating, Jesus took a loaf of bread, and after blessing it he broke it, gave it to the disciples, and said, "Take, eat; this is my body." Then he took a cup, and after giving thanks he gave it to them, saying, "Drink from it, all of you; for this is my blood of the covenant, which is poured out for many for the forgiveness of sins."*

This ancient practice is known by a number of names, such as *Communion*, *Eucharist*, and the *Lord's Supper*. The New Testament writer Paul used the term Last Supper in 1 Corinthians 11:20. The meaning of the blessed and shared bread and wine varies widely among Christians. Catholics, Orthodox, and some Protestant Christians believe that Jesus is actually present in the bread and wine. Others understand communion as a memorial. The frequency and manner in which it is shared also varies. Some Churches worship with the Word (scripture and prayer) only, while others worship with Word and Eucharist.

Baptism

The second major practice of the first Christians was **baptism**. The first Christians were baptized in water as Jesus was. After Peter completed his first sermon, many of those gathered in Jerusalem asked him what they must do. "Repent, and be baptized," he said, "every one of you in the name of Jesus Christ so that your sins may be forgiven; and you will receive the gift of the Holy Spirit" (Acts 2:38). With baptism, Christians believed that their sins were forgiven and that they were inserted into the very life of Christ. Baptism establishes a link with Jesus and confers church membership.

Christian baptism can be traced to the New Testament where Jesus' cousin, John the Baptist, baptized his followers: "And people . . . were baptized by him in the river Jordan, confessing their sins" (Mark 1:5). Jesus asked John the Baptist to baptize him, which John reluctantly did. "And when Jesus had been baptized, just as he came up from the water, suddenly the heavens were opened to him and he saw the Spirit of God descending like a dove and alighting on him. And a voice from heaven said, 'This is my Son, the Beloved, with whom I am well pleased' " (Matthew 3:16–17).

Communion
the sharing of sacramental bread and juice or wine as part of a Christian church service, commemorating or reenacting Jesus' last supper with his friends before he died; communion in some churches is also called the Lord's Supper and, in some churches, the Eucharist

baptism
the rite or ceremony by which people enter into the Christian faith

According to the Gospels, Jesus offered a different kind of baptism, which John the Baptist described: "I baptize you with water; but he who is more powerful than I is coming; I am not worthy to untie the thong of his sandals. He will baptize you with the Holy Spirit and fire" (Luke 3:16–17). Before Jesus ascended into heaven, he instructed his closest disciples to baptize: "'Go therefore and make disciples of all nations, baptizing them in the name of the Father and of the Son and of the Holy Spirit . . .' " (Matthew 28:19).

Most Christian traditions baptize infants as well as adults. Others baptize only adults. Although Christians today differ on when one should be baptized or on how it should done, they nevertheless continue this very early Christian practice.

In Christianity, water is used to baptize people. To baptize, it is necessary to sprinkle or pour water on a person's head or to immerse (submerge) the person in a pool of water or body of water. Water is sprinkled, poured, or the person is immersed and the words "I baptize you in the name of the Father and of the Son and of the Holy Spirit" are said. Various Christian churches clothe the person who is baptized in white, which symbolizes new life. Chrism (perfumed oil) representing the Holy Spirit's presence and a candle representing Christ's light are incorporated into the baptismal ceremony in some Christian churches.

Baptism is not only a rite or ceremony of belonging; in the Christian faith it is also seen as a gateway to life after death. Death has always been a mysterious, frightening eventuality for humankind. According to Christianity, death is not the end of life, but merely a change to another and better kind of life. Christians believe that their union with Christ will ensure them of a life after death. Death is not to be feared but accepted with courage. In the afterlife, they will live with God forever. They will fulfill the end for which they were created. Christians today continue to believe that Christ conquered death through his death and resurrection.

The Lord's Prayer

Since ancient times, Christians have recited the Lord's Prayer, or Our Father. According to the New Testament (Matthew 6:9–13 and Luke 11:2–4), Jesus himself gave this prayer to his disciples. The prayer contains elements of praise, petition, and yearning for the kingdom of God which are found in many Jewish prayers of the period. The words "for yours is the kingdom, and the power, and the glory, forever and ever" comprise a doxology (expression of praise). These words appear in several ancient manuscripts, and have been used in the context of worship since the sixteenth century. This is one version of the prayer:

Our Father, who art in heaven, hallowed be thy name. Thy kingdom come. Thy will be done on earth, as it is in heaven. Give us this day our daily bread, and forgive us our trespasses, as we forgive those who trespass against us, and lead us not into temptation, but deliver us from evil. For the kingdom, the power, the glory are yours, now and forever. Amen.

The Jesus Prayer

*Lord Jesus Christ, Son of God,
have mercy on me, a sinner.*

*This is an ancient Christian prayer that is still used by many Christians.
Its purpose is to bring the person praying to a profound sense of Jesus'
presence. After quieting the body, senses, and inner self, the person
begins to coordinate each phrase with the movement of breath in and out
of the body. Gradually the person becomes more still, unaware of outside
distractions, and focused on Jesus.*

Christmas
the Christian feast celebrating the incarnation of the Son of God, the birth of Jesus; celebrated on December 25

Easter
the Christian celebration of Jesus' resurrection from the dead; scheduled according to the lunar calendar in the spring

A Greek Orthodox Holy Week service in San Francisco

Christian feasts

Christians celebrate many special days throughout the year. Three common to all Christians are Christmas, Easter, and Pentecost. **Christmas** celebrates the incarnation of the Son of God; it celebrates the birth of Jesus. Christmas celebrates not only the past event of Jesus' birth, but also the presence of God among people today. Most Christians celebrate Christmas on December 25.

Easter Sunday celebrates the resurrection of Jesus from the dead. On Easter Sunday Christians celebrate not only Jesus' resurrection, but also the belief that they too will conquer death and rise from the dead. The date of Easter is established by a lunar calculation. For Western Christians, it is on the first Sunday following the first full moon after the vernal equinox. Eastern Christians follow the same schedule except that Easter must also be after the Jewish Passover.

On **Pentecost** Christians celebrate the descent of the Holy Spirit upon the first followers of Jesus. As mentioned earlier, this is considered the birth of the church. Again, it is not only a past event that is commemorated, but also the presence of the Holy Spirit among Christians today. The celebration of Pentecost follows fifty days after Easter.

These practices are common to nearly all Christian denominations today. Beyond these are many other rites, or ceremonies, and/or sacraments which various Christian denominations celebrate. They also celebrate many other events in the life of Jesus or the saints or aspects of church life which are particular to their own denomination. Some of these will be discussed within the context of each denomination.

Growing and Blooming

Christianity established (313–1054)

As we have seen, the period from Pentecost to 313 was a time when Christians formulated their essential beliefs and practices. It was also a time in which church and state were in opposition, with the state (Roman Empire) persecuting Christians. After 313, there grew a collaboration between church and state. The Roman emperors supported and promoted the development of churches, monasteries, missionary efforts, and theological discussions. In 380, Christianity became the official religion of the empire. The church, for its part, began to adopt the ceremonial style and trappings of the imperial court.

Christian belief continued to be discussed and further defined in the centuries following the formation of the Nicene Creed. Sometimes there were disagreements, and these led to **schisms** in the religion. For example, one such schism followed the Council of Ephesus in 431. Nestorius, the patriarch of Constantinople, taught a sharp distinction between the human and divine nature of Christ. He believed that God was living in Christ and that Mary gave birth to the human nature of Christ only, not the divine nature. The Council of Ephesus rejected his teachings and ruled that Mary was the mother of God and that the human and divine natures of Christ are inseparably bound together in the one person of Christ. The followers of Nestorius continued to spread his teaching. Today they are known as the Assyrian Church of the East. Recently, the Catholic Church and the Assyrian Church of the East reached agreement on this teaching concerning Christ.

There were other schisms in these centuries, usually connected with theological disagreements over church teaching. Generally speaking though, Christianity remained intact until the eleventh century when a split between East and West occurred. Because of dangers to the empire caused by migrating Germanic tribes in the fourth century, Constantine in 330 moved the capital of the empire from Rome in the West to Byzantium in the East (which he renamed Constantinople). Thus this city became the focal point of political, social, religious, and artistic developments. Meanwhile, the center of the Christian church and the pope remained in Rome. The growing tension between these two centers led to the **Great Schism**, the split in Christianity between East and West. The eastern branch developed into the Eastern Orthodox family of churches. The western branch developed into Roman Catholic and Protestant Christianity.

schism
split within a religion over disputed beliefs or practices

Great Schism
the split in Christianity between the eastern and western branches

Eastern Christianity

The Great Schism refers to the split between the eastern and western branches of Christianity. Although scholars typically identify the year 1054 as the date of the Great Schism, it is more accurate to think of the division as a growing tension between the years 810 and 1204. The seeds of this tension were sown even earlier in the years following the peace of the church. With the decline of the Roman Empire in the West, Christians there became preoccupied with the migrating Germanic tribes. In 410, Rome was sacked by the Vandals. Then western Christians sought to convert the Germanic peoples, a task which concerned them for the next 500 years. Christians in the West also had to combat several heresies.

Meanwhile, Christians in the East were preoccupied with their own concerns. The Roman Empire survived in the form of the Byzantine Empire centered in Constantinople. Christianity in the East became very much linked with the civilization and culture there. The church too had its own heresies to deal with, and then, later, wandering intruders. In 640, many of the areas where the eastern Christians lived were overrun by the Moslems; the church in these areas was either destroyed or severely weakened.

Thus each branch became more and more isolated within its own sphere of concern. The two groups were geographically distant from one another. Linguistically the West used Latin, the East used Greek. Culturally, each began to develop its own liturgical style and ways of thinking theologically. Politically there was a growing tension between the pope in the West who lived in the ancient imperial city of Rome and the bishops and imperial power in the East centered in Constantinople.

From 726 to 843, the eastern Christians became embroiled in a bitter dispute over the reverence of religious images. Following the resolution of this controversy, Pope Nicholas I declared the election of Photius, patriarch of Constantinople, uncanonical. Although Photius was later reinstated, the Eastern church resented the interference of the western church in their affairs. Political tension increased between the two centers. In 1054 the papal legates to Constantinople and Patriarch Michael Cerularius excommunicated (excluded from the church) each other. The schism was certainly sealed in 1204 when western Christians on the fourth Crusade sacked Constantinople instead of following their plan to go to Palestine.

Even though there was a deepening gulf between the two branches of Christianity, the essential differences between the two became focused on two key issues: the role of the pope in the church and the *filioque* clause in the Nicene Creed.

The role of the pope in Rome had gradually grown in influence over the first centuries of the Christian Church. It seems that from early on Christians throughout the known world gave the bishop of Rome (the pope) a special honor or respect as the successor to Peter. Eventually the pope exerted more and more influence on the other churches. This was sometimes welcomed and sometimes interpreted as interference and resented by Christians in other cities. Thus the issue was: What is the role of the pope? Is it only a primacy of honor?

Or is it also jurisdictional authority over the whole church?

The second major issued revolved around the **filioque** clause in the Nicene Creed. *Filioque* is Latin for "and the Son." The clause was not originally in the creed. As a response to a heresy, sixth-century Christians in Spain began to add the expression "and the Son" when they prayed the Nicene Creed: "We believe in the Holy Spirit . . . who proceeds from the Father and the Son." This practice gradually spread throughout the Western church and was accepted by the popes in the ninth century. Eastern Christians objected to this change for two reasons.

The first was a theological disagreement. It seemed that Christians in the two branches of Christianity were expressing differing beliefs about the Trinity. Second and even more important, eastern Christians disputed the way in which the change occurred. They claimed that changes in the Nicene Creed could not be made by a single person—namely, the pope—but that such changes required the consent of an ecumenical council. Thus authority in the church also became an issue.

Ukranian Orthodox church in Winnipeg, Manitoba

filioque

a Latin word meaning "and the Son," added to the Nicene Creed in western Christianity and one reason for the controversy between Christianity in the East and in the West

ecumenical

pertaining to openness among religions, especially strong among Christians in the latter half of the twentieth century; also a council to which all bishops have been invited

In recent decades, both the Catholic Church centered in Rome and Eastern Orthodoxy have been intensely involved in **ecumenical** discussions in order to restore unity between these two ancient branches of Christianity. Relations between the two have not been better in centuries. Yet progress toward unity has been slow. The *filioque* clause still separates the two, even though attempts have been made to clarify the meaning and intent of this expression. Of greater significance is the role of the pope in the church. This issue remains a major obstacle to unity, even though the Eastern church is willing to recognize him as the first among equals.

Eastern Orthodox Christians are those Christians who follow the teachings of the first seven ecumenical councils held between 325 and 787. They believe that these are the essential teachings of the Christian faith and that there is no need to add any further doctrines.

The structure of the Eastern Orthodox churches is hierarchical. Each of the churches is headed by a patriarch or bishop. They consider themselves a "family of churches," with the patriarch of Constantinople enjoying a "primacy of honor" among all. He does not have jurisdictional authority over the others. Each national church is governed by a council of bishops.

This family of churches derives from the four ancient patriarchs, or cities, where Christianity was first established: Alexandria, Antioch, Jerusalem, and Constantinople. Since Rome was one of the original five patriarchs, the pope is recognized by the East as the patriarch of the West. In recent years, other patriarchs have been recognized, such as those of Russia and Bulgaria. Autocephalous churches are those headed by a bishop without a patriarch. Autonomous churches are headed by a bishop and are self-governing on internal matters, but depend upon a patriarch for the appointment of their bishop.

Some Groups in the Americas

Worldwide there are about 175,000,000 Orthodox Christians. In the United States, several different Orthodox Churches have in total about 3.5 million members. The Canadian section of the Orthodox Church in America has about one million members.

Orthodox Christianity came to North America in 1794 when ten Russian monks founded a mission in Alaska. Missionary efforts were so successful that a diocese was created in Alaska in 1799. In 1840, Ivan Venyaminov became Alaska's first resident bishop. In 1848, he built the Cathedral of St. Michael at Sitka. Later, as metropolitan of Moscow and primate of Russia, he strengthened the Alaska diocese by separating it from its Siberian province and, in 1872, moving the headquarters to San Francisco. At that, the Russian Orthodox Church had 12,000 communicants.

Beginning in 1891 and in the years following, membership in the Russian Orthodox Church in North America increased significantly. Many of the new members were emigrés from central Europe who were at the time united with Roman Catholicism, even though they had once been Russian Orthodox. Upon arriving in the United States, many sought reunion with the Russian Orthodox Church. By 1904, half of the membership could be attributed to these transfers. In 1915, Archbishop Tikhov Belavin moved the headquarters of the church to New York.

Meanwhile, because of upheavals in Europe, members of many other Orthodox churches were immigrating to North America.

Most of these were Greek Orthodox Christians. The first Greek Orthodox Christians came to the United States in 1768 as indentured servants. Many other Greek Orthodox immigrated in the 1880s and 90s, and large numbers continued to arrive until strict immigration laws were implemented in the United States in the 1920s. The first Greek Orthodox parish was organized in 1891 in New York. By 1920, one hundred and fifty Greek Orthodox churches had been constructed.

Greek Orthodox Christians were served by priests from the Churches of Constantinople and Greece, both of which were Greek-speaking. The Greek Orthodox Archdiocese of North and South America was established in 1922 as a province of the Church of Constantinople. In September 1996, Archbishop Spyridon was installed as archbishop of Greek Orthodox Christians in America. He is the first native-born leader of this church. Today the Greek Orthodox Archdiocese in North and South America has about 1.5 million members.

In the seventeenth century, the first member of the Armenian Apostolic Orthodox Church came to the thirteen colonies. Coworkers referred to him as "Martin the Armenian." Waves of Armenians followed, and the first Armenian Apostolic Orthodox church in the United States was built in 1891 at Worcester, Massachusetts. In 1889, the Supreme Patriarch and Catholics of All Armenians responded to the needs of Armenian Americans by creating the Diocese of the Armenian Church of America. A period of rapid growth followed. An archbishop presides over the diocese, with headquarters in New York. The Armenian Apostolic Orthodox Church is the only Eastern church to use unleavened bread for Holy Communion. At different points in history, it has had considerable contact with the Church of Rome, which has long used unleavened bread.

Through the sufferings of thine Only-Begotten all creatures are renewed and mankind hath once more been made immortal, clad in a garment that none can take away. . . .

O chalice of fiery rain poured out on the apostles in the upper room, O Holy Ghost pour thy wisdom also upon us as we put on these vestments. . . .

O Thou who didst spread thy creating arms to the stars, strengthen our arms with power to intercede when we lift up our hands to thee. . . .

Supreme, divine Sovereign of all beings, Thou hast covered us with a robe as with love to be ministers of thy holy mystery.

Heavenly King, keep thy Church immovable, and preserve in peace all them that worship thy Holy Name.

—From the Vesting Hymn, recited by priests of the Armenian Apostolic Orthodox Church as they put on their sacred vestments. The hymn can be found in Prayers of Preparation in the Sacristy (the first part of the Badarak).

The migration of Orthodox Christians to North America from their ancient lands has been stressful. Orthodoxy is intimately tied to the land, culture, language, folk customs, and political structures of a particular country. Thus it is difficult to be uprooted from this background. Stress is also caused by separation from the church of origin thousands of miles away and by starting over in a culture which supports independence, mobility, and a plurality of beliefs. Orthodox Christians have had to struggle to find stability and unity among themselves in a very different western culture.

In 1970, the Orthodox Church in America became an autocephalous (independent) church within Orthodox Christianity. The Church seeks to unite all Orthodox Christians living in the northern hemisphere, regardless of their church of origin (the church to which they belonged in their native country).

Beliefs

As stated earlier, Eastern Orthodox Christians accept and believe all the teachings of the first seven ecumenical councils. They believe in the ancient creeds: the Apostles' Creed and the Nicene Creed. They believe in the incarnation of Jesus, the divinity of Christ, the Trinity, the virginity of Mary, the resurrection of the dead, the need for salvation in Christ, and eternal life with God after death. They believe in the **real presence** of Christ in the Eucharist.

Orthodox Christians place a high emphasis on the Holy Spirit. The Holy Spirit is the sanctifier of life. The consecration of the bread and wine by the priest at the Eucharistic liturgy is not considered complete without the invocation of the Holy Spirit. The Holy Spirit sanctifies the church.

Practices

The clearest way to gain insight into Orthodox Christianity is through their principal liturgical action: the **Divine Liturgy**. This liturgy is based upon the liturgy of St. John Chrysostom. For Eastern Orthodox Christians, the Divine Liturgy is a grand drama reenacting the life of Christ. Participation in this liturgy brings one into this drama.

The Divine Liturgy

The Divine Liturgy is divided into three parts:

- **Part one** is the preparation. This is when the materials for the Divine Liturgy are prepared. It recalls the incarnation and birth of Jesus.

- **Part two** consists of the "processions." The first procession is the entrance procession when the litany is said, prayers are offered, and the sermon is given. This is followed by the "Gospel Procession" when the book of Bible readings is brought out, an epistle is read, and the gospel is chanted or read by the priest. This symbolizes Jesus coming to the people to teach them and to heal their illnesses. The third procession is the "Great Entrance" when the prepared gifts of bread and wine are brought out and prayers said. The Creed is then recited.

- **Part three**, the highlight of the Orthodox liturgy, is the communion service. Since Orthodox Christians believe that the bread and wine become the body and blood of Christ, they believe that each individual receives the body and blood in holy communion. The priest brings the consecrated bread and wine to the people. This symbolizes Christ's self-giving for human salvation. The Divine Liturgy ends with a Dismissal Service which includes a prayer of thanksgiving to God and a blessing.

Like Roman Catholics in the West, Eastern Orthodox Christians have seven sacraments. They are called "mysteries" because the original Greek word for the Latin word *sacramentum* is translated as "mystery." In addition to the Eucharist, the mysteries are: baptism, chrismation, confession, holy orders, matrimony, and anointing.

---

real presence

the belief of some Christian churches that the risen Jesus is actually present in the consecrated bread and wine of Communion

Divine Liturgy

the principal liturgical action of Eastern Orthodox Christians; an elaborate ceremony which engages all the human senses

Orthodox Christians believe in infant baptism. The infant is also confirmed at the same time and receives a portion of the consecrated bread dipped in the consecrated wine. The sacrament of matrimony is celebrated in an elaborate liturgical service. Married men may be ordained priests, but bishops are chosen from the celibate clergy, usually monks. Confession of sins is made to a priest, and the sick are anointed with oil.

John Chrysostom

John's surname, Chrysostom, means "Golden Mouth." He was born about 347 in Antioch in Syria. Baptized at the age of twenty, John joined a group of hermits from 374 to 381. He became a priest and, in 398, the archbishop of Constantinople. However, he was forced from the position in 404 because of disputes with the archbishop of Alexandria and a complex political situation. John's last words before dying in exile in 407 were: "Glory to God for all things."

The *Liturgy of St. John Chrysostom* was probably not written by John. Rather, the widespread use of this liturgy in the East reflects the importance of Constantinople to the Eastern Christian Church of the time.

This is one of the prayers attributed to John Chrysostom:

Almighty God, who has given us grace at this time with one accord to make our common supplication to you, and has promised through your well-beloved Son that when two or three are gathered in his name you will be in the midst of them: Fulfill now, O Lord, the desires and petitions of your servants as may be best for us; granting in this world knowledge of your truth and in the world to come life everlasting.

Let's talk about It . . .

1. Why might someone be called "Golden Mouth"?
2. What Christian beliefs are reflected in John's prayer?

Mary and icons

Eastern Orthodox Christians have a high devotion to the saints, especially to Mary, the mother of Jesus. In an Orthodox church, one is surrounded by images of the saints. These saints are arranged in hierarchical significance. In the front of the church is an **iconostasis,** a screen on which are images of Jesus, Mary, John the Baptist, and the patron of the church. One has a sense of being surrounded by these heavenly hosts.

These images are called **icons.** Western Christians are used to seeing stained-glass windows, frescoes, oil paintings, wood carvings, and statues. Virtually the only religious images in an Orthodox church, other than a crucifix, are the icons. The Greek word *icon* means "image." An icon is a two-dimensional image of a saint or event in the life of Christ or Mary. The icon is painted on wood in an ancient stylized way. The figures do not have a "real" presentation; usually the figures are elongated, with bold, piercing eyes and large hands to symbolize the spiritual.

iconostasis

a wooden screen on which are painted images of Jesus, Mary, John the Baptist, the saints, and the patron saint of the church, found in Eastern Orthodox churches

icon

a two-dimensional image of a saint or event in the life of Christ or Mary painted on wood in an ancient stylized way

Mary as God-bearer is a common subject for icons.

An icon contains several elements of creation. The wood on which it is painted represents the plant world. Chalk or alabaster is used to smooth the wood, thus representing minerals. Animals are represented in the egg-based paints, and the artist represents humans and the spiritual. The artist fasts and prays before working on an icon. Most icons are not original conceptions but are copies of much older icons thought to be miraculous.

Icons are not pictures to be admired for their beauty; rather, they are images intended to draw the observer into the mystery presented. One does not really look at an icon. The image in the icon looks at the observer. They are like looking out of a large window to a beautiful scene outside. They convey the sense that there is another world beyond.

Conclusion

Eastern Orthodox Christians have demonstrated an unwavering commitment to the early Christian response to the question: Who is Jesus? They have held fast to the earliest beliefs about Jesus through all the stresses of the past two thousand years of history. They especially stand as witnesses to the sufferings caused by persecution. In recent times, this was evident in the Russian Orthodox Church during the communist domination of the Soviet Union. Orthodox Christians are a reminder to all Christians of their rich ancient heritage. They bring a dignity and solemnity to worship often lost in streamlined western Christian liturgies. Mystery and awe remain present in their liturgical experiences and daily life.

Reaping the Fruit

A Christian Calendar (Northern Hemisphere)

Many Christian churches follow a liturgical calendar which begins with the first Sunday of Advent. Included here are the major seasons and feasts celebrated in many Christian churches, along with some of the feasts particular to the Orthodox traditions.

Winter

The **Season of Advent** (four to seven Sundays/weeks before Christmas). Christians, especially Catholic Christians and most mainline Protestant sects, prepare for Christmas by observing Advent. Throughout Advent, the themes of expectation and joy are emphasized. The level of expectation and joy rises as Christmas approaches.

Christmas Day (December 25). Most Christians celebrate the birth of Jesus of Nazareth on this day. Some Christians observe Christmas on the ancient date of January 6.

Epiphany (January 6). On this day, Orthodox Christians celebrate Jesus' baptism. Catholic, Anglican, and other Christians celebrate the magi's visit to the child Jesus and Jesus' manifestation to the Gentiles.

The **Season of Christmas** (Christmas until mid-January).

Ordinary Time, from the end of the Christmas Season until Lent.

World Religions' Day (observed in January). On this day, Christians and peoples of other faiths celebrate the good in the world's religions. People mark the day by praying and meditating.

Feast Day of the Three Hierarchs (January 30). On this day, Orthodox Christians celebrate the contributions of Saint Basil the Great, Saint Gregory of Nazianzus (also known as Saint Gregory the Theologian), and Saint John Chrysostom. All were Greek (Eastern) Church Fathers. Selections from their writings are often read on this day.

Spring

Pre-Lent. In addition to Great Lent, Orthodox Christians observe Pre-Lent, which consists of the four Sundays immediately preceding Great Lent. Each of these four Sundays is known by a particular name, and stresses a specific theme: (1) The Publican and the Pharisee (humility), (2) The Prodigal Son (returning to the Father), (3) Meatfare Sunday (judgment), (4) Cheesefare Sunday (forgiveness).

Lent or **Great Lent** (the six to eight weeks preceding Easter). Many Christians prepare for Easter by observing Lent. Throughout Lent, these Christians try to live up to their baptism by fasting, giving to those in need, and praying.

Lazarus Saturday (Saturday before Palm Sunday). On this day, Orthodox Christians celebrate Jesus' raising of Lazarus from the dead. According to the New Testament, Jesus brought the dead back to life on only three occasions. Orthodox Christians emphasize the raising of Lazarus because he was one of Jesus' friends.

Palm Sunday or **Passion Sunday** (Sunday before Easter). On this day, Christians commemorate Jesus' final entry into Jerusalem. The New Testament Passion (story of Jesus' suffering and death) is read, and blessed palm branches are distributed. This day marks the beginning of Holy Week.

The **Triduum:** Maundy (or Holy) Thursday, Good Friday, Holy Saturday. The Triduum is observed by Eastern, Orthodox, Roman Catholic, and some Protestant churches.

Maundy or **Holy Thursday** (Thursday before Easter Sunday). On this day, many Christians share the Eucharist in a special way; they are especially mindful of how Jesus and his closest disciples shared in this sacrament at the Last Supper. Many Christians demonstrate their love for one another by imitating Jesus washing his disciples' feet.

Good Friday commemorates the saving death of Jesus.

Holy Saturday, the day after Good Friday, which is celebrated with the Easter Vigil in many Christian Churches. The celebration includes the baptism of infants and adults and the blessing of the paschal (Easter) candle and of water intended for use as holy water and for baptisms.

Easter Sunday or **Holy Pascha** (first Sunday after the full moon following the vernal equinox; between March 22 and April 25). On this day, most Christians celebrate the resurrection of Jesus of Nazareth. For Western Christians, Easter falls on the first Sunday after the full moon following the vernal equinox (between March 22 and April 25). Eastern and Orthodox Christians wait until after the start of Passover before beginning the Easter celebration.

The **Season of Easter**, the time between Easter and Pentecost.

Ascension Thursday (fortieth day after Easter). On this day, Eastern, Orthodox, Catholic, Anglican, and some other Christians commemorate the ascension of Jesus (his return to heaven in glory).

World Day of Prayer (observed in March). On this day, Christians and those of other faiths pray for solutions to the world's problems. They also pray for the unity of humankind.

Pentecost (fifty days after Easter Sunday). On this day, many Christians celebrate the coming of the Holy Spirit on Pentecost. For these Christians, the first Pentecost marked the formal creation of the Christian Church.

Summer

Ordinary Time, the time after Pentecost until the end of the liturgical year in November.

Transfiguration (August 6). Many Christians celebrate Jesus' transfiguration on this day.

Assumption of Mary or **Dormition of the Theotokos** (August 15). Catholic Christians honor Mary on this day by attending mass. Orthodox Christians honor Mary on this day as the "God-bearer" or *Theotokos*.

Holy Cross Day (September 14). On this day, Eastern, Orthodox, Catholic, and Anglican Christians mark the discovery of the true cross (the cross on which Jesus died). Holy Cross Day is known by three other names: Adoration, Elevation, or Exaltation of the Holy Cross.

Autumn

All Saints' Day (November 1). On this day, Catholic and Anglican Christians rejoice in the blessedness of persons (saints) known and unknown.

"Death is the supreme festival on the road to freedom."
—*Dietrich Bonhoeffer*

Feast Day of Saint Andrew the Apostle (November 30). This day is important to Orthodox Christians, especially to the Greek Orthodox. According to tradition, the Apostle Andrew established the Church of Constantinople. Istanbul (Constantinople), Turkey, is the headquarters of Orthodox Christianity's spiritual leader, the Ecumenical Patriarch, Archbishop of Constantinople and New Rome.

Discovering

1. Be sure you can explain the meaning of each of the vocabulary words.
2. Explain the difference between the Jesus of History and the Christ of Faith.
3. According to Christian tradition, what are the two historic covenants? Where are the histories of these two covenants found?
4. With what event did Christianity begin? Why is this event considered the beginning of Christianity?
5. What are the Apocrypha? What Christian traditions include it in the Old Testament?
6. How does the Old Testament differ among the various Christian traditions?
7. What is the New Testament? Does it differ among Christian traditions?
8. What is the Apostles' Creed? What significance does it have in the Christian faith?
9. Explain the basic doctrines Christians formulated in the first centuries of the church.
10. What does baptism signify for most Christians?
11. Why do Christians share sacramental bread and wine or juice?
12. Explain the Christian practices shared by all Christians.
13. Explain the organization of the Eastern Orthodox Churches.
14. What are the beginnings of Eastern Orthodoxy in North America?
15. Name and explain the three parts of the Divine Liturgy.
16. What is an icon?

Exploring

1. Discuss why you think Jesus taught in parables. What is an advantage of this type of teaching? What is a disadvantage?
2. Meet with two or three classmates and discuss the Nicene Creed. What is the meaning of each phrase? How does the creed express the beliefs of the early Christians and Eastern Orthodox Christians?
3. The text states that the Beatitudes are a kind of "prescription for happiness." Explain how this might be. How could following the Beatitudes lead to happiness? How do the Beatitudes compare/contrast with popular ideas about happiness? Compare and/or contrast each of the Beatitudes with popular ideas about achieving happiness.
4. Meet with two classmates and discuss the causes of the Great Schism.
5. Visit an Orthodox church. Every aspect of an Orthodox church is symbolic. Study the architectural style. Examine the interior. See if you can discover the symbolic meaning of each aspect. Visit with a parishioner or the priest; ask them to explain the symbolic significance of the items in their church.

Integrating

1. Choose one of the Beatitudes. Consider its meaning and how it contrasts with popular ideas about happiness. Then attempt to live that Beatitude for one week. At the end of the week, write a one-page reflection paper on successes and obstacles to living that Beatitude.

2. Visit the celebration of the Divine Liturgy at an Orthodox church. Allow yourself to get caught up in the drama of the liturgy. How are your senses—sight, smell, hearing, and touch—stimulated? Afterwards, reflect upon how this experience touches you interiorly.

3. The Orthodox have demonstrated unwavering commitment to their beliefs. Discuss in a small group the advantages and disadvantages of such commitment. How does commitment to religious beliefs help one to grow? Or hinder growth? Is it ever appropriate to modify one's beliefs?

4. What is your answer to the question, "Who is Jesus?"

Words to Know

apocalyptic
Apocrypha
apostle
baptism
Beatitudes
Christ of Faith
Christianity
Christmas
Communion
creed
Divine Liturgy

doctrine
Easter
ecumenical
Edict of Milan
filioque
Great Schism
icon
iconostasis
incarnation
Jesus

Jesus of History
New Testament
Old Testament
parable
Pentecost
real presence
schism
sect
testament
Trinity

Chapter 5

After reading this chapter, you will be able to

- Describe how Catholic Christianity goes about renewing itself
- Explain essential beliefs and practices of the Catholic Church
- Assess characteristics of the Catholic world-view

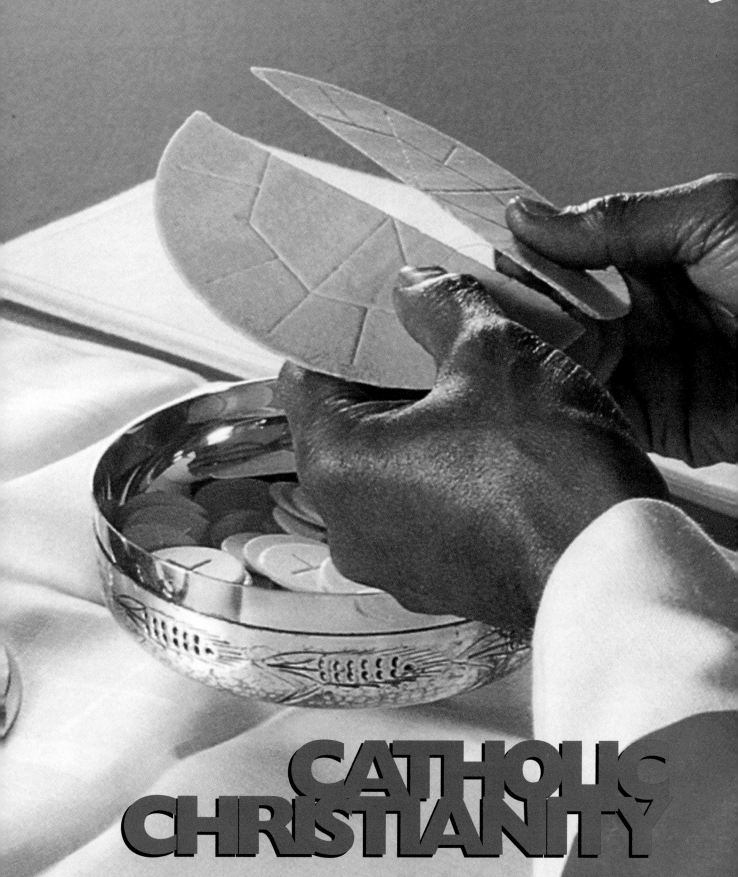

CATHOLIC
CHRISTIANITY

Introduction

❖ *Fourteen-year-old Todd Lambert was not looking forward to school. Today was "service day" and Todd, along with three other students, had been assigned to do service work for the elderly poor of his community. In addition to this, Todd was asked to bring a rake and garbage bags to school with him! While he appreciated the opportunity to be out of classes for a day, Todd did not understand why he had to rake leaves for "some old people" he didn't even know.*

*Each fall Todd's entire Catholic school community—teachers, staff, and students—took a day off from classes to serve the needs of the elderly poor in their area. Typically, they did general fall clean-up, such as raking leaves, cleaning out gardens, and washing windows. The day began with a **mass** for the school community. The homilist explained how service is part of their Catholic faith. To serve the needs of the poor, he said, is part of what it means to be a Catholic.*

Todd's group worked hard throughout the morning. The enthusiasm of the upper class students in his group helped Todd feel comfortable and involved in the work of the day. By 1:30 P.M., the group had finished its assigned tasks. The kids were tired, but pleased that they had been of genuine service. At one home, the elderly woman had invited the group into her home for homemade cookies and a soft drink. Todd noticed the smallness of the house, the old-time worn furniture, and pictures of the woman's family on a shelf in the living room. He realized that she was an ordinary person, a grandmother just like his own.

Later that day, Todd reflected upon his experience. "I never realized there were so many poor people in our town. When I look at the house I live in and the many things I have, I guess I really am lucky."

❖ *Karen Smith, 42, divorced and mother of two, was anxious about today's mass. Today was her first day to **lector** at her parish's Saturday evening mass. Karen had long wanted to get involved in her **parish** community, but had hesitated for one reason or another. Finally she decided that she could best serve her parish by lectoring on a regular basis at the weekend masses. Karen discussed this desire with her parish's director of liturgy. She had gone to the preparation sessions and was ready to proclaim God's word to her fellow parishioners for the first time.*

❖ *Greg, 25, from a small town in the foothills of the Appalachian mountains, proudly displayed his new book of prayers and instructions for being a Eucharistic minister. After completing the preparation classes, Greg was commissioned as a Eucharistic minister for his parish community, one who helped distribute Holy Communion. Living in an area where Catholics were only 2 percent of the population, Greg had been challenged in his faith. But he grew to appreciate the traditions and values of his religion. Greg was proud to be a Catholic and looked forward to serving his church as a Eucharistic minister. He was assigned to bring communion to six homebound members of his parish.*

mass
the eucharistic service in the Catholic Church

lector
reader of scripture at a religious service

parish
local religious congregation, especially Catholic and Anglican

✤ *Ellen Fischels ruminated about the parish council meeting this evening. Ellen had served on her parish council for three years and was now president of the council. Tonight's meeting, six months after her election as president, would be the first real test of her leadership abilities. In recent years, the number of Spanish-speaking people in her parish had grown to a sizable minority. The social concerns committee was now presenting several proposals on responding to the needs of these new families. While some members of the council would wholeheartedly promote full implementation of the proposals, Ellen knew that there would also be some council members who would argue that parish resources, especially financial resources, could not be found at this time to respond to the needs of these new families. Yet Ellen was confident that with patience and honest dialogue, the council could find ways to fully include these newest members of the parish.*

✤ *Bishop Simmons, a bishop from a diocese in the western part of the United States, thoughtfully packed the last few items into his suitcase as he prepared for his 3:00 P.M. flight to Washington, DC. Bishops from all over the United States were gathering in Washington the next day for their annual meeting. The major item on the agenda was a vote on a controversial new pastoral letter. Three years in development, the letter had gone through several drafts. It was now ready for a vote by all the bishops. The letter had sparked sharp differences of opinion not only among the bishops themselves, but also among the Catholic community at large and even in the nation. A favorable vote on the document would mean that the Catholic leaders would be expanding their dialogue in the public arena on an issue of urgent concern to the entire nation. Yet Bishop Simmons was thoroughly convinced that the teachings of this new letter were completely consistent with the teachings of the scriptures, the tradition of the Catholic Church, and contemporary teaching of church leadership in Rome.*

The Inspiration for these Catholic Christians

The joys and the hopes, the griefs and anxieties of the [people] of this age, especially those who are poor or in any way afflicted, these too are the joys and hopes, the griefs and anxieties of the followers of Christ. Indeed, nothing genuinely human fails to raise an echo in their hearts. For theirs is a community composed of [people]. United in Christ, they are led by the Holy Spirit in their journey to the kingdom of their Father and they have welcomed the news of salvation which is meant for every[one]. That is why this community realizes that it is truly and intimately united with [hu]mankind and its history.

—*The Documents of Vatican II*, "The Church in the Modern World," #1.

These words capture the spirit of the Catholic Church's twenty-first **ecumenical council**. All Catholic Church leaders, as well as invited observers from other churches and religions, met in four sessions at the Vatican in Rome, Italy, from 1962 to 1965. The sixteen documents of this council present a vision of the Catholic Church which points to a new

ecumenical council
a worldwide gathering of church leaders; since the Reformation, Catholic bishops in union with the pope have held their own councils, with other churches limited to observers

direction for relating to the people, needs, and problems of the world today. Until this time, the Catholic Church had been more separate, more guarded, more protective of its members from "the world" at large. In this way, the church had sought to protect its faith and members from the "dangers" of the outside world.

Under the leadership of **Pope** John XXIII and the Second Vatican Council in the 1960s, the Catholic Church opened up to the larger world. In this new perspective, the church accepted the risks and dangers of being a "pilgrim people." Being on pilgrimage means that the next step in the journey is not always clear. The temptation to return to safer, more stable, ways or to take a mistaken new way is always present. Thus, there is often disagreement among church members about how best to live as Catholics.

Yet Catholics in North America have taken the vision of this council to heart. The examples you read in the opening pages of this chapter are only a sampling of countless ways in which North American Catholics have sought to implement this new vision. Catholics have sought to renew their interior church life in the way they pray and celebrate their sacraments. They have expanded institutional structures in order to involve more members of the church in leadership and decision making. As individuals, Catholics have been challenged to renew and deepen their own faith and their response to the needs of people in their local communities. The Catholic Church, as a world church, has sought to respond to and lead in addressing the major issues facing humankind today. In short, the Catholic Church is attempting to open itself to the world: to embrace the joys and the hopes, the griefs and anxieties of the modern era.

Tilling the Soil

The early history of Christianity and the events leading up to the Great Schism were explained briefly in chapter 4. **Catholicism**, sometimes referred to as *Roman Catholicism*, derives from the western branch of Christianity and, like eastern Christianity, traces itself back to those foundations of Christianity. While Christians in the East were facing their own set of historical developments, so too were Christians in the West.

The Problems of the West

Constantine's removal of the capital of the Roman Empire from Rome to Byzantium in 330 caused a leadership vacuum in the West. With imperial power concentrated in the East, it became more and more difficult to maintain order and defend the borders of the empire in the West. Civil authority became weaker and weaker, and migrating Germanic tribes overran vast areas of Europe. This left the Christian Church as the only institution in the West which had any kind of unity and authority throughout the area.

This fact, along with the official status given to Christianity in 380, led to the development of a union between church and state. The Christian

pope
in the Catholic Church, the bishop of Rome, who has authority over the entire church

Catholicism
the branch of Christianity which acknowledges the leadership of the pope in Rome (Roman Catholicism)

Pope John XXIII

Church, because of both the leadership vacuum created and the support of the state, gradually took on more and more civil authority. Bishops were not just religious leaders of faith communities—they also took on temporal authority for their area. Eventually they became an elite ruling class. This led to many abuses and a confusion about the role and nature of the church. The union of church and state continued to be the norm until the establishment of the United States of America, which officially separated church and state. Reactions against the union of church and state and debates concerning the relationship of church and state continue until the present day.

Pope Gregory the Great (590–604), is credited with beginning the centralized structure of the Catholic Church. He negotiated peace with the Germanic tribes and sent missionaries to the far reaches of the empire in order to convert the tribes. Gregory called for a greater unity among the dioceses of the church. He disciplined the clergy and removed unworthy clerics. He was generous to many charities; he protected Jews from unjust coercion and saw to the feeding of the victims of a famine. He wrote many treatises and hundreds of sermons and letters. He reformed the liturgy. Gregory the Great is considered the founder of the medieval papacy.

Union between church and state continued to build in the following centuries. Charlemagne managed to dominate the various Germanic peoples in the ninth century. On Christmas Day in the year 800, the pope crowned Charlemagne Emperor of the Holy Roman Empire.

Charlemagne considered it his duty to christianize all the peoples in his realm. Unfortunately he did so by force. On the other hand, Charlemagne did much to support the work of the church by establishing dioceses and parishes, promoting education, and encouraging reform of the worship ceremonies. The union between church and state becomes complete with Charlemagne. Roman Catholic Christianity emerged as a separate and distinct variety of Catholic Christianity in the year 1054.

In the years following 1054, the Church of Rome began to look inward. A succession of strong popes, such as Nicholas II (?–1061) and Gregory VII (1020–1085), enacted much-needed reforms. In part, these reforms helped the church respond to and survive the momentous events of the fourteenth, sixteenth, seventeenth, and twentieth centuries.

The abuses which resulted from the union of church and state were unfortunately only one of many other causes contributing to the Reformation of the sixteenth century. The **Avignon Papacy** further exacerbated the ties between church and state. This term refers to the time from 1305 to 1377 when seven popes lived in Avignon in France rather than in Rome; the papacy took on greater wealth during this time, but lost much credibility in papal leadership, since the pope was not living in the traditional city of Rome. This period is sometimes referred to as the *Babylonian Captivity*, a reference to the seventy years of exile endured by the Jewish people in Babylon.

When the pope finally returned to Rome, the French elected another pope, who remained at Avignon. For thirty-one years, there were two popes. At the Council of Pisa (1409), the two popes resigned and a new pope was elected. Things did not go according to plan, however, and the Church of Rome ended up with three popes, causing further loss of credibility in papal leadership among members of the church. The Council of Constance (1414–1418) finally resolved the matter.

The bubonic plague or black death, which began in the years 1347–1350, ravaged Europe throughout the fourteenth century. Scholars estimate that at least one-third of the population and one-half of the clergy died during this time. Wretched living conditions and pessimism engendered by the plague deepened superstitious beliefs and reinforced negative ideas about a vengeful God. Furthermore, the clergy were hastily replaced by unprepared men with the hope that they would learn their responsibilities after ordination. Now the general populace was led by men who were themselves uneducated and superstitious. Add to this the rise of **nationalism** and the spirit of the **Renaissance**, and conditions became ripe for reform movements.

Many efforts were made by leaders and other individuals in the church to work for reform. Most laudable was the rise in the thirteenth century of mendicant religious orders, the Franciscans and the Dominicans. Members of these religious communities renounced material possessions and sought to live more according to the model of Christ.

Avignon Papacy

the period of time, 1305–1377, when seven popes lived in Avignon in France rather than in Rome

nationalism

a sense of national consciousness over and above other nations and supranational groups; the division of the Holy Roman Empire into independent nations

Renaissance

rebirth; usually refers to the rebirth of the spirit of the Classical Age during the late fifteenth and early sixteenth centuries

religious order

a group of men or women who live a vowed life in community, pray together, and generally share a common work, either within a monastery or among the people; more common in the Catholic Church and Orthodox Churches than in other Christian denominations

Francis of Assisi

Francis of Assisi is probably the most well-known saint in the history of the Christian Church. Francis lived from c. 1181 to 1226 in Italy. At about the age of twenty, Francis gave up his comfortable life and began a life of service to people who were sick or poor. Soon other men joined him in his life of poverty and charity; they took the name *Friars Minor* ("Little Brothers").

Francis is known as the originator of the Christmas crèche and for his love of all God's creatures. But more importantly, he, along with St. Dominic, was the guiding force in the development of active orders of men religious who moved beyond the monastery walls to live out their ministry.

Francis of Assisi was the only perfect Christian since Christ. His great originality lies in his having undertaken—with boundless faith and love—to carry out the program of Galilee . . . . he was a faithful mirror of Christ. . . . After Christianity itself, the Franciscan movement is the greatest popular achievement known to history. One sees it in the simplicity of men who know only nature and what they have seen or heard in church, and who combine the whole in the freest fashion.

—Ernest Renan

What a fine place
this world would be
if Dualist Humanists
tried to be human
to men.
What a fine place
this world would be
if Personalist Theists
tried to be
their brother's keeper
as God
wants them to be.
What a fine place
this world would be
if Fundamentalist Protestants tried to exemplify
the Sermon on the Mount.
What a fine place
this world would be
if Roman Catholics
tried to keep up
with Saint Francis of Assisi.

— Peter Maurin

I was perfectly happy, as a nothing could be perfectly happy. I also was perfectly sad as well. It occurred to me one day that a personal friend of Jesus named Francis has made it possible for a fraternity to exist among people that theretofore had not been recognized by the official church and therefore by anyone else. The faithful, in terms of having not just a position but an obligation, were increased and encompassed. By this encompassing they changed their nature. The people took seriously their baptism and what it implies. Maybe it has taken eight hundred years for that to be actualized. In some ways it is going to take longer. It hasn't occurred yet. It is not enough to sing "Priestly People" every two months. Francis made it possible for us in a way that is within the limits and structures of the church to be a community.

— Arlo Guthrie

Let's Talk about It . . .

1. Why is Francis of Assisi respected by so many people of many religions?
2. For each of the people quoted above, name the one thing about Francis that appealed to the writer.

The Reformation and Its Aftermath

Despite the many abuses and problems resulting from the union of church and state, the Christian Church in the West did much for society. The ancient writings of Christianity were preserved and recopied in the monasteries. The church gave stability to society and promoted education and the development of the arts. In many ways, the Christian Church oriented people to God. Nevertheless, the reformers of the sixteenth century and the European expansion to the New World did much to correct the abuses and problems that had arisen. Led by Martin Luther (1483–1546), the Protestant Reformation began as a reform movement within Catholic Christianity in the West, but led to the emergence of a number of independent churches. In the aftermath of the Reformation, the church centered in Rome underwent a renewal known as the Counter-Reformation, which gave rise to clerical reform and to the Council of Trent (1545–1563).

In the late seventeenth century, the Catholic Church in France asserted its autonomy. In 1682, it drafted the Gallican Articles:

1. In matters of state, rulers are independent of the church.
2. In spiritual matters, the authority of the pope is subject to that of a general (church-wide) council.
3. The history and practices of the French Church must be respected by the Church of Rome.
4. In matters of faith, decisions of the pope require the approval of a general council.

The Gallican Articles sparked an ongoing church-state dispute. Each claimed rights that the other said it did not have. Pope Pius VII (1742–1823) and Emperor Napoleon Bonaparte (1769–1821) finally settled on a compromise in 1801.

The Second Vatican Council, also known as Vatican Council II, or Vatican II, and held in the late twentieth century, was one of the most important councils in the history of Catholic Christianity. It ranks next to Nicaea (325), Chalcedon (451), and Trent (1545–63). Pope Paul VI (1897–1978), who was Pope John XXIII's successor, implemented the council's far-reaching conclusions. As a result of Vatican II, people now worship in their everyday language and participate more fully in all aspects of church life, including decision-making. As has been noted, the Second Vatican Council brought spiritual renewal to the church and redefines the church's place in the world.

Planting the Seed

The word **catholic** comes from a Greek word which means "universal." *Universal* in this sense means "totality" or "wholeness." The Catholic Church sees itself as being "total" or "whole" in two ways. First, Christ is considered the head of the church and is united with all members of the church. Thus the church possesses in a unique way the fullness or totality of what Christ intended for his church.

Second, the Catholic Church sees itself as being sent on a mission to the entire human race. This commission comes from Matthew 28:19–20 in which Jesus says, "Go therefore and make disciples of all nations, baptizing them in the name of the Father and of the Son and of the Holy Spirit, and teaching them to obey everything that I have commanded you. And remember, I am with you always, to the end of the age." In this sense of universal, the Catholic Church sees itself as reaching out to embrace the joys and hopes, the griefs and anxieties of all people.

catholic
universal, total, whole; sent on a mission to the entire human race

Catholic Church Structure

The Catholic Church is **hierarchical** in structure. This means that there are varying levels of authority united under a central authority. The pope is the head of the Catholic Church and the source of unity within Roman Catholic Christianity. He is the spiritual leader of a local church known as the Church of Rome (diocese of Rome), as well as the spiritual leader of a community of local churches (dioceses). In short, Roman Catholic Christianity can be seen as a community of some 2,500 local churches (dioceses) that recognize the authority of pope.

The Catholic Church traces the authority exercised by the pope to the apostle Peter. According to the New Testament, Peter played an important role in Jesus' life and in the affairs of the early church. Peter was the first person to be called by Jesus to discipleship, and the first of the disciples to be given power over unclean spirits. Moreover, he was the first of the apostles to receive news of Jesus' resurrection. Catholics believe that Jesus commissioned Peter as the head of his church:

hierarchical
having varying levels of authority united under a central authority

"And I tell you, you are Peter, and on this rock I will build my church, and the gates of Hades will not prevail against it. I will give you the keys

of the kingdom of heaven, and whatever you bind on earth will be bound in heaven, and whatever you loose on earth will be loosed in heaven."

—*Matthew 16:18–19, NRSV.*

The New Testament book, the Acts of the Apostles, chronicles events in the early church. In the Acts of the Apostles, Peter emerges as a powerful healer, exorcist, and leader. According to various ancient traditions, Peter traveled to Rome, founded a Christian community there, became the community's leader, and met death as a martyr. While Roman Catholic Christians regard Peter as the first bishop of Rome, or pope, this office was in a very early stage of development in the early church.

Today, united with the pope are the bishops who head the dioceses around the world. It can be said that (1) the pope is the highest authority in the Catholic Church, and (2) the bishops in union with the pope are the highest authority in the Catholic Church. A bishop especially focuses on his diocese. Each **diocese** is divided into parishes, each of which is headed by a pastor. The pastor works with the pastoral council which is composed of lay members of the parish who provide the leadership for the parish. While there are several other administrative levels in between, these three constitute the central structure: pope, bishop, and pastor.

Cardinals are ordinarily very visible leaders in the Catholic Church. While they generally head very important dioceses or serve in influential positions in the **Roman Curia**, the primary role of the cardinals is to serve as the body of electors for the next pope. They serve in this capacity until the age of 80 when they are no longer eligible to vote.

Rites

Observers of Catholicism in North America may not realize another form of organization present in the Catholic Church, namely, that the Catholic Church is composed of many different **rites**. The largest and thus most well known in North America is the Latin or Roman rite. Generally, rites designate different styles of worship, but the term also determines organization. A particular diocese is for the Catholics of one rite, and may overlap with the diocese of another rite. The Latin or Roman rite stems from the style of worship in Rome.

An **Eastern Catholic church**:

1. is or originated as a national church, usually consisting of a number of local churches (dioceses)
2. follows a specific pattern of worship (rite)
3. originated in the East (eastern part of the Roman empire)
4. was more than likely once part of Eastern (Oriental Orthodox) Christianity or Orthodox Christianity, although some eastern churches, such as the Maronite rite, have always been in union with Rome
5. recognizes the authority of the bishop of Rome
6. is considered to be part of Catholic Christianity centered in Rome

diocese

a jurisdictional division or geographical area of parishes or congregations, headed by a bishop

Roman Curia

the central offices of the Catholic Church at the Vatican in Rome

rites

diverse liturgical traditions within the Catholic Church, for example, the Latin Rite or the Maronite Rite

Eastern Catholic church

church originating in a national church in the East and in union with the Catholic Church centered in Rome

There are twenty-one Eastern Catholic churches that follow five different rites. The term *Eastern Catholic* applies to:

1. The Alexandrian rite: Coptic and Ethiopian churches

2. The Antiochene rite: Syro-Malankara, Maronite, and Syrian churches

3. The Armenian rite: Armenian churches

4. The Byzantine rite: Albanian, Belorussian, Bulgarian, Krizevci (Croatian), Greek, Hungarian, Italo-Albanian, Melkite (Greek Melkite), Romanian, Russian, Ruthenian (Carpatho-Russian), Slovak, and the Ukrainian (Galician Ruthenian) churches

5. The Chaldean rite: Chaldean and Malabar churches

Even though their church buildings may look different and their style of worship may be more elaborate, members of these churches are, nonetheless, members of the Catholic Church. Many of these rites have churches in North America. The casual observer may not realize that these churches are different from other eastern churches, such as the Greek or Russian Orthodox Churches.

> *The heritage of the East is open to the whole Church. It is a treasure of understanding that can enrich the lives of all Christians. . . . The Eastern Church has an awareness that the liturgy is the mystery of God acting among us, and treats liturgical traditions with the greatest respect. . . .*
>
> —*David M. Petras*, Eastern Catholic Churches in America, *page 35.*

Taking Root

The Catholic Church in the Americas

Catholicism came to North America with the arrival of the first explorers, who came from "Catholic countries." French and Spanish missionaries accompanied the early explorers. Their primary goal was the conversion of Native Americans. In the very first entry in his journal, Columbus "remarked that among the principal aims of his voyage one was to contact the native peoples so that he might observe what he termed 'the manner in which may be undertaken their conversion to our Holy Faith' " (Ellis, John Tracy. *American Catholicism* [Chicago: University of Chicago Press, 1969], page 3).

The Spanish colonized the southeastern parts of the United States from Florida west along the Gulf coast. Nombre de Dios, built at St. Augustine, Florida, in 1565, was the first Roman Catholic parish. The Spanish also colonized Mexico and moved north from there into the southwestern parts of the United States and all along the western coast of the present-day United States. Because of their efforts and success, many of these areas today are predominantly Catholic.

Some scholars today question the merits of these colonizing efforts. Some say that the Native American way of life was destroyed. Others say that the establishment of the missions among the Native Americans was truly formative and fruitful. There are certainly more than enough examples of the Spanish conquistadors mistreating the Native Americans—and worse. It is also fair to say that the evangelizing goals of the missionaries enabled many of the explorers and settlers to be respectful of and honestly helpful to the Native Americans. The missionaries in general believed that the Native Americans had souls and were truly human. Thus the missionaries intended to convert the Native Americans and help them to live better lives. Spanish missionaries, for example, in the southern part of the United States and California taught Native Americans how to build permanent homes; to plant crops; to tend cattle, sheep, and goats.

French colonial activity centered on eastern and southern sections of Canada along the St. Lawrence River. Montreal and Quebec were principal settlements. Missionaries moved east as far as the state of New York. French colonists were also active along the Mississippi River valley beginning at New Orleans and moving north to St. Louis and on into the north central regions of the present-day United States. Because of the French exploration, large concentrations of Catholics live in southeastern Canada and Louisiana today.

Father Jacques Marquette accompanied Louis Jolliet on an exploration of the upper Mississippi.

Chapter 5

Catholicism came to the eastern seaboard of the United States later. Catholics escaping persecution in Europe were often met with discrimination in the original thirteen colonies. Only Maryland and Pennsylvania accepted Catholics. In 1788, there were only 25,000 Catholics among four million people living in the thirteen states. Even though Catholicism came to the New World with the arrival of the first explorers, Catholics did not have any bishops in the colonies until after the American Revolutionary War. John Carroll (1735–1815) was consecrated the nation's first bishop in 1789. To him fell the responsibility of organizing the Catholic Church in the United States.

Catholics remained in the minority in this area until the great waves of Irish and German immigration in the middle and late nineteenth century. Between 1820 and 1900, ten million German and Irish Catholic Christians entered the United States. Membership in the Catholic Church continued to increase, especially in the north and eastern parts of the United States and in the midwest. The large increase resulted in the formation of the National Catholic Welfare Conference, the forerunner of the National Conference of Catholic Bishops.

The erection of new dioceses and the recruitment of priests and religious orders from Europe reflected the rapid expansion of Catholicism. The remarkable career of Elizabeth Bayley Seton is one example of innovative missionary work in the newly established United States. Elizabeth was an Episcopalian, the daughter of Richard Bayley, a professor of anatomy at King's College in New York. She married William Seton in 1794 and became involved in social work for poor widows as early as 1797. She was widowed with five children in 1803 while on a trip to Italy with her husband who died of tuberculosis.

Influenced by the friendship of Catholics she met in Italy, Elizabeth Seton converted to Catholicism, an act which ostracized her from her family. With four companions, she started a religious community in 1809 and a school for poor children near Emmitsburg, Maryland. The new order was approved in 1812, and she, with eighteen sisters, took vows in 1813 in the community now called the Sisters of Charity. The order spread throughout the United States, and by the time of her death in 1821, there were over twenty communities established. Her work in education is considered the beginning of the Catholic parochial school system in the United States.

Contributing to the strength of Catholicism in the St. Louis area was Rose Philippine Duchesne (1769–1852). Born in Grenoble, France, Duchesne joined the newly founded teaching order, the Society of the Sacred Heart, in 1804. Responding to the missionary needs described by Bishop Dubourg of New Orleans, Rose Philippine went to St. Louis in 1818. With her sisters and the Jesuits, she founded many schools. She began to work among Native Americans when she was seventy-one years old.

Working among Italian immigrants toward the end of the nineteenth century was Frances Xavier Cabrini. She was born on July 15, 1850, the daughter of Augustine and Stella Cabrini, at Sant' Angelo Lodigiano, Italy. She had originally intended to become a teacher, but when she was orphaned at age eighteen, she decided to enter the religious life. Frances Cabrini founded the Missionary Sisters of the Sacred Heart and worked in education.

In 1889, she came to New York at the invitation of Archbishop Corrigan to work among Italian immigrants. For the next twenty-seven years, facing great obstacles, she traveled extensively as the order spread all over the United States. Frances once said, "But don't think that my Institute can be confined to one city or to one diocese. The whole world is not wide enough for me." By the time of her death in 1911, she had begun sixty-seven hospitals, schools, orphanages, convents, and other foundations.

Today, Roman Catholicism is the single largest denomination in North America. In the United States, Catholics account for approximately 25 percent of the population. Twice each year, the Catholic bishops of the United States come together as the National Conference of Catholic Bishops, which was created in 1966. The conference allows the bishops to speak with a single voice on a wide variety of issues, both religious and political, such as the growing gap between rich and poor. The National Conference of Catholic Bishops has its offices at Washington, DC.

Growing and Blooming

God's Revelation through Scripture and Tradition

Catholics believe in the doctrines expressed in the ancient Christian creeds and shared by all mainline Christian Churches. Catholics regularly recite the Nicene Creed at their Sunday mass.

God the Father

Catholics believe in the God revealed in the Hebrew and Christian Scriptures. As stated in the Nicene Creed, this God created everything, "all that is seen and unseen." Just as the quality of a painting reveals something of the character of the artist, so too do the immensity of the universe, the fresh smells of a spring day, the colors of a sunset and the delicacy of a tulip reveal something of the character of God. All of the created order reveals God. This sense, that creation reveals the grandeur of God and that creation is good, is a characteristic of the Catholic worldview.

God the Son

Catholics believe, as do mainline Christians, that the often expected messiah of the Jewish people was made manifest in Jesus of Nazareth.

Thus God, in the history of forming a people, becomes one of us. Jesus taught people how to live in greater harmony with God and with each other and made it possible by redeeming humans. The greatest commandment Jesus gave was to "love one another." Catholics see themselves as a Christian denomination which carries this message through history to every people in every time.

God the Holy Spirit

Catholics believe that the Holy Spirit, the third person of the Trinity, sent by Jesus to the disciples at Pentecost, is active within the Catholic Church, as well as the entire Christian Church, until the end of time. The Holy Spirit prepares people to be open to God's presence and to hear God's word, especially as it is expressed by Jesus Christ. The action of the Holy Spirit nourishes, heals, and organizes the members of the church. It sends them to bear witness to the world of the saving action of Christ. The Holy Spirit is active within the whole church body as well. "In her whole being and in all her members, the church is sent to announce, bear witness, make present, and spread the mystery of the communion of the Holy Trinity."

Tradition

Catholics believe the formation of the church began with the commissioning of Peter. Catholics also see in the commissioning of Peter a special teaching authority given to the church. One may ask the question, "Where is the truth to be found?" Or "What is it that God wants us to know?" Protestant theology responds by saying that the "truth" is found in scripture. Catholic theology (and Eastern Orthodox) responds by saying that the "truth," what God wants us to know, is found both in scripture and the tradition of the church as it has developed over the centuries. **Tradition** is seen as a channel of the word of God entrusted to the apostles and handed on through their successors.

An analogy might be this. The Constitution of the United States has guided that country since 1788. It has served the United States well. But by itself, the Constitution would provide a chaotic life. It needs an authoritative body, the Supreme Court, to consider how the intent and meaning of the Constitution is to be applied to particular cases. In a similar way, the Catholic Church sees itself as an interpretative body of scripture.

Thus, for Catholics, scripture and tradition go together to help them understand what it is that God wants them to know. These are in some ways one. Rather, scripture and tradition are seen as a single source of God's revelation. Together they help Catholics know God's will. The Holy Spirit guides the church in understanding, interpreting, and teaching God's truth as it is revealed in scripture and tradition. This is a characteristic of the Catholic Church (and Eastern Orthodoxy) that distinguishes it from a Protestant understanding of church.

tradition
for Catholics, the word of God entrusted to the apostles and handed on through their successors; scripture and tradition are seen as a single source of God's revelation

A Sacramental Church

A second distinguishing characteristic of the Catholic Church is its concept of church as a special means of coming into contact with God. For Catholics, the church is not a mere human organization with leaders and members, rules and guidelines. Somehow, in a mysterious way, the human dimension of the church is united with the divine dimension. Christ is united with the church. The whole church mediates God's presence. While all of creation can mediate God's presence, Catholics see this happening in a special way in the church body.

The Sacraments

sacrament

in some Christian groups, a reality imbued with the hidden presence of God; signifies Jesus' contact with the church and causes an encounter between Jesus and the church

Throughout the centuries, Roman Catholic theologians have devoted considerable time and energy to developing church teaching on the sacraments. Pope Paul VI, a pope of the late twentieth century, defined a sacrament as "a reality imbued with the hidden presence of God." A sacrament signifies something and causes what it signifies. Therefore, each of the seven sacraments signifies Jesus' contact with the church, and causes an encounter between Jesus and the church.

The Catholic Church's seven sacraments correlate closely with basic human needs and experiences. For example, every person is born and needs to belong, matures, dedicates his or her life to a particular purpose, experiences illness, and dies. In the journey of life, every person "sins" or hurts others and every person needs to be nourished.

Basic human experience	Sacrament	Meaning
1. Belonging/acceptance	1. Baptism	1. Removal of original sin and forgiveness of personal sin; being filled with God's life leads to acceptance into the community
2. Maturity/independence	2. Confirmation	2. Celebrates the presence of the Holy Spirit and membership in the church
3. Need for nourishment	3. Eucharist	3. Nourished by the body and blood of Christ
4. Failure/sin/alienation	4. Reconciliation	4. Forgiveness of sin/healing, through the church, of division caused by sin
5. Physical and mental illness	5. Anointing of the Sick	5. Healing presence of Christ
6. Need to love/commitment to a purpose in life	6. Holy Orders	6. The commitment of a man to serve as a deacon, priest, or bishop
7. Need to love/commitment to a purpose in life	7. Matrimony	7. The commitment of a man and woman to love each other until the death of one

The Sacraments of Initiation: Baptism, Confirmation (Chrismation), and Eucharist

The sacraments of baptism, confirmation (or chrismation in the Eastern Rites), and Eucharist are called the sacraments of initiation; once all three are celebrated, the person is fully initiated into full membership in the church.

Baptism

Baptism is the first sacrament celebrated; it brings the new member into the church community. The sacrament confers a character (a spiritual mark) on the person and cannot be repeated. The waters of baptism are believed to wash away **original sin** and its effects. The minister of baptism is a bishop, priest, deacon, or lay person. The minister of baptism pours water on the person's head or immerses the person in water, and says, "I baptize you in the name of the Father, and of the Son, and of the Holy Spirit." The minister also anoints the person with oil to show that the newly baptized person now shares in the ministry of Christ. A baptismal candle is lit to show that the new Christian is united with Christ who is known as the "light of the world." The newly baptized, the parents, and the godparent(s) are told to keep the light of Christ burning brightly in their life.

The baptism of infants has been commonplace since the fifth century. The parents of the infant are responsible for making the arrangements at their parish and are often required to undergo some form of preparation. The parents also choose one or two **godparents** to assist them in raising and instructing the child in Christianity. At least one of the godparents is required to be Catholic.

Adults who are seeking membership of the Catholic Church usually participate in the **Rite of Christian Initiation of Adults**. This is the process that prepares adults for baptism, confirmation, and Eucharist, and membership in the Catholic Church. The process allows for an in-depth study of the beliefs and practices of the Catholic Church and encourages the involvement of the parish community. Those people seeking membership in the Catholic Church are referred to as either *candidates* or *catechumens*. A **candidate** is someone who has already been baptized in the Christian tradition. A **catechumen** is someone who has not been baptized in the Christian tradition. Those who have already been baptized Christian are not rebaptized, but a person must be baptized Christian before receiving the other sacraments of the Roman Catholic Church.

The candidates and catechumens choose a sponsor to help guide them through the process. The **sponsor** serves as a personal mentor and a parish representative throughout the process and presents the candidate or catechumen to the parish during the process. Once the person is baptized or received into the Catholic Church, he or she is confirmed and receives the Eucharist for the first time. The celebration of initiating the candidates and catechumens usually occurs in front of the congregation at the Easter Vigil on Holy Saturday night.

original sin

the condition of and tendency toward sinfulness present in humans since the beginning of the human race

godparent(s)

one person or two people chosen by an infant's parents to be witness(es) at the child's baptism and to assist them in raising the child in Christianity

Rite of Christian Initiation of Adults

a process that prepares adults for baptism, confirmation, and Eucharist, and membership in the Catholic Church

candidate

in the Catholic Church, a baptized person seeking membership in the church

catechumen

in the Catholic Church, an unbaptized person seeking membership in the church

sponsor

a person chosen to help guide a candidate or catechumen through the process of the Rite of Christian Initiation of Adults

Confirmation

confirmation

the second sacrament of initiation, believed to confer the fullness of the gifts of the Spirit; called *chrismation* in the Eastern Catholic churches

As the second sacrament of initiation, **confirmation** affirms the faith of baptism; it celebrates the gifts of the Holy Spirit received in the fullest sense in this sacrament. Confirmation confers a character, and cannot be repeated. The Eastern Catholic churches refer to this sacrament as *chrismation*.

At this time, the age of confirmation varies. It occurs at the time of baptism (in the Eastern Catholic churches, the three sacraments of initiation are celebrated together at this time), the age of discretion, or during adolescence. When confirmation does not occur at the time of baptism, there is usually an extensive time of preparation for the sacrament. In the beginning stages of the preparation process, the candidate usually chooses a sponsor. The sponsor may be the godparent, but it can also be someone else who has been positive influence in the candidate's faith life.

At the rite of confirmation, the minister of confirmation, a priest or bishop

1. dips his right thumb in the chrism (perfumed oil),
2. makes the sign of the cross on the person's forehead, and
3. says "Be sealed with the Gift of the Holy Spirit."

The sponsor accompanies the candidate and stands beside him or her throughout the ceremony.

Eucharist

Eucharist is considered the "source and summit" of church life, the "sacrament of sacraments." Just as a person must eat frequently, so Catholics return to celebrate this sacrament time and time again. Catholics believe that the living Jesus is present whenever they come together to celebrate the Eucharist (the mass).

The Eucharist is a sacrifice and a sacramental meal. Whenever Roman Catholic Christians celebrate the Eucharist, the sacrifice of Jesus, who was crucified to redeem humanity, is reenacted in a sacramental way. Moreover, the bread and wine used in this sacrament become the body and blood of Christ. Catholics do not believe that the bread and wine literally become flesh and blood, but rather that the body and blood of the Risen Christ is uniquely present sacramentally. Catholics believe that when they receive the body and blood of Christ, Christ himself enters into them. This is a belief about Eucharist that distinguishes Catholic (and Orthodox and Anglican) theology. Protestant Christians have many different interpretations of the Eucharist.

The minister of Eucharist is a bishop or priest. It is he who consecrates the bread and wine (recites the words of Jesus that change the bread and wine into the body and blood of Jesus). He repeats the words of Jesus "This is my body . . . . This is the cup of my blood."

For Catholics, the Eucharist is the third sacrament of initiation. Children who have reached the age of discretion (the age of seven or eight) begin receiving the Eucharist. The first time a person receives the Eucharist is known as *First Communion*. Reconciliation, which involves the confession and forgiveness of one's sins, usually precedes a person's first communion.

Liturgy, or Mass

The eucharistic liturgy, or mass, is the celebration of the Eucharist. Catholic Christians are expected to participate in this liturgy, or attend mass, every Sunday. Daily mass is offered in most parishes. Catholics who do not follow one of the Eastern Catholic rites celebrate the Eucharist according to the Latin rite.

Order of the Mass

Introductory Rites

Entrance Song—accompanies the procession of the ministers

Greeting—sign of the cross and presider's greeting

Penitential Rite—acknowledgment of sin

Gloria—hymn of praise to God

Opening Prayer—priest's prayer on behalf of the community

Liturgy of the Word

First Reading—scripture passage from the Old Testament (ordinarily)

Responsorial Psalm—verses of a psalm are said or sung

Second Reading—scripture passage from the New Testament

Alleluia Acclamation—praise for the gospel

Gospel—scripture passage from one of the Gospels

Homily—presider's remarks, often rooted in scripture passages

Profession of Faith—Nicene-Constantinopolitan Creed is said

General Intercessions—people pray in litany form

Liturgy of the Eucharist

Preparation and Offering of Gifts—people carry bread and wine to the altar and present them to the presider

Prayer over the Gifts—presider's prayer on behalf of the people

Eucharistic Prayer—prayer of thanksgiving and consecration of bread and wine

Lord's Prayer—prayer given by Jesus is said or sung

Sign of Peace—people share a sign of peace

Breaking of the Bread—presider prepares the Eucharist for distribution

Reception of Communion—communion is distributed

Prayer after Communion—presider's prayer on behalf of community

Concluding Rite

Blessing—priest blesses the people

Dismissal following announcements

The Sacraments of Service: Matrimony and Holy Orders

Matrimony

matrimony
for Catholics, the sacrament that celebrates the commitment of a man and woman to marriage for life

The sacrament of **matrimony** celebrates the lifelong commitment of a man and woman in marriage. In matrimony a man and a woman pledge a lifelong love for each other and a willingness to meet their children's needs, especially the need for religious education. The man and the woman marry each other; a bishop, priest, or deacon witnesses the marriage on the church's behalf. In Eastern Catholic churches, the presider is considered the minister of the sacrament.

If a marriage fails and it can be determined that the requirements for a sacramental marriage had not been met at the time of the marriage, the couple may receive a decree of nullity (after receiving a civil divorce) and permission to marry someone else in a Catholic wedding.

Holy Orders

holy orders
the sacrament that authorizes a man to work in the Catholic Church as a bishop, priest, or deacon

A Catholic ordination to the priesthood

The sacrament of **holy orders** celebrates the commitment of a man to serve the Catholic Church as an ordained minister. The sacrament of orders authorizes a man to work in the church as a bishop, priest, or deacon. *Order* comes from the Latin *ordo*, which means "group." In the one ancient Christian Church, there were three orders (groups) of ministers (workers): episcopate (to which bishops belonged), presbyterate (to which priests belonged), and diaconate (to which deacons belonged). To

ordain is to authorize a man to do the work of an order. The sacrament confers a character, and cannot be repeated.

The minister of the sacrament is a bishop. Three or more bishops ordain a man to the episcopate, the rank of bishop. A single bishop can ordain a man to the presbyterate (priesthood) or to the diaconate. Men who are preparing for priesthood are first ordained as deacons about a year before they are ordained as priests. Men who remain in the diaconate are called permanent deacons. At the time he is ordained, it is allowed that a permanent deacon be a married man. Priests and bishops of the Roman Catholic tradition are required to remain celibate.

However, married men who become Catholic after having served as a minister in another Christian tradition are sometimes ordained and may remain married.

The Sacraments of Healing: Reconciliation and Anointing

Two sacraments which touch upon the brokenness of life are the sacraments of healing. These are the sacraments of reconciliation and anointing of the sick.

Reconciliation

The sacrament of **reconciliation** celebrates God's forgiveness and reintegrates the sinful person back into the life of the community. The basic elements of the sacrament are sorrow for sin, confession of sin (telling a priest the sins committed), resolution not to repeat the sin, reparation (making up for the sins committed), and absolution (the forgiveness granted by God through the words of the priest). The minister of reconciliation is a bishop or priest. He absolves the person with the words "I absolve you from your sins in the name of the Father, and of the Son, and of the Holy Spirit."

reconciliation
the Catholic sacrament that celebrates God's forgiveness and reintegrates the sinful person back into the life of the community

Anointing of the Sick

The sacrament of **anointing of the sick** celebrates God's healing presence when a person is ill or is dying. As in all of the sacraments, Catholics believe that Christ is present to respond to their needs at that time. Anointing of the sick is a prayer for spiritual and physical healing and comfort. The minister of the sacrament is a bishop or priest. The minister anoints the person's forehead and hands with the oil of the sick (usually perfumed olive oil) and says the words, "Through this holy anointing, may the Lord in his love and mercy help you with the grace of the Holy Spirit. May the Lord who frees you from sin save you and raise you up." The ill and the elderly are encouraged to receive the sacrament as needed.

anointing of the sick
the Catholic sacrament that celebrates God's healing presence when a person is ill or dying

Marks of the Church

In Roman Catholic thought, there are four characteristics of the Christian Church. These characteristics indicate essential features of the church and its mission; the church is *one*, *holy*, *catholic*, and *apostolic*. The Catholic Church understands these marks to apply not just to itself, but the entire Church of Christ. The church is *one* in its source—God, one in its faith, born of one baptism, united into one body, and given life by the one Spirit. The *holiness* of the church comes from Christ who makes her holy; sinful though we are, all are called and empowered to be holy. The church is *catholic*, or universal, in that it is united with Christ and has a mission which reaches out to embrace the whole world. The church is *apostolic* because it is founded upon the twelve apostles and their ministry and teaching.

Other Characteristics

A characteristic of the Catholic Church which is often misunderstood is that of **infallibility**. Catholics believe that the pope and the bishops in union with him are sometimes infallible "in matters of faith and morals." *Infallible* means "to be correct and without error." Some people mistakenly believe that this means everything the pope teaches is infallible. Indeed, the pope's teachings are to be highly respected and taken very seriously. They are important teachings. But the pope is believed to be infallible only when he speaks of behalf of the whole church and in union with the bishops "in matters of faith and morals" and only when he does so on solemn occasions proclaiming this teaching as part of Catholic faith. The bishops, united with the pope, may also claim to speak infallibly, such as at a council—although this is not often done. Infallibility in any form has been exercised very rarely.

The Catholic Church is known for its strong and clear teachings in matters of morality. These teachings include matters of family life, sexuality, honesty, business ethics, personal integrity, rights of labor, distribution of goods, health care, war and peace, and care for the environment. These teachings are to be taken very seriously and in good conscience obeyed. The teachings are based upon the church's two-thousand year experience and often express profound reflections which are invaluable resources for personal decision making. They are intended to help Catholics live good, virtuous lives. In the final analysis, Catholics must develop their own well-formed conscience.

Reaping the Fruit

Liturgy and Devotions

Catholics reap the fruits of their faith in two ways. One way is the celebration of their faith through their various liturgies and sacraments. Most important is the celebration of the Eucharist each Sunday; Catholics are expected to participate in the Eucharist in their parish communities.

Devotions are prayers that are not part of the official liturgical prayer of the church. They are often private or shared with a small group. Devotions include special prayer services, **novenas**, and special devotions to Mary. Catholics also sponsor days of recollection, retreats, and other kinds of renewal experiences for all age groups and many different needs. For example, there are renewal opportunities available for youth, young adults, singles, married people, divorced, the grieving, and people who are elderly.

infallibility

quality of a teaching by the pope and/or the bishops in union with him that is a matter of faith and morals and is declared free from error

novena

a Catholic devotional prayer said for nine days, the prayer usually asks for the intercession of Mary or one of the saints

The Canticle of Brother Sun and Sister Moon

This is one of many prayers written by Francis of Assisi.

Most High, all-powerful, all-good Lord!
All praise is yours, all glory, all honor, and all blessing.
To you alone, Most High, do they belong.
No mortal lips are worthy to pronounce your name.
All praise be yours, my Lord, through all that you have made,
And first my lord Brother Sun,
Who brings the day; and light you give to us through him.
How beautiful he is, how radiant in all his splendor!
Of you, Most High, he bears the likeness.
All praise be yours, my Lord, through Sister Moon and Stars,
In the heavens you have made them, bright
And precious and fair.
All praise be yours, my Lord, through Brothers Wind and Air,
And fair and stormy, all weather's moods,
By which you cherish all that you have made.
All praise be yours, my Lord, through Sister Water,
So useful, lowly, precious, and pure.
All praise be yours, my Lord, through Brother Fire,
Through whom you light the night.
How beautiful he is, how playful! Full of power and strength.
All praise be yours, my Lord, through our Sister Earth, our mother,
Who feeds us in her sovereignty and produces
Various fruits and colored flowers and herbs.
All praise be yours, my Lord, through those who grant pardon
For love of you; through those who endure
Sickness and trial.
Happy those who endure in peace,
By you, Most High, they will be crowned.
All praise be yours, my Lord, through Sister Death,
From whose embrace no mortal can escape.
Woe to those who die in mortal sin!
Happy those She finds doing your will!
The second death can do no harm to them.
Praise and bless my Lord, and give him thanks,
And serve him with great humility.

Let's Talk about It . . .

1. What do you like about this prayer?
2. What puzzles you in the prayer?
3. What does the prayer tell you about Francis of Assisi?

This procession in honor of Our Lady Of Guadalupe is in Brooklyn, New York.

Mary

Catholics have traditionally had a high respect for Mary. She is seen as having played a critical role in the life of her son, helping him to fulfill his mission. Catholic Christians refer to Mary as ever-virgin, believing that she gave birth to Jesus while a virgin and remained a virgin for the rest of her life.

Throughout the centuries, Catholic Christian beliefs about Mary have taken shape. In 431, the Council of Ephesus gave her the title *Mother of God*. The words of the third Eucharistic Prayer, which the presider prays during the celebration of the Eucharist, contain this title: "May he [the Holy Spirit] make us an everlasting gift to you [the Father] and enable us to share in the inheritance of your saints, with Mary, the Virgin Mother of God. . . ." Catholics also pray the *Hail Mary*, which makes mention of the title: "Holy Mary, Mother of God. . . ."

In the Middle Ages, various writers emphasized Mary's role as intercessor (carrier of prayers to her son). Today this is particularly true of Spanish American and Mexican Catholics. A feast of special importance is that of Our Lady of Guadalupe, celebrated on December 12.

This feast is based upon an apparent apparition of Mary to Juan Diego in the year 1531 near Mexico City. According to the story, Juan Diego, a Native American who was studying to become a Catholic, was hurrying to mass on December 9, 1531. On the way, a lady appeared to Juan and told him to go to the bishop. He was to tell the bishop that she wanted a church built on that spot. When he went to the bishop, the bishop asked for a sign. The next day, Juan Diego avoided the spot. On December 12, the lady again appeared to Juan Diego near the same hill and asked about the building of a church. When Juan told her that the bishop wanted a sign, she instructed him to go to the top of the hill and pick some roses—a flower which did not grow in the area and especially not in winter. Nevertheless, Juan Diego went to the top of the hill and found the roses just as she had said. He wrapped them in his mantle and presented himself to the bishop. When Juan opened his cloak, the roses fell out and an image of Mary was seen on the cloak. His mantle is now preserved in the church built on this spot. Our Lady of Guadalupe is a feast in which Mary's special concern for the poor is revealed.

A devotion to Mary used by many Catholic Christians is the rosary. They use the rosary to meditate on fifteen events in the lives of Jesus and Mary. These events are grouped in three sets of five: the joyful mysteries, the sorrowful mysteries, and the glorious mysteries. When a person prays with a rosary, he or she concentrates on the mysteries. The rosary begins with the recitation of the Apostles' Creed, followed by the Lord's Prayer, three Hail Marys, and one Prayer of Praise. One person announces the mystery, and leads the praying of the Lord's Prayer, ten Hail Marys, and one Prayer of Praise. As people say the ten Hail Marys, they think of the mystery just announced. This completes a decade (referring to the ten beads) of the rosary. A full rosary is comprised of fifteen decades, but is most commonly recited in one of the sets of mysteries or five decades. A decade consists of one mystery, one Lord's Prayer, ten Hail Marys, and one Prayer of Praise.

Saints

The Catholic Church has a very extensive calendar of saints. These saints include people from the earliest days of Christianity to the present. They are martyrs, great leaders, teachers, innovators, as well as simple people. They include men and women, young and old, and people from all walks of life. **Canonization** is the act by which an individual is named a saint. As of 1990, the Roman Martyrology listed 4,500 saints. Since 1900, over 445 men and women have been canonized (declared saints). From the Catholic perspective, an officially recognized saint must be someone

1. who was martyred and/or lived a virtuous life to a heroic degree (practiced Christian virtue to a heroic degree),

2. who enjoys the glory of God in heaven,

3. who deserves honor from the whole church, and

4. whose life serves as a model and source of inspiration for Christian living today.

canonization
the act by which an individual is named a saint in the Catholic Church

Work for Justice

Another way Catholics reap the fruit of their faith is in the way they live their lives. Since the Second Vatican Council, Catholics have become much more aware of how they might live their faith on a daily basis: in their homes, at work, and in their recreation. Since Pope Leo XIII's **encyclical**, *Rerum Novarum*, in 1891, the Catholic Church has developed a very strong tradition in matters of social justice. These concerns include a strong commitment to education, health care, and peace issues, concern for those who are homeless, poor, discriminated against, elderly, young, and those yet unborn and those sentenced to die for their crimes. The church's voice for justice can be found at all levels of the church, from the international level to the local parish.

encyclical
a letter from the pope addressing issues of major importance

An Attempt at Unity

Taizé is an ecumenical community of one hundred brothers located in a small village in eastern France (southwest of Paris, north of Lyons, due west of Geneva, Switzerland, between the towns of Chalon-sur-Saone and Macon). The brothers belong to various Christian traditions, and come from many different countries.

In the 1940s, Brother Roger, a Protestant of the Reformed Tradition, founded the ecumenical religious community of Taizé. He came to the nearly abandoned village and offered shelter to Jews and others fleeing Nazi persecution. A few years later, Brother Roger was joined by other men. In 1949, they committed themselves to a life of celibacy and material and spiritual sharing. The nascent community dedicated itself to living out "the gospel call to reconciliation day after day."

Life at Taizé revolves around prayer, work, and hospitality. The brothers come together three times a day to pray. The prayer is more akin to silent meditation; singing, however, plays an important role in both prayer and worship. The community has always supported itself by its own labor, refusing donations of any sort. The brothers have shown hospitality to tens of thousands over the years, including refugees and spiritual searchers.

Each year, thousands of young people between the ages of seventeen and thirty spend a week at Taizé. They focus on returning to the roots of the Christian faith. The young people join the community for work and for prayer, Bible study, and silent reflection. They also meet in small sharing groups.

Interest in Taizé prompted the community to send brothers throughout the world to organize the "pilgrimage of trust on earth." The pilgrimage takes place every year at a different location. Pilgrimages have been held at Budapest, Dayton, Johannesburg, London, Madras, Manila, Munich, Paris, Prague, Rome, and Vienna. Above all, those who come seem to be searching for more meaning in their lives. Some want to deepen their relationship with God, and others simply want to meet Christians their own age who are also struggling and searching in their faith.

Christine Anderson, an eighteen-year-old from New York, was able to hear the Taizé brothers speak when they visited her community. She describes her experience:

When I agreed to go listen to the Taizé brothers with my youth group, I wasn't sure what to expect. I surely didn't expect to see such a large group of people. There were at least four hundred other students from different faiths present. As I listened to the brothers' message, I was overcome with a sense of unity. I felt connected to the other students. Although we were of different backgrounds and traditions, we were all searching for the same thing—a deeper understanding of God.

Since listening to the Taizé brothers speak, my youth group has been planning to attend the next World Youth Day celebrations. We are all very excited. I am sure that it will be an event that I will never forget.

Let's Talk about It . . .

1. What brings people to Taizé?
2. How are the brothers of Taizé promoting the unity of the Christian Church?

Conclusion

Sixteen students from a central Catholic high school in the Midwestern part of the United States had just completed a week of service in the Appalachian mountains. Riding home in a hot van, Neal asked his priest chaplain, "Hey, Father, did you enjoy the service trip?"

"Yeah, I enjoyed it."

"Did you feel like you sort of got back to yourself?" asked Neal.

"Well . . . yes. Yes, I did! I did feel like I got back to myself," reflected the priest.

"So did I," said Neal. "So did I."

In the years since the Second Vatican Council, the Catholic Church is one which has been trying to "get back to itself." It has been searching through the Scriptures, sifting through its traditions, and reflecting upon the issues present in the modern world. At the same time the Catholic Church has embarked upon a pilgrim journey into the future, a journey fraught with risks, but filled with hope.

People from all backgrounds find the expression of their religious faith in Catholicism. The Catholic Church, in turn, reaches out and seeks to embrace people in all groups. In its journey, the church is seeking to fulfill its mission to embrace the joys and hopes, the griefs and anxieties of all people, especially those who are poor or in any way afflicted. The extent to which it succeeds will show how well the church lives up to its name as a "catholic" church.

A Catholic Calendar

Winter

Advent prepares Catholic Christians for Jesus' birth. Throughout the four or so weeks of Advent, the themes of expectation and joy are emphasized. The level of expectation and joy rises as the birth of Jesus approaches. For Catholic Christians, the First Sunday of Advent is the beginning of the church year. The colors violet and rose are associated with Advent.

Christmas (December 25). This feast celebrates Jesus' birth. For Catholic Christians living in the United States, Christmas is one of six holy days of obligation. Catholic Christians observe these days by celebrating the Eucharist. White is the liturgical color of Christmas.

Solemnity of Mary, Mother of God (January 1). For Catholic Christians living in the United States, the Solemnity of Mary, Mother of God, is a holy day of obligation.

Chair of Peter (February 22). This day is important to Catholic Christians, especially those living in Italy. According to tradition, the apostle Peter established the Church of Rome. The Vatican City state, which borders Rome, Italy, is the headquarters of Catholic Christianity's spiritual leader, the bishop of Rome, the pope.

Spring

Lent prepares Catholic Christians for Jesus' resurrection. Throughout Lent, Catholic Christians fast, give to those in need, and pray. Lent spans six weeks (six Sundays) for Catholics; the first day of Lent is Ash Wednesday. Violet is the liturgical color of Lent.

Palm Sunday or **Passion Sunday** (Sunday before Easter). On this day, Catholic Christians commemorate Jesus' final entry into Jerusalem. The New Testament passion (story of Jesus' suffering and death) is read, and blessed palm branches are distributed. This day marks the beginning of Holy Week. Red is the color of Palm Sunday.

Holy Thursday (Thursday before Easter). On this day, Catholics commemorate the Last Supper (the night before his death when Jesus washed the feet of his disciples and gave the Eucharist to them). Catholics mark the day by celebrating the Eucharist with great solemnity. On this day many Christians demonstrate their love for one another by imitating Jesus washing the disciples' feet.

Good Friday (Friday before Easter) commemorates Jesus' crucifixion (public execution). Catholics do not celebrate the Eucharist on this day, although they do receive communion. Red is the color of Good Friday.

The lighting of the new fire and the Easter candle at the Easter vigil

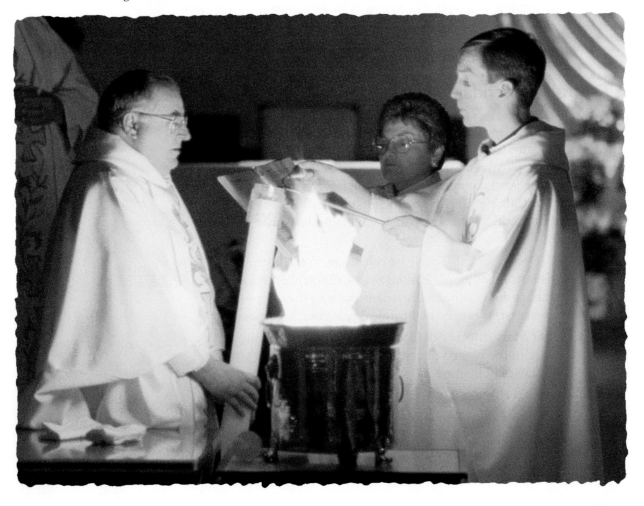

Holy Saturday Easter Vigil (Saturday before Easter). Catholics await Jesus' resurrection on this night. Most churches hold a liturgical vigil that culminates in the celebration of the Eucharist. The vigil includes the baptism of children and adults, blessing of the paschal (Easter) candle, and the blessing of water intended for use in baptism and as holy water. White is the color for the Easter Vigil.

Easter celebrates Jesus' resurrection and is the high point of the church year. Easter marks the victory of life over death, of the powerless over the powerful, of holiness over sinfulness, and of God's will over evil. For Latin-rite Catholics, Easter falls on the first Sunday after the full moon following the vernal equinox (between March 22 and April 25). Some Eastern Catholics may wait until after the start of Passover before beginning the Easter celebration. White is the color associated with Easter.

Ascension Thursday (fortieth day after Easter). On this day, Catholic Christians commemorate the ascension of Jesus (his return to heaven in glory). For Catholics in the United States, Ascension Thursday is a holy day of obligation. White is the color for this feast.

Pentecost (fiftieth day after Easter) celebrates the establishment of the one ancient Christian Church. According to the New Testament, the Holy Spirit descended on Jesus' apostles and disciples, empowering them to build up the church. Red is the color of Pentecost.

Summer

Trinity Sunday (first Sunday after Pentecost) celebrates the mystery of the Trinity.

Assumption of Mary (August 15). For Catholics in the United States, this is a holy day of obligation.

Feast of the Holy Cross (September 14). On this day, Catholics mark the discovery of the true cross (the cross on which Jesus died).

Autumn

All Saints' Day (November 1) recalls the blessedness of saints known and unknown. For Catholics in the United States, All Saints' Day is a holy day of obligation.

Immaculate Conception (December 8). For Catholics in the United States, the feast of the Immaculate Conception is a holy day of obligation. The doctrine of the immaculate conception means that Jesus' mother Mary was born without original sin.

Our Lady of Guadalupe (December 12) is the feast of the patron of Mexico. This is an important day for many Hispanic Catholics.

Christ the King (Sunday preceding the first Sunday of Advent) is the last Sunday of the church year. It is a feast that recognizes the sovereignty of Christ in our lives.

Discovering

1. Be able to explain each of the terms in the vocabulary list.

2. Explain the challenges which Christians in the West faced from the time of the peace of the church until the sixteenth century.

3. Name the factors which led up to the Reformation of the sixteenth century.

4. Explain the structure of the Catholic Church.

5. On a map of North America, locate the areas colonized by French and Spanish Catholics.

6. For Catholics, where is the "truth" of God found?

7. Explain how each of the sacraments relates to a basic human experience.

8. What beliefs do Eastern Orthodox share with Roman Catholics?

Exploring

1. Name and explain the ways the Catholic Church in North America is implementing the vision of the Second Vatican Council.

2. In a small group, analyze the strengths and weaknesses of a hierarchical church structure.

3. Which of the seven basic human experiences have you experienced? How do these relate to the meaning of the corresponding sacraments?

4. In a small group, discuss how scripture and tradition working together can help to maintain a balance in religious belief and practice.

5. Why do you think that there is such a variety of beliefs and practices surrounding the Eucharist within the Christian traditions? Which of the beliefs and practices do you find the easiest to accept? Why?

Integrating

1. Attend a Catholic Church service. How do you see the characteristics of Catholicism described in this chapter evident in the service?

2. Interview a Catholic. How does this person interpret the renewal going on within the church? What are the positive aspects of this renewal? How does this person think the church needs to renew itself further?

3. What aspects of the Catholic worldview are particularly helpful to you?

Words to Know

anointing of the sick

Avignon Papacy

candidate

canonization

catechumen

catholic

Catholicism

confirmation

diocese

Eastern Catholic church

ecumenical council

encyclical

godparent(s)

hierarchical

holy orders

infallibility

lector

mass

matrimony

nationalism

novena

original sin

parish

pope

reconciliation

religious order

Renaissance

Rite of Christian Initiation of Adults

rites

Roman Curia

sacrament

sponsor

tradition

Chapter 6

After reading this chapter, you will be able to

- Explain the evolution of the four main branches of Protestantism
- Compare the founding ideas of each
- Appreciate more fully the range of belief and practice in Protestantism

REFORMATION CHRISTIANITY

Introduction

A father and his son parked the car and together approached the large, new building. It was open house for the new police station and jail. As they toured the building, they were met by a police officer who explained how suspects are processed. Then they were shown the cells. The cells were clean and neat, but when the iron bars clanked loudly behind them, the son realized this was no place in which he wanted to spend time.

As they stood in the cell, the father turned to his son and said, "Jay, no member of our family has ever done anything to wind up in a place like this. Our family just doesn't break the law. If you ever have to be put in jail, we will love you, but you will have to suffer the consequences of your actions."

On their way home, the father said, "Son, you are a member of this family; we expect you to act like it. But more importantly, you are a member of God's family. God brought you into his family by bringing the blessings of forgiveness and salvation through his death and resurrection as you were baptized and as you were brought to faith in his word and promises. You don't keep God's law in order to become his child . . . you don't keep his laws to gain God's favor . . . you don't keep his laws to stay out of the prison of eternal death.

"You keep his laws because you are a member of his family. When you do fail God, as we all do, God still loves you, and even though you may have to face the consequences of your sin, God will receive you back because of his grace and mercy. The only way you can not receive God's grace and mercy is if you refuse to live as his child."

This story captures the sense of the Protestant denomination, Lutheranism. For Lutherans, a person receives God's love and forgiveness not because of his or her own worth and not because the person does anything to deserve it. One receives God's forgiveness because of God's love given through Jesus Christ. This perspective was carried forward throughout the mainline churches of the Reformation in the sixteenth century.

The **Reformation** was a sixteenth-century movement that sought to reform the Catholic Church. The Reformation moved through four phases: the Lutheran tradition, the Reformed tradition, the Anabaptist tradition, and the English tradition. Each of these traditions has its roots in the first half of the sixteenth century. Nearly all Protestant churches today are derived from these four traditions or a combination of them. In this chapter we will present the background of each tradition and discuss specific examples of each.

Reformation

the sixteenth-century movement that sought to reform the Catholic Church

Tilling the Soil

The Lutheran Tradition

The first phase of the Reformation began with **Martin Luther** (1483–1546). Luther had graduated from the University of Erfurt and then began to study law in 1505. But as a result of a vow he made during a lightning storm, Luther changed his course of study to theology. He became a professed religious in the Augustinian order in 1506, was ordained a priest one year later, and earned his doctor's degree in theology in 1512. He then taught scripture at the Univer-sity of Wittenberg. During the course of his teaching at the university, Luther's theological ideas began to take shape.

The central question which vexed Luther was "How can I be justified; how can I be saved?" In other words, Luther never felt he was in a "right relationship" with God. All the penance he performed, all the fasting, all the long hours in the confessional, never led Luther to the feeling that he was "right" before God. A tremendous feeling of guilt hung over him. This may seem like a strange problem for us today, but given Luther's medieval world steeped in superstition and simple ideas about God, sin, human nature, and church, it is quite understandable.

Finally, while studying the Letter to the Romans, Luther found the answer to his dilemma. "For in [the gospel] the righteousness of God is revealed through faith for faith; as it is written, 'The one who is righteous will live by faith' " (Romans 1:17). This was the solution! A person is saved—not by good works such as prayers, penance, and fasting—but by God's grace alone (*sola gratia*) and faith alone (*sola fide*). In Romans 3:28, Saint Paul used similar language: "For we hold that a person is justified by faith apart from works prescribed by the law." God freely bestows his grace upon undeserving human beings (*sola gratia*). Human beings accept this grace through faith (*sola fide*). This is the principle of justification by faith, a fundamental principle of Reformation theology.

A second question pursued by Luther was: "What is the source of truth (revelation)?" In other words, how do I know what is right or correct? Looking at the decadent medieval church, Luther could not see how it could be a source of truth. At first, Luther would have settled for the authority of a council, but later he rejected that idea. He was drawn to the conclusion that the Bible alone (*sola scriptura*) is the source of truth. The truth which God wishes to communicate to us is found only in the Bible.

Church Abuses

Luther saw many abuses in the church. His own theology was taking him in a direction away from Catholic Church teaching. The final precipitating cause of his protest against the evils around him was the work of one Johann Tetzel. Tetzel had been preaching in neighboring towns on indulgences. The church taught that the treasury of merits (good works accomplished by Jesus, Mary, or one of the saints) could

Lutheran tradition
the first phase of the Reformation, flowing from the teaching of Martin Luther

Martin Luther
the reformer who was the first strong guiding force behind the Reformation and the establisher of the Lutheran Church, the reformed Christian Church, especially in Germany and the Netherlands

justification by faith
the principle espoused by St. Paul and Martin Luther that we are saved (justified) by God's free grace and our faith, rather than being saved by what we do "to earn" God's approval

prevent or lessen temporal punishment. Temporal punishment due to sin, even when forgiven, could be lessened through these merits by the performance for some "good work." Punishment occurred either on earth or in purgatory (an intermediary state between earth and heaven); it was this latter that Tetzel preached on. An example of a good work might be prayer, a penance, or even a pilgrimage. An **indulgence** referred to the church's application of these good works for the purpose of remitting or lessening a person's punishment in purgatory. The indulgence could be "earned" for oneself or for a soul in purgatory.

It is one thing to treat a good work as a religious act. It is quite another to collect money, as did Tetzel, for the granting of indulgences. The money was collected to pay for the rebuilding of St. Peter's basilica in Rome and was thus named a "good work" by Tetzel, who had been sent out to gather funds. The archbishop of Mainz, Germany, authorized the sale of indulgences in order to send money to Rome in return for being named an archbishop. Tetzel preached throughout the archdiocese, convincing many people to buy indulgences for their dead loved ones. In order to capitalize on the sale of indulgences, Tetzel distorted the Catholic Church's original teaching about indulgences and made people believe that as soon as their donations were received, their loved ones would be allowed to enter into heaven.

The Ninety-Five Theses

This was the final straw for Luther. Luther posted his famous **Ninety-five Theses** on the door of the castle church at Wittenberg on October 31, 1517. The theses included Luther's opposition to the selling of indulgences. Ironically, the Church of All Saints, where the theses were posted, contained relics that had been donated in return for indulgences. Luther's intention was to raise questions for discussion, so he sent copies of the Ninety-five Theses to his bishop and to the archbishop of Mainz. But without Luther's knowledge, printers copied and circulated the theses. The ensuing controversy led to a hardening of positions.

indulgence

the remission by the church of the temporal punishment due to sin, forgiven by virtue of the merits of Jesus, Mary, and the saints

Ninety-five Theses

Martin Luther's list of items for discussion regarding beliefs and practices of the Catholic Church

Martin Luther posting his Ninety-five Theses.

A Sampling of Luther's Ninety-Five Theses

1. *Our Lord and Master Jesus Christ, in saying "Repent ye," etc., intended that the whole life of believers should be penitence.*

5. *The pope has neither the will nor the power to remit any penalties, except those which he has imposed by his own authority, or by that of the canons.*

6. *The pope has no power to remit any guilt, except by declaring and warranting it to have been remitted by God; or at most by remitting cases reserved for himself; in which cases, if his power were despised, guilt would certainly remain.*

21. *Thus those preachers of indulgences are in error who say that, by the indulgences of the pope, a man is loosed and saved from all punishment.*

27. *They preach mad, who say that the soul flies out of purgatory as soon as the money thrown into the chest rattles.*

28. *It is certain that, when the money rattles in the chest, avarice and gain may be increased, but the suffrage of the Church depends on the will of God alone.*

32. *Those who believe that, through letters of pardon [indulgences], they are made sure of their own salvation, will be eternally damned along with their teachers.*

37. *Every true Christian, whether living or dead, has a share in all the benefits of Christ and of the Church given him by God, even without letters of pardon.*

40. *True contrition seeks and loves punishment; while the ampleness of pardons relaxes it, and causes men to hate it, or at least gives occasion for them to do so.*

43. *Christians should be taught that he who gives to a poor man, or lends to a needy man, does better than if he bought pardons.*

44. *Because, by a work of charity, charity increases and the man becomes better; while, by means of pardons, he does not become better, but only freer from punishment.*

50. *Christians should be taught that, if the pope were acquainted with the exactions of the preachers of pardons, he would prefer that the Basilica of St. Peter should be burnt to ashes, than that it should be built up with the skin, flesh, and bones of his sheep.*

51. *Christians should be taught that, as it would be the duty, so it would be the wish of the pope, even to sell, if necessary, the Basilica of St. Peter, and to give of his own money to very many of those from whom the preachers of pardons extract money.*

59. *St. Lawrence said that the treasures of the Church are the poor of the Church, but he spoke according to the use of the word in his time.*

62. *The true treasure of the Church is the Holy Gospel of the glory and grace of God.*

81. *This license in the preaching of pardons makes it no easy thing, even for learned men, to protect the reverence due to the Pope against the calumnies, or, at all events, the keen questionings of the laity.*

93. *Blessed be all those prophets who say to the people of Christ, "The cross, the cross," and there is no cross!*

94. *Christians should be exhorted to strive to follow Christ their Head through pains, deaths, and hells.*

95. *And thus trust to enter heaven through many tribulations, rather than in the security of peace.*

The Ensuing Conflict

In 1520, Pope Leo X condemned forty-one points of Luther's teaching, and Luther's writings were publicly burned at Rome. On January 3, 1521, Luther was formally **excommunicated** (excluded from membership in the church). During this same time, the rise of nationalism was lending support to efforts to take control from both the emperor and the pope. It is no coincidence that the move to separate the German nation from the Holy Roman Empire prospered at this time. The empire's territories were no longer united.

On April 17, 1521, Luther appeared before the imperial Diet at Worms, Germany. Holy Roman Emperor Charles V (1500–1558) was deeply troubled by the unrest. When told to withdraw his objections, Luther refused to recant. He explained that the Bible and reason were his only guide. While Luther was able to win the favor of many German princes who were present, the emperor abruptly ended the proceedings. A ban was placed on Luther, allowing anyone in the empire to hand Luther over to the emperor's soldiers.

Luther went into hiding at the Wartburg castle at Eisenach, Germany, where he continued to write. He began the task of translating the Bible from Hebrew and Greek into German. So successful was his translation that the structure of the modern German language grew out of it.

Luther repeatedly called on people to do two things: one, to look critically at the clergy; two, to deepen their spirituality. He never asked people to break with the Church of Rome. According to some, this explains the widespread acceptance of his message. That message appeared in the form of cartoons, pamphlets, and plays. One million pieces of Reformation literature were printed in the first decade of the Reformation.

In 1525, Luther married a former nun by the name of Katherina von Bora (1499–1552). Together they had six children and adopted eleven others. On February 18, 1546, Luther died at Eisleben, Germany. He was buried at All Saints Church, Wittenberg, Germany.

Thus began **Protestantism**. The term *Protestant* was first used at the Diet of Speyer in 1529. An earlier Diet of Speyer in 1526 determined that each prince could order church affairs in his realm. Charles V, with the pope's backing, called a new Diet and attempted to end laws that favored the toleration of religions. Six princes and fourteen cities made a formal "protest" to the archduke. From then on, the reformers were known as *Protestants*. Sixteenth-century reformers saw themselves as successors of medieval churchmen who had sought to renew (*reformare*) the church of that time.

In 1530, Charles V faced a Turkish military threat. Above all, he wanted to unify the territories of the empire. For this reason, he endorsed the Peace of Nuremburg (1532). This document gave Luther's supporters legal recognition until a church-wide council could be held. In response,

excommunicate
formally exclude a person from a church community or organization

Protestantism
the churches that separated from the Catholic Church in the sixteenth century as a result of the Reformation; the beliefs of these churches

the empire's Protestant territories formed the Smalcaldic League, fearing that the emperor would eventually use force against them. In 1546, Charles V attacked the Protestant troops, in hopes that this move would enhance the central government's power. His plan backfired, and he had to abdicate. Charles's brother, Ferdinand V (1503–1564), finally acknowledged the victory of the Reformation. In the Peace of Augsburg (1555), Ferdinand permitted each territory to decide for itself what religion would be practiced within its borders.

The Reformed Tradition

Zwingli and Calvin

Ulrich Zwingli (1484–1531), from Switzerland, and **John Calvin** (1509–1564), a Frenchman, carried the Reformation movement into its second phase. The **Reformed tradition** refers to the non-Lutheran churches that emerged during the sixteenth-century Protestant Reformation. Zwingli became attracted to the writings of Luther in 1518. Soon Zwingli disagreed with Luther on the nature of the real presence of Christ in the Eucharist. Luther believed in the real presence; Zwingli said that the Lord's Supper was simply a memorial service. This difference of view on the Eucharist marks the separation between the Lutheran tradition and the Reformed tradition.

John Calvin is called the *Second Father of the Reformation*. While Luther left many writings, he did not leave a systematic presentation of his thinking; it was John Calvin who organized the theological views of the Reformation and carried this movement forward. His most important work, *Institutes of the Christian Religion*, remains the classic formulation of Reformation theology and has been called the most important piece of Protestant Christian literature in existence. The theology of the Reformed tradition has had a major influence upon the religious experience of North America. Reformed Christians share three important beliefs with other Protestant Christians: justification by faith, priesthood of all believers, and scripture alone.

For Calvin, the doctrine of justification by faith highlights the distance between God and people, a distance that cannot be bridged. We can become justified only through faith. This doctrine also says something about the nature of God and human nature; it stresses the absolute sovereignty of God and the utter depravity of humankind. The "depravity" of humankind means that people are helpless before God. Calvin stressed this even more than Luther and called it *total depravity*. He felt that the Fall had so changed human nature that humans were no longer capable of willing or doing anything but sin. Only Christ's merits and God's grace brings justification.

Ulrich Zwingli
reformer whose teachings and leadership resulted in a break from the Lutheran tradition in Switzerland and parts of Germany

John Calvin
Second Father of the Reformation; systematic writer of Protestant theology and a major influence on the Reformed tradition

Reformed tradition
the non-Lutheran churches that emerged during the Reformation

Tenets of Reformed Christianity

There are four tenets of Reformed Christianity that flow from the above view of God and humans: election for service and salvation; good stewardship; decency and order; and presbyteral government.

Election for service and salvation

Election for service and salvation is often expressed or understood as **predestination**. From the Reformed perspective, to be elected means "to be chosen." Churches of the Reformed tradition believe that Jesus' chosen followers will be rewarded both in this life and in the next. Thus, predestination means that God has decided certain individuals will be saved for heaven and some will be damned to hell. If only some people go to heaven, then this means that Jesus died only for them (the elect). Jesus did not die for those going to hell. This is called **limited atonement**. Further, those who are saved cannot resist God's grace; they cannot backslide. Over time, there was a moderation of this rigid view among many Calvinists.

Good stewardship

Reformed Christians commit themselves to following Jesus. That commitment enables them to be of service in this life and is a sign of their salvation in the next. Reformed Christians believe that God is present in the world. Therefore, they involve themselves in the world's affairs.

Reformed Christians use their resources of land, money, time, and talents (including a developed intellect) very carefully.

From the Reformed perspective, a Christian's life must involve study. Study sharpens the mind; a sharpened mind enables people to better devote themselves to God's service. In Calvin's view, belief and action are linked together: What a person thinks determines what he or she does. Within the Reformed tradition, the sermon became the center point of public worship because it was a vehicle of instruction, shaping the beliefs of the entire congregation.

Decency and order

The Church must preach the "pure doctrine of the gospel" (emphasis in Calvin's teachings) and maintain the "pure administration of the sacraments" (celebrate baptism and Holy Communion). Baptism

predestination
election for service and salvation, as taught by John Calvin; God's predetermination of who will be saved and who will not

limited atonement
the Calvinist belief that Jesus died only for the elect

Preaching is central in many Protestant churches.

and Holy Communion are the only recognized sacraments among Reformed Christians. Baptism is a communal sacrament; the whole community welcomes the baptized person into the church. Reformed Christians believe that Jesus is spiritually present, not bodily present, in the eucharistic bread and grape juice. They observe the sacrament of Holy Communion once a month.

Presbyteral government

Most churches of the Reformed tradition have a presbyteral form of government. Preaching elders (ordained) function as ministers. They preach the gospel and administer the sacraments. Ruling elders are lay people who assist the preaching elders. Deacons help the elders to carry out service work.

In each local church, ministers, elders, and deacons make up a **consistory**, or session. Ministers and elders are elected. Local consistories form a **presbytery**. The presbytery gives advice and facilitates cooperation. Three or more presbyteries form a synod. Synods come together in a general assembly.

Results

The teachings of Calvin, Zwingli, and other reformers spread throughout Europe—especially in France, Germany, the Netherlands, and Switzerland. John Knox (1505–1572) brought the Reformed tradition to Scotland, which influenced the Puritan movement in England. No religious denominations today call themselves *Calvinist*. But many religious denominations today hold to basic Calvinist theology and many cultures have been influenced by his thinking. Much of Calvin's theology has been nuanced or interpreted less rigidly than Calvin taught. Nevertheless, the effect of Calvinism upon religious thinkers in North America is inestimable.

The Anabaptist Tradition

The Baptist tradition of today has a rich history. Some Baptists trace their roots directly to John the Baptist, who baptized Jesus. Others trace their roots to the Anabaptists of sixteenth-century Germany, who believed in the baptism of believers and that infants should not be baptized. Still others trace their roots to seventeenth-century Puritanism.

Anabaptist reformers said that Luther, Calvin, and Zwingli had laid a fine foundation for the needed reformation of western Christianity, but they had not gone far enough. The church needed to be reformed **in its very structure**. Many individuals and groups throughout Europe began to ask questions well beyond those of Luther and Calvin.

- Is it legitimate for Christians to go to war, or should they avoid all use of weapons?
- Should the sacraments be retained or discarded all together?
- If baptism is practiced at all, should it not be for adults only?
- Is scripture a normative pattern for life, or is it a document of a simple church which should now be ignored?

consistory
part of the presbyteral form of government in the Reformed tradition, unique to each local church and made up of ministers, elders, and deacons

presbytery
part of the presbyteral form of government in the Reformed tradition, made up of local consistories; gives advice and facilitates cooperation

Anabaptist tradition
movement of sixteenth-century reformers who believed in the baptism of believers and that infants should not be baptized

These questions obviously carried the Reformation to a radical new dimension. The reformers were now reacting against not only the Catholic Church but the first two phases of the Reformation as well. The first Anabaptist group gathered around Conrad Grebel in Zurich in 1525.

The early years of the Anabaptist tradition are mired in appalling controversy, persecution, and bloodshed—thousands died for their beliefs. So radical were some views that they drew the condemnation of Luther, Calvin, and other Reformation leaders. Anabaptist leaders were hung, burned, and drowned. "Few of the leaders of the Anabaptist movement died in bed" (footnote: John Dillenberg, *Protestant Christianity—Interpreted Through Its Development*, New York: MacMillan, 1988, 58). Nevertheless, Anabaptist communities sprang up throughout north-central Europe, even though persecution would follow them for more than four centuries. Eventually, Moravia and Holland became the centers of the Anabaptist tradition. From Moravia came Jakob Hutter and from Holland, Menno Simons.

Differences with Luther and Calvin

Anabaptist thinking departs significantly from Luther and Calvin. For the Anabaptist reformers, justification by faith is not the issue. What is more important is the role of the Holy Spirit and the living experience of Christ now. They believed in the direct inspiration of the Holy Spirit and focused on the spiritual experience of members of the church and the importance of Christian living in the present. "Theology was considered a highly suspicious enterprise in which theologians spun out theses which were a stumbling block to those of simple but genuine faith" (footnote, Dillenberg, 60).

Anabaptists insisted that the church must be restructured in every detail according to the New Testament pattern. For them, this means that the church is a voluntary association of Christians living in a disciplined community. Thus it must be composed of adults who have experienced the work of the Spirit and can accept baptism. Anabaptists did not accept infant baptism and baptized adults only. They rebaptized adults who had been baptized as infants. Thus they were called "rebaptizers," from which the word *Anabaptist* comes. This is called the **baptism of believers**. The church is composed of members who are already holy and live out that holiness within a defined community.

Groups which descend from this tradition often stress faith lived in a simple lifestyle and in isolation from the world. Most adherents refuse to take oaths, oppose capital punishment, and reject military service. The Hutterites in South Dakota are the descendants of the community started by Jakob Hutter. From Menno Simons come the Mennonites. Also included in this tradition are the Church of the Brethren and the Amish.

baptism of believers
within the Anabaptist tradition, the baptism of adults

The English Tradition

According to the early Christian writers Tertullian (155–220) and Origen (185–254), Christianity came to England sometime during the early third century. By the fourth century, English bishops resided at Londinium (London), Eboracum (York), and Colonia Linum (Lincoln).

In 597, Pope Gregory I (540–604) sent a monk, Augustine (540–604), to England. Augustine converted the Anglo-Saxon peoples to Christianity and became the first archbishop of Canterbury (601). He is known as Augustine of Canterbury.

In the succeeding centuries, a number of developments took place within the Church of England. In the eighth century, the English clergy became well known for their scholarship. In the tenth century, a series of church reforms were enacted. In the eleventh century, the Norman conquest of England increased contact between the churches of England and Rome. In the thirteenth century, the English theologian John Wycliffe (1330–1384) criticized the papacy, which served to influence the Reformation.

The Reformation in England, or **English Reformation** as it is commonly called, differed in substance from all that was going on in continental Europe. The reformers in Europe dealt with theological issues. The beginning of the Reformation in England had nothing to do with theology; it had to do with jurisdiction—or authority—in the church. For this reason, and because of the way it developed later, it is perhaps best to think of the **English tradition** as "Protestant" in a different way —and for its own reasons.

Henry VIII

It all began with King Henry VIII (1491–1547). Henry sought to have his first marriage, to Catherine of Aragon, annulled so that he could marry Anne Boleyn. The king and Catherine had had a number of children, but only one of them (a daughter, Mary) survived. Thus, Henry sought a new wife, hoping for a son to carry on after him. When Pope Clement VII denied the annulment, Henry took matters into his own hands. He replaced the Archbishop of Canterbury, Cardinal Wolsey, with Thomas Cranmer, who was more sympathetic to Henry's wishes. Henry ordered the clergy to continue functioning even if they were excommunicated by Rome. And he coerced Parliament to issue the **Act of Supremacy,** which declared that the king was "the only supreme head on earth of the Church of England. . . ." Other than this change of leadership for the Church in England, Henry made few changes on the practical level. The Ten Articles of Religion of 1536 made little substantive changes in the faith. On his death bed, Henry would have considered himself a Catholic.

Tension and Change

Real change happened only after Henry's death. His male heir, Edward VI (son of his third wife, Jane Seymour), was a sickly boy when he became king in 1547. During Edward's brief time on the throne, the church at first took on more of a Lutheran flavor and then more of a Reformed flavor. Christians began to worship in English, not Latin. And church rituals were brought together in a single book known as the *Book of Common Prayer.*

English Reformation
the Reformation in England, based on jurisdiction rather than theology

English tradition
the reformed Christian Church in England, dating from the time of Henry VIII and his ruling children

Act of Supremacy
declaration initiated by Henry VIII that the king of England was the supreme head on earth of the Church of England

Book of Common Prayer
the Church of England's collection of its church rituals

After six years, Mary, Edward's Catholic sister from King Henry's first marriage, became queen. She attempted to restore Catholicism to England, but died after five years of reigning. Reversing her father's and brother's policies caused much bloodshed, and Mary I became known as *Bloody Mary*. Then Elizabeth, daughter of Henry and Anne Boleyn, began a forty-five-year reign. She steered a middle path between the extremes of Roman Catholicism and Protestantism. Elizabeth I (1533–1603), helped to define Anglican Christianity in a number of ways:

1. She advocated publication of a new prayer book (1559) that struck a balance between the versions of 1549 and 1552.

2. She favored the Act of Supremacy (1559) and made the English monarch "supreme governor" of the church, not "supreme head on earth of the Church of England." This demonstrated that the Church of England's spiritual leader is the archbishop of Canterbury, not the English monarch.

3. She preserved apostolic succession (the apostles' practice of ordaining bishops who ordained bishops who ordained bishops, and so on). At the queen's request, two bishops from the reign of Henry VIII and two bishops from the reign of Edward VI consecrated (ordained) Matthew Parker (1504–1575) Archbishop of Canterbury.

4. She advocated parliament's approval of the *Thirty-Nine Articles* (1571), a summary of Anglican Christian doctrine.

In 1570 relations between Catholic Christians (who looked to Rome) and Anglican Christians (who looked to Canterbury) reached an impasse. In that year, Pope Pius V (1540–1572) released the subjects of Elizabeth I from allegiance to her, and subsequently excommunicated her.

England's National Church

Thus, over time, Christianity in England became a national church with the Thirty-Nine Articles guiding its theology. The church became more Protestant in flavor, emphasizing the importance of justification by faith over good works. The importance of scripture is affirmed, while the real presence of Christ in the Eucharist is understood in a "heavenly and spiritual manner," but real rather than symbolic. As with Catholicism, the positive aspects of tradition are stressed, with the church having a responsibility for proper interpretation of scripture. Strong emphasis is placed on the unity of worship; the *Book of Common Prayer*, revised several times, has guided Anglican churches since that time. The church in England retained the episcopal structure of the church and considers it a symbol of unity in the church.

Planting the Seed

Having looked at the origins of each of these Reformation traditions, we will now discuss specific examples of each tradition.

Lutheranism

A Lutheran is a Christian who subscribes to and follows Martin Luther's interpretation and reform of Christianity. The term *Lutheran* was actually used for the first time in a papal document condemning Luther. It was then used in derision by Luther's opponents. But the name stuck, over Luther's intention to reform the existing Catholic Church and his insistence that members of the movement be known as **evangelicals**, that is, "believers in the gospel."

The Augsburg Confession

Luther's interpretation of Christianity was first expressed in the **Augsburg Confession**. The Augsburg Confession (or formal profession of belief) is a statement of belief, doctrine, and practices as formulated by Philip Melancthon (1497–1560), Luther's associate and theologian. It was presented at the Diet (Conference) of Augsburg, Germany, in 1530, and became the principal statement of belief, or creed, of all Lutheran churches. German Protestant churches became known as the churches of the Augsburg Confession. From the seventeenth century onwards, they were known as Lutheran churches.

Later other documents were added. These include the *Large Catechism* and *Small Catechism* (1529) written by Luther, the Schmalkaldic Articles (1537), the Apology of the Augsbury Confession and the Formula of Concord (1577). Added to this are three creeds from early Christianity: the Apostles' Creed, the Nicene Creed, and the Athanasian Creed. All of these were collected into the ***Book of Concord*** in 1580 and constitute the basic collection of Lutheran doctrinal writings.

The teachings of Luther quickly spread beyond Germany to other European countries: Sweden, Denmark, Norway, Iceland, the Baltic countries, Hungary, and Transylvania. In some of these countries, Lutheranism became the state church. In Europe, most Lutheran churches are episcopal, that is, governed by bishops.

Lutheran Beginnings in North America

The first stable Lutheran community in North America was established at Fort Christina on the Delaware River in 1638. Swedish settlers were followed by German immigrants who were escaping poverty, famine, and war, and who settled in Pennsylvania, a colony which proved to be especially tolerant. In 1748, a German immigrant, Henry Melchior Muhlenberg (1711–1787), organized the Ministerium of Pennsylvania, and is credited as the organizer of Lutheranism in the United States. This was the first **synod** in the thirteen colonies; the creation of additional synods followed. During his forty-five-year ministry,

Lutheranism
the way of thinking that subscribes to and follows Martin Luther's interpretation and reform of Christianity

evangelicals
"believers in the gospel," self-description of early Protestant churches

Augsburg Confession
the Lutheran formal profession of belief, doctrine, and practices formulated by Philip Melancthon, Luther's associate and theologian

Book of Concord
the basic collection of Lutheran doctrinal writings and the definitive statement of Lutheran orthodoxy

synod
group of churches, within Lutheranism especially

Muhlenberg worked among the scattered Lutheran communities and organized them on a permanent basis.

In Europe, Lutheranism was closely tied to the state. This association continued when citizens of various countries immigrated to North America. During the 1830s, Lutherans emigrated from Denmark, Finland, Iceland, Norway, and Sweden. Upon arriving in North America, they stayed within their own ethnic groups. The immigrating groups founded churches which preserved their customs and language. Each linguistic group established a synod and thus an independent Lutheran church. They were independent of other linguistic groups and of churches in other regions.

As more immigrants came to North America, more synods were formed, and Lutheranism broke out of the original settlements on the East Coast and spread to the central parts of the United States. It became especially strong in the Midwest. By 1850, there were one hundred fifty Lutheran churches in the United States clustered in several synods.

The structure of the Lutheran Church in the United States follows a congregational and synodical form of government. Congregations are independent but are linked together for common purposes. In general, a president and bishops are elected for a limited time, and their authority is restricted. Ordained ministry became an option for Lutheran women in the United States in the late 1960s.

The Synods Today

Since the later nineteenth century, Lutherans of all ethnic backgrounds have been merging, or combining, into a few synods. In the United States, the largest Lutheran body is the Evangelical Lutheran Church in America—ELCA. This body was formed in 1987 from the union of three Lutheran bodies: the Lutheran Church in America, the American Lutheran Church, and the Association of Evangelical Lutheran Churches. The Evangelical Lutheran Church in America has its headquarters in Chicago, Illinois. The presiding bishop oversees the church. In the United States the ELCA has about 5.2 million members.

The roots of the ELCA are in the earliest colonial Lutheran churches and the nineteenth-century settlers from Scandinavia, Germany, and Eastern Europe. The American Lutheran Church was mainly a nineteenth-century creation. The church produced the missionary Johannes Konrad Wilhelm Loehe (1808–1872), who helped newly arrived Lutheran immigrants adjust to their new country. Historically, the church placed emphasis on the cultivation of spirituality. The Association of Evangelical Lutheran Churches constituted the theologically liberal wing of the Missouri Synod. The association was formed by faculty and students who left Concordia Seminary, St. Louis, Missouri, protesting against a lack of academic freedom. The Seminex, or Concordia Seminary in Exile, provided the impetus behind the creation of the association.

The second largest group is the Lutheran Church—Missouri Synod, with 2.6 million members. The Missouri Synod rose from mid-1800s German congregations in the Midwest. The church grew up around Martin Stephan (1777–1846); Stephan and his followers believed that they were the last remnant of authentic Christianity in Germany. By 1838, a group of six hundred had made their way to Missouri. Stephan was succeeded by Carl Ferdinand W. Walther (1811–1887). Walther founded a number of hospitals, orphanages, and schools. The German Evangelical Lutheran Synod of Missouri, Ohio, and Other States dates from 1847. The name *Lutheran Church–Missouri Synod* was chosen during World War I because of anti-German sentiment in the United States.

Church headquarters continue to be located at St. Louis, Missouri. The convention, which meets every three years, elects the president of the Lutheran Church—Missouri Synod. Members of the Missouri Synod believe that the Bible is free of error. This belief is known as **inerrancy**. They also accept the entire *Book of Concord* as authoritative.

The third largest group is the Wisconsin Evangelical Lutheran Synod, with about 500,000 members. This group is also primarily German in origin and was founded by John Muehlhaeuser (1804–1868) in 1850. Under the leadership of John Bading (1824–1913) and Adolf Hoenecke (1835–1908), the church emphasized its faithfulness to Luther. It regards itself as the most traditional Lutheran church in the United States, upholding the inerrancy of the Bible and adherence to the Lutheran confessions (the *Book of Concord*). The denomination's headquarters are in Milwaukee, Wisconsin. Denominational churches, found in all fifty states, meet on the national level every three years.

inerrancy
the belief that the Bible is free of error

Responsibility for Creation

The earth is a planet of beauty and abundance; the earth system is wonderfully intricate and incredibly complex. But today living creatures, and the air, soil, and water that support them, face unprecedented threats. Many threats are global; most stem directly from human activity. Our current practices may so alter the living world that it will be unable to sustain life in the manner we know.

Twin problems—excessive consumption by industrialized nations, and relentless growth of human population worldwide—jeopardize efforts to achieve a sustainable future. These problems spring from and intensify social injustices. Global population growth, for example, relates to the lack of access by women to family planning and health care, quality education, fulfilling employment, and equal rights.

—Caring for Creation: Vision, Hope, and Justice *(1993),*
a document approved by the Third Churchwide Assembly
of the Evangelical Lutheran Church in America.

Let's Talk about It . . .

1. Why do you think the ELCA is so concerned about the state of the planet today?
2. If Martin Luther were living today, what might he say about this issue?

Beliefs

For all Lutherans, the *Book of Concord* holds the articulation of their central beliefs. More important than this, of course, is the Bible, especially the Gospels and writings of Paul in the New Testament. Three key teachings of Luther—faith alone, grace alone, and scripture alone—remain the central threads of Lutheran belief.

Word

Scripture possesses ultimate authority for Lutherans. Not all Lutherans, however, interpret scripture in the same way. Some believe that scripture has relevance only in certain situations, while others maintain that scripture can guide people in every age and situation. Some Lutherans regard scripture as free of error (biblical inerrancy). Most Lutherans, especially of the ELCA, do not understand the Bible as a record of history or science. For them, it is a book of religious truth.

The *Book of Concord* contains several documents and consists of eight parts:

1. a preface signed by civil (state) and ecclesiastical (church) authorities
2. the Apostles' Creed, the Nicene Creed, and the Athanasian Creed
3. the Augsburg Confession (1530)
4. Apology (explanation) of the Augsburg Confession
5. the Schmalkaldic Articles (1536–1537)
6. Philipp Melanchthon's "Treatise on the Power and Primacy of the Pope" (1537)
7. Martin Luther's *Small Catechism* and *Large Catechism* (1529)
8. the Formula of Concord (1577)

The Augsburg Confession is looked upon by Lutherans "as a true witness to the gospel." Lutherans hold to the central Christian beliefs of the early centuries; for example: the Trinity, Christ's divinity, the incarnation, the reality of sin and the forgiveness of sin, baptism, the efficacy of God's grace, and eternal life. They also believe in a liturgical form of worship. In his *Small Catechism*, Luther listed six fundamentals of faith:

- the Ten Commandments
- the (Apostles') Creed
- the Lord's Prayer
- the sacrament of holy baptism
- confession
- the sacrament of the altar

Sacraments

As a result of his central teaching on "scripture alone," Luther concluded that there are only two sacraments that are based in scripture: baptism and Eucharist. Thus Lutherans practice only these two sacraments. For Lutherans, baptism and Holy Communion allow God's grace to penetrate people's lives, and that grace creates and strengthens faith.

Baptism is the beginning of the life of faith; through baptism the first taste of God's grace is bestowed upon a person. Through baptism God builds up a community of faith. The Lord's Supper (Eucharist) is an encounter with the living (resurrected) Lord, who is truly present in Holy Communion to forgive sins and renew the faith-life of believers. In general, mostly as a result of ecumenical dialogue, Lutheran churches are celebrating the Lord's Supper more frequently than in former years. The frequency will vary from one congregation to the next.

A very important event in the life of Lutherans is **confirmation**. Lutheran students prepare diligently for this event. They may spend several hours a week for a year or more preparing for confirmation at the age of thirteen or fourteen. The service is usually held on Pentecost or Palm Sunday. It marks an important time in life when the Lutheran youth affirm their faith for themselves.

Lutherans also celebrate other events, of course, such as matrimony, ordination, and burial. These are considered "rites," not sacraments. Some groups also have a confessional rite. The anointing of the sick is considered a pious Christian action which is believed to be therapeutic only.

confirmation

in some Protestant denominations, a rite of mature affirmation of the faith rather than a sacrament

"Religion is the best armor, but the worst cloak."
—Thomas Fuller

Worship

A pamphlet on Lutheran worship states: *As we worship so we believe; as we believe so we worship.* The principal religious act of Lutherans is their Sunday worship service. Because there is no official liturgical form that all Lutheran churches must follow, there is a wide variety. Some are very close to the Catholic order and style of worship, including vestments and candles. Others move more toward a simple traditional Protestant style.

The typical service includes a confession of sin, a declaration of salvation by God's grace, an entry psalm or song, the recitation or singing of the traditional "hymn of praise," and the official prayer of the congregation. This is followed by the Bible readings, the recitation of the creed, a Lutheran hymn, and a sermon by the minister on the scripture readings. The readings and the sermon are the highlights of the typical Lutheran Sunday service. When the sermon is finished, the congregation joins in a prayer, makes an offering, sings more hymns, and receives a blessing invoked by the minister.

On Communion Sundays, the service includes the consecration ceremony of the bread and the wine and the reception of the bread and wine, usually while kneeling at the altar railing. In many Lutheran churches, the Sunday service is followed by a period of "fellowship" when members of the congregation meet with each other and their pastor.

Lutherans observe the traditional Christian feast days, such as Christmas, Easter, and Pentecost, and follow the traditional church calendar of seasons: Advent, Christmas, Lent, Easter, and Pentecost. They also observe Reformation Sunday at the end of October. They do not have any special religious devotional services, cult of the saints, shrines, or pilgrimages.

The Lutheran worship book is diverse in culture and time. Lutheranism has given to the western Christian Church a great heritage in hymns. Most widely known is Luther's "A Mighty Fortress Is Our God." Luther published two hymn books in 1524. The popular hymns spread Luther's ideas on human sinfulness and God's grace. They became an integral part of Lutheran worship.

Taking Root

Reformed Tradition

Puritans
English Protestants in a strict Calvinist model, some of whom immigrated to the thirteen colonies

To a degree, the **Puritans** helped to promote Reformed Christian ideas in the thirteen colonies. Between 1650 and 1776 most of the immigrants who came to America belonged to churches of the Reformed tradition. Thus Calvinist theology has had a profound effect upon many North American denominations that exist today. Numerous denominations have evolved through various stages as they clarified their theology, broke away from one another or other Protestant bodies, and merged with other denominations.

Churches in the Reformed tradition share similarities with ancient Christianity and the Lutheran tradition, but they also have distinctive new ideas. They affirm the beliefs of early Christianity as articulated in the ancient creeds. They agreed with the key ideas of Martin Luther: faith alone, grace alone, and scripture alone. Their contribution to the Reformation movement was in a new definition and model of church. When studying the New Testament, leaders in the Reformed tradition did not see a sharp distinction between the bishop and priest as it existed in Catholicism. They noted that "elders" were appointed over the early Christian communities (Acts 14:23) and that sometimes the term *elder* was used interchangeably with the Greek word for *bishop*. John Calvin concluded that Jesus Christ himself was the sole ruler in the church and that he exercised that rule through four kinds of officers: preachers, teachers, deacons, and lay elders. Thus churches in this tradition organize themselves differently from Catholic and Lutheran churches.

Today the characteristics of the Reformed tradition can be found in three main groupings of denominations: Reformed,

Congregationalist, and **Presbyterian**. Presbyterians and Congregationalists take their names from their organization as church. *Congregationalist* comes from the Latin word *grex* which means society or company. Congregation-alists believe that each congregation should govern itself. The word *Presbyterian* comes from the Greek word for elder, *presbyterios*.

The churches of the Reformed tradition contributed to the First Great Awakening, a revival of American Christianity that occurred during the mid-eighteenth century. *The new birth* was its central theme. During this time, Reformed Christians were led by dynamic ministers. Among these ministers were Dutch Reformed Theodore Frelinghuysen, Presby-terian Samuel Davies, and Congregationalist Jonathan Edwards. These ministers emphasized the Holy Spirit's role in bringing people to Jesus.

In the mid-nineteenth century, Reformed Christians helped to ignite the Second Great Awakening. This awakening focused the nation's attention on ending slavery, improving education, promoting international peace, and reforming prisons. The Congregational ministers Lyman Beecher, Timothy Dwight, and Asahel Nettleton played an important role in its success. After the Second Great Awakening, the influence of Reformed Christians began to decline. In 1750, 80 percent of Americans belonged to the Reformed tradition. By 1850, 70 percent of the U.S. population were Baptists and Methodists.

Reformed Church in America

In 1628, Jonas Michaelius built the first Reformed Christian church in America. He had undertaken missionary work on behalf of the Reformed Church in the Netherlands. During the late seventeenth and early eighteenth centuries, a number of French and German Reformed Christians joined the church congregation begun by Michaelius. In 1792, the church became independent of the Dutch mother church. Under the leadership of John H. Livingston (1746–1825), the church assumed the name *Dutch Reformed Church*. Since 1867, the church has been known as the *Reformed Church in America*. The church adheres to the Belgian Confession (1561), the "Five Points of Calvinism" from the Canons of the Synod of Dot (1619), and the Heidelberg Catechism (1693).

The General Synod, the church's highest authority, meets once a year. The Reformed Church in America belongs to the National Council of Churches of Christ in the USA and to the World Council of Churches. It is headquartered in New York City.

United Church of Christ

The United Church of Christ is a church of the Reformed tradition. The United Church of Christ, by that name, came into existence in 1957 when two churches combined. Each of these churches was in turn the product of mergers. The United Church of Christ, therefore, represents the coming together of four churches: the Congregational Churches, the Christian Church, the Reformed Church in the United States, and the Evangelical Synod of North America. The General Synod is the church's highest authority, and meets every year. The United Church of Christ belongs to the National Council of Churches of Christ in the USA and to the World Council of Churches. Its headquarters are in New York City.

Congregationalist
Reformed tradition denomination(s) in which each congregation is self-governed

Presbyterian
Reformed tradition denomination in which each church is governed by presbyters or elders

A Just World

So many of God's people suffer. So many are maltreated. God's good earth cries out in pain. Our world needs those who will pursue justice, show mercy, and seek peace. That is the Church we hear God calling us to be. We want "to join oppressed and troubled people in the struggle for liberation . . . and to work for justice, healing, and wholeness of life."

We envision a world wherein "justice will flow down like mighty waters." Therefore, we will stand alongside those who hurt so that the hungry may be fed, the excluded embraced, and the creation renewed.

—Statement of Commitment (1993), approved by the General Synod of the United Church of Christ.

Let's Talk about It . . .

1. What is the relationship between religion and justice?
2. What is your vision of a world where justice will flow down like mighty waters?

Presbyterian Church (USA)

Presbyterianism is a good representative example of the Reformed tradition. Thus, this denomination will be covered in more detail than those Reformed groups mentioned above.

Each Presbyterian community is governed by teaching elders who are ordained ministers and ruling elders who are elected from the ranks of the community. These elders together form a session. At least five sessions form a presbytery, which is composed of each of the ministers and one elected elder from each community. Each presbytery is responsible for matters pertaining to that presbytery: settling doctrinal and disciplinary questions within the presbytery, examining and ordaining candidates for the ministry, checking the records of local churches, and starting new communities. The next level of structure is the synod which is composed of at least three presbyteries. The highest level of organization is the General Assembly; it is composed of equal numbers of ministers and ruling elders. The General Assembly has the right to suppress heresy and schism, reorganize synods, settle doctrinal and disciplinary controversies, and ratify mergers with other denominations.

Today there are about fifty million Presbyterians in the world. Many are found in Scotland, Northern Ireland, England, the Netherlands, Switzerland, Hungary, France, South Africa, Indonesia, and Korea. In the United States there are approximately 4.3 million in eight groupings. About 216,000 members comprise the Presbyterian Church in Canada. The church's headquarters are in New York.

Presbyterianism in North America

Presbyterianism began in Scotland with **John Knox** (1505–1572) who was a devoted follower of John Calvin. He had spent three years in Geneva with Calvin before returning to his home country. Knox opposed the Catholicism of Mary Queen of Scots and the Anglicanism of Elizabeth. He convinced the Scottish parliament to establish Presbyterianism as the state religion. Scotland is the only country remaining today that has at least a nominal connection between Presbyterianism and the government. Presbyterianism came to Northern Ireland through Scottish colonists who settled on land confiscated by the King of England from Irish landowners. From 1729 to 1809 many of these Scotch-Irish immigrated to North America. They settled mostly in New York, New Jersey, Pennsylvania, Maryland, Delaware, and Georgia.

John Knox
follower of Calvin and founder of Presbyterianism in Scotland

One of the early immigrants to North America was Rev. Francis Makemie who is considered the father of Presbyterianism in the United States. Upon his arrival in 1683, Makemie began to organize the various Presbyterian communities. Sometime around 1705 he organized the first presbytery in Philadelphia. By 1717 the Synod of Philadelphia had nineteen ministers, forty churches, and 3,000 members.

With the westward movement in the United States, Presbyterianism spread rapidly. It split into groups, most notably into the Northern and Southern synods during the Civil War. Since then, there have been several mergers among Presbyterian bodies. In 1958 the United Presbyterian Church in the USA resulted from the union of the northern Presbyterians and the United Presbyterian Church of North America. In 1983 the United Presbyterian Church in the USA and the Southern Presbyterian Church formed the Presbyterian Church (USA). This group accounts for about 3.8 million members.

Presbyterianism spread rapidly in North America.

In Canada, Presbyterianism took root after 1763 when Irish Presbyterians from New Hampshire settled in Nova Scotia. They were joined by large numbers of Scottish Presbyterians in 1773. From there the denomination spread westward, and in 1875, all Presbyterian churches formed the Presbyterian Church in Canada. In 1925 the Presbyterian Church in Canada joined with the Methodists and the Congregationalists to form the United Church of Canada. Those Presbyterians who did not join the merger remain the Presbyterian Church in Canada. The United Church of Canada is essentially Presbyterian in government, but in doctrine and religious practice, both the Methodists and the Congregationalists have retained most of their own traditions.

Reformation Christianity

Beliefs

Westminster Confession

the standard of faith for Presbyterians in North America; sets doctrinal and ecclesiastical standards

The Westminster Assembly, held in London from 1643 to 1649, produced the **Westminster Confession**, which is the standard of faith for Presbyterians in North America. The Confession sets doctrinal and ecclesiastical standards for Presbyterians. The document also includes a *Larger* and *Shorter Catechism* and a *Directory for Public Worship*. These documents have guided Presbyterian bodies in North America and in other English-speaking areas of the world.

As explained earlier, Presbyterians share certain beliefs with ancient Christians and reformers in the Lutheran tradition. They believe in the Trinity, the divinity of Christ, the incarnation and resurrection of Christ, the Bible as revelation ("the only infallible rule in faith and practice"), eternal life, the reality of sin and the need for forgiveness, the law of love as the guiding principle in morality, the need for community worship service, and two ordinances: baptism and the Lord's Supper.

American Presbyterians do not believe that baptism is necessary for salvation, nor do they believe in the physical presence of Christ in holy communion. For them, baptism is only a sign of God's covenant, and so it is important only as a ceremony of entrance into the Church. The Lord's Supper is only a commemoration of the sacrifice of Christ, and Christ is spiritually present in the bread and the wine. The Lord's Supper is a common-participation sacrament in which the entire Church is brought into fellowship with Christ; it brings them into the presence of God.

Worship

For Presbyterians, worship is not something done for God or even simply to worship God. It is part of God's total work in redeeming the world through Jesus. For them, God's self-revelation is in all things, but particularly in the "Word"—God's self-communication in baptism, the Lord's Supper, the scriptures, preaching, and community prayer. For this reason, the Sunday worship service includes these elements. In a typical worship service, there is a call to worship, prayers, hymns, reading of the word of God in scripture, and the "going forth" ceremony of blessings and dismissal. When the Lord's Supper is included, it takes place after the preaching.

In addition to the Sunday worship service, Presbyterians have confirmation, marriage, burial, and ordination services for its ministers. These are not sacraments for Presbyterians. In all their ceremonies, Presbyterians now employ rich and elaborate symbolism—a departure from the original Presbyterian practice. Their services are now relatively solemn, and their rituals elaborate. Where once they had simple rooms or plain churches, they now have church buildings on the medieval plan or modern, and they use candles, vestments, the cross, other decorations, and well-trained choirs. Ordination of women was approved in 1956.

Presbyterians do not have shrines, special devotions, a cult of the saints, or religious feasts, aside from the major Christian feasts of Christmas, Easter, and Pentecost, and the traditional seasons of the church year.

Growing and Blooming

Anabaptist Tradition

The Mennonite Church of the Anabaptist Tradition

Since the sixteenth century, the Anabaptist tradition has diversified into a wide spectrum of church bodies. Even though this spectrum manifests a variety of emphases, the churches maintain a high level of adherence to central Anabaptist beliefs. The concept which is key to all churches in this tradition is that the church consists of a free association of adult believers. This concept leads to a distinctive pattern of beliefs and practices that permeate Anabaptist church bodies.

Denominations in this tradition are non-creedal; this means they do not have a specific creed which all members must believe. Nevertheless, two documents guide the beliefs and practices of specific denominations. The first of these is the **Schleitheim Confession** (1527, formerly known as "The Brotherly Union of a Number of Children of God Concerning Seven Articles") which expresses the central ideas of the Anabaptists. These include the affirmation that the church consists of adult believers only and things of this world—such as war, violence, the taking of oaths, civic affairs, and worldly amusements—are to be strictly avoided.

The **Dordrecht Confession of Faith** (1632) systematized beliefs in the emerging Mennonite body. These include affirmations of basic Christian beliefs such as the Trinity, the incarnation of Christ, and the redemptive work of Christ. It also defines the nature of the church and counsels respect for the state, but strict separation of church and state. It advocates the use of the ban (excommunication) and shunning (avoidance).

Organization

Even though Mennonite churches essentially share common beliefs, they are not united in a common organization. Many factors account for this. First of all, from the very beginning Anabaptist theology stressed the union of the church through belief rather than church structure. Others factors include separations which resulted from a continuous pattern of migration and ethnic and linguistic differences. Many Mennonite church bodies, however, hold regional and national conferences in order to share ideas and discuss common concerns, but not to define doctrine. Some denominations do not hold conferences.

There are about 566,000 Mennonites in the world. Almost 200,000 members belong to various Mennonite churches in the United States. The largest among these is the Mennonite Church with almost 100,000 members. The Canadian Conference of Mennonite Brethren Churches has almost 30,000 members.

History

As suggested earlier, the history of churches in the Anabaptist tradition is one of persecution and pilgrimage. Because of their radical views, Anabaptists were persecuted by Catholics, Lutherans, Calvinists,

Schleitheim Confession
document of 1527 expressing the central ideas of the Anabaptists

Dordrecht Confession of Faith
a 1632 document systematizing beliefs of Mennonites

and the state. Consequently, members of these traditions frequently migrated to countries more tolerant of religious diversity.

Menno Simons (1496–1561) was a Dutch Catholic priest who began to question the real presence of Christ in the Eucharist. After the execution of an Anabaptist in 1531, Simons was moved to investigate the meaning of infant baptism. Eventually he began to believe that Anabaptist views were correct. In 1536, Menno Simons gave up his Catholic faith and soon thereafter became a leader in the Anabaptist community. His moderation probably helped to bring some stability to the Anabaptist movement. Simons sought to protect the communities from state authorities, guard against militarism, and avoid ideas such as apocalyptic beliefs that the world would end soon. His followers were first called *Menists.* This, of course, led to the name **Mennonites.**

After initial persecution, the Reformed Church in Holland was established, and the Mennonites eventually flourished in that country. They made important contributions to industry and became poets, artists, writers, and patrons of the arts. In time Mennonites migrated across northern Europe into Prussia, Poland, Russia, and the Ukraine. Some Mennonites settled in Switzerland and central Germany. In southern Russia, the Mennonites flourished in an unusual situation. The Russian government granted the Mennonites the right to be self-governing. This continued until the 1870s when the government demanded military service for all. Immigration in large numbers to North America began at this time.

Mennonites generally identify 1683 as the official beginning of the Mennonite Church in North America. In this year, the first permanent settlement of Mennonites was established at Germantown, Pennsylvania. These settlers were from Switzerland and the central regions of Germany. Immigrations from northern Germany, Poland, and Russia continued throughout the eighteenth, nineteenth, and twentieth centuries. Mennonites moved west from Pennsylvania to Ohio, Indiana, Illinois, and on into the prairie states. They also settled in the provinces of Ontario and Manitoba in Canada. Some Mennonites then emigrated from Manitoba to Mexico and Paraguay.

Beliefs and Practices

In general, Mennonites today hold the following Anabaptist beliefs:

1. Authority of the Bible

2. Voluntary membership and commitment to Christ

3. Sent into the world: the ministry of reconciliation and healing

4. Covenanted community life: responsibility for the welfare of the faithful

5. Ethical seriousness: this includes a rejection of violence and military service

6. Mutual aid, which "sets the stage for service to the needy of the world"

—*Source: Pamphlet,* One family of faith, *Council of International Ministries, Elkhart, IN.*

Mennonite
the Anabaptist denomination begun by Menno Simons in Holland in the sixteenth century

Mennonites hold to the baptism of believers. Thus, the church is made up of adults who have come to believe in Christ. Mennonites do not baptize infants or young children.

Since the church consists of believers only, Mennonites also believe that the visible church should mirror the invisible church of the saints. This often leads to strict discipline and high moral standards. Included among these is often a strong admonition to avoid worldly attractions and pleasures. These worldly things may include the use of modern conveniences and education. However, there is a wide of range of interpretation of this belief among Mennonite churches. Their understanding of church leads to a definite separation between church and state. Mennonites have high respect for the state and pray for it, but they do not participate in civic activities, take oaths, or serve in the military. Mennonites are members of the church first, then the state.

The Bible, the highest authority for faith and life, is often interpreted literally. Mennonites do not have sacraments. Baptism and the Lord's Supper (which is celebrated two to four times annually) are called *ordinances*. Some congregations also have the foot washing. Mennonites believe that peace is an integral part of the scriptural message. Thus they have steadfastly maintained pacifism since the time of Menno Simons; they are opposed to capital punishment and refuse to bear arms.

Practices of the Mennonite churches include the election of deacons and bishops by lot. In order to maintain the integrity of the community, Mennonites usually practice the **ban** and **shunning**. The ban is excommunication from the Church. Shunning is avoiding the person until he or she repents and is reconciled with the community. The strictness with which these practices have been carried out has led to controversy and often schism.

ban
excommunication from a Mennonite group

shunning
the practice of deliberately and habitually avoiding a Mennonite member who has seriously veered from the beliefs or practices of the group

The Amish broke with Swiss Mennonites before coming to North America and settling in farm communities.

Commitment to the Earth

The following items are two of ten commitments adopted by the Mennonite Central Committee in 1993.

We will work together to discern what God's reign means for our lifestyles and economic systems. As Christians we are called to be compassionate and just in our economic practices, domestically and internationally, and to critique all economic systems according to their impact on the poor. In our nations military expenditures are used to sustain and shape our economic systems. We seek to resist being trapped by the consumerism so prevalent in our societies, and to live modestly as witnesses against greed and militarism.

We will work to restore the earth which God has created. God made the earth good, and wills the redemption of the whole creation. The threats to the future of the creation posed by nuclear weapons and environmental degradation are the result of human sinfulness. We seek to live in sustainable ways as inhabitants of the earth, and to respect all of God's creation.

Let's Talk about It . . .

1. What problems are addressed in these two commitments?
2. What solutions do you think are suggested?
3. What ideals come through in these statements?

Good Works

The Mennonite Church supports several high schools, three colleges, a hospital, retirement centers and mental health centers. They are generous in helping their neighbors; some reach out to people in their communities, many extend their care to the world. The Mennonite Central Committee, founded in 1920, seeks to unite Mennonite efforts to reach out to the poor of the world. They promote this care for others because they believe that their words should be demonstrated in their actions.

Bear in mind that, while Mennonites share certain core beliefs, the ways they interpret and express those beliefs may vary widely. Some groups support a college education; others accept education only until the eighth grade. Some use modern conveniences; others strictly avoid them. Some are active in government, the sciences, business, medicine (as in Holland today); others seek a rural, agricultural way of life. Some live immersed in the world; others live in isolated, strict communities.

While specific beliefs and practices of Mennonite communities may seem odd and out of sync with modern life, it is wise to take a second look. Mennonites are universally perceived by their neighbors as honest, hard working, God-fearing people. Their rejection of violence and war and their love for peace are indeed important statements in this world. Their concern for world poverty and economic and social justice in the world cannot be faulted. These themes ought to give the thoughtful student of comparative religions reason to pause and ponder.

Reaping the Fruit

English Reformation— Episcopalians

The many independent churches that stem from the Church of England form a worldwide fellowship called the **Anglican Communion**. The word *anglican* comes from the Latin *anglicus*, which means "English." This communion is comprised of twenty-seven provinces or national churches, over 430 dioceses, and seventy million members. While these independent churches range considerably in belief and liturgical practice and are self-governing, they do hold to a common heritage which includes the Thirty-Nine Articles, the *Book of Common Prayer*, and the hierarchical orders of deacon, priest, and bishop. The Episcopal Church in the United States is one of these independent churches. The archbishop of Canterbury, who leads the Church of England, is a source of unity within Anglican Christianity, although in a moral sense rather than a judicial sense. The Church of England is the "Mother Church."

Anglican Communion
the worldwide fellowship of independent churches that stem from the Church of England

Groupings

Anglicanism and the **Episcopal Church** in the United States (members are known as *Episcopalians*) can be divided into three main groupings: the "High Church" or Anglo-Catholic, the "Low Church" or Evangelical, and the broad or Modernist group. The High Church retains many of the beliefs and practices of Catholicism; the Low Church is a mainline Protestant church; and the Modernist group includes elements of each. The reason for such a wide spectrum of belief and practices comes from Anglicanism's historical roots. The turmoil of the sixteenth century in England caused Christians to swing back and forth between Catholicism and extreme forms of Protestantism until they followed the middle course steered by Queen Elizabeth I. Elizabeth was determined to avoid submission to Roman authority and at the same time did not want to dispense with the hierarchical structure of the church. Her leadership, as well as various controversies and schisms throughout the years, led Anglicanism, as a family of churches, to seek a middle path between Protestantism and Catholicism.

In 1867, the archbishop of Canterbury, Archbishop Langley, invited all Anglican bishops to meet at his palace of Lambeth in London. Since then the Lambeth Conference has been called approximately every ten years by the archbishop of Canterbury. The conference deals with internal Anglican church matters, ecumenical activities, and discussion of social and ethical issues. The conference now carries binding authority over the Anglican churches.

Episcopal Church of America
the Anglican Communion Church in the United States

Establishment in North America

Anglicanism came to North America with the first English explorers. The first church was established in 1583 at St. John's in Newfoundland. Another was established on August 13, 1587, in the Roanoke colony in Virginia. Anglicanism was permanently established with the Jamestown colony in 1607. While the Puritans dominated in New England, the Church of England became the established or primary church in the Carolinas, Maryland, and Virginia. From the founding of Anglicanism at Jamestown in 1607, the American branch had no bishop for the next 177 years. This meant that candidates for the priesthood had to travel to England for ordination and that there was no confirmation in the colonies—since confirmation (of new members) was the responsibility of the bishops. Thus Anglicanism in North America languished in these years.

After the Revolutionary War, Anglican Christians confronted the reality of being cut off from the Church of England and broke ties with the mother church in England. The clergy, who had been required to take an oath of loyalty to the king, scattered to Canada or England at the outbreak of the Revolution. With the independence of the colonies, the Church of England in America had serious organizational problems. On September 27, 1785, a general convention convened at Philadelphia. Representatives gave the church the name *Protestant Episcopal Church*. In this case, the word *Protestant* means "non-Catholic," and the word *episcopal* means "governed by bishops." The representatives also began looking for Anglican bishops to ordain bishops for the new church.

A struggle between the Low Church party and the High Church party ensued. Samuel Seabury, representing the High Church, was elected bishop, but was unable to obtain consecration in England since he could not take the oath. He was finally consecrated a bishop in 1784 by bishops from the Episcopal Church in Scotland. Bishops in England considered this schismatic and convinced Parliament to allow them to consecrate bishops without the required oaths of obedience to the monarchy and archbishop of Canterbury. They subsequently consecrated two more American bishops. William White, representing the Low Church, was consecrated in 1787. Seabury and White worked together to form the American Protestant Episcopal Church in 1789. At the general convention that year, the Protestant Episcopal Church had three resident bishops: Samuel Seabury, William White, and Samuel Provost. The convention approved a church constitution, canons (church laws), and a newly-revised version of the *Book of Common Prayer*.

But the Episcopal Church was unable to compete with Methodist and Baptist preachers on the frontier. By 1830, there were only about 30,000 members of the church. In 1873, a group of Low Church members broke away to found the Reformed Episcopal Church. They wanted to move further away from any "Catholic" elements left in Episcopalian-ism. In their revised edition of the *Book of Common Prayer*, they deleted such terms as *priest*, *altar*, *sacrament*, and *holy communion*.

Anglicanism prospered in Canada as a missionary branch of the Church of England. The Constitutional Act of 1791 made specific provision for the support of the Church of England. As a result of the Act, new parishes were established, schools started, and new ministries initiated. This Act facilitated the Church of England's success across Canada. However, governmental support of the Church of England, especially income from lands set aside for the support of the clergy and church, was not without opposition. By 1853, the church lost the revenue from these land reserves. A further side-effect of the years of opposition was that the Protestant churches in Canada united against the Church of England in Canada.

Until this time, each diocese had operated independently, responsible directly to England. In the 1850s, the Church of England in Canada established its own province. By the end of the century, the Anglicans in Canada became an independent member of the growing worldwide Anglican Communion.

The Episcopal Church in the United States has about two and one-half million members. The Reformed Episcopal Church has about 6,500 members. The Anglican Church of Canada has about 848,000 members.

In Praise of the Creator

God of all power, Ruler of the Universe, you are worthy of glory and praise. . . .

At your command all things came to be: the vast expanse of interstellar space, galaxies, suns, the planets in their courses, and this fragile earth, our island home. . . .

From the primal elements you brought forth the human race, and blessed us with memory, reason, and skill. You made us the rulers of creation. But we turned against you, and betrayed your trust; and we turned against one another. . . .

Again and again, you called us to return. Through prophets and sages you revealed your righteous Law. And in the fullness of time you sent your only Son, born of a woman, to fulfill your Law, to open for us the way of freedom and peace.

—The 1979 version of the Book of Common Prayer (The Holy Eucharist: Rite Two, Eucharistic Prayer C).

Let's Talk about It . . .

1. What reasons are given to praise the Creator?
2. Do you think of the human race as rulers of creation?
3. What would make freedom and peace more of a reality today?

Beliefs

Episcopalians believe in the basic Christian doctrines established in the first centuries of the Church. Most would affirm the Apostles' and Nicene creeds as part of their belief system. All would consider the Bible as revealing God's truth, and many would hold to the role of tradition, especially as it reveals God's truth before the Great Schism.

Thirty-Nine Articles

The Thirty-Nine Articles spell out the Anglican position on a variety of subjects, such as the Bible, the creeds, the sacraments, and the episcopate.

Bible

Regarding the Bible, Article VI (Of the Sufficiency of the Holy Scriptures for Salvation) reads: "Holy Scripture containeth all things necessary to salvation; so that whatsoever is not read therein, nor may be approved thereby, is not to be required of any man, that it should be believed as an article of the Faith, or be thought requisite or necessary to salvation." According to this article, Anglican Christians are not required to submit to beliefs not found in scripture or to beliefs prohibited by scripture.

Creeds

Regarding the creeds of the one ancient Christian Church, Article VIII (Of the Three Creeds) reads: "The Three Creeds, Nicene Creed, Athanasius's Creed, and that which is commonly called the *Apostles' Creed* ought thoroughly to be received and believed: for they may be proved by most certain warrants of Holy Scripture." This article says that Anglican Christians assent to beliefs contained in the historic, biblically-based creeds.

Sacraments

Regarding Baptism and the Supper of the Lord, Article XXV (Of the Sacraments) reads: "Sacraments ordained of Christ be not only badges or tokens of Christian men's profession, but rather they be certain sure witnesses, and effectual signs of grace, and God's good will towards us, by which he doth work invisibly in us, and doth not only quicken, but also strengthen and confirm our faith in him. There are two Sacraments ordained of Christ our Lord in the Gospel, that is to say, Baptism and the Supper of the Lord." According to this article, Anglican Christians recognize the sacraments of baptism and Holy Eucharist because they are rooted in the Gospels.

Episcopate

Regarding the episcopate, Article XXXVI (Of the Consecration of Bishops and Ministers) reads: "The Book of Consecration of Archbishops and Bishops, and Ordering of Priests and Deacons . . . doth contain all things necessary to such Consecration and Ordering. . . . And therefore whosoever are consecrated or ordered according to the Rites of that Book . . . we decree all such to be rightly, orderly, and lawfully consecrated and ordered." This article says that Anglican Christians acknowledge apostolic succession (the apostles' practice of ordaining bishops who ordained bishops who ordained bishops and so on).

Let's Talk about It . . .

1. Which of the above beliefs do you find consistent with the other denominations discussed in this chapter?
2. What are the differences?

Worship and Sacraments

The Episcopal Church considers itself to be a sacramental church. The Holy Eucharist is the celebration of the Supper of the Lord. In most Episcopal churches, people gather for the Holy Eucharist every Sunday. In some churches, Holy Eucharist takes place early Sunday morning, and is followed by the principal Sunday service known as Morning Prayer. The Holy Eucharist consists of two parts: (1) Word of God and (2) Holy Communion.

High Church Episcopalian services appear to be very similar to those of Catholicism. Both groups include the liturgy of the word and the liturgy of the Eucharist (as in Rites One and Two above), use vestments, and to some extent have the same seven sacraments. Baptism and Eucharist have the highest importance and are seen by Episcopalians to be ordained by Jesus as the church's chief sacraments. Episcopalians on the Protestant (Low Church) end of the spectrum, on the other hand, reject most things that look Catholic. Their services appear to be very "Protestant."

A bishop is the head of a diocese (area of the church) and looks out for the spiritual, liturgical, and doctrinal aspects of a diocese. He also ordains priests (or ministers as they are sometimes called), appoints them to parishes, and looks after the religious orders or monasteries in his area. The Episcopal tradition in the United States allows for both men and women to be ordained; the first woman was ordained in 1973. Since the Episcopal Church in Canada is more closely connected with the Church of England, there were no ordinations of women until after the Church of England approved such ordinations in 1996.

New Controversies

In the twentieth century, controversies over new issues have caused tensions and further schisms in the Episcopal Church. Included among these issues are questions concerning the nature of morality, the ordination of women (still not the practice in some countries), the use of funds to support political issues, and the church's involvement in social issues. In 1976, the general convention of the church approved extensive revisions in the *Book of Common Prayer*, which caused further tensions with some groups. Disagreement over these issues has led to the formation of several new church bodies, some of whom have moved closer to the Catholic Church in overall theology and practice.

All versions of the *Book of Common Prayer* used throughout the Anglican Communion are based on the 1549 original. The version of the *Book of Common Prayer* used by the Episcopal Church in America first appeared in 1789, and was revised in 1892, 1928, and 1979. The latest *Book of Common Prayer* spells out two distinct ways of performing each ritual. These ways are known as Rite One (traditional) and Rite Two (contemporary). In Rite One, the bishop or priest presiding at the Lord's Supper says: "It is very meet, right, and our bounded duty, that we should at all times, and in all places, give thanks unto thee, O Lord, holy Father, almighty, everlasting God." And in Rite Two, the bishop or priest says: "It is right, and a good and joyful thing, always and everywhere to give thanks to you, Father Almighty, creator of heaven and earth."

Ecumenism

The Anglican Church has been instrumental in the ecumenical movement. In 1988 the Lambeth Conference proposed a fourfold basis for negotiations with other churches. This is known as the Lambeth Quadrilateral.

1. the Scriptures as the rule and ultimate standard of faith

2. the Apostles' and Nicene creeds as sufficient statements of the Christian faith

3. the sacraments of baptism and Eucharist as instituted by Christ

4. the historical episcopacy adapted to varying local needs

Anglicans planned the first World Conference on Faith and Order at Lausanne, Switzerland, in 1927. This movement became part of the World Council of Churches in 1948. Anglicans have fostered extensive dialogues with many Protestant Churches and the Catholic Church.

Small and large gatherings of Christians claim the move toward ecumenism.

A Reformation Christianity Calendar

Winter

The Season of **Advent** is observed during the four weeks before Christmas. The colors violet (or blue) and pink (or white) are associated with Advent.

Christmas, on December 25, celebrates the birth of Jesus, the entrance of the Son of God into human history. White is the liturgical color of Christmas.

On **Epiphany** (January 6), Anglican Christians celebrate the Magi's visit to the child Jesus and Jesus' manifestation to the Gentiles.

Spring

Lent is observed with varying degrees of solemnity. For Anglican Christians the first day of Lent is Ash Wednesday. Violet is the liturgical color of Lent.

Holy Week is the week before Easter Sunday. Many Protestant Christians observe Palm Sunday, Maundy Thursday, and Good Friday. In most Reformation churches, the observance of these days is optional.

Palm Sunday or **Passion Sunday** (Sunday before Easter). This day commemorates Jesus' final entry into Jerusalem. The New Testament passion (story of Jesus' suffering and death) is read, and blessed palm branches are distributed. This day marks the beginning of Holy Week. Red is the color of Palm Sunday.

Holy Thursday or **Maundy Thursday** (Thursday before Easter). On this day, many Christians commemorate the Last Supper (the last occasion on which Jesus shared bread and wine with his disciples). *Maundy* comes from the Latin word *mandatum*, which means "command." In John 13:34, Jesus commanded his disciples to love one another. On this day many Christians demonstrate their love for one another by imitating Jesus washing his disciples' feet.

On **Good Friday** or **Holy Friday** (Friday before Easter), Christians commemorate Jesus' crucifixion (public execution).

Eve of Easter or **Holy Saturday** (Saturday before Easter). On this night, Anglican Christians await Jesus' resurrection. Many churches hold a prayer vigil that culminates in a midnight celebration of the Lord's Supper or Eucharist. The celebration may include the baptism of infants and adults.

On **Easter**, Christians celebrate Jesus' resurrection. Easter marks the victory of life over death, of the powerless over the powerful, of holiness over sinfulness. For Protestant Christians, Easter falls on the first Sunday after the full moon following the vernal equinox (between March 22 and April 25). White is the color associated with Easter.

Ascension Thursday (fortieth day after Easter) commemorates the ascension of Jesus of Nazareth (his return to heaven in glory).

Pentecost (fiftieth day after Easter). On this day, many Christians celebrate the establishment of the one ancient Christian Church. According to the New Testament, the Holy Spirit descended upon Jesus' apostles and disciples, empowering them to build up the church. Red is the color of Pentecost.

Feast of Saint Augustine of Canterbury (May 26). This day is important to Anglican Christians everywhere. According to tradition, Saint Augustine established the Church of Canterbury. Canterbury, England, is the headquarters of the Anglican Communion's spiritual leader, the Archbishop of Canterbury.

On **Trinity Sunday** (first Sunday after Pentecost), Anglican Christians celebrate the mystery of the Trinity. For them, Trinity Sunday is a principal feast.

Summer

Transfiguration (August 6). On this day, Anglican Christians celebrate Jesus' transfiguration.

Holy Cross Day (September 14). On this day, Anglican Christians mark the discovery of the true cross (the cross on which Jesus died).

Autumn

All Saints' Day (November 1). On this day, Anglican Christians rejoice in the blessedness of persons known (saints) and unknown.

World Communion Sunday (observed in October). On this day many Protestant Christians celebrate the significance of sharing bread and wine. This sharing is known as Communion, Eucharist, or the Lord's Supper. This practice serves to unite Christians everywhere.

Reformation Day (October 31). On this day, Lutherans remember Martin Luther. On October 31, 1517, Luther posted his ninety-five theses on the door of the Church of All Saints at Wittenburg, Germany.

Discovering

1. Be able to explain each of the words in the vocabulary list.
2. Name the four phases of the Reformation and briefly explain how each developed historically.
3. Gather with two or three classmates. As a group write a paragraph for each of the four Reformation traditions and clearly state the central ideas of each.
4. Explain why the Anglican Communion churches are theologically diverse.

Exploring

1. Choose one of the Reformation traditions. State its main beliefs. Then state the practices which flow from those beliefs.
2. Develop a chart in which you show the main beliefs and practices of each tradition. On the left side, list each of the traditions. Across the top, write these column headings: *Central Beliefs, Main Texts, Sacraments or Rites, Church Organization,* and *Liturgical Practice.* Fill in the chart.

3. Do you agree with Calvin that belief and action are linked? Why?

4. The Reformed tradition places a great emphasis on study. It believes that study better enables a person to serve God. What is your reaction to this belief?

Integrating

1. In which tradition did you learn the most? What were your new insights?

2. What do you believe about the relationship between God and human beings? In there a great distance between them? How is the relationship brought close?

3. What do you believe about human nature? Are humans "totally depraved"? Flawed but good?

4. Why do you think *sola gratia*, *sola fide*, and *sola scriptura* became the key elements of the Lutheran faith? How do they compare and contrast with your beliefs?

Words to Know

Act of Supremacy

Anabaptist tradition

Anglican Communion

Augsburg Confession

ban

baptism of believers

Book of Common Prayer

Book of Concord

confirmation

Congregationalist

consistory

Dordrecht Confession of Faith

English Reformation

English tradition

Episcopal Church of America

evangelicals

excommunicate

indulgence

inerrancy

John Calvin

John Knox

justification by faith

limited atonement

Lutheranism

Lutheran tradition

Martin Luther

Mennonite

Ninety-five Theses

predestination

Presbyterian

presbytery

Protestantism

Puritans

Reformation

Reformed tradition

Schleitheim Confession

shunning

synod

Ulrich Zwingli

Westminster Confession

Chapter 7

After reading this chapter, you will be able to

- Identify major trends in nineteenth- and twentieth-century religions
- Compare different theological viewpoints
- Begin to assess the influence these religions have had upon life in North America

The 19th- and 20th-Century

CHRISTIAN
SEARCH

Introduction

Six years ago, a group of Quakers began renovating an apartment building in the inner city of Wichita, Kansas. Today, that apartment building is home to the Friends of Jesus, a community of men, women, and children committed to eradicating poverty and prejudice. The community is a stable influence in a low-income neighborhood long plagued by drug trafficking. Members of the community describe their work as "witnessing to Christ's reconciling power among and between the races."

Friends of Jesus focuses much of its attention on Hope Street, an empowerment program for students in elementary and secondary school. Hope Street offers young people an opportunity to escape poverty and violence through education. It does this by teaching them how to make good choices—choices regarding their education, their career, and their life.

The Hope Street high school program consists of three phases: academic instruction, college/vocational study, and leadership. In phase one, students meet two evenings a week to discuss character development, leadership skills, and spiritual growth. African American culture and history also receive attention, as do various issues confronting teens. Completion of high school with a GPA of at least 3.0 is the goal of phase one.

In phase two, students who have completed phase one receive scholarships which enable them to attend college or vocational school. In phase three, students who have completed college or vocational school return to the neighborhood for at least two years. During this time they serve as leaders and role models for young people.

Sara Mitchell is now in phase three and enjoys sharing her experience and knowledge with her peers. Below, she shares some of her thoughts and feelings about Friends of Jesus and the Hope Street high school program.

I am so grateful to the Quaker community and Friends of Jesus for helping me turn my life around. They gave my family a safe place to live and direction for our lives. Thanks to them I have a college education. So do my brothers, Mark and Daniel. Now that I have graduated, I enjoy giving back to Hope Street what they have given me. In my spare time, I tutor a fifteen-year-old high school student, Michael. He wasn't very cooperative until I told him that I also came from a poor family and had a hard time learning to read. I think my story has helped Michael realize that poverty isn't something to be ashamed of. People don't make themselves poor. Poverty presents challenges that can be met. Michael is now getting a "C" in the English class that he was once failing and has hopes of one day being a teacher. I no longer look at my childhood of poverty as a curse, but rather as a blessing. Because of my experiences, I am more sensitive to the needs of others and more in tune with what is really important in life.

Tilling the Soil

Religion in North America at the dawn of the nineteenth century stood poised for diversity in religious belief and practice far beyond the vision of sixteenth-century Reformers. This diversity was primarily fueled by the climate of religious freedom and tolerance fostered in North America, especially in the United States. The emphasis on individualism was also a major contributing factor. Although never totally free from persecution and intolerance, religious people in North America were at least living in a climate where they could feel more free about religious expression than in Europe.

This diversity of expression took new forms. In the last chapter we discussed the four main movements within Protestant Christianity. We saw how these movements distinguished themselves as more or less distinct denominations. This pattern continued in the nineteenth and twentieth centuries. The slavery issue in the United States, for example, was a major cause for the birth of many new denominations. At times a new form crossed denominational lines. For example, fundamentalism and evangelism are movements found in many traditions. Millennialism and Pentecostalism, discussed in this chapter, are also movements found in several denominations.

In this chapter, we will discuss two major denominations in North America which stem from the original denominations of the Reformation: the Baptists and Methodists. The Methodists are also part of a religious movement called Pietism. We will discuss two movements which crossed denominational lines: Millennialism and Pentecostalism; then, Unitarians and Quakers. Finally, we will discuss a denomination which has uniquely American roots: the Church of Jesus Christ of the Latter-Day Saints. Along the way, several denominations will be briefly discussed. All of these church bodies contributed significantly to the religious diversity of North America.

Baptists

Origins

Baptist historians have proposed three perspectives on their origins. One view proposes a *continuity of organization* by claiming that the Baptists descend from the baptizing activity of John the Baptist and the baptism of Jesus. In this case, they would say they predate Protestantism. A second view proposes a *continuity of doctrine* by associating the origins of the Baptists with the Anabaptist movement of the seventeenth century. Proponents of this view are seeking a theological connection with the Anabaptist movement. A third view claims a historical connection with British Puritanism in England. In this case, the history of the Baptists would begin in 1610 in England.

English Baptists
seventeenth-century
forerunners of the
Baptist tradition in the
United States

While **English Baptists** were influenced by Anabaptist thought in the seventeenth century, they were more strongly influenced by Calvinist thought. Two groups of English Separatists (from the Church of England and influenced by Calvinism) escaped persecution in England by going to Holland in 1608. While there, a group led by John Smyth came into contact with Dutch Mennonites and had themselves rebaptized as adults. However, a difference arose concerning the Mennonite belief in free will. While some in the group wanted to maintain the Calvinist belief in predestination, others wanted to adopt the Mennonite belief in free will.

English Baptists fell into two groups: Particular Baptists and General Baptists. Particular Baptists believed that Jesus' crucifixion, resurrection, and ascension saved only particular individuals. General Baptists believed that these events saved everyone. Among these two groups were Separatists and Non-separatists. Separatists disavowed any contact with the Church of England. Non-separatists believed that the local church (parish) could still be purified. Whether Particular, General, Separatist, or Non-separatist, English Baptists were persecuted by both civil and ecclesiastical authorities.

John Smyth returned to England and, in 1611, founded the first Baptist church there. This group believed in **"general atonement,"** which means that they believed that salvation is possible for all people, not just for some—as taught by Calvinist theology. This group became known as *General Baptists*.

A second group became known as *Particular Baptists*. A group of Puritans (people who wanted to "purify" the Church of England of any Catholic elements) began to move toward the Baptist views. They retained the Calvinistic view of predestination, and thus the name "Particular" was attached to them. It was the Particular Baptists who wrote the London Confession, a list of basic beliefs, in 1644.

A third group began to believe that Saturday was the correct day for celebrating the Sabbath. This group started in 1617. Seventh-day Baptists have been a small group of the larger family of Baptists, but they are the oldest continually existing Baptist body. They also influenced the development of the Seventh-day Adventist Church in North America.

The Baptist Tradition in North America

In the thirteen colonies, Baptists prospered under the leadership of Roger Williams (1603–1683). Williams had been banished from the Plymouth and Massachusetts Bay colonies. At Plymouth, he insisted that settlers purchase land directly from Native Americans. And at Massachusetts Bay, he told civil magistrates (state authorities) that they could not meddle in religious matters. In 1636, Williams set out for Narragansett Bay. Once there, he purchased land from the Narragansetts and founded the city of Providence, Rhode Island. He later served as Rhode Island's president. The first Baptist church in North America was founded by Roger Williams in Providence in 1639.

A second congregation was founded by John Clarke in Newport, Rhode Island, in 1648. Baptists moved into the middle colonies in the 1680s. In the years before the Revolutionary War, Baptists prospered more in the middle colonies than in the North or South.

The first Baptist association in North America was formed in 1707 in Philadelphia when five Baptist churches united to form the Philadelphia Baptist Association. The group adopted the 1689 London Confession of the Particular Baptists in 1742, thus associating themselves with Calvinist theology. They supported Baptist missionary endeavors throughout North America.

Baptists came to the South in the late 1600s and established the first church in 1714. A home missionary, Shubal Stearns (1706–1771), was influential in the Baptist tradition as it spread through the southern colonies. These Baptists opposed the Calvinist teaching of predestination and believed in free will. From them came the Free-Will Baptist associations.

During the nineteenth century, Baptist church bodies grew significantly and became successful and well-organized. Institutions of higher education were established, publishing and missionary efforts were begun. In 1814, the missionaries Adoniram Judson and Luther Rice spearheaded the General Missionary Convention of the Baptist Denomination in the United States for Foreign Missions. This was the first time that Baptists came together on a national level. The Triennial Convention was formed in 1824. This group met every three years and concerned itself with missionary efforts. It also became the forum for many other issues.

Baptist Conventions

Since the beginning of a Baptist presence in North America, a wide range of Baptist churches have emerged. Initially these were autonomous and were unrelated to one another. Eventually, however, the need for cooperation among the church bodies became evident.

In the mid-nineteenth century, Baptists clashed over the issue of slavery. Southern Baptists, who believed slavery was supported by scripture, broke away from the Triennial Convention and formed the Southern Baptist Convention in 1845 in Augusta, Georgia. Within a few years, the convention successfully unified Baptist congregations throughout the South. The group has established a Sunday-school board that provides a single set of materials for the Church's educational program. Various other boards, commissions, and programs supported by member churches are under a single budget.

This is the largest Baptist body of churches in the United States, with over 15 million members. Denominational headquarters are in Nashville, Tennessee. The Southern Baptist Convention is organized by congregations. These congregations are related to one another through county, state, and national associations.

Southern Baptists fall squarely within the Reformed theological position. They emphasize a person's right and freedom to interpret scripture on his or her own. From their perspective, God is the Bible's author. A fundamental approach to scripture is strong among many Southern Baptists.

In 1907, anti-slavery Baptists formed the Northern Baptist Convention, which became the American Baptist Churches in the USA in 1973. This convention is the historic counterpart to the Southern Baptist Convention. Members of the denomination have a wide range of theological views. American Baptists helped create the Social Gospel movement. Members of this body of Baptist churches tend to be ecumenically active, liberal, and socially conscious. They have over 1.5 million members. Headquarters are located in Valley Forge, Pennsylvania.

Participation of African Americans in the Baptist Church extends back to the church founded by Roger Williams in Rhode Island. Evangelization among African Americans grew throughout the years until they formed their own conventions. Following the Civil War, African American Baptists created church structures that were responsive to their needs. They formed the Foreign Mission Baptist Convention (1880) and the National Baptist Convention (1895).

The National Baptist Convention of the USA, Inc. is the merger of three African American Baptist Conventions, a merger that took place in 1895. It is the largest African American Baptist denomination in existence. The administration offices to the convention are in Baton Rouge, Louisiana. In time, a board for the purpose of publishing educational materials was added. The convention continues the beliefs and church structure of the white Baptist church, but has been able to develop its own worship style, adapted to African American cultural life. The National Baptist Convention of the USA has about 8.2 million members. Overall, 9 million African Americans in the United States are Baptist.

Most Baptist conventions belong to the National Council of Churches in the USA and to the World Council of Churches.

The Baptist Federation of Canada was the result of a merger of three regional Baptist bodies in 1944. Today the union is known as the Canadian Baptist Federation. The presence of the Baptist Church in Canada can be traced back to the 1760s, especially to the work of Henry Alline who evangelized throughout Nova Scotia. His congregations were initially Congregational, but eventually became Baptist. In time, other Baptist groups from the United States started churches in Canada. After the American Revolution, Baptists moved into Quebec and Ontario. The Baptist Church also grew in western Canada. Canadian Baptists are moderately Calvinist in belief. The Canadian Baptist Federation has about 131,000 members. Total Baptists in Canada are about 355,000. North America is the predominant location of Baptist churches, although they are gaining in importance in other areas of the world.

Baptists have developed many institutions of higher learning. These include colleges and universities as well as a private school system which has an estimated 90,000 students. Baptists have always demonstrated strong missionary zeal. Each of the Conventions promotes missionary efforts in other countries. Baptists are strong advocates of separation of church and state. This is one of the characteristics which distinguishes it (in its origins) from other Protestant bodies.

Participation in the ecumenical movement varies from one Convention to the next. The Southern Baptist Convention does not participate in the ecumenical movement. The American Baptist Churches in the

USA participate actively. In the twentieth century, Baptist organizations heavily debated two issues: the power of national conventions and the interpretation of scripture.

Baptist Beliefs

Baptists are non-creedal. Nevertheless, many attempts have been made over the years to articulate Baptist belief. The Westminster Confession of English Puritans was also a guide for Baptist theology. Baptists wrote their own version of this in 1644, 1677, and 1689. The New Hampshire Confession of Faith was written in 1833 and became an important document for Baptists in the United States. This confession was often adopted and amended by various Baptist Conventions. Of course, the scriptures themselves are the most important religious writings for Baptists. Baptists strongly affirm the divinity of Christ and Christian teachings on his incarnation and redemption of humankind. They believe in the Trinity, the virgin birth, original sin, heaven and hell. Baptists profess that their practices are in conformity with the commands and practices of the New Testament.

Baptist churches are called *free churches*. This means that they are a free association of adult believers. Differences on doctrinal issues and social issues have caused the development of many different Baptist bodies. Yet there are three common characteristics.

The first characteristic is baptism of adults by total immersion; this is considered the authentic and truly scriptural form of baptism. From the Baptist perspective, baptism does not make a person believe, baptism shows that a person believes. Those desiring baptism believe that Jesus is their savior who died for them, and they commit themselves to following him. Church membership is restricted to baptized adults who have turned away from sin. "Baptism of adults" is for persons who have reached the age of knowing right and wrong, which would include adults and children over the age of six or so.

The second characteristic is the observance of two **ordinances**—baptism and the Lord's Supper. Baptists believe that Jesus ordered his followers to observe these practices, hence the word *ordinance*. An ordinance is a rite that commemorates a practice of the early Church.

"We honor God precisely by honoring scripture as his written word."
—James I. Packer

Baptists

members of non-creedal, free (members are not under the authority of a church) churches who practice baptism of adults

ordinance

a rite in Christianity that commemorates a practice of the early Church, for example, the Lord's Supper

Another distinguishing characteristic of Baptists is the doctrine of Church. Baptists believe in the free church. Ideally, no individual Baptist is under the authority of a Church. The only authority for the individual Baptist is the authority of the Bible itself. From the Baptist perspective, a person can interpret the Scriptures on his or her own. A person can also approach God directly—relate to God one on one. This concept is sometimes referred to as *soul liberty*.

From the Baptist perspective, only regenerated persons can become members of the church. To *regenerate* is to "bring into existence again." A regenerated person publicly declares his or her commitment to follow Jesus. From the Baptist perspective, all church members have equal rights and none have special privileges. A majority, not a minority, rules the congregation. Historically, Baptists have placed great emphasis on the autonomy of the local congregation. Over time, a more complicated structure has evolved.

Unlike the Puritans who looked to the state to enforce religious observance, Baptists believe in a strict separation between church and state. This belief can be traced to the influence of Roger Williams, who, in the end, became more a seeker than a traditional church member.

Liturgical practice is determined by the local congregation. Usually it is very simple, with little symbolism or ritual. Baptists remember the death of Jesus by observing the Lord's Supper. Many Baptists observe the Lord's Supper, or Communion, on the last Sunday of the month. They usually do not observe feast days, other than Christmas and Easter.

Responsibility for Creation

Today the human race faces an unprecedented challenge. . . . The explosive growth of population, the depletion of nonrenewable resources, tropical deforestation, the pollution of air, land, and water, waste of precious materials and the general assault on God's creation, springing from greed, arrogance and ignorance present the possibility of irreversible damage to the intricate, natural systems upon which life depends. At the same time nuclear weapons threaten the planet. . . . The danger is real and great. Churches and individual Christians must take responsibility. . . .

—American Baptist Policy Statement on Ecology *(1989), adopted by the General Board of American Baptist Churches.*

Let's Talk about It . . .

1. What do you see as the greatest danger to creation today?
2. What can churches do to counteract some of the problems mentioned in this statement?

The Restoration Tradition

The **Restoration tradition** is the product of the Restoration movement, a nineteenth-century American movement that sought to restore the New Testament basis of the Christian Church. The churches of the Restoration tradition never conceived of themselves as churches. They were part of a broad movement that aimed at purifying all of Christianity.

Several personalities and forces came together to create the Restoration movement. They included the Methodist minister James O'Kelly, the Baptist lay preachers Abner Jones and Elias Smith, the Presbyterian minister Barton W. Stone, and the Scottish Seceder Presbyterian minister Thomas Campbell.

James O'Kelly had separated himself from the Methodist Episcopal Church and founded the Republican Christians. In 1794, they adopted the name *Christians*. Abner Jones and Elias Smith became disenchanted with the Baptist tradition and felt called to unite with other Christians. Their followers merged with O'Kelly's Christians in 1811.

Barton W. Stone and his followers concluded that the Presbyterian form of church government was non-scriptural. They formed the Presbytery of Springfield. Later, they adopted the name *Christian* and pledged themselves to the promotion of Christian unity. Stone's followers joined those of Jones and Smith in 1826.

Thomas Campbell espoused the causes of Christian unity and reliance on the Bible. The phrase "where the Bible speaks, we speak; where it is silent, we are silent" originated with him. Campbell was joined by his son Alexander Campbell. Together they formed the Campbellites. Thomas Campbell's *The Declaration and Address* helped to shape the group by outlining its goals. The Campbells favored baptism by immersion and weekly observance of the Lord's Supper. In 1831, followers of the Campbells and Stone joined together. The Campbells preferred the name *Disciples of Christ* and Stone preferred the name *Christian Church*. It was agreed that both names would be used. The Christian Church, or Disciples of Christ, grew considerably but refused to call itself a denomination. Members believed that any such label would smack of Christian division.

By 1906, a division did occur in the Christian Church (Disciples of Christ) itself. At issue was the organization of missionary societies and the use of instrumental music (the use of musical instruments during worship). In essence, the controversy had to do with *biblical silence*. If the Bible does not mention a particular thing, should it be permitted? Those who disapproved of missionary societies and instrumental music became known as the *Churches of Christ (Noninstrumental)*.

In 1927, a group of Christians, or Disciples of Christ, condemned nonliteral interpretations of the New Testament. They separated themselves from the Christian Church, or Disciples of Christ, and organized the North American Christian Coalition. Member churches refer to themselves as Christian Churches/Churches of Christ (Independent).

Restoration tradition
the product of the Restoration movement, a nineteenth-century American movement which sought to restore the New Testament basis of the Christian Church

The Churches

In sum, there are three churches of the Restoration tradition: the Christian Church, or Disciples of Christ; the Churches of Christ (Noninstrumental); and the Christian Churches/Churches of Christ (Independent). The Christian Church, or Disciples of Christ, looks upon itself as a denomination. Of the three Restoration branches, it has the most central organization.

Christian Church, or Disciples of Christ

In the late nineteenth century, the Disciples of Christ was the fastest growing religious group in the United States. It was also the largest religious group to have originated on American soil. The Christian Church, or Disciples of Christ, has preserved the autonomy of the local congregation. The practices of baptism by immersion and Communion every Sunday have been upheld. Those desiring membership in the Disciples of Christ are required to make a good confession (Matthew 16:16):

> [Jesus] said to them, "But who do you say that I am?" Simon Peter answered, "You are the Messiah, the Son of the living God." And Jesus answered him, "Blessed are you, Simon son of Jonah! For flesh and blood has not revealed this to you, but my Father in heaven."
>
> —Matthew 16:15–17, NRSV.

The General Assembly, which meets every two years, constitutes the church's highest authority. Church headquarters are located in Indianapolis, Indiana.

Churches of Christ (Noninstrumental)

The Churches of Christ (Noninstrumental) observe the basic teachings of Alexander Campbell. These teachings recognize

1. scripture as the sole authority in Christian life
2. Jesus as messiah and savior
3. the order of the ancient Christian Church
4. the authority of Jesus and his apostles (not the authority of Old Testament figures)
5. the need to cooperate closely with other Christians

Members of the Churches of Christ (Noninstrumental) reject the doctrine of the Trinity, as they believe it is non-scriptural. The Church has offices in Cincinnati, Ohio.

Christian Churches/Churches of Christ (Independent)

Above all, these churches believed that only those who had been baptized by immersion could become members. These churches did not immediately separate from the Disciples of Christ. Instead, they trained their own missionaries, who immersed already baptized Christians. The commitment of these churches to baptism by immersion stems from their reading of Acts 2:38:

> Peter said to them, "Repent, and be baptized every one of you in the name of Jesus Christ so that your sins may be forgiven; and you will receive the gift of the Holy Spirit (NRSV).

Around 1960, churches affiliated with the North American Christian Coalition began withdrawing their names from the Year Book of the Disciples of Christ. The church's headquarters are located in Austin, Texas.

Beliefs and Practices

Note: In this section, the term *Disciple* refers to someone who belongs to a church of the Restoration tradition.

The beliefs and practices of the Disciples reflect the religious background of their founders and their desire to be like the New Testament Church. One Disciple described the diversity of the church's beliefs and practices in these words:

> We baptize by immersion, so we look like Baptists. We have Communion every Sunday, so we look a bit like Roman Catholics. We stress the ministry of the laity, so we look a little like Quakers. Our congregations call their pastors rather than accepting assigned ministers, so in that respect we look like Presbyterians. We rely heavily on preaching and teaching, so we look somewhat like Methodists. We have congregational government, so we look a lot like the United Church of Christ.

"No creed but Christ." This popular slogan is heard throughout the Restoration tradition. Disciples have long believed that creeds are a source of division. In light of this conviction, they do not require a new member to recite a creed, or summary of beliefs and practices. Instead, they ask the question, "Do you believe that Jesus is the Christ, the Son of the living God, and do you accept him as your personal savior?" The person desiring membership responds, "I do."

A distinguishing mark of the entire Restoration tradition is the desire to promote Christian unity. Disciples look upon their quest for unity as "a sign of God's unity for the human community." Thomas Campbell reflected on the importance of unity. He wrote: "The church of Christ upon earth is essentially, intentionally, and constitutionally one."

In imitation of Jesus' baptism, the Disciples practice baptism by immersion. From their perspective, baptism binds a person more closely to God and to other people. Unlike many Protestant Christians, the Disciples observe Communion every week. When Disciples gather for the Lord's Supper, they recall Jesus' life, death, and resurrection. Above all, they celebrate the continuing presence of Jesus in their midst.

The Quality of Life

The quality of human life is not dependent upon increasing consumption of material goods but is based on those things which have permanence; the care of the spirit, relationships of justice and equity, creativity, cultural and artistic expression, reverence for all God's creation, and celebration of the gift of being.

—Resolution for Sustainable Community *(1993), adopted by the* General Assembly of the Christian Church, or Disciples of Christ.

Let's Talk about It . . .

1. What do you mean when you talk about the quality of life?
2. Does the above statement agree with your own understanding of quality of life? Explain.
3. What would improve the quality of life?

Planting the Seed

Millennialism

millennialism

apocalypticism; the belief that Christ will soon bring this evil world to an end and replace it with a new order of happiness and goodness—a thousand-year reign (millennium) of Christ

Millennialism, or apocalypticism, is a theme in Christianity which recurs through the course of history. It is a theme which also thread its way through religious thought in the United States during the nineteenth and twentieth centuries. In fact, sometimes events, such as the Civil War or the Gulf War, have been interpreted from a millennialistic perspective.

Millennialism is the belief that Christ will soon bring this evil world to an end and replace it with a new order of happiness and goodness. This will be a thousand-year reign (millennium) of Christ. Time is clearly perceived as linear, the world is evil, God is on the side of those who are on God's side, and people should prepare for the end. The belief that there will be a second coming of Christ is a mainline Christian belief. Millennialism is a perfect example of highlighting an aspect of Christian belief, emphasizing its importance, and fashioning a religious system around it. It is also a classic example of how actions flow from belief as discussed in chapter one.

Apocalyptic belief has its roots in Jewish apocalyptic writings, especially the Book of Daniel. This book tells the story of Daniel and his companions who are faithful to God while under domination of a foreign power. The book also includes visions of the future. It is this kind of writing that became a model for later Christian apocalyptic movements of the first two centuries C.E.

The belief that Christ would return soon was a major issue in early Christianity. The first Christians, even Paul in his early writing, spoke of Christ returning soon, perhaps within their own lifetimes. When Christ's return did not seem imminent and the first Christian generation began to die, Christians had to reassess their thinking and come to terms with the issue. The Book of Revelation became the point of focus for settling the issue. The Book of Revelation is filled with visions written in a style very similar to the Book of Daniel. Was this book to be considered part of the New Testament? Eventually it was accepted, largely through the influence of mainline theologians. Still it was not clear how literal millennialism (the thousand-year reign of Christ) could be reconciled with his apparent delay and the fact that the book was becoming accepted as part of scripture. The question was resolved with St. Augustine who argued that the Church may not be living at the end times, but that God is still with the Church, helping it to combat evil.

Millennialism appeared several times throughout European Christian history. In the seventh century, for example, Syrian Christians under Moslem rule expected a battle with the Anti-Christ, followed by the last judgment. The centuries preceding the Reformation saw several millennial movements, some of which were connected with the Crusades. During the Reformation era, the milliennialist Thomas Muntzer believed that the Turks were the Anti-Christ and that Christians should rise up to overthrow them. Millennialism is represented in North America by the group of Christian churches called the *Adventist churches*.

Adventist Churches

The churches of the Advent tradition take their name from the word *advent*, which means "coming." **Adventist** churches are those churches who believe that the second coming of Christ is imminent. Christ will return soon and establish his thousand-year reign. Members of Adventist churches live in a way which prepares for this imminent coming. There is also an urgency to tell others of these coming events. As explained above, millennialism is an idea which recurs throughout Christian history. In this case, however, its presence in North America is not a European transplant, but has its roots in the United States in the nineteenth century.

Millennialism in North America stems from William Miller, a Baptist layman who lived in New York after the War of 1812. Miller's early thinking centered on the use of reason over faith in religion. After studying the Bible, he became more convinced of its teachings. He also

Adventist
those churches who believe that the second coming of Christ is imminent

began to believe that Jesus would soon return—thus that he was living toward the endtime of the world—and that he must tell others about this approaching second coming. Gradually his preaching attracted interest. In 1833, the Baptist Church licensed him to preach, and for the next ten years Miller spread his message of the imminent return of Christ. Members of many different Protestant congregations were among his followers.

In 1836 Miller published his first book: *Evidences from Scripture and History of the Second Coming of Christ about the Year 1843: Exhibited in a Course of Lectures*. In this book, Miller revealed his calculations concerning the endtimes. Working with the Book of Daniel and the Book of Revelation, Miller came to the conclusion that the second coming of Christ would occur in about the year 1843. On January 1st of that year, he committed himself—the second coming would happen sometime between March 21, 1843, and March 21, 1844.

Miller's ideas were promoted by Joshua Himes, a minister from Boston who invited Miller to preach there in 1839. Himes had great organizational talent, which he applied to the growing movement. A conference to discuss the second coming was held on October 13, 1840. The movement continued to attract followers from many denominations, all of whom waited anxiously for March 21, 1843. When Christ did not return on March 21, excitement only grew. Opposition to the Adventist movement from other denominations also increased. This led Charles Fitch to plead that all Adventists should "come out" of their parent churches and form new ones. By March 21, 1844, Miller had over 50,000 followers in the East and Midwest. When Christ did not return on this date, Miller was bitterly disappointed. In May he wrote: "I confess my error and acknowledge my disappointment."

Nevertheless, the enthusiasm of the movement did not wane. Samuel S. Snow recalculated the timing and set October 22, 1844 as the date of the second coming. On this date, Adventists gathered to witness Christ's coming. The date came and went. This day is known as the *Great Disappointment*. Chaos ensued. Adventists now had to reassess their beliefs. Some set new dates for Christ's coming. A few went back to their parent churches. Many began to interpret the events of 1843/44 in a spiritual way. From this time on, Miller forbade the practice of giving precise dates for the second coming.

Two representative groups of millennialism in North America are the Jehovah's Witnesses and the Adventists. Jehovah's Witnesses number almost one million in the United States and 100,000 in Canada. Adventist churches in the United States number about 800,000. Of these, the Seventh-day Adventist Church is the largest, with 760,000 members. There are about 43,000 Seventh-day Adventists in Canada.

Jehovah's Witnesses

Jehovah's Witnesses began with a Bible study group in Allegheny City, Pennsylvania, in the 1870s. In 1879, Charles Taze Russell (1852–1916), an Adventist and a member of the group, published a magazine, *Zion's Watch and Herald of Christ's Presence*, the beginning of an extensive publishing program under the *Watchtower* name. In the early twentieth century, Russell's followers joined those of Joseph Franklin Rutherford (1869–1942) and adopted the name *Jehovah's Witnesses*. Congregations grew along with the printed sermons, Bible tracts, and books. In 1912, an audiovisual program went into production; it was eventually seen by up to 35,000 people per day. Radio programs were added in the 1920s and 1930s. The group's headquarters are in Brooklyn, New York.

Most people are familiar with Jehovah's Witnesses because of their door-to-door visits. During these visits, they attempt to witness to the good news of Jesus and share their literature on scripture and other related topics. Frequently, entire families engage in this witnessing, a result of the group's emphasis on family life. At the Witnesses' Kingdom Halls, there are weekly meetings on biblical topics; these meetings are open to the public.

Jehovah's Witnesses refer to God as *Jehovah*. They do not believe in the Trinity, and look upon Jesus as the first of Jehovah's creations. In their view, scripture passages that point to the Trinity are corruptions of the original. Their translation of the Bible, the New World translation, has corrected all such mistranslations.

While the human soul is believed to no longer exist at death, Jehovah's Witnesses believe that there is hope in resurrection. In their understanding, 1914 marked a significant shift in the history of the world and they point to the many terrible events of the twentieth century as evidence. They believe that the world is now in a time of transition between human rule and the reign of Christ. The wicked will be eternally destroyed, but the elect, faithful Jehovah's Witnesses, will be saved. They believe that Jesus died to save this remnant. In the future, the kingdom of God will exist on earth, and the Witnesses will live on earth forever as princes. While some people will go to heaven, most of the resurrected will be part of this kingdom of God on earth. Those in heaven, the 144,000 "spirit-anointed Christians," will rule with Jehovah.

Jehovah's Witnesses

an Adventist group that believes the world is at present in transition between human rule and the reign of Christ

The worship space of Jehovah's Witnesses is called Kingdom Hall.

Jehovah's Witnesses do not take part in interfaith endeavors, and some of their literature is very critical of many other churches. Witnesses believe that Christians should stay separate from the world. They do not participate in wars, which they associate with the "things of this world."

There is a natural respect for the earth in the teachings of Jehovah's Witnesses. In their literature, these two scripture quotes are used to support the emphasis:

"The nations raged,
but your wrath has come,
and the time for judging the dead,
for rewarding your servants, the prophets
and saints and all who fear your name,
both small and great,
and for destroying those who destroy the earth."

—*Revelation 11:18, NRSV.*

For thus says the LORD,
who created the heavens
(he is God!),
who formed the earth and made it
(he established it;
he did not create it a chaos,
he formed it to be inhabited!):
I am the LORD, and there is no other.

—*Isaiah 45:18, NRSV.*

Seventh-day Adventists

It was a group of New England Millerites who were to form the nucleus of the Seventh-day Adventist Church. This group included Joseph Bates, Hiram Edson, James White and his wife, Ellen G. White, and they met in Washington, New Hampshire. In time, Ellen White became the undisputed leader of the new church. She is considered to be a prophetess by **Seventh-day Adventists** and often had visions, during which she dictated many of her twenty books and three thousand articles. She also confirmed an idea advanced by Hiram Edson concerning the interpretation of the events of 1843–44. Edson proposed that Miller had been right in the date, but wrong in the location. In 1843–44 Christ did not come to cleanse the earthly sanctuary, but to cleanse the heavenly sanctuary as described in Hebrews 8:1–2. When this work is finished, Christ will then come to earth.

In 1861, the group adopted the name *Seventh-day Adventist*. Many of the church's beliefs and practices have a Baptist character because of William Miller's Baptist background. Due to the influence of Seventh-day Baptists, the church observes the Jewish Sabbath (Saturday—the seventh day of the week). The General Conference and its Executive Committee constitute the Church's highest authority. Church headquarters are located in Washington, DC.

Seventh-day Adventists

a strict Adventist group which worships on Saturday and holds many beliefs similar to Baptists

Beliefs

Seventh-day Adventists are non-creedal, although they have published several statements detailing their beliefs in order to assist their missionaries and explain their beliefs to others. Generally, Adventist churches reflect the main beliefs of the parent church, with some modifications to allow for an emphasis on millennialism. Since Miller was a Baptist, the Seventh-day Adventist Church has many beliefs in common with Baptists. Currently, Seventh-day Adventists list twenty-seven fundamental beliefs.

Seventh-day Adventists believe the scriptures, both the Old and New Testaments, are the revealed word of God and contain all that is necessary for salvation. They accept the Reformation principle that the Bible alone is its own interpreter and the basis of all doctrines. Also very important, but not having the same status as scripture, are the writings and prophecies of Ellen G. White. Her work is considered a guide for understanding scripture. White wrote more than eighty books, two hundred tracts and pamphlets, and 4,600 periodical articles. Her other writings total up to 60,000 pages.

Seventh-day Adventists believe human beings are created in the image of God; they reject predestination, believe in the incarnation and the Trinity. An important difference between Adventist belief and mainline Christian belief is that Adventists believe a human being becomes a living soul—they do not receive a soul. Adventists see human beings as an organic unity of body, mind, and spirit.

One distinctive belief and practice is the observance of the day of rest on Saturday, rather than on Sunday. This practice came to the group from a former member of the Seventh-day Baptist Church. Mrs. White confirmed the practice through her own study of the Bible and later through a vision. Since churches of the Adventist tradition interpret the Old Testament story of creation literally, they believe that God created the world over a period of six days and rested on the seventh day. They point out that the commandment pertaining to the Sabbath begins with the word *remember*. Therefore, they remember that God rested on the seventh day; on the seventh day, they also rest.

Another belief of Seventh-day Adventists concerns the second coming. In 1844, they believe, Christ entered into the heavenly sanctuary and is now involved in the work of cleansing that sanctuary. Satan and Christ are locked in a struggle, called the *Great Controversy*. All of the universe, including humanity, is part of this struggle. This world is the arena of this universal conflict; distress among nations and natural disasters are signs of this struggle. "To assist His people in this controversy, Christ sends the Holy Spirit and the loyal angels to guide, protect, and sustain them in the way of salvation."

Soon Christ will complete this work and will return to earth for the second coming and to judge all people. The righteous will go to heaven with him to reign for a thousand years. During the thousand-year reign, the earth will be desolate and Satan will be as in prison on the earth.

The Great Controversy will ultimately be resolved after the thousand-year reign, when the wicked will be raised and, along with Satan, destroyed. Since human beings are souls, the body turns to dust at death, but the soul returns to God. At the resurrection of the dead, the body and soul will be reunited. Christ will establish a new life on earth where all things, animate and inanimate, will declare that God is love.

Adventist leaders no longer follow the once widespread practice of providing an exact date for Jesus' return.

God's Gift

God gave our first parents the food . . . that the race should eat. It was contrary to [God's] plan to have the life of any creature taken. There was to be no death in Eden. The fruit of the trees in the garden was the food [humankind's] wants required.

—Ellen G. White, Testimonies for the Church *(1864).*

Let's Talk about It . . .

1. Why might it be contrary to God's plan to take any creature's life?
2. If this were your belief, how would your life differ from that of people of other Christian groups?

Practices

The Seventh-day Adventist Church considers itself the holy remnant of God's people. All members of the Church are expected to participate in the mission of the Church and to use their talents for the good of others. Seventh-day Adventists teach stewardship over body, abilities, time, material possessions, and the earth. This includes abstinence from tobacco, alcohol, and the irresponsible use of harmful drugs and narcotics. They advocate a healthful style of living, including vegetarianism, exercise, and good nutritious food. Members of the Church are to monitor their use of TV, movies, radio, and videos. Gambling, card playing, theater going, and dancing are to be avoided.

Seventh-day Adventists believe that Jesus instituted the ordinances of baptism by immersion, the Lord's Supper, and footwashing. Baptism is by immersion for adults or young people who are old enough to understand its meaning and accept the teachings of the Church. The Lord's Supper is a special memorial of Jesus' death; unleavened bread and grape juice are used. The Lord's Supper is preceded by a footwashing service, which represents Jesus' spiritual cleansing of his followers. This is followed by preaching and a communion service. The Lord's Supper and footwashing are observed every three months.

Since Seventh-day Adventists believe that they are the remnant of God's church, they do not participate in the ecumenical movement. However, they do not believe that they are the only Christians. They recognize that Christians may also be in the various other Protestant Churches and in the Catholic Church.

Worldwide Church of God

The Worldwide Church of God grew out of the Church of God, a small Adventist church with headquarters in Stanberry, Missouri. Shortly after the Great Depression, the church's Oregon Conference became independent. In 1931, the conference ordained Herbert W. Armstrong (1892–1986). A short time later, Armstrong became an influential leader in the church. Three years later, he launched the Radio Church of God. This enterprise included the radio broadcast, *The World Tomorrow*, and the periodical, *The Plain Truth*. A television broadcast was added in 1960. In 1968, the name *Worldwide Church of God* was adopted. Headquarters are in Pasadena, California. A pastor general presides over the church.

Members of the Worldwide Church of God observe the Jewish festivals spelled out in scripture. The church has reinterpreted the festivals so that they have Christian significance. From their perspective, these festivals "serve as memorials of God's great acts of salvation in history and as annual celebrations of God's power, love, and saving grace in Jesus Christ."

Taking Root

Methodism

The Methodist tradition began as a spiritual practice, with the aim of deepening a person's relationship with God and other people. Methodism was influenced by Pietism through the Moravians in England. The denomination began with John Wesley (1703–1791), the son of an Anglican clergyman. While attending Oxford, Wesley started the Holy Club, partially in response to the lax morals of fellow students. Club members studied scripture and developed strict daily schedules; it is believed that because of this methodical discipline, they became known as the **Methodists**.

In 1735, after graduating from Oxford and being ordained as Anglican priests, John Wesley and his brother Charles (1707–1788) left England for the colony of Georgia in order to serve as missionaries there. On their voyage to North America, John met a group of Moravians and was very impressed with their piety. While in America, the Wesleys had a very frustrating experience. The Native Americans with whom they had been asked to work were not interested in the Wesleys' religion. John, while trying to convert them, did not feel converted himself.

Believing that they had failed, John and Charles Wesley returned to England. John joined a Moravian society and, on May 24, 1738, had a conversion experience, a turning point in his life. John recalled this moment. A member of the Moravian society was reading from Luther's preface to the Romans. John writes: "About a quarter before nine, while he was describing the change which God works in the heart through faith in Christ, I felt my heart strangely warm. I felt I did trust in Christ; Christ alone, for salvation; and an assurance was given me, that he had taken away my sins, even mine, and saved me from the law of sin and death." John began preaching outdoors, thus launching the Methodist revival.

Methodist Church
Protestant denomination which grew out of the methodical Bible-based discipline developed by John Wesley

Shortly after this, Wesley broke with the Moravians and started the United Societies. The United Societies were a group of Anglicans concerned about the application of their faith to life. They remained within the Church of England. In 1753, Wesley defined a typical *practitioner* as "one that lives according to the method laid down in the Bible." In time, practitioners were generally referred to as *Methodists*. Methodism in England appealed to many people who were unchurched and to disaffected Anglicans.

The Return to North America

Once again, the Wesleys became interested in ministering in the United States, as America had experienced a shortage of Anglican clergy since the Revolutionary War. Methodist preachers and laymen came to the American colonies in the 1760s. The first society was established at Leesburg, Virginia, in 1766. Methodism spread throughout the middle colonies. Because of their strong ties with the Church of England, their loyalties to the cause of the revolution were suspect. After the war, John Wesley sent Thomas Coke (1747–1814), along with two other newly ordained presbyters, to the United States to set up Methodism. Coke in turn ordained Francis Asbury (1745–1816), who had previously been a lay preacher.

John Wesley

By 1784 Asbury was the undisputed leader of Methodism in the United States. In that year, the Anglican bishop of London refused to ordain a Methodist to the presbyterate (priesthood). Under these circumstances, John Wesley and other presbyters began ordaining men for service in America. Asbury was ordained bishop. A general conference was held at Christmas of 1784, and the Methodist Episcopal Church was founded.

Methodism came to Canada with the arrival of Cornish immigrants to Nova Scotia around 1775. William Black Jr. emerged as their leader. After the American Revolution, Black attended the Christmas Conference of 1784 and sought the assistance of Methodists in the United States. This assistance continued for a number of years. Eventually, however, Black looked to Methodists in England for support. For some time, Methodists ministered to African Americans who had been transported to Nova Scotia by the British after the Revolution.

A second beginning for Methodism in Canada occurred in Upper Canada in the 1780s and 1790s. The first Methodist chapel was built there, and an Anglican family, the Ryersons, was influential in supporting the movement. Egerton Ryerson was especially known as an educator. Unfortunately, relations were strained between Methodists in Canada who were British subjects and the revolutionary Methodists in the United States. After the War of 1812, the two groups separated.

Circuits and Other Innovations

Some of Wesley's innovations in the frontier of the developing United States included field preaching, lay preachers, and discipline in the way one lived. Traveling preachers, known as **circuit riders**, carried the tenets of Methodism across the continent. Circuit riders traveled to the various congregations within their region and thus were able to minister to the people's needs in a timely fashion. These Methodist ministers remained at one church for a short period of time (a few years). During this time, they traveled from meeting place to meeting place to preach. Over the course of three or four weeks, they would make up to twenty or thirty stops. These stops comprised their circuit.

circuit riders
traveling Methodist preachers who carried the tenets of the religion through many parts of the developing United States

The revival was an open-air meeting where people celebrated God's love and promise of salvation. Charles Wesley wrote more than six thousand hymns for the revivals; many of these hymns remain in use. A period of dramatic growth began at this time and lasted into the twentieth century.

The Use and Abuse of Creation

All creation is the Lord's and we are responsible for the ways in which we use and abuse it. Water, air, soil, minerals, energy resources, plants, animal life, and space are to be valued and conserved because they are God's creation and not solely because they are useful to human beings. Therefore, we repent of our devastation of the physical and nonhuman world. Further, we recognize the responsibility of the church toward lifestyle and systemic changes in society that will promote a more ecologically just world and a better quality of life for all creation. . . .

We support regulations that protect the life and health of animals, including those ensuring the humane treatment of pets and other domestic animals, animals used in research, and the painless slaughtering of meat animals, fish, and fowl. Furthermore, we encourage the preservation of animal species now threatened with extinction. We also recognize the necessity of the use of animals in medical and cosmetic research; however, we reject the abuse of the same.

—*General Conference of The United Methodist Church*, Social Principles: The United Methodist Church, 1992. ¶ 70, I, I.C.

Let's Talk about It . . .

1. What does it mean to repent of our devastation of the physical and nonhuman world?
2. What lifestyle changes could you make?
3. What is your reaction to medical and cosmetic research which uses animals?
4. What is your reaction to a church taking a stand on this research issue?

Organization of Methodism

Methodists are those bodies of Christian churches who adhere to the Wesleyan tradition. They reacted against a certain rigidity and emptiness they perceived in the Anglican Church and emphasized more the heartfelt experience of faith and its application to daily life. Theologically they follow the Reformed tradition, but reject predestination. They have been very active socially. Historically their first appeal and missionary activity was to members of the poor and lower class of society; in time this appeal spread to the middle class.

United Methodist Church

Since arriving in the North America, the Methodist Church has suffered many schisms. These schisms have generally revolved around two issues. One issue was that of church governance: to be episcopal or non-episcopal. (Methodists in England elected to be non-episcopal.) The second issue was slavery, which split the Methodist Episcopal Church in 1844.

At the same time, the history of Methodism in North America is a history of mergers. In 1939, the northern and southern Methodists united to form the Methodist Church of the United States. In 1946, another merger occurred between the United Brethren and the Evangelical Church. And in 1968, the Methodist Church merged with the Evangelical United Brethren to form the United Methodist Church. Members of the church have actively promoted the cause of Methodist unity and have been strong advocates of ecumenism (Christian Unity Movement). The General Conference, the Church's highest authority, meets every four years. Church offices are located in Dayton, Ohio. The United Methodist Church belongs to the National Council of Churches of Christ in the USA and to the World Council of Churches.

African Methodist Episcopal Church

In the late eighteenth century, the issue of racial equality brought division to the Methodist Episcopal Church. In 1787, a group of African American Methodists were turned away at St. George Methodist Episcopal Church in Philadelphia. Under the leadership of Richard Allen (1760–1831), the group formed the African Methodist Episcopal Church, which first met in an old blacksmith shop. The church, known as Bethel Church, provided a place where African American Methodists could worship without fear of harassment.

Church membership grew after the U.S. Civil War, and a publishing house began. AME Book Concern was the first African American-owned press in the United States. The African Methodist Episcopal Church is the largest of the African American Methodist churches. An international General Conference is the Church's highest authority; it meets every four years. Church headquarters are in Nashville, Tennessee. The Church belongs to the National Council of Churches of Christ in the USA and to the World Council of Churches.

Nine years after the beginnings of the African Methodist Episcopal Church, a similar discriminatory incident occurred at John Street Methodist Episcopal Church in New York. When the church's African American members were barred from full participation, they formed the African Methodist Episcopal Zion Church.

Structure

The Methodist conference grew out of the meetings between John Wesley and his assistants (lay preachers). In the United States, the conference is the basic structure of the Methodist organization on four levels.

The local church conference deals with the business affairs of the local congregation. The district conference serves primarily as a means of communication between the local church conferences and the annual conference. The annual conference is chaired by the bishop whose job it is to assign ministers to their parishes. The general conference is composed of representatives from all of the annual conferences. This conference meets every four years and is the church's highest legislative body. Participants discuss national and international issues confronting Methodists. Jurisdictional conferences (regional conferences) also meet every four years. Their purpose is to elect the church's bishops.

The Methodist Church is highly organized. This trait enabled the church to have a significant influence upon the development of religion in North America, even though it arrived relatively late. Because of this organization, Methodist ministers were able to move quickly with the advancing frontier and settlers. The unusual circuit riders were part of this advance. Another factor contributing to the success of Methodism was that their less-harsh theology was attractive to many of the more independent-minded settlers.

The number of Methodists is second only to Baptists among Protestant Christians. In the United States, there are approximately thirteen and one-half million. The largest group is the United Methodist Church, numbering about nine million. There are about 12,000 Methodists in Canada. Worldwide Methodists number about twenty-five million.

Beliefs

Only very late in Wesley's life did doctrinal issues become important. The development of Methodism in North America caused Wesley to formulate a set of doctrinal standards. In his instruction to ministers in the Americas, Wesley directed them to his four-volume *Sermons*, his *Notes on the New Testament*, and his *Large Minutes of the Conference*.

Wesley also abridged Anglicanism's Thirty-Nine articles to twenty-four articles. Methodists in the United States added a twenty-fifth article stating the independence of the United States, thus the *Twenty-Five Articles of Religion*. The *Articles* state basic Christian doctrines; theologically they reflect a Reformed tradition. However, Wesley rejected Calvinist predestination and emphasized the witness of the spirit and Christian perfection. These constitute a common core of belief for almost all Methodists today. The *Heidelberg Catechism* has also had a significant effect on Methodism.

Practical divinity

The term **practical divinity** was the central theme of John Wesley's teaching. Above all, Wesley wants people to become holy, which would spread holiness. He taught people to put faith and love into practice. Wesley explained that God wants people to be happy and holy.

practical divinity
John Wesley's teaching that God wants people to be happy and holy; thus, faith and love must be put into practice

Grace

A distinctive doctrine of Methodism is the doctrine of **sanctification**. This doctrine says that one can experience a blessing after justification which frees the person from all sinful desires. This takes one to a higher level than simple justification by faith. After justification, the person grows in grace; the second blessing ratifies that perfection has taken place. This doctrine within Methodism can be credited as an impetus behind the Great Awakening and revivalism in the United States. It also led to the Holiness movement.

The Methodist tradition teaches that **grace** pervades life. Methodists define grace as "the undeserved, unmerited, and loving action of God in human existence through the ever-present Holy Spirit." They distinguish among prevenient grace, justifying grace, and sanctifying grace.

- *Prevenient grace* offers people the first awareness of having done wrong and prompts them to please God.
- *Justifying grace* leads people away from sin and toward God. It reconciles people with God and leads to their regeneration.
- *Sanctifying grace* leads people to Christian perfection. John Wesley described Christian perfection as "a heart habitually filled with the love of God and neighbor and as having the mind of Christ and walking as he walked."

Grace helps to preserve the unity of believing and doing. According to Wesley, a person's faith shows itself in three ways:

1. "Doing no harm, by avoiding evil of every kind"
2. "Doing good of every possible sort"
3. "Attending upon all the ordinances of God"

The ordinances of God include worship of God, participation in the Lord's Supper, family and private prayer, reading and discussion of scripture, the practice of turning to scripture for guidance, and fast and abstinence.

Other beliefs of Methodists follow mainline Christian teachings. They accept two sacraments: baptism and holy communion. Baptism is for infants and adults; its form varies, but usually it is performed by sprinkling. At baptism, a person is recreated and transformed. Baptism initiates and incorporates people into the community of faith.

Methodists do not have a uniform liturgical practice, so the style of worship varies considerably from congregation to congregation. Holy communion is in the form of bread and grape juice and may be celebrated anywhere from quarterly to weekly. The Lord's Supper is considered a memorial "after a heavenly and spiritual manner." Holy communion nourishes people so that they can be faithful disciples.

While few Methodists are fundamentalists, they traditionally have had a strict moral code. This has included total abstinence from alcohol, tobacco, and gambling. Other prohibitions in earlier years included dancing, card playing, and the theater; today these are all tolerated in moderation.

sanctification

the doctrine that one can experience a blessing after justification which frees the person from all sinful desires

grace

the undeserved, unmerited, and loving action of God in human existence through the ever-present Holy Spirit

Methodist churches have a distinguished record in social justice activities. Methodists have over seventy colleges and universities and over seventy hospitals in the United States. Goodwill Industries was started by Methodists in 1907 to help people with disabilities to help themselves by repairing and selling old furniture and clothes. Worldwide missionary activity of the Methodist Church is directed by the Board of Global Ministries, and missionary work is carried on in most countries. Methodists have gained international acclaim for their ability to respond to emergencies and natural disasters with relief assistance.

The Methodist Church has been heavily involved in the ecumenical movement. The United Methodist Church is a member of both the National Council of Churches and the World Council of Churches.

Methodist Social Creed

We believe in God, Creator of the world, and in Jesus Christ the Redeemer of creation. We believe in the Holy Spirit, through whom we acknowledge God's gifts, and we repent of our sin in misusing these gifts to idolatrous ends.

We affirm the natural world as God's handiwork and dedicate ourselves to its preservation, enhancement, and faithful use by humankind.

We joyfully receive, for ourselves and others, the blessings of community, sexuality, marriage, and the family.

We commit ourselves to the rights of men, women, children, youth, young adults, the aging, and those with handicapping conditions; to improvement of the quality of life; and to the rights and dignity of racial, ethnic, and religious minorities.

We believe in the right and duty of persons to work for the glory of God and for the good of themselves and others, and in the protection of their welfare in so doing; in the rights to property as a trust from God, collective bargaining, and responsible consumption; and in the elimination of economic and social distress.

We dedicate ourselves to peace throughout the world, to the rule of justice and law among nations, and to individual freedom for all people of the world.

We believe in the present and future triumph of God's Word in human affairs, and gladly accept our commission to manifest the life of the gospel in the world. Amen.

—Social Principles: The United Methodist Church, *General Conference of The United Methodist Church, 1992, ¶ 76.*

Let's Talk about It . . .

1. What beliefs in this statement surprised you?

2. What beliefs in the statement would you like to discuss in more detail?

Growing and Blooming

The Unitarian Tradition

In the United States, the **Unitarian tradition** exists in the form of the Unitarian Universalist Association. The association represents the coming together of two Reformation movements.

The Unitarian movement took its name from the Latin *unitas*, which means "one." Unitarians asserted that God is one person, not three. Unitarianism can be understood as a reaction against Trinitarianism. Trinitarian comes from the Latin *trinitas*, which means "three." Classical Unitarians rejected the ancient Christian doctrine of the Trinity. (Most Christians are Trinitarians, asserting that the one God is three persons.)

Sixteenth-century Unitarianism originated in what is today Hungary, Poland, and Romania (Transylvania). Leading Unitarians included Michael Servetus (1511–1553), Faustus Socinus (1539–1604), and Lelius Socinus (1525–1604). In the eighteenth century, an English scientist, Joseph Priestly (1733–1804), brought Unitarianism to the thirteen colonies. Once there, it influenced several Christian groups, including Anglicans and Puritans. In fact, King's Chapel (an Anglican church) at Boston became the first Unitarian church in North America. In 1785, the church published a version of the *Book of Common Prayer* that omitted references to the Trinity.

The character of Unitarianism began to change in the mid-nineteenth century. In 1838, the poet Ralph Waldo Emerson (1803–1882) addressed the graduating class of Harvard Divinity School. In his address, he questioned whether Unitarians should espouse belief in Jesus' miracles. From this time forward, American Unitarianism was no longer exclusively Christian.

Around this time, John Murray began spreading the Universalist message: *God will save everyone and punish no one* (hell does not exist). The Universalist movement derived its name from the notion of universal salvation. An independent Universalist minister, Hosea Ballou, defined the basic beliefs of Universalism in his *Treatise on the Atonement* (1805). The Universalist Church of America was organized in 1833.

The **Unitarian Universalist Association** came into existence in 1961. In that year, the American Unitarian Association and the Universalist Church of America voted to become one religious body. The General Assembly, the association's highest authority, meets every year. The Unitarian Universalist Association has its headquarters in Boston.

Principles

A summary of Unitarian Universalist beliefs and practices does not exist. A member of this group may be a theist, a Christian, or a humanist. Every Unitarian Universalist has his or her own creed. There are, however, principles that unite Unitarian Universalists.

Unitarian Universalists believe that every person has dignity and worth. People are not asked or required to change. They are accepted. They look upon one another's differences as sources of strength. Unitarian Universalists do not discriminate on any basis. They strive for justice, equity, and compassion in human relations. Every individual is part of the world community. Unitarian Universalists stress this point by speaking of the "interdependent web of all existence."

Unitarian Universalists support the "free and responsible search for truth and meaning." Each person determines the source of his or her own truth. The group celebrates reason and pluralism. Unitarian Universalists study the religions of the world to enrich their ethical and spiritual lives. They look upon Jewish and Christian teachings as calling humankind "to respond to God's love by loving our neighbors as ourselves." From the Unitarian Universalist perspective, humanist teachings help people "to heed the guidance of reason and the results of science. . . ." They understand the spiritual teachings of earth-centered traditions as helping people "to live in harmony with the rhythms of nature." They may be influenced by modern therapies, as well as by Eastern religions.

Unitarian Universalists uphold the "right of conscience." A person's decision to do or not to do something must be respected. Relatedly, they promote the democratic process in all areas of their lives. Unitarian Universalists work to create a world filled with "peace, liberty, and justice for all." To ensure the existence of such a world, the "powers and structures of evil" must be confronted with "justice, compassion, and the transforming power of love."

In their bylaws, Unitarian Universalists list the following sources for their living tradition:

1. Direct experience of transcending mystery

2. Words and deeds of prophetic people

3. Wisdom from the world's religions

4. Jewish and Christian teachings

5. Humanist teachings

Emerson's Unitarianism

The grass grows, the buds burst, the meadow is spotted with fire and gold in the tint of flowers. The air is full of birds, and sweet with the breath of pine. . . .

Through the transparent darkness the stars pour their almost spiritual rays. [A human being] under them seems a young child, and . . . the huge globe a toy. The cool night bathes the world as with a river, and prepares . . . again for the crimson dawn.

The mystery of nature was never displayed more happily. One is constrained to respect the perfection of this world in which our senses converse.

—Ralph Waldo Emerson, Unitarian minister, Harvard Divinity School Address (1838).

Let's Talk about It . . .

1. What Unitarian beliefs are present in Emerson's words?
2. Does the reader have to be Unitarian to appreciate and understand what Emerson is saying? Why?

Quaker Tradition

Quakers, Friends
the Religious Society of Friends, a non-creedal religious group that attempts to live simply and meets for silent prayer

The Religious Society of Friends is another name for the **Quaker** tradition. In part, the name Religious Society of Friends comes from Scripture. In John 15:15, Jesus referred to his followers as "friends." In time, members of the society were known as *Friends*. Some called them *Quakers* because they supposedly quaked (trembled) when praying.

The experiences of George Fox (1624–1691), an Englishman, gave birth to the Religious Society of Friends. Seeking closeness to God, Fox spent long hours reading Scripture and studying religious writings. On one occasion, Fox heard a voice which said: "There is one, even Christ Jesus, who can speak to thy condition." This experience changed Fox. From this time forward, he welcomed the presence of Jesus into his life and trusted this presence more than anything else.

Fox taught that Scripture is not the word of God, but points to the word of God who is Jesus. He believed that Christians could not participate in war or armed struggle, basing this view on Jesus' Sermon on the Mount. On eight occasions, Fox was imprisoned for spreading his ideas.

In the mid-seventeenth century, the Religious Society of Friends came to the thirteen colonies when the first Friends arrived in Boston. These Friends were immediately greeted with hostility. In 1656, Ann Austin and Mary Fisher were charged with witchcraft and expelled. By 1657, members of the Religious Society of Friends had been barred from Boston. Between 1659 and 1661, the colony of Massachusetts executed (hung) four members of the society.

In 1681, the fortunes of the Religious Society of Friends changed. In that year, William Penn (1644–1718), a Friend, founded Pennsylvania. The colony soon became a sanctuary for those fleeing religious persecution. The freedom of religion enjoyed in Pennsylvania helped to inspire the Bill of Rights. For the remainder of the seventeenth century, the Religious Society of Friends prospered and members of the society began to exert their influence. A Friend, John Woolman (1720–1772), was among the first Americans to condemn slavery. Levi Coffin, the first president of the Underground Railroad, was a Friend. Throughout the eighteenth and nineteenth centuries, the Religious Society of Friends worked to improve the lives of minorities. It helped to abolish slavery and to give women the right to vote.

Friends General Conference

In the United States, there are more than one thousand local Quaker groups. Many of these Meetings have formed umbrella organizations known as *Yearly Meetings*. And some of these organizations have banded together to form even larger meetings, such as the Friends General Conference, which began in 1827. In that year, Friends met in Philadelphia to debate the teachings of Elias Hicks, a popular Quaker preacher who placed great emphasis on the role of inner light. His followers, known as Hicksites, withdrew and soon organized a Yearly Meeting of their own. Today, the Friends General Conference brings together more than a dozen Yearly Meetings who meet every year at the Gathering of Friends. The conference's headquarters are in Philadelphia. The Friends General Conference belongs to the World Council of Churches.

> We shall respect that of God in all creation. We shall live in loving harmony with the earth. Humankind shall be a joyful gardener of the world given us by God, and shall use its fruits wisely and moderately.
>
> —Taken from Quaker Writings (1979).

Beliefs and Practices

Inner Light

Friends believe that an "element of God's own Spirit and divine energy" can be found in every human soul. Early Friends described this element as "that of God in everyone." Sometimes they used the term "the seed of Christ" or "the seed of Light." The idea of Inner Light is grounded in Scripture. Friends point to John 1:9, which reads: "The true light, which enlightens everyone, was coming into the world." Friends teach that the Inner Light accomplishes two things.

1. It exposes good and bad; people can't choose between the two.
2. It reinforces human equality: every member of the human race has the same light inside.

Ongoing revelation

Revelation can be defined as "what God reveals to humankind." Revelation (knowledge of God's will) is not confined to the past, nor to the Bible. Revelation (knowledge of God's will) is ongoing; it can be found in the present. On more than one occasion, George Fox stressed this very point: "You will say Christ saith this, and the apostles saith this, but what canst thou say? Art thou a child of Light and hast thou walked in the Light, and what thou speakest, is it inwardly from . . . God?"

Meetings

Quakers do not have sacraments, believing that all human experiences are meant to be sacramental. Friends use the term *meeting for worship* to describe their service. Some congregations use pastoral prayer, readings, hymns, Scripture, and sermons in their meetings. These groups often have a pastor.

Other groups have silent meetings. Most of these hour-long meetings are conducted entirely without words. The silence of the meeting gives Friends an opportunity to open themselves to the God within. The silence helps them to know God's will. They share the silence—they are silent together. On occasion, a person may be prompted to share his or her insights. Children are free to comment. This commenting is known as ministry; it gives voice to what is already known in silence.

Quakers are well known for their opposition to war.

Chapter 7

A Quaker Meeting

A member of the Quaker community, Douglas Steere, describes what he experiences at a meeting.

I attend a meeting that usually has from sixty to ninety persons present. We meet together in an old meeting house each Sunday morning for an hour. The little meeting house where I worship lies well out in the country. I get there just before eleven, enter in silence and sit down. There is no altar before me, no choir loft, nor organ. Only three rows of "facing benches," each of the back two being slightly elevated above the one in front of it. . . .

Our meetings are made up of a group of people gathered together in silent prayer. The first thing that I do is close my eyes and then still my body, in order to get it as far out of the way as I can. Then I still my mind and let it open to God in silent prayer, for the meeting, as we understand it, is the meeting of the worshiper with God. I thank God inwardly for this occasion, for the week's happenings, for what I have learned at God's hand, for my family, and the work there is to do. I often pause to enjoy this presence. Under God's gaze I search the week and feel the piercing twinge of remorse that comes at this, and this, and this. I ask forgiveness for my faithlessness and ask for strength to meet this matter when it arises again. There have been times when I had to re-weave a part of my life under this auspice.

When I have finished these inward prayers, I quietly resign myself to complete listening, letting go in the intimacy of this friendly company and in the intimacy of the Great Friend who is always near. At this point, one could use Robert Barclay's words in describing our silent sitting together, "As our worship consisted not in words so neither in silences as silence, but in a holy dependence of the mind upon God; from which dependence, silence necessarily follows in the first place until words can be brought forth which are from God's spirit." I do not know what takes place here. Often I am sure it is nothing at all. But there are times when a certain slowing-down takes place, a certain healing seems to go on, certain tendering, a certain "dependence of the mind upon God." This, however, may come in at any point in my own directed prayers and take precedence over them. Someone asked another how long he ought to pray, and received the answer, "Long enough to forget time."

When this tendering happens in a meeting, one feels knit very closely to one's fellow worshipers, and a particular sense of our common ground in the Spirit and of our life in "holy obedience" to it often develops. With this we may be brought very low and into a realization of the condition of some group with which we stand out of unity, whether it be the suffering millions in India or neglected friendless senior citizens, or an underprivileged group in our own neighborhood.

Let's Talk about It . . .

1. If you spent an hour in silence, what would you think about?
2. How does the Friends' practice of silent prayer compare with your understanding of worship?

Testimony

testimony

for Quakers, the demonstration of a living truth, bearing witness to a value

Friends demonstrate the living truths of the human heart. The demonstration of a living truth is known as a **testimony**, a bearing witness to a value. The precise form of a testimony varies. Community, equality, peace, and simplicity are among the more basic testimonies. Friends' literature on the peace testimony states that:

The Peace Testimony is perhaps the most widely known of these [testimonies]. Taken as a whole, the Society of Friends is strongly opposed to war and to conscription. It seeks to remove the causes of war; it tries to reconcile factions and nations; it ministers to suffering on both sides of conflicts; it helps to rebuild at war's end. It witnesses creatively to the power of nonviolence in the movement toward social change.

—Friendly Answers, *Friends World Committee for Consultation, Philadelphia.*

Friends' long heritage of witness to peace can be found in public statements and personal reflections, in their refusal to bear arms in times of civil and international conflict, in acts of prophetic confrontation and of quiet, reconciling diplomacy. But these are merely outward and visible signs of inward conviction. This conviction springs from a living Spirit, mediated through the human experience of those trying to understand and follow its leadings. It grows afresh in every life, in every worshiping group, in every generation.

—Quaker Peace Testimony, *Philadelphia Yearly Meeting.*

Because of the non-creedal nature of this religious group, there exists a wide range of convictions. Even the strong testimonies are not universally held. However, Friends are united in their transforming experience of God.

Christian Science Tradition

Christian Science

the religious tradition which believes in healing people by spiritual means and in working for universal salvation from evil, including sin and death

Christian Science is the rediscovery of the divine laws (science) that Jesus understood, taught, and proved. These laws cured people. In addition to healing people by spiritual means, the higher purpose of Christian Science is to work for "universal salvation from every phase of evil—including sin and death."

The Christian Science tradition was developed by Mary Baker Eddy (1821–1910). Eddy's study of the Bible led her to discover the foundation of Jesus' healing ministry. Eddy's association with Phineas P. Quimby convinced her that a person could promote his or her own health. She resolutely refused to accept the view that God caused pain and suffering.

Shortly after Quimby's death, Mary Baker Eddy had an experience that changed the course of her life. In February of 1866, Eddy slipped on ice and fell. Because of the seriousness of the injury, doctors did not think she would survive. A few days later, she asked to be left alone with her Bible. While meditating, she realized two things: one, her life was in God; two, God was the sole reality of existence. These insights caused instantaneous healing. In the years ahead, Eddy devoted herself to studying the Bible and explaining the notion of God as healer. During this time, she wrote *Science and Health with Key to the Scriptures.*

Church of Christ, Scientist

Following the publication of Eddy's *Science and Health with Key to the Scriptures*, Eddy founded the Christian Science Foundation (1876). Those who studied at the foundation spread her teachings across the country. In 1892, Mary Baker Eddy founded the First Church of Christ, Scientist, in Boston. This is the Mother Church of the Christian Science tradition. Today a five-member board of directors governs the church according to the Church Manual, which Eddy wrote (1895). The *Christian Science Monitor* was founded by Eddy in 1908 and has the aim of healing the nations. This greatly respected daily newspaper is published by the Mother Church.

Beliefs and Practices

Mary Baker Eddy declared the Bible and her *Science and Health with Key to the Scriptures* to be the "pastor of the Church." Eddy developed the concept of the Pastor in these words, "Your dual and impersonal pastor, the Bible, and 'Science and Health with Key to the Scriptures,' is with you; and the Life these give, the Truth they illustrate, the Love they demonstrate, is the great Shepherd that feedeth my flock, and leadeth them 'beside the still waters.' " Christian Scientists regard *Science and Health with Key to the Scriptures* as a companion to the Bible. It enables them to completely and fully understand the word of God.

Sunday worship includes readings from the Bible and from the works of Mary Baker Eddy and the singing of hymns. At the local church level, those authorized to publicly read from *Science and Health with Key to the Scriptures* are elected by the membership for a short term.

Christian Scientists believe people can be healed through **scientific prayer**, or spiritual communion. Because Jesus was a healer, they believe that they are following Jesus whenever they use scientific prayer for healing. They see their Christian duty as praying for the healing of the sick as well as the sinners. Christian Scientists believe that God, or the Divine Mind, is the source of all healing. Scientific prayer brings the idea of divine love to the patient's consciousness. It aims to change the patient's thought so that his or her condition will change. Sickness is seen as part of the same unreality as evil and sin; faith in God's healing power banishes these unrealities. Christian Science Practitioners are those who devote themselves to the ministry of Christian healing.

Christian Scientists look upon God as the creator and governor of the universe. They often call God by names such as *Life, Love, Mind, Principle, Soul, Spirit,* and *Truth.* According to Christian Scientists, the term *Christ* denotes the divine nature or spiritual sonship of Jesus. For them, Christ is the mediator between God and humankind. Christian Scientists accept the Gospels' portrayal of Jesus—virgin birth, ministry, crucifixion, resurrection, and ascension. Christian Scientists do not observe baptism or communion. They understand "baptism" as the process of purifying one's actions and thoughts. For them, communion is spiritual communion with God; silent prayer and clean living promote this communion.

scientific prayer
the Christian Science process of turning human thought to the enlightening and saving power of God in order to bring about healing

The Unity Tradition

Unity tradition

a Christian tradition which originated in the late nineteenth century and which believes that people's acts, feelings, thoughts, and words exert power over their lives

The **Unity tradition** originated with Charles (1854–1948) and Myrtle (1848–1931) Fillmore in the late nineteenth century. Charles Fillmore used these words to describe the Unity tradition: "Unity is a link in the great educational movement inaugurated by Jesus Christ; our objective is to discern the truth in Christianity and prove it. The truth that we teach is not new, neither do we claim special revelations or discovery of new religious principles. Our purpose is to help and teach [humankind] to use and prove the eternal Truth taught by the Master."

While living in Kansas City, Missouri, Charles and Myrtle Fillmore went to a lecture on healing that changed them forever. The lecture was delivered by Eugene B. Weeks—a representative of an independent Christian Science school. The Fillmores had attended the lecture to find a cure for Myrtle's tuberculosis. Weeks believed that Myrtle's condition could be treated. He told her to repeat the words "I am a child of God and therefore do not inherit sickness." Within a period of months, Myrtle Fillmore made a complete recovery.

The Fillmores wanted to bring healing to others, and founded the Society of Silent Help (1890). In 1891, they named their movement *Unity*. Two of their closest students, Harriet Emilie Cady and Annie Rix Militz, wrote important works and helped to spread Unity teachings. Harriet Emilie Cady's *Lessons in Truth* and Charles Fillmore's *Christian Healing and Metaphysical Bible Dictionary* are the chief texts of Unity.

The Association of Unity Churches and the Unity School of Christianity comprise the Unity movement. The Association of Unity Churches oversees the training of ministers and the formation of churches. The Unity School of Christianity is the movement's publishing arm, publishing, among other things, *Daily Word*, a monthly guide to day-to-day living. The Society of Silent Help, now known as Silent Unity, maintains a twenty-four hour prayer vigil. Unity Village, Missouri, is the headquarters of the movement.

Beliefs and Practices

Unity believes that God is Spirit. It understands God as "the one and only Spirit behind, in, and through all things, visible and invisible." Unity teaches that love is the most important of God's attributes. Nothing is more powerful than this love. Members of Unity do not believe in the existence of an evil force, power, or presence. In their view, the ignorance of humankind and the misapplication of God's laws comprise the root of all suffering.

From the perspective of Unity, every human being is a child of God— every human being is divine. Unity looks upon Jesus as a great model.

He showed human beings how to express their divine potential. People attain salvation if they live like Jesus—realize their divinity and perfection.

Unity teaches that a person's mind links him or her to God (the Divine Mind). The mind has an effect on the body and on all circumstances and situations. The Unity movement makes the point that people's acts, feelings, thoughts, and words exert power over their lives. Unity stresses the importance of the present, which it sees as a part of eternal life.

Unity embraces the truths offered by the world's religions. It likens God to the hub of a wheel and the religions of the world to spokes. Unity stresses the goodness of religions, and emphasizes that they look to the one God. The Old and New Testaments are Unity's main textbook. Members are encouraged to relate its lessons to their experiences and lives. The Unity movement promotes intellectual freedom; its members are free to hold their own beliefs.

According to Unity, worship of God must glorify and uplift the God within—the spirit of God that dwells inside of a person. All worship should emphasize the goodness of people and their potential to transform themselves and their lives.

Responsibility

Is God responsible for all that occurs on this earth, and if not all, how much of it?

By right thinking [humankind] can have the co-operation of God in producing manifestations and thereby can set up the kingdom of God in the earth; or [humankind] can ignore God and attempt to form a world and govern it without divine aid. We are now living in a civilization dominated by human thought, and confusion is the result. . . .

The taproot of all this confusion is our failure to use our minds intelligently. . . . We must therefore begin at once to develop this unity with the Father mind by incorporating divine ideas into all that we think and speak.

—*Charles Fillmore*, Atom-Smashing Power of Mind, *noncopyrighted.*

Let's Talk about It . . .

1. According to Charles Fillmore, is God responsible for everything that happens on earth?

2. What are the results when people fail to use their minds intelligently?

Reaping the Fruit

The Holiness and Pentecostal traditions grew out of the **Evangelical movement**. *Evangelical* comes from the Greek *euangelion*, which means "gospel." Early members of the Evangelical movement were referred to as gospel believers. They stressed faithfulness to the gospel—the message preached by Jesus.

The Evangelical movement was the successor to the First Great Awakening, which occurred in the thirteen colonies during the mid-eighteenth century. New birth was the central theme of this revival of American Christianity which enriched the lives of thousands of Christians. Followers became known as Evangelical Christians. Evangelical Christians have a number of core beliefs:

1. For Christians, there is no authority greater than the Bible.

2. A person must be "born again" to enjoy eternal salvation (eternal happiness with God).

3. A Christian has to trust Jesus completely and fully.

4. The life of a Christian includes praying, spreading the gospel, studying the Bible, and supporting missionary work.

The Evangelical movement's emphasis on supporting missionary work gave rise to a number of missions and social service projects. Evangelical Christians believed that they were spreading holiness throughout the world. But rising immigration and severely over-crowded cities posed problems greater than the reach of Evangelical social service projects.

Some Evangelical Christians began to emphasize and cultivate personal holiness. In time, a more inward-looking Evangelicalism known as the Holiness movement gathered force. The leading spokesperson of the new Holiness movement was Dwight L. Moody (1837–1899). The Moody Bible Institute, Chicago, Illinois, was named after him. The Holiness movement taught that the New Birth could, and should, be completed. This completed New Birth was sometimes described as a "second blessing." It was associated with the presence of the Holy Spirit.

The Holiness Movement

The **Holiness movement** is an outgrowth of Wesley's doctrine of sanctification. While Methodism did not particularly emphasize this doctrine, other people of the nineteenth century picked up on Wesley's teaching of leading a strict moral life and rejecting worldliness. Pentecostalism, in turn, is an extension of the Holiness movement.

Foundational Beliefs

The Holiness and Pentecostal traditions can be understood only if the experiences of justification, sanctification, and Spirit baptism are explained.

A person who accepts Jesus of Nazareth as his or her personal savior has been justified. This is the first blessing, or the first work of grace.

Justification is also known as regeneration, new birth, or being born again. This is the *moment of justification*. The person is now justified (accepted by God). The person has been born again (regenerated).

A person whom the Holy Spirit perfects, or makes holy, has been sanctified. **Sanctification** is the second blessing, or the second work of grace. Belief in **entire sanctification** sets Holiness Christians apart from other Christians. From their perspective, a person does not earn either justification or entire sanctification—the Holy Spirit controls the entire process. A person touched by the Holy Spirit has been baptized in the Holy Spirit. One result of this is that the person speaks in tongues. Pentecostal Christians believe that Christians should expect to be justified, sanctified, and baptized in the Holy Spirit.

The Salvation Army

The **Salvation Army** dates from 1878. The Salvation Army evolved out of the East London Christian Mission. William (1829–1912) and Catherine (1829–1890) Booth founded the mission so that people who were poor in nineteenth-century London would have a place to worship. The Booths did not regard the Army as an independent Christian church. In 1878, William Booth decided to give the mission a military-like structure and renamed it the *Volunteer Army*. His son, William Bramwell, and a close associate, George Railton, feared that people might confuse the Volunteer Army with the Volunteers, part-time soldiers in the British army. Booth agreed and gave the mission the name *Salvation Army*.

Members of the Salvation Army are officers and salvationists. Each local church is known as a *corps*. A commissioner presides over the Salvation Army in the United States, and the army's headquarters are in Verona, New Jersey.

Adult members sign the Articles of War, which require members to wage salvation warfare—to ease people's material and spiritual suffering. In place of a piano or pipe organ, a brass band provides music. Salvation is knowing God through a personal relationship with Jesus Christ. Thus the mission of the Salvation Army centers on Jesus—"to proclaim His gospel, to persuade men and women to become His disciples, and to engage in a programme of practical concern for the needs of humanity." Members of the Army are dedicated to "the advancement of the Christian religion . . . of education, the relief of poverty, and other charitable objects beneficial to society or the community of mankind as a whole." Members of the Salvation Army affirm their belief in entire sanctification in these words: "We believe that it is the privilege of all believers to be wholly sanctified, and that their whole spirit and soul and body may be preserved blameless unto the coming of our Lord Jesus Christ."

From its inception, the Salvation Army has sought to reach people neglected by other Christian groups. Their social service has taken the form of aid to families, Christmas relief, counseling, day care, natural disaster assistance, senior citizen residences, and summer camps. The Salvation Army operates an extensive network of rehabilitation facilities for homeless alcoholics.

justification
the first blessing, or work of grace; accepting Jesus as one's personal savior; being born again

sanctification
the second blessing, or work of grace; perfected by the Holy Spirit, thus sanctified

entire sanctification
for Holiness Christians, the point when the Holy Spirit erases any trace of sin from the person's life and fills the person with love

Salvation Army
a holiness Christian church with a military structure, an emphasis on moral living, and no sacraments

> *As people made in the image of God (Genesis 1:27), we have a responsibility to use the resources of the earth in a way that ensures that people in this and future generations do not suffer from poverty and injustice. This is part of our stewardship of the earth and our love for others.*
>
> —Salvation Army's Position on Responsibility for the Environment *(1992), approved by the Commissioners' Conference.*

Church of the Nazarene

Church of the Nazarene

a holiness church with some Pentecostal roots and strong moral guides

During the late nineteenth century, a number of small Holiness organizations banded together to form churches. One of these churches was the First **Church of the Nazarene**, founded by Phineas Bresee in 1895 in Los Angeles. Since that time, seven different Holiness churches and organizations have merged with Bresee's church. In 1907, the church adopted the name *Pentecostal Church of the Nazarene.* The present-day Church of the Nazarene came into existence on October 13, 1908. On that date, the Holiness Church of Christ and the Pentecostal Church of the Nazarene combined to form one church. In 1919, the new church dropped the word *Pentecostal* from its name to prevent confusion with the growing Pentecostal movement.

Members of the Church of the Nazarene affirm their belief in entire sanctification in these words: "Believers are to be sanctified wholly, subsequent to regeneration, through faith in the Lord Jesus Christ." There is a strong emphasis in the church on moral living. Ministers, elders, and deacons serve the local church, and each local church conducts its own affairs. The General Assembly, which meets every four years, elects the six-member Board of General Superintendents. This board interprets the *Manual of the Church of the Nazarene,* which governs the church. The national offices of the Church of the Nazarene are in Kansas City, Missouri.

Pentecostalism

Pentecostalism

Christian expression with a belief that persons who have been born again and sanctified should ask for baptism in the Spirit

glossolalia

speaking in tongues; believed to be "initial, physical evidence" of baptism in the Spirit

Pentecostal Christians believe that after a person has been regenerated (born again) and sanctified (made holy), he or she should ask for baptism in the Spirit. Pentecostals teach that all early Christians were "baptized in the Holy Ghost and fire" and "spoke in tongues" immediately afterwards. From the Pentecostal perspective, the experience of these Christians conformed to the experience of Jesus' disciples on the day of Pentecost.

According to Pentecostals, baptism in the Holy Spirit changes a person. The person baptized in the Holy Spirit feels the Spirit's presence more strongly, reveres God deeply, consecrates (gives) himself or herself to God, dedicates himself or herself to God's work, and actively loves Jesus, Scripture, and those less fortunate. Pentecostalism refers to those churches who have experiences similar to those of Pentecost and present in the New Testament Church. Primary among these is the phenomenon of speaking in tongues (**glossolalia**). Other gifts include healing, prophecy, wisdom, and the discernment of spirits.

New Testament writings state that when the first Christians experienced the Holy Spirit, they received one or more gifts. These gifts included speaking in tongues as well as the gifts of healing, working miracles, and prophecy. Speaking in tongues means having the ability to speak in a language which one has never heard or learned. To the outsider it is only so many meaningless sounds; to the believer it is a language spoken under the control of the Holy Spirit.

After the first century, there is little evidence of this phenomenon in Christianity until the twentieth century.

Charismatic prayer enthusiastically involves the whole person.

Apparently some people spoke in tongues in France in the seventeenth century during the persecutions of the Huguenots (French Calvinists). There are some isolated examples from the early nineteenth century in North America, but most examples come from members of the Holiness movement late in the century.

While many specific Pentecostal churches have developed, Pentecostalism crosses denominational lines and is found in many churches, including Methodist, Lutheran, Reformed, Baptist, Presbyterian, Episcopalian, and Catholic. The members of those churches who accept Pentecostal beliefs and practices are known as **charismatics**. In 1959, an Episcopal priest, Dennis Bennett, reported that he had been baptized in the Holy Spirit. The cross-denominational charismatic movement is said to have begun with him.

charismatics
members of many Christian Churches who accept Pentecostal beliefs and practices

Development of Pentecostalism

The modern Pentecostal movement can be traced to January 1, 1901, in Topeka, Kansas. Rev. Charles Parnham, a former member of the Methodist Episcopal Church, entered into a healing ministry and founded Bethel Bible College in Topeka in 1900. Over the Christmas holidays, he assigned his students the task of investigating the scriptures for evidence of the **baptism of the Holy Spirit**. When he returned from a speaking engagement, he learned that the students concluded that the one evidence that this baptism had been received was that people spoke in tongues. Parnham and his students immediately prayed for the baptism of the Holy Spirit. On January 1, 1901, the Spirit fell on Agnes Ozman who spoke in tongues during a student prayer meeting. This is the beginning of the modern Pentecostal movement.

baptism of the Holy Spirit
Pentecostal understanding of the special gift of the Spirit with resulting speaking in tongues, interpretation of tongues, and healing

The second phase of the Pentecostal movement happened in Los Angeles. W.J. Seymour, an African American Holiness minister, had been invited to speak to a congregation there. The congregation turned him away after one sermon, but he was invited to speak at a member's home. Within three days, people began speaking in tongues. The movement grew rapidly, fueled by news of people in Wales and Armenia experiencing the same phenomenon. Further impetus to the urgency of the movement came from the San Francisco earthquake which occurred just nine days after the first experience. By the end of 1906, Pentecostalism claimed 13,000 members in the United States and Canada, as well as members in India, Norway, and Sweden.

Holiness preachers came to San Francisco to receive their baptism in the Spirit. At first, efforts were made to promote Pentecostalism within the established churches, but eventually adherents were forced to organize their own denominations. Three churches are central to Pentecostalism: the Assemblies of God, the Church of God (Cleveland, Tennessee), and the Church of Our Lord Jesus Christ of the Apostolic Faith. Many other Pentecostal churches have been organized as well, but they tend to be modeled on these or directly stem from them.

Beliefs

Early Pentecostals looked to the Holy Spirit to direct their worship. Speakers were not designated beforehand; the Holy Spirit chose them on the spot. They were chosen to give testimony, to sing, to deliver a sermon, to prophesy, to pray, to heal, or to speak in tongues. One Pentecostal Christian used these words to describe Pentecostal worship, "The Lord was liable to burst through anyone. It might be a child, a woman, or a man. It might be from the back seat or from the front. It made no difference. We rejoiced that God was working."

Pentecostalism carries Luther's doctrine of justification by faith one step further. Recall that Luther taught that people are saved (justified) by faith in Jesus as Lord and savior. Methodism and the Holiness movement taught that after justification, one grows in holiness and becomes more perfect. Thus one asks for the blessing of sanctification as a sign that one is perfect. The third step is that of Pentecostalism, which prays for the baptism of the Holy Spirit. Evidence of being baptized in the Holy Spirit are the gifts evidenced at Pentecost, especially the gift of speaking in tongues.

In the early twentieth century, Pentecostals disagreed over the nature of sanctification and the existence of the Trinity. Some Pentecostal Christians believed that sanctification was an ongoing process. They are known as *non-Wesleyan Pentecostals*, given this name because they disagree with John Wesley, who more or less defined sanctification as an experience. Some Pentecostals argued that the words "in the name of the Father, Son, and Holy Spirit" had the same meaning as the words "in the name of Jesus." They taught that a person could be baptized "in the name of Jesus." Today these Pentecostals are known as advocates of "Jesus-only" or "Jesus' name" teaching.

Pentecostals are actively engaged in evangelization. Most churches have missionaries in foreign countries. They publish Christian literature extensively and sponsor TV and radio programs. The radio program "Revivaltime," is a weekly radio program sponsored by the Assemblies of God and has an estimated audience of twelve million.

Assemblies of God

Disputes over sanctification and the Trinity fragmented the Pentecostal movement. In 1913, the editor of the Pentecostal periodical *Word and Witness* called on Pentecostal leaders to convene a convention. The call was answered. On April 2, 1914, more than three hundred Pentecostal leaders met at Hot Springs, Arkansas. After three days of prayer, they created a "voluntary cooperative fellowship" known as the **Assemblies of God**. The thrust of the Assemblies of God has been described as full-gospel and Bible-based. In 1916, the Assemblies of God formulated a *Statement of Fundamental Truths*, which is contained in the *Constitution of the Assemblies of God*. Its purpose is to promote agreement among member churches.

Assemblies of God
full-gospel and Bible-based Pentecostal churches

The General Council of the Assemblies of God, with offices in Springfield, Missouri, is a fellowship of Pentecostal churches with a total membership of about twenty-five million (1992). In the United States, there are about 2.3 million, and in Canada 200,000. The General Council has centralized control over missionary, educational, ministerial, and publishing concerns. They have an active ministry to Native Americans, Jews, people who are deaf and blind, prisoners, and teen gangs. Their Gospel Publishing House is one of the major publishers of Christian literature in the United States. The Assemblies of God have missions in 132 countries.

The Assemblies of God believe in a process view of sanctification. In contrast to "Jesus only" Pentecostals, the Assemblies of God strongly affirm belief in the Trinity. They also believe in the Bible as the word of God, the fall of humankind, salvation in Christ, baptism by immersion, divine healing, and the resurrection.

Men, women, and children, created in God's image . . . have a unique responsibility for creation. . . . We recognize that poverty forces people to degrade creation in order to survive; therefore we support the development of just, free economies which empower the poor and create abundance without diminishing creation's bounty. . . . We commit ourselves to work for responsible public policies which embody the principles of biblical stewardship of creation.

—An Evangelical Declaration on the Care of Creation *(1994), released by the Evangelical Environment Network (EEN).*

The EEN has the support of many members of the Assemblies of God, which belongs to the National Association of Evangelicals.

Let's Talk about It . . .

1. How does poverty force people to degrade creation?
2. What kind of policies would reflect the principles of biblical stewardship of creation?

Church of Jesus Christ of Latter-day Saints

Church of Jesus Christ of Latter-day Saints
the uniquely American church founded by Joseph Smith which claims to be the restoration of the original church of Jesus Christ; often called the Mormon Church

Nearly all religions present in North America have roots in other parts of the world. The major exception, of course, is the Native American religions. There are, however, a few others which may have traces of other religious belief, but have their own unique American origin. One of these is the **Church of Jesus Christ of Latter-day Saints**. While members of the group are often referred to as *Mormons*, a more correct term is *Latter-day Saints*. Members of the Church of Latter-day Saints follow the teachings set forth by Joseph Smith. Church members believe that Smith replaced the Church of the past with the Church of the present and that all other churches are in error. Smith restored the original church of Jesus Christ.

Beginnings

Joseph Smith, a Vermonter, moved to western New York in 1815 at the age of ten. The time following the War of 1812 and the area in which Smith lived was inundated with wave after wave of religious fervor. Smith, like many of his time and place, was confused by all the different religious sects, each claiming to speak God's word. In this context, according to Smith, he began to have visions in which the true nature of the Church was revealed to him, along with what he must do to restore it. Smith described his first vision in these words:

> When the light rested upon me, I saw two personages, whose brightness and glory defy all description, standing above me in the air. One of them spake unto me, calling me by name, and said, pointing to the other— "This is my beloved son, hear him!". . . I asked the personages who stood above me in the light, which of all the sects [religious groups] was right—and which I should join. I was answered that I must join none of them, for they were all wrong. . . .

Smith later identified the two personages as God the Father and Jesus. Other visions followed as Smith conversed with John the Baptist and various angels. The glorified, resurrected being Moroni (often referred to as an angel) appeared to him in 1827 and told him to dig near the top of the Hill Cumorah near Palyrma, New York. There he found a box of golden plates inscribed in "Reformed Egyptian." Members of the religion believe that the *Book of Mormon* was inscribed on these tablets. The *Book of Mormon* told the story of the first North Americans, from 600 B.C.E. to 400 C.E. This ancient history had been written by a number of prophets. In the year 400, a man by the name of Mormon began collecting this history. Around 421, his son Moroni completed the task and hid the tablets in a hill near Smith's boyhood home.

Moroni also reportedly gave Smith two stones, like crystals or spectacles, and called *Urim* and *Thummim*, with which to read the tablets. (The Urim and Thummim were sticks or stones that the Hebrew high priest wore fastened to a breastplate; they were said to be used by seers.) Smith translated the Book of Mormon over a period of sixty-five days. After Smith had translated the golden tablets, Moroni showed them to Martin Harris, Oliver Cowdery, and David Whitmer—the Three Witnesses. Later, Smith himself showed the tablets to eight other witnesses.

The Development of a Church

The *Book of Mormon* was published in 1830, and a church organized. More revelations followed and new works were written. An inspired translation of the Bible was also developed. Almost immediately the *Book of Mormon* was attacked by other religious groups, and the Mormons became outcasts. This criticism followed the Mormons in their journey across the United States until their settlement in Utah.

The church organized by Smith moved to Kirtland, Ohio. Here the new church was welcomed, a first temple built, and twelve apostles chosen to assist President Smith. Another group continued on and settled in Jackson County, Missouri. Soon the Mormons drew the antagonism of Missourians, and they were expelled from the state in the winter of 1838–39. Eventually the group settled near Nauvoo, Illinois. In Nauvoo, the 20,000 Mormons built the largest city in the state, a city with broad streets, big homes, factories, and a new temple.

Soon trouble visited the Mormons again. Fear of the Church's political power, rumors of polygamy, and envy of their prosperity caused non-Mormons to take matters into their own hands. In addition, Smith himself was involved in several legal allegations. In 1844, a group of Latter-day Saints led by Charles and Robert Foster, C.L. Higbee, and Wilson Law formed their own church. They began the *Nauvoo Expositer*, a newspaper critical of Joseph Smith. Smith denounced the newspaper, and the Legion of Nauvoo, a pro-Smith group, destroyed the newspaper's office and press. As a result, Smith and his some of his closest associates were jailed at Carthage, Illinois. On June 27, 1844, a mob broke into the jail and killed Smith.

Mormon Temple in Salt Lake City, Utah

The movement was now in chaos, and the Latter-day Saints split into several factions. Brigham Young, a Methodist minister from Vermont, had joined Smith in Kirtland. Now he was able to gain the confidence of many church members and began to organize them for a great march west. In 1846, the first group left on a grueling journey in the middle of the winter. By April, all had left Nauvoo and were on their way to Utah. Upon arriving in the valley of the Great Salt Lake, Brigham Young declared, "This is the place." Here Mormons were to stay and prosper.

The group centered in Salt Lake City is known as the Church of Jesus Christ of Latter-day Saints. The First Presidency (one president and two counselors) and the Twelve Apostles constitute the Church's highest authority.

The Latter-day Saints were not, however, unchallenged. A dispute arose with the United States government concerning the practice of polygamy or plural marriage, which had been publicly announced in 1852. War almost broke out, but Mormon leaders decided to compromise. In 1862 and 1882, Congress passed anti-bigamy laws, and the Supreme Court ruled in 1870 that religious freedom could not be claimed as grounds for polygamy. The practice was officially ended in 1890.

From the very beginning, the church was plagued by several schisms. Some members of the Church claimed to have visions like the prophet Joseph Smith, and this led to the development of new sects. The most important such group decided not to follow Young after Smith's death, claiming that the new leader should be a relative of Joseph Smith. Thus they broke away and started the Reorganized Church of Jesus Christ of Latter-day Saints.

In 1994, the church reported a worldwide membership of about 9 million. In 1995, there were at least 4.5 million members of the Church of Jesus Christ of Latter-day Saints in the United States. The Reorganized group reported about 150,000. Numbers for Canada were not reported.

Writings

Mormons have four groups of writings. They are the Bible "insofar as correctly translated," *The Book of Mormon*, *Doctrine and Covenants*, and *The Pearl of Great Price*.

The Book of Mormon, Another Testament of Jesus Christ, tells the story of two groups of people, the Jeredites and the Israelites. The Jeredites came to North America immediately following the attempt to build the Tower of Babel. The Israelites came following Lehi after the destruction of Jerusalem in the sixth century B.C.E. (here is the connection with the ten "lost tribes" of Israel). The Israelites were the descendants of Lehi: the Lamanites and the Nephites. The Lamanites take their name from Laman, the eldest son of Lehi, and the Nephites from Nephi, another son of Lehi. The groups were rivals. The Jeredites were destroyed shortly after the arrival of the Israelites. The Israelites were mostly destroyed in the fourth century C.E., and Native Americans are the only remnant. The last of the prophets of the second group wrote a history which was buried and later found by Joseph Smith. Still another group, the Mulekites, were survivors of the Babylonian invasion and take their name from Mulek, who led them. They began making their way to North America in 588 C.E.

The *Book of Mormon* contains fifteen books: 1 Nephi, 2 Nephi, Jacob, Enos, Jarom, Omni, Words of Mormon, Mosiah, Alma, Helaman, 3 Nephi, 4 Nephi, Mormon, Ether, and Moroni. In 3 Nephi 11 (Third Book of Nephi, chapter 11), Jesus visits the ancient Lamanites and the Nephites. This chapter is regarded as the climax of the entire *Book of Mormon*. Jesus' visit occurred about a year after his resurrection. The chapter opens with a group of Nephites discussing the pending collapse of their society; 3 Nephi 11:8–10, 33, 41 reads:

> And it came to pass, as they understood, they cast their eyes up again towards heaven; and behold, they saw a Man descending out of heaven; and he was clothed in a white robe; and he came down and stood in the midst of them; and the eyes of the whole multitude were turned upon him, and they durst not open their mouths, even one to another, and wist not what it meant, for they thought it was an angel that had appeared unto them.
>
> And it came to pass that he stretched forth his hand and spake unto the people, saying:
>
> > Behold, I am Jesus Christ, whom the prophets testified shall come into the world. . . .
> >
> > And whoso believeth in me, and is baptized, the same shall be saved; and they are they who shall inherit the kingdom of God. . . .
> >
> > Therefore, go forth unto this people, and declare the words which I have spoken, unto the ends of the earth.

The *Doctrine and Covenants* is a collection of revelations from God to Joseph Smith and a revelation to Brigham Young. *The Pearl of Great Price* includes the *Book of Moses*, the *Book of Abraham*, the collected writings of Joseph Smith, and the Articles of Faith.

Joseph Smith's Articles of Faith

1. *We believe in God, the Eternal Father, and in His Son, Jesus Christ, and in the Holy Ghost.*

2. *We believe that men will be punished for their sins, and not for Adam's transgression.*

3. *We believe that through the Atonement of Christ, all mankind may be saved, by obedience to the laws and ordinances of the Gospel.*

4. *We believe that the first principles and ordinances of the Gospel are: first, Faith in the Lord Jesus Christ; second, Repentance; third, Baptism by immersion for the remission of sins; fourth, Laying on of hands for the gift of the Holy Ghost.*

5. *We believe that a man must be called of God, by prophecy, and by the laying on of hands by those who are in authority, to preach the Gospel and administer in the ordinances thereof.*

6. *We believe in the same organizations that existed in the Primitive Church, namely, apostles, prophets, pastors, teachers, evangelists, and so forth.*

7. *We believe in the gift of tongues, prophecy, revelation, visions, healing, interpretation of tongues, and so forth.*

8. *We believe the Bible to be the word of God as far as it is translated correctly; we also believe the Book of Mormon to be the word of God.*

9. *We believe all that God has revealed, all that He does now reveal, and we believe that He will yet reveal many great and important things pertaining to the Kingdom of God.*

10. *We believe in the literal gathering of Israel and in the restoration of the Ten Tribes; that Zion (the new Jerusalem) will be built upon the American continent; that Christ will reign personally upon the earth; and that the earth will be renewed and receive its paradisiacal glory.*

11. *We claim the privilege of worshiping Almighty God according to the dictates of our own conscience, and allow all men the same privilege; let them worship how, where, and what they may.*

12. *We believe in being subject to kings, presidents, rulers, and magistrates, in obeying, honoring, and sustaining the law.*

13. *We believe in being honest, true, chaste, benevolent, virtuous, and in doing good to all men; indeed, we may say that we follow the admonition of Paul—We believe all things, we hope all things, we have endured many things, and hope to be able to endure all things. If there is anything virtuous, lovely, or of good report or praiseworthy, we seek after these things.*

—Pearl of Great Price, *Articles of Faith.*

Let's Talk about It . . .

1. What basic Christian beliefs are expressed in these Articles of Faith?
2. What belief(s) do you see as unique to Latter-day Saints?

Beliefs and Practices

The Articles of Faith were written shortly before Smith's death, and the thirteen points of doctrine are still used by Latter-day Saints. While the articles are primarily Protestant in tone, Mormons have several distinct doctrines which separate them from mainline Christianity.

Although the first article sounds like faith in the Trinity, it is belief in three gods. God did not create matter; God organized it from the chaos. God did create a tremendous number of spirits or souls. These souls are united with a body and sent to earth. Mormons believe in the eternal progress of humans from a spiritual state to mortality and then to an afterlife where resurrected individuals receive their reward.

Latter-day Saints practice baptism by immersion at the age of eight or older. They also believe in vicarious baptism. This means they believe that members of the Church can stand in for ancestors who have died and be baptized in their place. Latter-day Saints promote genealogical research so that ancestors can undergo vicarious baptism.

Marriage may be for time or it may be for time and eternity. "For time" means for this world only. "For time and eternity" means for this world and the next. Couples must be married in one of the temples in order to be married for time and eternity.

There are two orders of priesthood. The lower order is the Aaronic Priesthood of which all adult males are members. From it are drawn deacons, teachers, and priests. The higher order is the Melchizedek Priesthood. From it comes the Church's leadership: elders, seventies, high priests, apostles, and the president-prophet.

Latter-day Saints think of the afterlife as having three levels. The celestial level is the highest and is reserved for Mormons who were married in the temple rites. The second level is the terrestrial, which is for lower-grade Mormons and exceptional Gentiles; they will be presided over by Christ. The lowest level is the telestial, which is for ordinary Gentiles, who will spend eternity visiting with angels. Only murderers and apostates go to hell.

Latter-day Saints believe that God continues to reveal God's word to individuals who seek it for their own benefit or to leaders of local units for their own jurisdiction. God's word is also revealed to the president-prophet for the Church as a whole. For example, in 1978, Church authorities announced that they had been instructed by revelation to strike down the Church's former policy of excluding African American men from the priesthood.

Missionary Work and Family Life

Religious education is thorough and often daily. At the age of nineteen, all males are expected to begin two years in missionary activity. Women have also begun to enter missionary work and now account for about one eighth of the total. About two-thirds of these young people go to other countries. Other practices of the church include abstinence from alcohol, tobacco, and "hot drinks" which are interpreted to mean tea, coffee, and colas. Mormons also have a reputation for taking care of each other, especially their poor. Church members pay a tithe to support numerous church activities and building construction.

The Church of Jesus Christ of Latter-day Saints places great emphasis on family life, and large families are typical. Family solidarity is encouraged through a weekly family evening of religious instruction and entertainment. The church's strong opposition to the equal rights amendment is based on its belief that the effects would be disruptive to family life. Each family keeps an extensive up-to-date supply of food, water, and other essentials in order to be prepared by a natural or human-caused disaster.

While the Church of Jesus Christ of Latter-day Saints is fairly new and rooted in the United States, it is also a good example of John Calvin's goal of a religious society. Members' beliefs determine to a large extent how they live out their lives.

Conclusion

In chapters 4 through 7, we have discussed a wide array of Christian churches. These represent only the broad outlines of Christianity as it exists in North America today. Many more denominations and movements, best left to your own personal study, could be covered. Altogether, they give evidence of a wide variety of belief and practice.

At several points throughout these chapters we have mentioned one or another church body's participation in the "ecumenical movement." The ecumenical movement is the modern-day movement to bring unity among the Christian churches. Over the centuries there have been many attempts to restore unity between disputing factions in Christianity. The modern-day movement is said to have begun in 1910 with the Edinburgh International Missionary Conference. This was a meeting of Protestant Christians to discuss ways in which they could work more closely in missionary lands. In the 1920s, two international councils were organized: the Faith and Order Conference and the World Council of Churches. Today almost 300 Protestant churches, representing 450 million Christians, belong to the World Council of Churches.

Although there were several individual Catholics who were involved in the modern ecumenical movement, the Catholic Church did not become officially involved until 1949 when it gave official recognition to the movement and set guidelines for Catholic participation. This openness eventually led to the *Decree of Ecumenism* promulgated by the Second Vatican Council in the 1960s. Today the Catholic Church is more directly involved in the ecumenical movement. It has established official dialogues with many Christian bodies and works toward greater unity among Christian churches.

Ecumenical service at Seaman's Church Institute in New York City

A Christian Calendar (Northern Hemisphere)

Winter

The Season of **Advent** (four to seven Sundays/weeks before Christmas). Many Protestant Christians observe Advent. This four-week period prepares Christians for the celebration of Christmas. Each week of Advent is marked by a Sunday.

Christmas Day (December 25). Most Christians celebrate the birth of Jesus on this day. Friends (Quakers) do not observe Christmas or Easter; they believe that every day of the year is equally holy. Seventh-day Adventists observe Jesus' birth on the Saturday closest to Christmas Day.

The **Season of Christmas** (Christmas until mid-January).

Watchnight (December 31). On New Year's Eve, Salvationists and others gather to reflect on the year that has passed. They recommit themselves to leading a sanctified life.

Junior Soldier Day of Renewal (observed in January). On this day, members of the Salvation Army between the ages of seven and eighteen renew their commitment to Jesus. They make this promise by signing a special card.

World Religions' Day (observed in January). On this day, Christians and people of other faiths celebrate their similarities and differences. People mark the day by praying and meditating.

Spring

Lent (the six to eight weeks preceding Easter). Many Protestant Christians prepare for Easter by observing Lent. Throughout Lent, these Christians fast, give to those in need, and pray.

Holy Week is the week before Easter Sunday. Many Protestant Christians observe Palm Sunday, Maundy Thursday, and Good Friday. In many churches, the observance of these days is optional.

Palm Sunday or **Passion Sunday** (Sunday before Easter). The New Testament Passion (story of Jesus' suffering and death) is read, and blessed palm branches are distributed. This day marks the beginning of Holy Week.

Maundy or **Holy Thursday** (Thursday before Easter Sunday). On this day, many Christians share bread and wine in a special way; they are especially mindful of how Jesus and his closest disciples shared bread and wine at the Last Supper. Many Christians demonstrate their love for one another by imitating Jesus washing the disciples' feet.

Festival of the Lord's Supper (observed in March or April). Members of the Worldwide Church of God observe the Jewish festivals spelled out in Scripture. The festival of the Lord's Supper recalls Jesus' last meal and his crucifixion on the day of Passover. On this day, bread and wine are shared.

Good Friday commemorates the death of Jesus.

Holy Saturday, the day after Good Friday, is celebrated with the Easter Vigil in many Christian Churches. On this day, Seventh-day Adventists observe Jesus' resurrection.

Easter Sunday (first Sunday after the full moon following the vernal equinox; between March 22 and April 25). On this day, most Christians celebrate the resurrection of Jesus. Protestant Christians tend to place more emphasis on the resurrection than on the crucifixion of Jesus.

The **Season of Easter**, the time between Easter and Pentecost.

World Day of Prayer (observed in March). On this day, Christians and those of other faiths pray for solutions to the world's problems. They also pray for the unity of humankind.

Birthday of the Lord and His Church (April 6). On this date, Joseph Smith founded the Church of Jesus Christ of Latter-day Saints. Smith taught that Jesus was born on this date. Many Latter-day Saints spend the day reflecting on the life of Jesus, as well as on the legacy of Joseph Smith.

World Heritage Sunday (observed in April). On this day, churches of the Methodist tradition celebrate the enduring legacy of Methodism.

Earth Day (April 22). On this day, people everywhere reverence the earth and its many gifts.

Festival of Pentecost (fifty days after the Festival of the Lord's Supper). Members of the Worldwide Church of God give this day the same meaning as other Christians give to Pentecost, celebrating the descent of the Holy Spirit on the apostles. The Festival of Pentecost coincides with the Jewish Festival of Shavuot (also known as Pentecost), which celebrates the harvesting of spring crops and God's giving of the Torah to the Jews atop Mount Sinai.

Pentecost (fifty days after Easter Sunday). On this day, many Christians celebrate the coming of the Holy Spirit on Pentecost. For these Christians, the first Pentecost marked the formal creation of the Christian Church. The observance of Pentecost is especially important to churches of the Holiness and Pentecostal traditions.

Aldersgate Sunday (May 24). On this day, Methodists recall the work of John Wesley. Aldersgate was the name of a chapel in London where Wesley dedicated his life to spreading holiness.

Summer

Baptist Heritage Month (June).

Decision Sunday (observed in July). Members of the Salvation Army ask themselves whether they have truly followed Jesus. They believe that only those who imitate Jesus attain salvation. Decision Sunday is also celebrated during the months of February, April, and October.

Pioneer Sunday (July 24). On this date, the first Mormons entered the corporate limits of Salt Lake City. Pioneer Sunday is a state holiday in

Utah, and many communities observe the holiday by holding a parade.

Sacrament Sunday (second Sunday of July). At the conclusion of the regular Sunday service, Christian Scientists kneel and recite together the Lord's Prayer. They renew their faith on this day. Sacrament Sunday also occurs on the second Sunday in January.

Rally Day (September 15). The Salvation Army rallies its members back to church. They are reminded that the distractions of summer are once again behind them.

United Nations International Day of Peace (September 16). Many Christians throughout the world support the work of the United Nations, which emphasizes the interdependence of all peoples. Christians and those of other faiths mark this day by calling attention to armed conflict and praying and working for solutions.

Autumn

Festival of Trumpets (observed in September). At the Festival of Trumpets, members of the Worldwide Church of God look forward to the second coming of Christ. According to the Book of Revelation, trumpets will sound at the second coming.

Festival of Tabernacles (observed in September). On the Festival of Tabernacles, members of the Worldwide Church of God reflect on Jesus' role in nourishing people. He is referred to as the *water of life*.

Senior Soldier Day of Renewal (observed in September). On this day, members of the Salvation Army who are eighteen or older renew their commitment to Jesus. They make this promise by signing the Articles of War.

Festival of Atonement (observed in September or October). On this occasion, the Worldwide Church of God rejoices because Jesus reconciled humankind with God.

League of Mercy Sunday (observed in October). Salvationists honor those who have dedicated themselves to visiting the sick. These people travel to homes, hospitals, and care centers to give comfort to the ill.

World Communion Sunday (observed in October). On this day, many Protestant Christians celebrate the significance of sharing bread and wine. This sharing is known as *Communion, Eucharist*, or the *Lord's Supper*. This practice serves to unite Christians everywhere.

International Human Rights Day (December 10). On this day, Christians and people of other faiths affirm the worth and dignity of every human being. They mark the day by focusing attention on the need to protect people's basic human rights.

Discovering

1. Be able to explain each of the words in the vocabulary list.

2. In addition to denomination as a way of thinking of Protestant Christianity, what is the new pattern emerging in the nineteenth and twentieth centuries? State an example.

3. Draw a chart. Along the left side, write the names of each religious system described in this chapter. Across the top write: *Origin*, *Central Belief*, *Practices*, and *Reaping the Fruit*. Fill in the chart. Under *Origin*, write in two or three sentences or just phrases about the history; under *Central Belief*, write the belief which seems central to this group; under *Practices*, write two or three practices that come from this belief; and in the fourth column, write examples of how this is lived.

4. Why do the Baptists restrict membership to baptized adults and young people?

5. Do you think that a creed can be a source of division? Why?

6. According to the Adventist tradition, what does the distress caused by nations and natural disasters indicate?

7. According to John Wesley (Methodist tradition), what are the three ways that a person's faith shows itself?

8. How is the Unitarian faith different from all other Protestant faiths?

9. Why do the Quakers spend their meetings in silence?

10. According to Christian Science, on what does healing depend?

11. What is the function of the *Book of Mormon*?

Exploring

1. Choose two groups described in this chapter. Then compare and contrast their beliefs. Look especially for how they are similar.

2. Meet with two classmates. Choose one of the groups described in this chapter and thoroughly discuss its central beliefs and practices. Try to find how this group's practices flow from their beliefs.

3. The Baptist faith requires that a person completely turn away from sin. What is your definition of sin? What do you think completely turning away from sin requires?

4. How do you define grace? According to your understanding, how important is it for daily living?

5. How could the issues of slavery and racial equality divide the Methodist Church that taught people to put faith and love into practice? What other Churches were affected by these issues? What issues are dividing Churches today?

6. Quakers believe that revelation is ongoing. Would most Christians share this view? Why or why not?

7. What do you find most helpful in Christian Science ideas of healing?

8. Often conversion experiences set the foundation for faith. Compare and contrast the conversion experiences of George Fox (Quaker tradition), and John and Charles Wesley (Methodist tradition) with the conversion experience of Joseph Smith (Mormon tradition). How did these experiences lay the foundations for the various traditions? Are the conversion experiences contradictory?

9. In a few brief paragraphs, give your own definition of *soul*. With what tradition, Christian or non-Christian, are your thoughts most in line?

10. The Salvation Army defines salvation as "knowing God through a personal relationship with Jesus Christ." How do you define salvation? How important do you think salvation is? Why?

11. Why do you think there are so many different beliefs about baptism?

Integrating

1. Imagine that you are a member of one of the church bodies described in this chapter. What would be some central concepts in your thought? How would you live? Be able to explain this to a classmate.

2. Which of the beliefs or practices described in this chapter most directly challenge your own belief and practice? Why do you think this is so? Clearly state your own belief or practice on this topic.

3. What is the dominant religious group in your area? How does the presence of this group affect life in your area? Do further research to find out how this group's presence may be felt. Do they sponsor special projects or provide programs for specific groups such as youth, handicapped, or aged? Does this group have political influence? How is this felt? Be prepared to share your research with your class.

4. Even though we live in a tolerant religious climate in North America, we can still cite instances of persecution, bias, and intolerance in our own times. Why do you think this is so? What can be done to overcome this?

5. What are the pros and cons of not having a written summary of beliefs and practices? If you were founding a Church, would you want to have a written summary of your beliefs and practices?

Words to Know

Adventist

Assemblies of God

baptism of the Holy Spirit

Baptists

charismatics

Christian Science

Church of Jesus Christ of Latter-day Saints

Church of the Nazarene

circuit riders

English Baptists

entire sanctification

Evangelical movement

general atonement

glossolalia

grace

Holiness movement

Jehovah's Witnesses

justification

Methodist Church

millenialism

ordinance

Pentecostalism

practical divinity

Quakers, Friends

Restoration tradition

Salvation Army

sanctification

scientific prayer

Seventh-day Adventists

testimony

Unitarian tradition

Unitarian Universalist Association

Unity tradition

Chapter 8

After reading this chapter, you will be able to
- Identify major beliefs of Islam and Bahá'í
- Compare Islam with other major religions
- Begin to assess the influence of Islam on the world today

ISLAM AND BAHA'Í

Introduction

Each year, Muslims eagerly await the arrival of Ramaḍān which begins at the first sighting of the new moon. Ramaḍān is the ninth month of the Islamic calendar. The first day of Ramaḍān signals the start of a month-long fast. From dawn to sunset, Muslims refrain from drinking, eating, or enjoying sensual pleasures, such as listening to music. Food and drinks are not the only things from which Muslims turn away during fasting. They are called upon to avoid negative feelings and to focus on charity and prayer.

The world's Muslims look forward to the great fast of Ramaḍān. It is an opportunity for them to increase their discipline and self-control. Fasting in Ramaḍān is one of the five Pillars of Islam. A young Muslim, Athar Tayyab, summed up one of the chief purposes of Ramaḍān: "During this time you learn not only how to control your appetite, but also how to control your anger. . . . It is a time that makes you stronger."

For many people, the thought of going without food and water for eleven hours seems incredible. Surprisingly, many Muslims do not find this kind of fasting difficult. In the words of sixteen-year-old Athar Tayyab: "Fasting is not that much of an adjustment because I grew up as a Muslim. . . . I'm used to it, so there isn't as much of a physical strain on me." For one of Athar's classmates, Saleem Abdul-Musawwir, the month-long fast, at least at the beginning, requires some effort.

According to Saleem, some hours of the fast are more difficult than others. "The hardest part of the day is lunchtime because this is when your hunger really hits," he said. "But what motivates me to continue the fast is a belief that what I'm doing is right." Saleem also notes the difficulty of observing the fast of Ramaḍān in a society that does not understand: "Most of the students in my school do not understand the importance of Ramaḍān, and thus they look at me very strangely when I spend my lunch hour in the library."

Muslims of all ages are quick to point out that Ramaḍān is a happy and joyous month. The evening meal takes place after sunset and is a festive time. People celebrate the temporary breaking of the fast. Evening prayer follows the meal, which, in turn, is followed by additional nocturnal worship. In Muslim neighborhoods, people normally visit with one another before retiring.

The great Muslim fast of Ramaḍān officially comes to an end on the Feast of the Fast Breaking, one of the two most important festivals of the Islamic calendar. For three days, the Muslim community celebrates a sense of achievement. During this time, people gather for family reunions and give new clothing and gifts to children.

Tilling the Soil

Islam is the religion preached by Muhammad. Followers of Islam are known as **Muslims**. Islam joins Judaism and Christianity as the third great religion of the West. It shares with these religions fundamental perspectives concerning God, human beings, and moral living. Of course, Islam also has its own contributions to make to the world's religious community. Events in recent years such as the oil crisis of the 1970s, the holding of hostages in the U.S. embassy in Iran in the 1980s, and the Gulf War of the 1990s have drawn the world's attention to the Islamic community. Events such as these have raised questions, caused confusion, and fostered prejudice against Muslims. An accurate understanding of Islam is crucial for understanding the events of our world today.

The word *Islām* is related to the Arabic words *silm* and *salam*, which mean peace, purity, acceptance, and commitment. One of the most beautiful names of God in Islam is "The Peace." As a religion, Islam calls for complete acceptance of the teachings and guidance of God. The full connotation of the word *Islām* means "the peace that comes when one's life is surrendered to God" or submission—"living in peace with the Creator, [within] one's self, with other people, and with the environment." A person becomes a Muslim when he or she utters the words, "There is no god except God, and Muhammad is the messenger of God." From the Muslim perspective, this declaration signifies that the person believes in one universal God and in all of God's messengers and the scriptures they gave to humankind.

Islam
the religion preached by Muhammad; based on submission to God which leads to peace with God, people, and the environment

Muslims
followers of Islam

The Birth of Islam

The birthplace of Islam, like Judaism and Christianity, is the Middle East. It began in the Arabian peninsula, present-day Saudi Arabia, in the sixth century C.E. The religion of the Arabs living in that area was polytheistic and animistic. This included the worship of inanimate objects and spirits. In this area and at this time, immorality ran rampant. The people were addicted to drinking, gambling, and sexual promiscuity. Murder and looting were common place. The only loyalty which existed was to one's tribe. Into this world was born **Muhammad** in about the year 570. Muhammad was born of poor parents in the area of Mecca, a caravan city in the Hijāz region of northwestern Arabia.

Muhammad lived near the **Ka'ba**, which means "house of God." According to tradition, the Ka'ba was built by Abraham and his son Ishmael. The ancient building was made of stone; some believe that it was the site of a sanctuary (holy place) constructed by Adam. It was intended to be a place where the true God would be worshiped, but Arabs before the time of Muhammad had placed more than 360 idols in the building and worshiped them.

Muhammad
founder and prophet of Islam

Ka'ba
Arabian house of God, traditionally thought to have been built by Abraham and his son Ishmael; holy shrine of Islam

Muhammad, the Prophet

Tradition tells us that Muhammad's father died before he was born, his mother when he was six, and his grandfather two years later; thereafter he was reared by an uncle. Because Muhammad spent most of his childhood among the desert Bedouins, who herded cattle, he developed a deep love for the Arabic language, learned patience and forbearance, and an appreciation of solitude.

As a young man, Muhammad became a caravan guide for Khadīja, a rich widow. This gave him the opportunity to make journeys to Yemen, Syria, Ethiopia, Persia, Egypt, and Palestine. On these journeys, he met and talked with Jewish and Christian merchants about their beliefs. Eventually, at the age of 25, Muhammad married Khadīja, who was fifteen years older than he. They had six children, of whom only a daughter, Fatima, survived.

However, Muhammad was not settled, nor at peace. Muhammad was deeply concerned about religion, and he suffered inner turmoil. The polytheistic animism and often irreligious lives of his fellow Arabs distressed him greatly. In 610, Muhammad had a religious experience in a cave on Mt. Hira, where he often went to meditate. There he received a revelation from the angel Gabriel who told him to proclaim.

> *READ in the name of your Lord Who creates,*
>
> *creates man from **a clot**!*
>
> *READ and your Lord is most Generous;*
>
> *[it is He] Who teaches*
>
> *by means of the pen,*
>
> *teaches man what he does not know.*
>
> —Qur'ān, *Sūra 96, 1–5; translated by T.B. Irving*
> *(Brattleboro, VT: Amana Books, 1988).*

"Faith does not increase, nor does it decrease; because a diminution in it would be unbelief."
—Abu Hanifa

As Muhammad left the cave, he heard a voice: "You are the messenger of Allāh, and I am Gabriel" (the name of an angel in both Judaism and Christianity). Like the prophets of old, Muhammad received his commission; he was the chosen bearer of a divine message. Muhammad returned to Khadīja, terrified, saying he was either a prophet or possessed. In time, Muhammad began to understand that he was the next prophet in the long line from Abraham to Jesus. At first Khadīja put him off, but eventually she came to believe him and became his first convert. Other members of his family became believers as well, but after three years of preaching, Muhammad had only a few dozen followers.

Islamic Beginnings

In a polytheistic, immoral, and unjust society, the reasons are clear for such a slow response. Muhammad preached one God, a high moral code, and a just society. Many merchants of the area made a good living selling idols to pilgrims on the way to the Ka'ba. Soon the merchants of Mecca plotted to kill him because they would lose money if the new religion won out. Opponents of Muhammad also sought to intimidate his followers through murder, torture, and trade embargo. On June 20, 622, upon learning of an attempt to assassinate him, Muhammad and his few followers fled 220 miles to the north to the city of Yathrib, now known as Medina. This emigration is called **Hijra**, or "night of the flight," and the date has become known as the *Anno Hijra*, or center of time for Arabs. In other words, this is the year 1; all events are dated from this great event which inaugurated the Islamic era.

According to the Qur'ān and Islamic tradition, the Hijra was preceded by the *Miraj*. The Miraj refers to Muhammad's visit to heaven and hell, during which he conversed with ancient prophets. The high point of the Miraj was Muhammad's conversation with Allāh.

Muhammad was welcomed in Medina. His ideas caught on, and soon he had thousands of followers and built the first mosque. In 629 or 630, Muhammad returned to Mecca with an army of thousands. Without bloodshed, his forces took control of the city. Muhammad removed the images housed in the Ka'ba and restored the building to its original purpose: the worship of the one God. In the face of these actions, the inhabitants of Mecca embraced Islam. From then on, Islam grew rapidly, and all the Arab tribes submitted to Allāh. Muhammad died in 632 at Medina.

The Arabs were now on fire with religious zeal to spread their new faith. They exploded out of their Arabian homeland on their famous horses and war camels, conquering every group along the way. Within a hundred years, Islam had spread throughout the Middle East and North Africa, ranging all the way from China to India to Spain. Their northern advance was finally stopped at the Battle of Tours in France in 732 by the Christian Franks under the leadership of Charles Martel.

Through "conversion, commerce, and conquest," the number of Muslims grew. Islam influenced the rise of civilizations and learning centers. Islam brought together Eastern and Western thought, and in doing so, contributed to the fields of architecture, art, astronomy, geography, history, language, law, literature, mathematics, medicine, physics,

Hijra
the night flight by Muhammad and his followers on June 20, 622; the beginning of the Muslim calendar

and science. It has been said that the "genius of Arab civilization set the stage for the European Renaissance." This Islamic empire, however, was too vast and eventually broke into three sections.

As the European nations began extending their influence throughout the Middle East, the influence of Islam on political affairs, and to some extent on people's lives, began to diminish. In the twentieth century, however, colonial rule began to give way, and new predominantly Muslim nations emerged. Consequently, Islam has returned to the world stage as an economic, political, and social force.

Schools of Islam

There are schools of Islam, akin to the traditions of Protestant Christianity such as Lutheran, Reformed, Baptist. In Islam, the Sunnī, Shī'i, and Sufi schools are predominant; those who belong to these schools are known as *Sunnīs*, *Shī'is*, and *Sufis*. The first major split in Islam was into the two factions, the Sunnīs and Shī'is. The Sufi school arose in the ninth century as a reaction against legalism.

Sunnīs

The Sunnī school emphasizes only two main sources for Islam: the Qur'ān and the Sunna. For **Sunnīs**, the Sunna (collected in the Ḥadīth) supplements the Qur'ān; it speaks where the Qur'ān is silent. The Sunnīs are the largest school, 90 percent of all Muslims, and are considered the orthodox or traditional Muslims.

Shī'is

The word *Shī'is* comes from the Arabic *shi'at 'Alī*, which means "party of 'Alī." 'Alī was the husband of Muhammad's daughter Fatima. The **Shī'is** were a group who believed that the immediate successor to Muhammad should be a member of his family; they claim that Muhammad chose 'Alī to succeed him. After the death of Muhammad, the first Shī'is came to regard 'Alī as their **imām** (leader). For Shī'is, the imām is "sinless, endowed with supernatural knowledge and power, and capable of interpreting infallibly the Qur'ān." Throughout the centuries, Shī'is have looked to the descendants of 'Alī and Fatima for leadership; every age has an imām. Twelver Shī'is, or Twelvers, believe that the Twelfth Imām never fully revealed himself; they await his return. In short, Shī'is see God, Muhammad, and 'Alī as intimately related. A large number of Muslims who live in Iran and Iraq are Shī'is.

Sufis

The ninth-century Sufi school arose as a reaction against legalism. It also promoted an intense personal relationship with God; thus, **Sufis** are known as mystics. Mystics are those holy people who have such a deep prayer-life that they experience an intense awareness of the presence of God. The Sufis finally became organized in the twelfth century when they began to group themselves into brotherhoods or tarīqas (paths). The Sufi way of life, which includes the wearing of woolen garments, the use of music in rituals, contemplation, and community living in special buildings, reflects the influence of Christian monasteries.

One of the greatest Sufi contributions is their literature. The Sufi masters used teaching stories to transmit spiritual insights to their disciples

Sunnīs
Muslims of the Sunnī school who reverence the Ḥadīth as a supplement to the Qur'ān; the large group of orthodox or traditional Muslims

Shī'is
Muslims of the Shī'i school who believe that the immediate successor to Muhammad should be a member of his family

imām
Islamic leader able to interpret the Qu'rān infallibly; for Shī'is a descendent of 'Alī and Fatima

Sufis
Muslims of the Sufi school, who are often mystics

and to awaken deeper levels of spiritual consciousness in them. While Sufi orders have been in decline for some years, and officially abolished in Turkey, sudden interest in Sufi wisdom has occurred throughout Europe and North America.

Planting the Seed

Islam in America

Like Christianity and Judaism, Islam was present in North America from the earliest years. The first real attempt to establish Islam came with Muhammad Alexander Russell Webb, who was converted to Islam in 1888. Webb came to New York in 1892 and opened the Oriental Publishing Company and began a periodical, *The Moslem World*, of which he was editor. It was also at this time that large-scale immigration from the Eastern Mediterranean began. People came from Syria, Lebanon, Iran, India, Turkey, and other Islamic countries. Wherever sizable numbers of Muslims gathered, attempts were made to organize communities. Detroit and New York were among the first Islamic centers. Other cities included Pittsburgh, Cleveland, Worchester, Boston, and Providence.

The Islamic Society of North America is one of the most inclusive Sunnī organizations. It is made up of several societies around the country, each of which focuses on organizing educational, social, and spiritual activities. The societies are committed to helping Muslims fulfill their religious obligations, educating young Muslims, and promoting better understanding of Islam. The Islamic Society of North America has a student organization known as the Muslim Students' Association of the United States, which serves "the best interest of Islam and Muslim students in the United States and Canada so as to enable them to practice Islam as a complete way of life." The Islamic Society of North America has its headquarters in Plainfield, Indiana.

Among Shī'i Muslims, the Islamic Center of America continues to play an important role. For example, it publishes Shī'i literature, which explains differences between Sunnīs and Shī'is, and helps to dispel general misconceptions surrounding Islam. The Islamic Center of America, founded by Imām Mohamad Jawad Chirri in 1962, began as the Islamic Center of Detroit and is one of the oldest Shī'i Muslim organizations on the continent of North America. In recent years, membership has risen dramatically. The Islamic Center of America has offices in Detroit, Michigan, and has affiliate centers around the country.

There are Sufi brotherhoods, or orders, throughout the world. The International Association of Sufism (IAS) was founded in 1983 for the purpose of bringing these orders together. In short, it seeks to unite the world's Sufis and educate people about Sufi principles. The IAS invites scholars, teachers, and students from every variety of Sufism to "join in the common purpose of seeking greater knowledge, mutual understanding, and the dissemination of Sufi principles." The IAS publishes materials in Arabic, English, French, German, Persian, and Spanish and is located in San Rafael, California.

Signs in Creation

In the creation of Heaven and Earth, the alternation between night and day, the ships which plow the sea with something to benefit mankind, and any water God sends down from the sky with which to revive the earth following its death, and to scatter every kind of animal throughout it, and directing the winds and clouds which are driven along between the sky and earth, are (all) signs for folk who use their reason.

—Qur'ān, *Sūra 2:164; translated by T.B. Irving (Brattleboro, VT: Amana Books, 1988).*

Let's Talk about It . . .

1. What is the relationship between creation and the works of humankind?
2. Of what are all the mentioned things signs?

Minaret of the mosque in Cedar Rapids, Iowa

Cedar Rapids, Iowa, is home to the oldest continuously existing Muslim community in North America. Thus its Islamic center is called the "Mother Mosque" of North America. In 1914, there were about forty-five Muslim immigrants in the area. By the mid-20s, Cedar Rapids boasted more than fifty shops and grocery stores owned and operated by Arabs. In 1925, Muslims first used a rented building as a temporary mosque. They began planning for building a permanent home which eventually opened in 1936; this was the first mosque constructed in North America. By the early 1950s, Muslims started to organize and establish active contact with other Muslim communities in the United States and Canada, and the Federation of Islamic Associations of the United States and Canada was founded. The first International Muslim Convention for the United States and Canada was held June 27–29, 1952, in Cedar Rapids. The headquarters of the Islamic Association is now in Detroit.

Today there are more than 250 mosques and Islamic centers in the United States and Canada, with more than 200 of these in the United States. California and New York have the largest numbers of Muslims. Other significant concentrations are in Illinois, New Jersey, Pennsylvania, Ohio, and Michigan. Islam grew from about one million members in the United States in 1965 to more than 5.5 million today. There are about 120,000 Muslims in Canada.

African American Muslims

According to the American Muslim Council, 40 percent of the Muslims who live in the United States are African American, and belong to a number of organizations. Other Muslim groups estimate the percentage at 25.

The Black Muslim movement in the U.S. began with Wallace Fard, who immigrated to the country from Arabia in 1930. Elijah Muhammad (1897–1975) took charge of the Lost-Found Nation of Islam in 1934, preaching a mixture of Islam and black separatism. For the ten years before his assassination by religious rivals, Malcolm X (1925–1965) was the well-known spokesperson for African American Muslims. He made the Hajj, pilgrimage to Mecca, in 1964, and thereafter moved toward the original Islam and away from the Nation of Islam. In a letter from Mecca, Malcolm X wrote:

There are tens of thousands of pilgrims, from all over the world . . . but we were all participating in the same ritual, displaying a spirit of unity and brotherhood that my experiences in America had led me to believe never could exist between the white and the non-white.

We were truly all the same (brothers)—because their belief in one God had removed the "white" from their minds, the "white" from their behavior, and the "white" from their attitude.

I could see from this that perhaps if white Americans could accept the Oneness of God, then perhaps, too, they could accept in reality the Oneness of Man—and cease to measure, and hinder, and harm others in terms of their "differences" in color.

> —*Quoted in* The Autobiography of Malcolm X *by Malcolm X with Alex Haley.*

Following Elijah Muhammad's death, leadership of the Nation of Islam passed to his son, Warith Deen Muhammed. Warith essentially disbanded the organization and encouraged many of its members to embrace Islam as it is practiced by Sunnī Muslims. Warith Deen Muhammad, described by his followers as a "sincere, humble and deeply religious" man, "speaks for more Muslims than any other Muslim leader in this country," according to Steven Elijah Muhammad Barboza, a Muslim who has written about Islam in America. "He was responsible for probably one of the largest mass conversions in American history, where there was no bloodshed or warfare, but he doesn't choose to put himself in the headlines." The Muslim community is located in Chicago and welcomes people of any race.

The Nation of Islam was revived in 1978 by Louis Farrakhan, who describes himself as the "spiritual son of Elijah Muhammad." Because of its tendency toward separatism, Farrakhan's group is viewed with mixed enthusiasm. Farrakhan's million-man march on Washington in the late 1990s brought the Nation of Islam to the attention of the world and impressed many with the ideology of that form of Islam in the U.S.

Taking Root

Beliefs of Islam

Allāh is the Arabic name for the One and Only God. "There is no God but Allāh and Muhammad is his prophet." This the central affirmation of Islam. Muslims share with Christians and Jews belief in one God. For Muslims, this belief is a strict monotheism without any hint of other gods or an incarnation into a human form. God is One. God's oneness, or unity, is expressed in Sūra 112 on The Unity, which reads, "Say: He, Allāh, is One. Allāh is He on Whom all depend. He begets not, nor is He begotten. And none is like Him."

God is infinite. God is personal. God is loving and kind. At the same time, God is a just and merciful judge who rewards the believers and damns the unbelievers. God is the creator of the universe and absolute ruler. Muslims believe that Allāh has ninety-nine beautiful names, such as The Gracious, The Merciful, The Beneficent, The Creator, The All-Knowing, The All-Wise, The Lord of the Universe, The First, The Last, and others. From the perspective of Islam, Allāh is the Creator of all human beings and the God of all. Muslims put their trust in him and they seek his help and his guidance. The Qur'ān speaks of Allāh in these words:

> He is God,
> besides Whom there is no [other] deity;
> Knowing the unseen and the Visible,
> He is the Mercy-giving, the Merciful!
> He is God [Alone]
> besides Whom there is no [other] god,
> the Sovereign, the Holy, the [Source of] Peace,
> the Secure, the Preserver, the Powerful,
> the Compeller, the Magnificent:
> glory be to God ahead of anything
> they may associate [with Him]!
> He is God,
> the Creator, the Maker, the Shaper.
> His are the Finest Names.
> Whatever is in Heaven and Earth
> celebrates Him. He is
> the Powerful, the Wise.

> —Qur'ān, *Sūra 59:22–24; translated by T.B. Irving (Brattleboro, VT: Amana Books, 1988).*

Allāh
Islamic name for the one God

God of Islam

God is the One Who splits the seed and the Kernel,

He brings the living from the dead, and is the One

Who brings the dead from the living.

Such is God; yet still you shrug Him off!

Kindler of morn, He grants night for repose,

and the sun and moon for telling time.

Such is the measure of the Powerful, the Aware!

He is the One Who has placed the stars

to guide you through the darkness on land and at sea.

We have spelled out signs for people who know.

It is He Who has reproduced you from a single soul,

and [granted you] a settlement [on earth]

and a resting place after [death].

We have spelled out signs for people who understand.

It is He Who sends down water from the sky. Thus we bring forth plants of every type with it . . . Look at their fruit as He causes it to grow and ripen,

In that are signs for folk who believe.

. . . Glory be to Him; Exalted is He over whatever they describe!

Deviser of Heavens and Earth! How can He have a son while He has no consort? He created everything and is Aware of everything!

Such is God, your Lord;

there is no deity except Him,

the Creator of everything,

so serve Him. He is

a Trustee for everything!

No powers of vision can comprehend Him, while He comprehends [all] vision; and He is the Subtle, the Informed.

—Qur'ān, *Sūra 6:95–103*

Let's Talk about It . . .

1. What specific attributes are given to Allāh in this passage?

2. What message does this passage convey?

3. How does the Qur'ān's description of God compare to the Bible's description of God?

Muslims believe that angels, such as Gabriel, Michael, Raphael, and Uriel, are messengers sent to carry out the will of Allāh. Prophets are also messengers whom God uses to bring divine revelations to people. For Muslims, the chain of prophets began with Adam, the first man. The chain includes twenty-eight prophets, including twenty-one well-known biblical figures, such as Noah, Abraham, Ishmael, Isaac, Jacob, Joseph, Job, Moses, Aaron, David, Solomon, Elias, Jonah, John the Baptist, and Jesus.

Muhammad is the last and greatest of the prophets, "the summation and the culmination"; this is where the chain ends. God sent Muhammad to explain the true mission of Abraham, Isaac, Jacob, Moses, and Jesus. Muhammad is "the seal of the prophets" who purified all previous messages, and gave humankind a final, complete, and eternal message. Islam is the message, and the Qur'ān is the revelation.

> *"A man walking along a path felt very thirsty. Reaching a well he descended into it, drank his fill and came up. Then he saw a dog with its tongue hanging out, trying to lick up mud to quench its thirst. The man saw that the dog was feeling the same thirst as he had felt so he went down into the well again and filled his shoe with water and gave the dog a drink. God forgave his sins for this action." The Prophet . . . was asked: "Messenger of God, are we rewarded for kindness towards animals?" He said, "There is a reward for kindness to every living thing."*
>
> —*The Ḥadīth of Bukhari.*

The Sacred Writings

Islam honors several holy books which predate the time of Muhammad. These scriptures are considered to be books of revelation:

- The Scrolls—ten scriptures given to Abraham and since lost
- The Torah, the "books of Moses"
- The Psalms, revealed to David
- The Gospels, revealed to Jesus

Qur'ān

the holy book of Islam; a record of the words that God gave to the angel Gabriel to deliver to Muhammad

The **Qur'ān** is the most important of the writings of Islam. Muslims believe that God's self-revelation happened gradually through the centuries and that this revelation culminated in the Qur'ān. The Qur'ān is a record of the words that God gave to the angel Gabriel to deliver to Muhammad. Muhammad memorized these words and then dictated them to his companions, who, in turn, gave them to scribes. Muslims regard the Qur'ān as the cornerstone of their faith, the holy book of Islam.

sūra

a chapter in the Qur'ān

The Qur'ān focuses on God's relationship with creation, which is its central theme. The Qur'ān contains 114 **sūras** (chapters). Every sūra but one begins with the words: "in the name of God, the Mercy-giving, the Merciful."

The **Sunna**, which means "way," is second in importance to the Qur'ān. It contains the **Ḥadīth**, a collection of the teachings, sayings, and actions of the Prophet Muhammad which were reported and collected by his companions. They explain and elaborate upon the Qur'ān. The Qur'ān and the Sunna provide the framework for **Sharī'ah**, the sacred law of Islam. Sharī'ah covers every aspect of a community's life—public and private, social and economic, religious and political.

Words of the Prophet

These are some of the sayings attributed directly to Muhammad:

"[The person] who eats his fill while his neighbor goes without food is not a believer."

"Powerful is not [the person] who knocks the other down, indeed powerful is he who controls himself in a fit of anger."

"God does not judge according to your bodies and appearances but he knows your hearts and looks into your deeds."

Let's Talk about It . . .

1. What do you think are the three messages being conveyed by the above sayings of Muhammad?
2. Do these messages speak to you?

Judgment

Muslims believe that there will be a final judgment day at the end of the world when Allāh will judge the merits of every human being. Some will enter paradise and others will be sent to hell. Heaven is called "The Gardens of Delight." A popular image of heaven is an oasis with cool water, fruit, and wine. A popular image of hell is hot winds and boiling water, a proper punishment for unbelievers and the wicked.

Jesus in Islam

Muslims respect and revere Jesus as a great prophet. Whenever they say or write his name, the words "peace be upon him" immediately follow. The Qur'ān says that God showed many miracles through Jesus. The Qur'ān attributes these words to him:

"I have brought you a sign from your Lord. I shall create something in the shape of a bird for you out of clay, and blow into it so it will become a [real] bird with God's permission. I shall cure those who are blind from birth and lepers, and revive the dead with God's permission" (Sūra 3:49).

Although they do not believe Jesus died on the cross, Muslims do believe that Jesus ascended into paradise (heaven) and eagerly await his second coming. They believe in Jesus' virgin birth and look upon Mary as the purest woman to have ever lived; the Qur'ān devotes an entire chapter to her.

Growing and Blooming

The Five Pillars

five Pillars of Islam

the five most
important obligations
or practices of Islam

The **five Pillars of Islam** are "acts of devotion, or service," the five most important obligations or practices of Islam. Every Muslim must fulfill these obligations over the course of his or her lifetime. The five Pillars of Islam are Shahāda (the profession of faith), Ṣalāt (prayer, or worship), Zakāt (almsgiving or charity), Ṣawm (fasting), and Ḥajj (pilgrimage). The five Pillars of Islam unite the Umma, or community of believers.

Profession of Faith

Shahāda

the professon of faith
to which a Muslim
witnesses

The first of the pillars is the **Shahāda**, the profession of faith to which a Muslim witnesses: "I bear witness that 'There is no God but Allāh'; I bear witness that 'Muhammad is his prophet.' " A Muslim, one who submits to God, worships the one God and affirms that there is no other god but Allāh. Muhammad is the final prophet of God, and the Qur'ān, revealed through him, is the final and totally accurate word of God. Muslims are to recite this profession daily. One becomes a Muslim simply by professing this article of faith in the presence of witnesses.

Daily Prayer

Ṣalāt

the recitation of
prayers five times daily
required of Muslims

The second pillar is the **Ṣalāt**, the recitation of prayers five times daily: at dawn, noon, mid-afternoon, sundown, and before retiring. Facing Mecca, the holiest city in the Islamic world, the Muslim bows down, kneels, and touches the ground with the forehead. Prayer keeps consciousness of God alive in every Muslim. The Muslim prays that the purpose of life shall not be lost amidst the confusion of worldly activities. Muslims seek God's guidance and ask God's help in following the right path.

Muslims at prayer in New York City

Muslims gather on Friday for their holy day. Friday is considered sacred because Muslims believe that the Day of Judgment will be on a Friday. They gather in the **mosque** at noon for prayer. A sermon is given by the imām, and he leads the group in prayer. In the Islamic world, there are three main holy places: the Mosque of Ka'ba in Mecca, the Mosque of the Prophet Muhammad in Medina, and the Mosque Aqsa in Jerusalem, which is adjacent to the Dome of the Rock. The word *mosque* comes from the Arabic *masjid*, meaning "place of prostration."

Worship in Islam, whether ritual or non-ritual, trains the individual to love his or her Creator. The Creator's love spurs him or her to do good, wipe out evil and oppression in human society, and make God's word supreme in the world.

mosque
place of worship for Muslims

Almsgiving

Zakāt, the giving of alms is the third pillar. For Muslims, giving to those in need demonstrates devotion to God. Every Muslim makes an obligatory payment of one-fortieth (2.5 percent) of his or her income to the annual charity. In addition, further almsgiving is encouraged and expected. This practice develops in the Muslim generosity of character and eliminates selfishness; it is an expression of love for our fellow human beings. Most of these funds provide for the basic needs of the poor in the community, for debtors and travelers, and for the work of making converts. Almsgiving redistributes wealth, which brings social justice and thereby eases tensions between the upper and lower classes. Almsgiving increases a society's stability and prevents social unrest.

Zakāt
the required almsgiving in Islam

Have you seen someone who rejects religion?
That is the person who pushes the orphan aside
and does not promote feeding the needy.
It will be too bad for the prayerful
who are absent-minded as they pray,
who aim to be noticed
while they hold back contributions.

—Qur'ān, *Sūra 107.*

Fasting

The fourth pillar of Islam is **Ṣawm**, the fasting during the month of **Ramaḍān**. This is the month in which the Qur'ān was revealed. According to the Qur'ān, a person who fasts demonstrates deep and personal devotion to God. Through fasting, Muslims gain a richer perception of God. The fast encourages the suppression of desires and passions; in this way it proclaims the supremacy of the law of God. Fasting allows a person to experience hunger—to understand the suffering of the poor. Throughout the month of Ramaḍān, Muslims fast from dawn to sunset, abstaining from drinking, eating, smoking, and other sensual pleasures during the hours of the fast.

Ṣawm
the fasting during Ramaḍān for Muslims

Ramaḍān
the month of fasting for Muslims

Pilgrimage

Ḥajj

the pilgrimage to Mecca which is to be performed once during life by every Muslim

The fifth pillar is the **Ḥajj**, which means "visit to the revered place." This is the pilgrimage to Mecca which is to be performed once during life by every Muslim whose health permits it and who can afford it. Muslims visit the Ka'ba, the location of the house built by Abraham. The Ḥajj is the realization of the universal human community in the worship of God and is considered to be the peak of a Muslim's religious life.

In part, the Ḥajj recalls the trials and tribulations of Abraham, his wife Hagar, and his eldest son Ishmael. The Ḥajj takes place every year, and its focus is the Ka'ba. Those who participate in the Ḥajj follow an ancient order of a ritual, which dates from the time of Muhammad. Three rituals must be observed while the faithful pilgrim is in Mecca:

- walk around the Ka'ba seven times and kiss the "black stone" each time
- walk between the two hills, Safa and Marwa, seven times in commemoration of Hagar's search for water
- climb the Mount of Mercy where Muhammad is said to have preached his farewell sermon

Other practices of Islam include the following: A Muslim must tell the truth at all times. Gambling, adultery, stealing, and murder are forbidden. Kindness to animals is necessary. The eating of pork is forbidden. Aged parents must be provided for. Muslims practice circumcision.

Reaping the Fruit

Bahá'í

Bahá'í

follower of Bahá (glory) or follower of Bahá'ulláh (glory of God)

Báb

a young Persian man, Siyyid [Mirza] 'Ali Muhammad, the originator of the Bahá'í faith

Bábí's

followers of the Báb of the Bahá'í faith

The word **Bahá'í** means "follower of Bahá (glory)," or "follower of Bahá'ulláh (glory of God)." The history of the Bahá'í faith begins with the emergence of the **Báb**, although it has some roots in Islam and Hinduism. The title *Báb*, which means "gate," refers to a young Persian man, Siyyid [Mirza] 'Ali Muhammad (1819–1850). In 1844, Siyyid [Mirza] 'Ali Muhammad told people that he was the promised Twelfth Imām of the Shī'is. He explained that he was an independent Messenger who had been sent to prepare people for another revelation from God, a new Manifestation. Within a six-year period, the Báb attracted tens of thousands of followers, which greatly alarmed the Shī'is clergy. Many of the Báb's followers (**Bábí's**) were either executed or imprisoned. In 1850, Siyyid' Ali Muhammad, or the Báb, was executed.

One of the imprisoned Bábí's was Husayn-'Ali (1817–1892). In 1863, Husayn-'Ali told his fellow Bábí's that he was the Manifestation of God whom the Báb had mentioned. Most Bábí's believed Husayn-'Ali's words and gave him the title *Bahá'ulláh*, which means "glory of God." In their eyes, he was the bearer, or deliverer, of a great message to humankind. They became known as Bahá'ís (followers of Bahá). On a number of occasions, Bahá'ulláh was forced to leave Persia (present-day Iran). He died at 'Akká (Acre), Palestine, in 1892.

After Bahá'ulláh's death, his eldest son, 'Abdu'l-Bahá (–1921), assumed leadership of the Bahá'ís and served as the official interpreter of his father's writings. Although Bahá'ís do not regard 'Abdu'l-Bahá as another Manifestation of God, or Messenger, they look upon his decisions and writings as divinely guided. The Bahá'í scriptures consist of the writings of the Báb, Bahá'ulláh, and 'Abdu'l-Bahá.

'Abdu'l-Bahá was succeeded by his eldest grandson, Shoghi Effendi, who was known as the Guardian of the Bahá'ís and carried the Bahá'í message throughout the world. During his thirty-six years of leadership, Effendi appointed twenty-seven people to serve as promoters and protectors of the faith. Six years after Effendi's death, this group was replaced by the Universal House of Justice. This governing body is made up of nine elected Bahá'ís from around the world.

Further organization includes an International Teaching Center and, in each country where Bahá'í is present, an elected National Spiritual Assembly which holds an annual convention. Each local group elects a Local Spiritual Assembly. All members of the faith are considered equal, and therefore there is no clergy. No one is bound by any other member's interpretation of Bahá'í writings.

Unity

Unity is the overall theme of the Bahá'í religion. It teaches three areas of unity:

• Oneness of God—one God

• Oneness of Religion—one religion progressively revealed by God

• Oneness of Humanity—equality of all people before God

Oneness of humanity

The earliest leaders of the Bahá'í faith devoted themselves to helping humankind find common ground in the face of their many problems. As a consequence, Bahá'ís have actively supported organizations that promote international cooperation, such as the United Nations, and support an international tribunal. They see humankind as one family and look upon earth as one home. In the words of Bahá'ulláh, "The earth is but one country and humankind its citizens."

Bahá'í dedication to fostering humankind's oneness has given rise to a number of commitments. Taken together, these commitments form the Bahá'í mission. Bahá'ís have pledged themselves to developing a single language for the world's peoples, to providing an equal level of education for people everywhere, to ending all forms of prejudice, to eradicating differences between the sexes, to closing the gap between rich and poor, and to bringing about a Great Peace which would make war illegal.

Oneness of religion and oneness of God

From the Bahá'í perspective, the religions of the world share the same essence or inner form. They have labeled this religious core *Truth*. Bahá'ís understand Truth as God's guidance, as light, as love, and as mercy. Bahá'í scriptures encourage people to investigate Truth for themselves: "God has not intended [human beings] to imitate blindly [their] fathers and ancestors. He has endowed [them] with mind, or the faculty of reasoning, by the exercise of which [they are] to investigate and discover the truth." Elsewhere, the Bahá'í scriptures suggest that people's investigation of Truth will achieve the same result—recognition of their common essence:

> There can be no doubt that whatever the peoples of the world, of whatever race and or religion, they derive their inspiration from one heavenly Source, and are the subjects of one God. The difference between the ordinances under which they abide should be attributed to the varying requirements and exigencies of the age in which they are revealed.

—"Gleanings," *Writings of Bahá'ulláh, 111.*

Simplicity of worship and religious practices

Bahá'ís believe that religion's outer forms are sources of division. In their view, ritual is a prime example. For this reason, there are no sermons, rituals, or clergy. Bahá'í worship is very simple, basically consisting of readings from Bahá'í scriptures and choral singing. Bahá'í houses of worship, however, are elaborate and magnificent—they exist to honor God. There are seven large Houses of Worship, at least one on each continent. Each House of Worship has nine sides and a central dome. The first House of Worship in the United States opened in 1953 in Wilmette, Illinois. This impressive structure is known for its filigree dome and beautiful ornamentation, which combines elements of Eastern and Western architecture.

Bahá'í house of worship in Wilmette, Illinois

An important celebration is the Nineteen Day Feast. Every nineteen days, Bahá'ís gather in their local communities for

- spiritual devotion
- administrative consultation
- social fellowship

Other Bahá'í practices include daily reading and prayer with the Bahá'í scriptures, the obligation to teach the Cause of God, observance of holy days, and contributions to the Bahá'í Fund. There is a period of fasting March 2 to 21 similar to the Islamic Ramaḍān and a prohibition against alcohol and non-medicinal drugs. Work is considered a form of worship. Moral guidelines include the observance of chastity before marriage, respect for government, and the avoidance of backbiting and gossip.

Evolving religion

Bahá'ís believe that religions must evolve and progress as humankind evolves and progresses. They have a progressive, evolutionary view of religion and believe that religions must be updated to reflect people's mental, social, and spiritual progress. In the Bahá'í view, God periodically sends a prophet to update the religions of the world; this prophet adds to the "depository of religious truth." From the Bahá'í perspective, Bahá'ulláh fulfilled this role for humankind. Bahá'ulláh summed up the notion of evolutionary and progressive religion in these words: "Every Prophet Whom the Almighty and Peerless Creator hath purposed to send to the peoples of the earth hath been entrusted with a Message, and charged to act in a manner that would best meet the requirements of the age in which He appeared."

Calendar for Islam and Bahá'í

The second caliph 'Umar ibn Al-KHaTTab (592–644 C.E.) introduced the Islamic calendar (Hijri calendar) in 638 C.E. The calendar began with the Hijra (Muhammad's flight from Mecca to Medina), which began on July 16, 622 C.E. Muslims write this date as Muharram 1, 1 A.H. For them, it is the first day of the first month of the first year. This is the beginning of Islamic Era or the Hijra calendar era. The letters A.H. stand for the Latin *Anno Hegirae*, which means "year of the Hijra." The Islamic calendar consists of twelve months: Muharram, Safar, Rabi' I, Rabi' II, Jumada I, Jumada II, Rajab, Sha'ban, Ramaḍān, Shawwal, Dhu al-Qa'dah, and Dhu al-Hijjah.

For the most part, the Bahá'í calendar, or Badi calendar, was the creation of the Báb. Bahá'u'lláh specified that the calendar begin in the year 1844. The Bahá'í calendar has nineteen months, each of which has nineteen days. The names of the months bear the names of God's attributes, for example, Glory, Splendor, Beauty, Grandeur, Light, and Mercy. Each day of the week, which begins at sunset, is also named for one of God's many attributes, for example, Saturday is Splendor, Sunday is Beauty, and Monday is Perfection.

Winter

Night of Isra' (Rajab 27 observed in the seventh month of the Islamic lunar calendar). On this day, Muslims remember Muhammad's flight from Mecca to Jerusalem as well as his Miraj (visit to heaven and hell, during which he spoke with the ancient prophets). Shortly thereafter, he ascended into heaven (620 C.E.). Chapters 17 and 53 of the Qur'ān mention these events. Muslims gather at homes and mosques to hear stories of the night flight and to share desserts and other foods.

Night of the Middle of the Sha'ban (Sha'ban 15—eighth month). Muslims pray throughout the night on this date. Muhammad visited cemeteries on this date and prayed for the dead. Muslims spend the night asking Allāh to forgive their sins as well as the sins of their dead loved ones. There are also no special prayers associated with this night. Muslims remember this day with varying degrees of enthusiasm and devotion. Some people do not celebrate it at all.

Ayyam-i-Ha (observed in February or March). Each year, Bahá'ís spend four or five days celebrating the goodness of life. These are intercalary days (extra days inserted into the calendar). This is a time for helping neighbors and giving presents to loved ones. Ayyam-i-Ha prepares Bahá'ís for the Bahá'í Fast.

Beginning of **Ramaḍān** (1 Ramaḍān observed in the ninth month). Muslims fast throughout Ramaḍān, which they consider to be a blessed month. Special prayers are said in the evenings, and donations of various sorts are given to the poor. According to Islamic tradition, Muhammad received his first revelations during Ramaḍān. It is a time for Muslims to improve their discipline and self-control.

Bahá'í Fast (observed during the entire month of Ala). Bahá'ís spend the entire month of Ala fasting. The fast's purpose is to bring about spiritual renewal and to lessen dependence on material things.

Spring

Feast of Naw-Ruz (Bahá 1, March 21). The vernal equinox begins a new year for Bahá'ís. The formal celebration of Naw-Ruz, which means "new day," occurs on this date. Naw-Ruz brings an end to the fasting undertaken during the month of Ala. Work of any sort is suspended on Naw-Ruz.

Lailat al-Qadr (Ramaḍān 27, observed on April 1). On this day, Muslims celebrate the descent of the Qur'ān from heaven. The angel Gabriel visited Muhammad for the first time on this date in 610 or 611 C.E. Muslims often spend the night studying the Qur'ān.

Eid al-Fitr—Feast of the Fast Breaking (Shawale 1—tenth month). This date marks the end of Ramaḍān. This is one of two main festivals of Islam. On Eid al-Fitr, Muslims give thanks for the benefits of Ramaḍān. They typically give money to those less fortunate. Muslims gather in the early morning for a worship service, which is normally held in a large, open space. The service consists of a prayer, a short sermon, and a greeting.

Twelve Days of Ridvan (observed during the month of Rivdan, April or May). The word *Ridvan* comes from the Garden of Ridvan, in which Bahá'ulláh formally declared his mission before going into exile for the second time (1863). Ridvan 1 (April 21), Ridvan 9 (April 29), and Ridvan 12 (May 2) mark various aspects of that declaration. Ridvan 12 commemorates Bahá'ulláh's departure and his followers' attempts to keep him from leaving. On these dates, Bahá'ís come together for prayer and reflection.

Declaration of the Báb (Azamat 7, May 23). On this date, Bahá'ís mark the Báb's declaration of his mission, which occurred at Shiraz, Persia, in 1844.

Ascension of Bahá'ulláh (Azamat 13, May 29). According to Bahá'í tradition, at the time of Bahá'ulláh's death, his spirit ascended into heaven. This took place in the year 1892. Bahá'ís gather at 3:00 a.m. (their time), the actual hour of Bahá'ulláh's death. They take turns reading a special prayer called the *Tablet of Visitation*.

Day of Stay at Mount Arafat (Dhu al-Hijjah 9, twelfth month). For Muslims, this day is the most important of the five days that make up the Ḥajj. The Ḥajj occurs during the twelfth month of the Islamic calendar. From mid-day until sunset, all pilgrims spend their time in deep prayer and reflection.

Eid al-Ad-ha (Dhu al-Hijjah 10). This is an important three-day festival in Islam. Muslims stress the importance of being faithful to God and remember Abraham's willingness to sacrifice his son Ishmael. For them, Abraham is a symbol of faithfulness (obedience) to God. Many Muslims recall Abraham's faithfulness by sacrificing (ritually slaughtering) cows, goats, and sheep. The meat is then distributed to the poor. Muslims begin this important festival by gathering for prayer in the early morning. Those participating in the Ḥajj go to the city of Mina to begin the festival.

Summer

Rass as-Sanah al-Hijriyah (Muharram 1—month varies). For Muslims, a new year begins on this date. This is the first day of the Islamic calendar, or Hijri calendar. The day serves to remind Muslims of Muhammad's migration from Mecca to Medina in the year 622 C.E. Many Muslims send greeting cards to friends and relatives at this time.

Martyrdom of the Báb (Ramat 16, July 9). On this day, Bahá'ís recall the murder of the Báb. They traditionally meet at 12 noon to recite prayers. Bahá'í music is very solemn on this day.

Ashura (Moharam 10, observed in June or July). After arriving at Medina, Muhammad made Moharam 10 a fast day. For this reason, many Muslims continue to fast on this day, though it is not obligatory. Muslims remember the life of Muhammad's grandson who was martyred on this day. Husain ibn 'Alt was killed in the battle of Karbalā' (680 C.E.).

Mawlid-an-Nabi (Rabi I, 12—month varies). Muslims celebrate the anniversary of Muhammad's birth. The celebration may have originated in Egypt in the early tenth century C.E. Many Muslims spend the day discussing Muhammad's life and work.

Autumn

Birth of the Báb (Iim 5, October 20). Bahá'ís celebrate the birth of the Báb. Bahá'ís mark this occasion by gathering with friends and family for a festive dinner.

Birth of Bahá'ulláh (Quadrat 9, November 12). On this date, Bahá'ís observe the anniversary of Bahá'ulláh's birth. It is a day of great rejoicing. The ethnic diversity of Bahá'ís is stressed. The celebration includes dancing, food, music, and presentations.

Day of the Covenant (Qawl, November 26). Since 1912, Bahá'ís have observed the Day of the Covenant. It was initiated by Bahá'ulláh's son, 'Abdu'l-Bahá. On this day, Bahá'ís reaffirm their commitment to leading a God-filled life.

Ascension of Abdu'l-Bahá (November 28). According to Bahá'í tradition, at the time of 'Abdu'l-Bahá's death, his spirit also ascended into heaven. He was the official interpreter of Bahá'ulláh's writings. Bahá'ís gather at 1:00 am (their time), the actual hour of 'Abdu'l-Bahá's death, to recite prayers.

Discovering

1. Be able to identify the meaning of the words in the vocabulary list.
2. Be able to tell the story of Muhammad's life and the founding of Islam.
3. Explain some of the beliefs of Islam.
4. Explain the five Pillars of Islam.
5. What is the central theme of the Qur'ān?
6. What is the relationship of the Qur'ān to the Old and New Testaments?
7. What is the relationship of the Prophet Muhammad to the preceding prophets?
8. What are the central beliefs of Bahá'ís?
9. What do Bahá'ís believe are sources of division? Why?
10. Why are Bahá'ís said to have a progressive, evolutionary view of religion?

Exploring

1. Compare the five Pillars of Islam with your own religious tradition (if you are not Muslim) or with another religion which is very familiar to you. How do you see each of these five pillars in that religion?
2. Explain how Muslims live out their beliefs. Which practices flow from their beliefs?
3. Gather with two or three classmates and discuss how living out the faith and practices of Islam can have an effect on society and even the world community. Consider, for example, how Muhammad's teachings would have affected the world into which he was born. How would they also affect the modern world? For example, what would life be like if everyone followed the five pillars?
4. What is your opinion of required almsgiving—2.5 percent of one's income to the community? Do you think this is a good way to deal with those in need in the community? Why or why not?
5. Do you think it is important for religion to be progressive and evolutionary? Why or why not? Which religions would be affected the most if they were to become progressive and evolutionary? Which would be affected the least? Why?

Integrating

1. Visit a mosque or Islamic center near you. Ask to visit with the imām or a member of the community to learn more about Islam.

2. If you were to construct your life around five pillars, what would they be? Write a short essay in which you explain your five pillars and how they will help you to live successfully. These should be five pillars which would serve you for the long term.

3. If you were to create a religion that could be universal, what elements would you include? What would you definitely not include?

Words to Know

Allāh	Muslims
Báb	Qur'ān
Bábí's	Ramaḍān
Bahá'í	Ṣalāt
five Pillars of Islam	Ṣawm
Ḥadīth	Shahāda
Ḥajj	Sharī'ah
Hijra	Shī'is
imām	Sufis
Islam	Sunna
Ka'ba	Sunnīs
mosque	sūra
Muhammad	Zakāt

Chapter **9**

After reading this chapter, you will be able to
- Identify characteristics of eastern thought
- Compare aspects of the eastern worldview with the western worldview
- Propose ways eastern thought can expand your own

EASTERN RELIGIONS

Introduction

Thousands Rush to Temples

For centuries, devout Hindus have placed offerings before statues of their gods. Most of the time these offerings are relatively ordinary things, such as candy, flowers, ghee (semi-fluid clarified butter), and milk. There is nothing extraordinary about placing such gifts before statues, unless, of course, the statues begin consuming the offerings.

In late September of 1995, the Hindu communities of India and the United States seemed to converge. The scene at Hindu temples in both countries was the same: statues of Ganeśa, the elephant-headed god who brings good fortune, could be seen drinking milk.

The phenomenon was first reported in India. In Bombay, Calcutta, New Delhi, and Madras, tens of thousands flocked to local temples. Police estimated that there were up to three hundred people at each temple, some of whom began waiting in line at 4:00 a.m. (There are nearly five thousand temples in New Delhi alone.) For days, people could be seen carrying cups, glasses, pots, jugs, and steel containers of milk to the temples. Milk shortages were reported throughout the country. As a result, milk sold for ten times its usual price.

At the New Delhi temple where it all began, a priest told this story: "A man, who is a frequent visitor to the temple, told me that he had had a dream about Ganeśa. In the dream, Lord Ganeśa asked him for a drink of milk. The next morning this man remembered the dream and came to the temple. When he lifted a spoonful of milk to Ganeśa's trunk, the milk disappeared." The priest exclaimed: "It is a miracle!" One of those who stood in line said, "It cannot be a hoax. Where would all the milk being offered go? It is such a small idol, it can't take in so much. The gods have come down to earth to solve our problems."

Upon learning of events in India, many Hindus in the United States rushed to local temples with offerings of milk. At the Sunnyvale Hindu Temple at Sunnyvale, California, the Indian phenomenon repeated itself. A statue of Ganeśa could be seen consuming milk. The news quickly spread among Hindus living in the Silicon Valley, and crowds began forming outside of the temple.

Sunita, a seventeen-year-old high school student from Sunnyvale, describes the crowds swarming outside of the temple to which she and her family belong. "Seeing the crowds still flocking to the temple is a constant reminder to me that God is active in my life. The statue of Ganeśa has been a real pillar of strength in my faith life. My fellow classmates never tire of hearing my story about Ganeśa's consumption of milk."

Tilling the Soil

Before reading this chapter, review charts 1 and 2 from chapter 1 on page 17. Recall that human beings think of "separation" as the fundamental human "problem." Humans perceive that they are separated from the divine, from Ultimate Reality. The cause of this separation, from the eastern point of view, is a type of ignorance. The consequences of this separation are that one must overcome ignorance and find the truth. God is an impersonal, absolute, unknowable "that" which does not relate to human beings. Salvation, in the eastern view, is from the state of being ignorant. The means of attaining salvation is to actualize oneself. Redemption is attaining oneness with Ultimate Reality. Consider how this way of thinking differs from western thought.

Hinduism

The name *Hinduism* first originated among Persian explorers. They described the beliefs and practices of the people living near the Indus River as "Induism." Thus, the history of Hinduism is closely tied to the history of India. Hinduism does not have a specific starting date nor a founder. Hinduism's many forms reflect its long history; this history can be divided into four periods.

- 6000–1500 B.C.E. The first, the Pre-Vedic Period, is the time before the invasion of India by Indo-Europeans. There is no clear picture of religious belief for this time period.

- 1500–500 B.C.E. The Vedic Period, beginning with the Indo-European invasions, was a time in which the people had a positive view of the world. India's oldest existing sacred writings, the *Vedas*, come from this time period. These writings present a polytheistic religion oriented to nature and an agricultural life. The survival of death was a continuation of the good life on earth.

- 500 B.C.E. to 650 C.E. This positive view of the world changed to a pessimistic view during the third period of Hinduism's history, the Epic Period. This view surfaced in the centuries following 1000 B.C.E. Reincarnation and the law of karma became part of Hindu thinking at this time.

- The fourth period of Hinduism's history follows closely and is marked by the development of the Brahmins, or priestly caste, and the idea of *māyā*.

Defining Hinduism

Hinduism does not fit categories of definition as easily as western religions. Strictly speaking, Hinduism is not really a religion; rather, it is a name for several religious traditions. While a basic worldview is common to all Hindus, Hinduism also contains within it an amalgamation of beliefs and practices which are often contradictory, even in opposition to

Hinduism
eastern worldview expressed in several religious traditions

one another. Like Christianity, it has innumerable groups. Unlike Christianity, these groups generally coexist peacefully. This is because Hinduism has a fundamental openness to all beliefs. It holds that all religions manifest some aspect of Ultimate Reality. Thus, Hindus do not condemn, or claim as false, other religions.

Hinduism constantly seeks the truth and is never content with a certain "definition" of the truth. It always pushes beyond, asks more questions, seeks further insight. This is another reason why Hinduism is deeply respectful of other religions; these religions may contain a new insight on the truth. Hinduism rejects nothing which is good. Hinduism has given the world the concept of nonviolence. With this principle Gandhi was able to shake off the powerful British Empire in India without resorting to violence. This concept of nonviolence was used by Dr. Martin Luther King Jr. during the 1960s in the civil rights movement in the United States.

Unity and Diversity

The Christian is not to become a Hindu or Buddhist, nor a Hindu or a Buddhist to become a Christian. But each must assimilate the spirit of the others and yet preserve his identity and grow according to his own law of growth.

—Swami Vivekananda, *World Parliament of Religions*, 1893.

Let's Talk about It . . .

1. How have western religions benefited from eastern religions?
2. Do you foresee more unity or more division among religions? Explain.

Hinduism in North America

The presence of practitioners of all eastern religions in North America is generally tied to immigration policies in the United States. The history of Hinduism in the United States, however, begins before such policies. In the seventeenth century, the translation of some Hindu sacred writings into English had a direct influence on some New Englanders. The writings especially affected members of the Transcendentalist Movement. Eastern religions then received a major impetus with the World Parliament of Religions held in Chicago in 1893. At this time, many Americans became acquainted with the teachings of eastern religions. However, growing anti-Asian sentiment in the first years of the twentieth century led to the Asian Exclusion Act of 1917. Thus growth of these religions slowed dramatically after this time. The repeal of the act in 1965 resulted in a correspondingly dramatic increase of Asian immigration and practitioners of eastern religions.

Similar to the denominations of Christianity, Hinduism exists in North America in a wide variety of beliefs and practices. The titles for such groups include *society, foundation, ashram, center, mission*, and *alliance*. A group is generally founded by a specific individual and continues to exist either under that individual's guidance or that of his or her followers. Three main divisions are Vaishnavism, Shaivism, and Saktism. Vaishnava Hinduism emphasizes bhakti yoga. Shaiva Hinduism worships Shiva, and Sakta Hinduism worships Sakti, the female consort of Shiva, the feminine cosmic energy. Saktas emphasize the presence of the female power within the human body.

ISKCON

The International Society for Krishna Consciousness (**ISKCON**) is a representative form of Vaishnava Hinduism which grew out of the work of Caitanya Mahaprabhu (1486–1534?). The work of Caitanya was brought to the United States in 1965 by A.C. Bhaktivedanta Swami Prabhupada (1896–1977). In 1966, ISKCON was founded, a magazine begun, and a center opened in San Francisco. Swami Prabhupada served as the leader and guru for the group of several thousand people. He was also a writer and translator of the scriptures, commenting on Krishna consciousness. His primary work is his translation and commentary on the Bhagavad-Gita, entitled *The Bhagavad-Gita as It Is*.

ISKCON
International Society for Krishna Consciousness, founded in the U. S. in 1966

Devotees of Krishna consciousness practice bhakti yoga by publicly chanting the name of God. In this case, they chant the Hare Krishna mantra:

Hare Kirshna, Hare Krishna.

Hare, Hare, Krishna Krishna.

Hare Rāma, Hare Rāma.

Hare, Hare, Rāma Rāma.

By chanting this mantra, practitioners seek to receive the pure consciousness of God who is thought of as the incarnation of Krishna and Rāma. Other devotional practices include homage to the deity statues in Krishna temples, marking the body with the names of God, and the eating and distribution of vegetarian food offered to Krishna. Practitioners also study Hindu culture, the history of bhakti yoga, and the writings of the founder.

ISKCON attracted much attention during the 1970s because of its colorful displays and public appearance. In 1987, the group split between conservatives who wanted to maintain the practices established by Prabhupada and reformers who wanted to adapt the practices. Controversy surrounded some gurus who were accused of illicit sexual relations and the use of psychedelic drugs, so the group has also been beset by legal problems. The result of the schism was the formation of a new group, the International Society for Krishna Consciousness of West Virginia.

Vedanta Society

vedanta

spiritual truth or spiritual wisdom of Hinduism

god-consciousness

in Hinduism, a constant awareness of God's presence

The oldest group of Hinduism in the United States, founded in 1894, is the Vedanta Society. **Vedanta** means "spiritual truth," or "spiritual wisdom." Vedanta as a group began in India with Sri Ramakrishna (1836–1886) who was a priest in a Calcutta temple of Kali, the goddess through whom God is worshiped as Universal Mother. Ramakrishna reached the state of **god-consciousness** and became convinced that the Divine Mother wished him to stay on the edge between God and the world so that he could help humanity. He also believed that all religions are different paths to the same goal and all gods are different aspects of the same God.

Sri Sarada Devi (1853–1920) was the wife of Sri Ramakrishna. To this day, Ramakrishna's followers refer to her as "the Holy Mother." On one

Sanskrit symbol for "om," Old Temple Vedanta Society, San Francisco

occasion, she said, "I am the Mother of the wicked, as I am the Mother of the virtuous. Whenever you are in distress, just say to yourself: I have a Mother." After her husband's death, Sri Sarada Devi carried on his work by helping to found the Ramakrishna Order of India, a monastic community.

Sri Ramakrishna's close disciple, Swami Vivekananda (1863–1902), brought the movement to the United States. From Vivekananda's perspective, there were four broad paths or yoga that led to God. He asserted that a person can realize God by following one, two, three, or all four of these paths. Regarding the four broad paths, he said: "This is the whole of religion. Doctrines or dogmas or rituals or books or temples are but secondary details." Swami Vivekananda spoke at the World Parliament of Religions held in 1893 at Chicago and continued to lecture for two years after that.

The Vedanta Society has emphasized the leading ideas of Hinduism rather than promoting the cult of an idolized founder. The society teaches the universal religion of Ramakrishna, modern Hinduism deeply rooted in ancient Indian traditions. The Vedanta Society's Hindu roots teach that:

1. There is a unity behind all reality.

2. We can learn to look beyond the variety (which is illusion, māyā) we see around us and know the unity of reality in this life.

3. Enlightenment can be achieved by following one of the four yoga.

Vedanta centers are located in both the United States and Canada. There are nearly twenty Vedanta societies located throughout the United States. The Vedanta Society, which is the oldest, has offices at New York.

Planting the Seed

Human Wants

What do human beings want? Hinduism observes the desires of people and proposes that they have four basic wants: pleasure, worldly success, to fulfill human duty, and liberation. The first three of these can be seen as the **path of desire**.

Path of desire

Hinduism says that, first of all, human beings want *pleasure*. They want to avoid discomforts, pain, and frustration, and they want to experience the pleasures of life. So Hinduism says: Within decent moral grounds, "go for it!"—Seek the pleasures of life. And then Hinduism waits patiently. Eventually we come to realize that this isn't really what we want after all; pleasure is too trivial to satisfy human nature.

What else do human beings want? Hinduism says they want *worldly success*: wealth, fame, and power. These are worthy goals and have the advantage of lasting longer than pleasure. So Hinduism says, "Go for it!" But there are certain problems with these desires. The quest for wealth, fame, and power lead to competition and exclusivity. This desire for worldly success can never be satisfied; no one ever has enough money! Goals remain self-centered and, in the end, do not last. In the West, we say, "You can't take it with you." The quest for worldly success does not satisfy human nature.

The third thing that Hinduism says human beings want is to *fulfill human duty*. People want to serve others; they want to give, to contribute to the good of their society. Once again, Hinduism says, "Go for it!" Once again, human beings discover that service to humanity, as laudable as that may be, does not satisfy human nature.

Path of renunciation

What human beings really want, says Hinduism, is *liberation (moksha)* from our limitations. We want *being* (existence). We want to *know*, to be aware. And we want *joy*, which is the opposite of boredom and frustration. Furthermore, Hinduism says we want these to an infinite degree. This is not impossible; they are within our reach. In fact, says Hinduism, we already possess these! The path of renunciation is the way.

Consider the human being: A human being is many layered. On the very surface is the self we present to the world: the way we look, our body, our mannerisms. On a deeper level is our conscious personality. Beyond that is our subconscious. At the deepest level, at the very center of the human being, is Being itself. This is a person's **ātman**, the true self, divine and eternal, the core of every human being. Some Hindus speak of the many layers around the ātman as five sheaths: bliss, intellect, mind, prāna (cosmic and human breath), and physical. In a sense, the five sheaths are concentric: the bliss sheath fits inside of the intellect sheath, which fits inside of the mind sheath, and so on. The bliss sheath

path of desire
in Hinduism, pleasure, worldly success, and the need to fulfill human duty

path of renunciation
in Hinduism, liberation, being, awareness, joy

ātman
Hindu understanding of the human person: the true self; the core of the person

is the lightest, and the physical sheath is the heaviest. The self, or ātman, has been likened to a lightbulb, and the five sheaths to pieces of cloth which cover it. Thus, the five sheaths can be viewed in this way: bliss—net, intellect—gauze, mind—silk, prāna—velvet, and physical—canvas.

One reason why human beings do not know they already possess their deepest wants is because of **māyā**. Māyā is illusion. All that we perceive around us in not really real; it is illusion. What is real is the unity which lies beyond the variety we perceive in the world. The goal of Hinduism is to become aware and reach the ātman (or bráhman) within.

māyā
in Hinduism, cosmic illusion

Ultimate Reality

Hindus do not believe in one Supreme Being (God), although sometimes they speak of a god who created 330 million other beings (gods). **Brahmā** is the creator, the "grandfather" of the gods. However, Vishnu and Shiva, the other two major gods, are more worshiped than Brahmā. Brahmā is frequently seen as the dispenser of knowledge and wisdom: "That which is hidden in the Upanishads which are hidden in the Vedas, Brahmā knows as the holy womb of the Vedas" (*Svetasvatara Upanishad* 5.6).

Brahmā
the creator, the "grandfather" of Hindu gods; the dispenser of knowledge and wisdom

Vishnu is the preserver god. Vishnu not only protects and maintains the physical universe, but also human spirituality. Some Hindus are particularly devoted to him; for them he is the source of life. Whenever the spiritual is in decline, Vishnu becomes incarnate; the incarnations of a deity such as Vishnu are called **avatārs**. Hindus especially honor Vishnu through Krishna and Rāma, two avatars. These Hindus are called Vaishnavites (followers of Vishnu).

Vishnu
Hindu preserver god who protects and maintains the universe; for some, the source of life

avatār
in Hinduism, a manifestation of the divine; the earthly form or appearance of a diety

Since ancient times, the figure of **Shiva** has been prominent in Hinduism. Shiva is commonly known as God the Destroyer. As God the Destroyer, Shiva is often portrayed as the Lord of Dance; his dance symbolizes his energy. Although Shiva is noted for destruction, he is not seen as evil. Shiva destroys the universe when it is old and worn out, making way for Brahmā to create a new universe. Thus, Hindus believe that our universe is not the first nor the last, but merely one in an eternal cycle of creation, preservation, and destruction. In addition to destruction, Shiva symbolizes fertility and sexuality. Shiva is the most popular of the three major gods; devotees of Shiva are called Shaivites.

Shiva
the Hindu god commonly referred to as God the Destroyer

The three together—Brahmā, Vishnu, and Shiva—are called the *Trimurti*. These three are sometimes referred to as creator, preserver, and destroyer of the universe.

Images of the Divine

You are the fire;

You are the sun;

You are the air;

You are the moon;

You are the starry firmament.

You are Bráhman Supreme;

You are the waters—You, the Creator of all!

You are woman, You are man;

You are the youth, You are the maiden;

You are the old man tottering with his staff;

You face everywhere.

You are the dark butterfly;

You are the green parrot with red eyes;

You are the thunder cloud, the seasons, the seas.

Without beginning are You,

beyond time and space.

You are He from whom sprang

the three worlds.

—Svetasvatara Upanishad, 4. 2–4.

Let's Talk about It . . .

1. In this excerpt, what is the image of the divine that most appeals to you? Why?
2. What images would you add to these?

Sacred Writings

The sacred writings of Hinduism are an extensive collection of ancient writings which include hymns, stories, legends, commentaries, ritual directives, myths, philosophy, and theological speculation. Unlike the sacred writings of western religions which are a specific selection of ancient writings, the writings of Hinduism are inclusive of religious wisdom gathered from the centuries. Western religions regard their sacred scriptures as the revealed word of God; the writings of eastern religions do not carry this sense of divine revelation. They are, instead, the religious wisdom of Hindus from the centuries.

śruti scriptures
the words of the Vedas, which the rishis heard

smriti scriptures
the words of the rishis, written down and remembered; include the Ramayana and Mahabharata, the Laws of Manu, the Puranas, and the Tantras

rishis
ancient Indian sages; possessors of knowledge regarded as the "spiritual founders" of Hinduism

Vedas
four collections of religious materials containing prayers, rituals, liturgy, hymns, and spells and charms of a popular nature

Hindu writings encompass a vast body of knowledge, often classified as the śruti scriptures (that which is heard from the gods) and the **smirti** scriptures (that which is remembered from the sages). The śruti are believed to contain knowledge, the words of gods, which comes through the **rishis**, ancient Indian sages and seers. The rishis were possessors of knowledge and are regarded as the "spiritual founders" of Hinduism. These writings are held in a higher regard than the smriti.

The śruti writings of the **Vedas** are the most ancient of Hindu writings. The Vedas are four collections of religious material which contain prayers, ritual, liturgy, hymns, and spells and charms of a popular nature. The Rig Veda, the oldest, longest, and most widely known, includes ancient creation hymns and hymns to various gods to be sung at sacrifices. The Yajur Veda is a collection of mantras, explanations, and instructions for sacrifices and ceremonies. The Sama Veda revises hymns and verses from the Rig Veda and arranges them for singing. Finally, the Atharva Veda includes spells, charms, incantations, and curses unrelated to sacrifices.

> *Universal Order and Truth were born of a blazing spiritual fire, and thence night was born, and thence the billowy ocean of space. From the billowy ocean of space was born Time—the year ordaining days and nights, the ruler of every moment. In the beginning as before, the Creator made the sun, the moon, the heaven and the earth, the firmament and the realm of light.*
>
> —*Rig Veda* 10.190.1–3.

The four Vedas were later supplemented with an extensive collection of explanatory texts. Taken together, this literature is called *Vedanta* (the culmination of the Vedas). This collection remains open, and the truth and wisdom of future sages can be incorporated into it. People of all religions can draw upon the insights in this literature, since it is meant to help them on their spiritual journey. The Vedanta teaches that:

1. Truth is one; sages call it by various names.
2. All that we see, including the human being, is a manifestation of divine consciousness; the human being's essential nature is divinity.
3. The goal of human life is to realize (manifest) this divinity.
4. There are innumerable (countless) ways to manifest this divinity.

The Bráhmanas are prose additions to the Vedas which spell out the way to perform the more complex rituals of the Sama Veda. The Aranyakas are mainly discussions of priestly rituals associated with the forest and are a supplement to the Bráhmanas. The Upanishads are sometimes presented as records of conversations between teachers and students on the subject of Absolute Truth. The word *upanishad* means "receiving knowledge at the teacher's feet." There are 108 Upanishads which are considered to be authentic. The Upanishads pick up from the Aranyakas; they are mythical and philosophical speculations about life in the cosmos. This is a famous passage from the Brihadaranyaka Upanishad (1.3.28), the first of thirteen primary Upanishads:

From the unreal lead me to the real!

From darkness lead me to the light!

From death lead me to immortality!

Om

While the Rig Veda Samhita praises the gods of the Aryan tribes who invaded India, the Upanishads speak of worship of only one God. All the other gods are manifestations of this one Ultimate Reality. These writings also introduce the idea of oneness of a person's ātman with this Ultimate Reality.

The smriti, the words of the ancient sages written down and remembered, include two important religious epics, the *Mahabharata* and *Ramayana*. The Mahabharata is the story of the earliest inhabitants of the Indian sub-continent. It was put in written form sometime between the second century B.C.E. and the third century C.E. Consisting of 100,000 verses, it is the longest poem ever written. The Mahabharata tells the story of the civil war that broke out between the Kauravas and Pandavas. The Kauravas clan, led by Duryodhana and counting a hundred heroes, are defeated by the Pandavas. The brave Arjuna and Krishna (an incarnation of the god Vishnu) lead the Pandavas to victory.

The Mahabharata is especially noteworthy because it contains the **Bhagavad-Gita**, which is the story of Lord Krishna, the source of the manifestations (avatars, incarnations) of Vishnu. Known as "India's favorite Bible," the Bhagavad-Gita has provided inspiration to millions, including Mahatma Gandhi. The Bhagavad-Gita, or Gita, asserts that life's goal of realizing God can be reached by many paths. Nevertheless, it leans heavily toward the yoga of devotion (bhakti yoga).

As the heat of a fire reduces wood to ashes, the fire of knowledge burns to ashes all karma. Nothing in this world purifies like spiritual wisdom. It is the perfection achieved in time through the path of yoga, the path which leads to the Self within.

—Bhagavad-Gita 4. 37–38

The Ramayana is a love story which tells the tale of Rāma (an incarnation of the god Vishnu) and Sita (the daughter of King Janaka of Videha). The tale revolves around the kidnapping of Sita and Rāma's attempts to rescue her from the clutches of Rāvana, the demon king of Lanka.

The Puranas are a collection of laws, philosophical reflections, and stories which illustrate themes contained in various older works. The Bhagavata Purana, the most well known, tells the story of Krishna's life and explains his teachings. The Linga, Garuda, Markandeya, Matsya, Shiva, Skanda, and Vishnu (which forecasts the future coming of Kalki, the manifestation of the divine) Puranas are also influential.

Reincarnation

In Hinduism, devotion to the various gods can help one become aware of Ultimate Reality. Unfortunately, human beings are unaware that they already possess the divine within. Thus, the goal of Hinduism is to become aware of the ātman within. This is rarely, if ever, achieved in a single lifetime.

Therefore, it is necessary to be reincarnated, born again and again in progressively higher life forms or higher levels in human life, until one is released from limitations. In Sanskrit, the word for **reincarnation** is *samsāra*. The English word *reincarnation* derives ultimately from the Latin *caro*, which means "flesh." To reincarnate means "to reflesh," to wrap oneself in flesh again. Reincarnation refers to the evolution or transmigration of the soul body, the process of being reborn. The process allows a soul body or lifebody to move from immaturity to maturity. A soul body becomes mature as it learns the lessons of the physical (material) world. Once the lessons have been learned, the soul body attains **moksha** (release from reincarnation).

Karma

The word *karma* means action or ritual work; it also has a "cause and effect" connotation. In short, whatever a person does—whatever action he or she takes—has an effect on him or her. Karma is both the action and the result of that action. A person's thoughts, words, and deeds contain energy—they *are* energy. Thinking, speaking, or doing releases energy, which returns to the thinker, speaker, or doer. If bad energy is released, bad energy eventually returns. And if good energy is released, good energy eventually returns.

The law of karma determines a person's next life form or the possibility of the person escaping the cycle of reincarnation. Fulfilling one's duties and performing rituals faithfully helps one to build up good karma and thus increase the chances one will be reincarnated into a higher life. Failing to do one's duties means one will likely be reborn in a lower form. Redemption, for Hinduism, is escape from this cycle of reincarnation and the achievement of oneness with the Ultimate Reality.

reincarnation
literally, "to reflesh"; born again and again in progressively higher life forms or higher levels in human life

moksha
in Hinduism, the release of the soul body from samsāra (reincarnation)

karma
action or ritual work, with a "cause and effect" connotation

Lotus Lantern Festival, Buddhist offering, in New York City

> *"You are a Hindu if you believe in karma, reincarnation, the existence of God everywhere in all things, and the existence of beings that are on a greater evolutionary path than ourselves."*

Paths to the Goal

The paths to the goal of oneness with the Ultimate Reality are called *yoga*. A **yoga** is a kind of discipline, "a method of training designed to lead to integration or union" with the divine. In Sanskrit, *yoga* means "yoke," as in "to yoke together." A yoke is also a restraint; through yoga, we restrain both body and mind. When preparing for a concert or athletic contest, you may train for endless hours. You will need to manage your time well, learn new skills, perhaps eat only certain foods and develop an ability to focus on the task at hand. You adopt a certain discipline so that you can perform well. In a similar way, a yoga is a spiritual discipline which leads the practitioner to spiritual awareness of the ātman within.

There are four main yogas. These yogas correspond to four personality types. For the intellectual person, there is jnāna yoga, the yoga of knowledge. Bhakti yoga is the yoga of devotion and is for people who are more in touch with their emotions. Those who like to be busy and active can use karma yoga. A fourth yoga is raja yoga, which is for a serious minded, disciplined person who can practice meditation and contemplation.

Jnāna yoga approaches God through reason; the practitioner seeks intuitive knowledge. The goal is to break through delusion and see God everywhere. The practice begins with listening to the wisdom of the ages—the sages, philosophy, and scripture—in order to understand that what is most important is Being itself. The person then distinguishes self from things in the world. For example, "This is 'my' book, but 'I' am not my book. 'I' am separate from it." What is this "I"? The person then sees self in the third person and meditates on the eternal part of me. Jnāna yoga is for a person who likes ideas; it is considered the shortest and steepest path to divine awareness.

While the practitioner of jnāna yoga perceives Ultimate Reality as impersonal, the practitioner of **bhakti yoga** takes a personalist perspective. One's energy is used to search for the God within. Bhakti yoga cultivates a relationship with the Ultimate Reality through prayer, ritual, and worship. Bhakti yoga is a yoga of love—all of one's love is directed toward the Ultimate Reality, just for the sake of loving Ultimate Reality. A person can love the personal Ultimate Reality through word and action. Interestingly, Hinduism describes Christianity as "one great big bhakti highway." Practitioners of bhakti yoga distinguish four kinds of devotion.

- To love Ultimate Reality as a protector: as a lord or master

- To love Ultimate Reality as a friend

- To love Ultimate Reality is as a parent to child; the practitioner is the parent and Ultimate Reality is the child; this elicits a parental kind of love for Ultimate Reality

- To love Ultimate Reality as an intimate lover

yoga
a method of training designed to lead to integration or union; unites aspects of one's being so that one can unite with the divine; allows one to restrain the body and the mind

jnāna yoga
a yoga discipline that emphasizes intellectual reflection

bhakti yoga
a yoga discipline that emphasizes love and a relationship with the Ultimate Reality through prayer, ritual, and worship

karma yoga
a yoga discipline that emphasizes work, which is done out of love for the Ultimate Reality

raja yoga
a yoga discipline that emphasizes the practice of meditation which leads the practitioner deeper through each layer of the self

guru
teacher, guide

samnyāsin
in Hinduism, the final stage of life, beyond the attractions of this world, preparing for the next life

Many people like to be active; most people have to work. **Karma yoga** is for this type of person. The practitioner of karma yoga seeks to be detached from the work itself. Work is done not for one's own sake but for the sake of the Ultimate Reality alone. A person's good works have the effect of worshiping the God within others. Thus, karma yoga reaches out to God by serving (helping) others. Work is performed with a calm detachment as though this were the only and last thing one must do. A spouse may work for many years, not for the sake of the work or the reward it brings, but rather out of love for family. In a similar way, the karmi is detached from work and works for love of the Ultimate Reality. Through work, the person identifies with the divine.

Raja yoga attunes a person's mind to God through concentration and meditation. Raja yoga is sometimes called the yoga of meditation and the soul of all the yoga. Raja yoga is a series of psychological exercises leading to union with the Ultimate Reality. Through these exercises, the practitioner is led deeper through each layer of the self. Raja yoga begins with eliminating five bodily addictions: abstain from injury, lying, stealing, sensuality, and greed. Then follow five observances: cleanliness, contentment, self-control, studiousness, and contemplation of the divine. The next six steps progressively lead the practitioner through bodily and mental disciplines until *samādhi* is reached. Samadhi takes place when the person is completely absorbed with God. This yoga is risky and must be done properly; thus the help of a guide is required. Raja yoga is called the royal road to integration with the divine.

Stages of Life

A life lived well has four stages. (These stages apply to men only.) The first stage is that of a learner or student, which may last up to twelve years. In this stage, the learner studies Hindu writings under the direction and guidance of a **guru**. The student has only one responsibility in this stage—and that is to study.

The second stage of life is that of the householder. During this stage, one takes up the responsibilities of marriage, vocation, and community. Eventually this stage is to be left behind as a person moves into the third stage.

The third stage of life is spiritual maturity. This stage may begin anytime after the birth of the first grandchild. At this point, the person begins a life as a hermit and seeks oneness with the Ultimate Reality. A man's wife may accompany him on this quest.

Having reached union with the divine, a person becomes **samnyāsin**. *Samnyāsin* means "one who renounces." A person in this stage neither loves nor hates, seeks nor desires, goes forth nor resists. The person simply rests in the presence of the divine and prepares him or herself for passage into the next life.

Castes

In addition to the four stages, Hindus live within castes. The **caste system** dates back to the time of the Indo-European invasions. Originally there were four castes.

- The highest is that of the *Brāhmana varna*—the priests, teachers, and artists.
- The next is that of the *Ksatriya varna*—the rulers and warriors.
- A third caste are the *Vaiśya varna*—craftsmen, bankers, merchants, and farmers.
- The fourth caste are the *Sūdra varna* who are the unskilled laborers. This group is not permitted to participate in many of the rituals and mantras of the other three castes.

Beyond these four are the *untouchables*, people who belong to no caste at all. Since its ancient beginnings, thousands of subcastes have evolved. The caste system, coupled with the law of karma, keeps people within rigidly defined stratas in society. It would be against the law of karma to try and change castes. One should be content in the caste one is born into and fulfill one's duties in that caste. In this way, rebirth to a higher caste is possible after death. The caste system has been opposed by such people as Buddha in the sixth century B.C.E., Mohandas Gandhi in the twentieth century, and by many of India's laws today. Still the caste system persists, especially in the countryside of India.

caste system

a series of social classes which have developed in Hindu India

A Holy Man

When Pope Paul VI made his historic visit to India, the people lined the streets by the hundreds of thousands, and they stood in silence. The pope, though deeply moved, was probably not surprised, for he knew that Hindus regard a high holy man of any religion as a visible and sacred manifestation of the great Bráhman [Ultimate Reality]. They would not view Catholicism as a false religion, but rather as one of the many expressions of truth which flow from Bráhman.

—*John T. Catoir,* World Religions, *The Christophers.*

Let's Talk about It . . .

1. Why would Hindus consider the leader of another religion to be a holy man?
2. What other holy men and women would you name?

Further Hindu Practices

Shlokas and mantras

Most shlokas and mantras are known in the ancient language of Sanskrit. Shlokas are post-Vedic affirmations, repeated in both Sanskrit and English. Repeating a shloka remolds the subconscious and increases alertness. Hindus utter shlokas before getting out of bed, before entering the shrine room of their home, before journeying to a temple, and before going to sleep. **Mantras** are sounds that can actually be seen in certain states of meditation. They sometimes appear as colored light. Repeating a mantra awakens latent brain cells. *Om*, or *Aum*, is a famous mantra. Repeating it brings harmony to all levels of one's being. Another great mantra contains five distinct syllables: "Na ma Shi va ya." "Hail to Shiva."

mantra
a sound that appears as colored light in certain states of meditation, repeated in an attempt to awaken latent brain cells

Kumkum

The kumkum is a dot of color worn on the forehead. Both women and men may wear a kumkum, which represents the third eye (spiritual awareness). Hindus then seek to increase spiritual awareness through the practice of one of the yogas. An unmarried woman wears a black kumkum, and a married woman a red one.

Morality

In Hindu society, it is important to fulfill one's duties in the state of life into which one is born. One's actions have consequences. Good thoughts and actions lead to rebirth in a higher life. Bad thoughts and actions lead to rebirth in a lower life form.

Morality in Hinduism is focused on the individual and his or her actions. There is little concern for the larger society. The law of karma and the caste system promote specific social strata and strongly discourage movement for change. Thus it would be wrong to try and change one's lot in life or to improve social conditions. The situation for women is further aggravated by law. Article 14 of the Indian Constitution guarantees equal rights for all citizens regardless of sex or creed, but this article is offset by Article 25 which guarantees freedom of religion. Freedom of religion means that people are subject to the laws of their religious community. In Hinduism, these laws generally favor an inequality between the sexes. A Hindu woman cannot head a household or inherit ancestral property, and she can inherit her father's or husband's personal property only if it is in his will. Thus Hinduism as a system supports the status quo and generally does not work for social change, since this is seen as unnecessary and contrary to the law of karma.

Rites

Unlike religions of the west, worship in Hinduism is individual. Hindus perform ritual washing or bathing. Offerings may be made to a god either at a household shrine or in the temple.

Hinduism has many sacred life-cycle rites called **samskāras**. One of the most beautiful and elaborate is for marriage. Other beautiful ceremonies may be performed on the day when a child is presumed to be conceived, during pregnancy, at birth, on the child's name day, when the child first takes hard food, at the first cutting of the child's hair, and especially at the time when the child receives the sacred thread that denotes full acceptance into the Hindu community.

samskāras
sacred life-cycle rites in Hinduism

Taking Root

Buddhism

Siddhartha Gautama

Much as Martin Luther and the Reformation which followed were a reaction to medieval Catholicism, so too were Siddhartha Gautama and Buddhism a reaction to Hinduism. Hinduism of the sixth century B.C.E. had become extremely complex and difficult to live. Siddhartha, having tried the ways of Hinduism in an attempt to achieve enlightenment, gave it up and sought his own path. **Buddhism** is a "Way of Life" based on the teachings of **Siddhartha Gautama**—the Buddha. The proper name *Siddhartha* means "one who has attained the goal"; the surname *Gautama* designates a family of warriors; the word *buddha* means "enlightened one."

According to Buddhist mythology, Siddhartha Gautama (c. 563–483 B.C.E.) was born at Kapila, Sakya (modern-day Rummindei, Nepal), the son of a prince. Shortly after Siddhartha's birth, a hermit made a startling prediction. As the old man looked at Siddhartha, he said: "This prince, if he remains in the palace after his youth, will become a great King to rule the Four Seas. But if he forsakes the household life to embrace a religious life, he will become a Buddha and the world's Savior."

Siddhartha lived a typical princely life filled with comforts and pleasures, a life of princely extravagance. When he turned sixteen, his father made arrangements for him to marry. Because his father did not want his son to cast aside a life of power and privilege, he did everything possible to shield the young couple from the outside world and its miseries. Theirs was a life of almost total seclusion.

"The Legend of the Four Passing Sights" recounts Siddhartha's discovery of life's miseries. One day Siddhartha ventured out into the world and came face-to-face with the "inevitable suffering of life." He encountered an old man, a sick man, a dead man, and a religious man (monk). The first three images symbolized the suffering of humankind—Siddhartha discovered old age, sickness, and death. These sights greatly disturbed Siddhartha.

Buddhism
the way of life based on the teachings of Siddhartha Guatama; the Middle Path

Siddhartha Gautama
the Buddha, the enlightened one, the founder of Buddhism

Buddhism . . . has been essentially the religion of tolerance.
—*Lafcadio Hearn*

The last image—the monk—pointed to Siddhartha's destiny. Thus at the age of twenty-nine, Siddhartha left his wife and his newborn son in good hands and went on a journey, determined to find the answers to his questions about why suffering exists. Siddhartha planned to live as an ascetic and to "relieve universal suffering."

Siddhartha spent the next six years seeking out the great teachers of his day, studying nearly every known form of meditation, and perfecting the ascetic practices and yoga of Hinduism. He meditated and fasted until he was little more than a walking skeleton. Nevertheless, the feeling of satisfaction eluded him.

Then, quite unexpectedly, a girl carrying a bowl of rice changed the course of his life. Siddhartha accepted the rice she offered, realizing that an ascetic life did not guarantee liberation (relief from suffering). He saw the wisdom of the Middle Way, and immediately decided to follow a path of balance (one between the paths of pleasure and pain). Having rejected the extreme of luxury (palace life), he now abandoned the extreme of self-torture and resolved to follow the middle way of balance. At nightfall, Siddhartha sat beneath a bodhi tree, and proceeded to lose himself in meditation, determined never to rise again until he found enlightenment. It is said he made this vow:

> Let my body be dried up on this seat,
>
> Let my skin and bones and flesh be destroyed,
>
> So long as Bodhi is not attained . . .
>
> My body and thought will not be removed from this seat.

Buddha
one who has reached enlightenment

Soon Siddhartha finished purifying his mind (erasing all defilements), and attained enlightenment. Siddhartha arose the **Buddha**, the "enlightened one." Siddhartha preached his first sermon at Benares, India, in the Deer Park. In this sermon, he spelled out the Four Noble Truths, which contain the Eightfold Path. Until his death at age eighty, the Buddha helped others reach enlightenment. According to one Buddhist tradition, six Buddhas (enlightened ones) preceded Siddhartha Gautama, and thirteen will follow him. No Buddhas have appeared since the Buddha's death.

Buddha modified many of Hinduism's teachings, for example, the many yoga and the necessity of indefinite reincarnations. His **Middle Path** between excessive sensual pleasures and the severe asceticism of Hinduism led to a movement. The first crisis in Buddhism occurred after his death. The First Council was called to decide basic questions concerning doctrine and discipline. But the Second Council was called in 377 B.C.E. after a group of monks revolted against the strict rules that were developing within Buddhism. The council decided in favor of the strict interpretation, and the dissenting monks seceded; this was the first schism.

Middle Path
Siddhartha Gautama's method of balance between excessive sensual pleasures and the severe asceticism of Hinduism

Buddhism is not so much about God, as it is about the *how* of human living. Thus, some people regard Buddhism as a philosophy, others look upon it as religion, and for still others it is a bit of both. Buddha never taught about God, and he rejected the idea of going to one or more gods to ask their divine assistance. He rejected the fatalism of Hinduism and the necessity of innumerable reincarnations in order to achieve oneness with the Ultimate Reality. He rejected the complexities of Hinduism in favor of a simple search for self. When the practices of yoga did not work for him, Siddhartha came to realize that happiness lay within each person and not in the various and uncertain revelations of many gods.

The Spread of Buddhism

The spread of Buddhism received a major impetus in 270 B.C.E. Asoka, emperor of a vast empire, regretted his wars of conquest and became a Buddhist. He acquired a strong missionary sense of Buddhism and helped it to spread throughout his realm to all of India, Ceylon, Nepal, and central Asia. Asoka's son, Prince Mahinda, took Buddhism to Ceylon. In time, Buddhism reached Burma and Thailand.

Buddhism came to China in about 200 B.C.E. It was aided in its growth in China when Hindus reasserted themselves in India and drove out nearly all Buddhists. Buddhism in China evolved into several forms, one of which is Zen Buddhism. Buddhism mixed with the native Chinese religions of Confucianism and Taoism. Each of these religions has its own historical basis and belief, but Chinese religions, especially in North America, are best understood within a Buddhist context.

From China, Buddhism spread to Korea in 372 C.E. An important note about Buddhism in Korea is that Buddhists there began to emphasize what the various manifestations of Buddhism had in common rather than how they differed. This led to the formation of a single organization called the *Chogye sect*. Buddhism then spread to Japan. Most American Buddhists are Japanese in orientation.

Forms of Buddhism

Buddhists today follow the essential teachings of the Buddha. They may be in one particular school of teaching, and they may interpret the teachings of Buddha differently. The various groups represent nuances produced by their own ethnic origins. Nevertheless, they all follow the Buddha's essential ideas.

Theravada Buddhism

Around the time of the emperor Asoka, Buddhism began to take on two dominant forms. One school of Buddhism is the Hinayana school (also called **Theravada Buddhism** or Lesser Vehicle, which is a conservative interpretation of Buddhism). Theravada Buddhism follows the teachings of Buddha closely and does not call upon the gods or divine forces to help people on the journey to enlightenment. A person's main task is to achieve enlightenment through meditation; the approach is something of a "self-help" method. Theravada Buddhism comes from Southeast Asia and looks to the writings of Sariputra, a disciple of Buddha, who emphasized the role of the monk and the monastic life as the way to enlightenment.

Theravada Buddhism
a conservative interpretation of Buddhism, emphasizing the search for nirvana apart from the world, as a monk

Mahayana Buddhism

Mahayana Buddhism

the larger branch of Buddhism, open to non-monks seeking enlightenment

The other school of Buddhism is **Mahayana Buddhism**, or Greater Vehicle, which does not accept the teachings of Sariputra. Rather, it stems from Ananda, another disciple of Buddha, who was more open to the role of non-monks in seeking enlightenment. The goal of Mahayana Buddhism is the ultimate enlightenment of all people. This perspective made Buddhism more accessible to people of other nations.

Mahayana Buddhists do not emphasize the Buddha's human origins. In their view, the Buddha is eternal; he existed before Siddhartha Gautama's birth. Therefore, Siddhartha Gautama was merely an earthly projection of the eternal Buddha. According to Mahayana Buddhists, the eternal Buddha can help people attain nirvana. Mahayana Buddhists believe that all people possess Buddha nature. If a person embraces his or her Buddha nature, he or she becomes a Buddha. A person can embrace his or her Buddha nature by being faithful and devoted to the Buddha and by being compassionate to all beings.

According to Mahayana Buddhists, nothing exists. All is empty; emptiness is everywhere. In other words, life on earth is an effect of an effect of an effect of an effect *ad infinitum*. It is empty—empty of existence. The same point can be made in a different way: Everything is interconnected; every single thing is dependent on another thing for its existence. Nothing exists in its own right. Therefore, nothing exists.

Mahayana Buddhism is the missionary branch of Buddhism, brought to China, Japan, Korea, Tibet, and Vietnam. As it extended into these countries, it encountered numerous other religious beliefs and practices. Adherents wanted to reconcile Buddhism with these native religions and believed that the teachings of the Buddha were for everyone of every time and place. They considered their perspective on Buddhism more compassionate and inclusive than the view of the Theravada Buddhists. Mahayana Buddhists incorporated the local gods into their perspective, built temples, and organized a religious system. In seeking enlightenment, one could call upon the help of the gods as well as one's own resources.

Zen Buddhism

Zen Buddhism

a Japanese refinement of Mahayana Buddhism; emphasizes enlightenment

satori

in Buddhism, the sudden glimpse of enlightenment about life; bodhi

The Japanese pronounce the Chinese word *Ch'an* as *Zen*, which means "meditation." Zen Buddhism is a refinement of Mahayana Buddhism in China and a reaction against a too formal and rigid Buddhism. **Zen Buddhism** is the mystical school of Buddhism. It seeks, by meditation under the guidance of a teacher, the **satori**, or glimpse of enlightenment about life. Zen teachers help their students attain enlightenment through the use of zazen (seated meditation), sanzen (teacher's instruction), and koan (paradoxical puzzle).

Zen Buddhism teaches that truth does not lie in any particular revelation, wise sayings, person, or particular way. It lies in existence itself. Zen maintains that meditating on the ordinary brings wisdom. For example, a student of Zen Buddhism once remarked, "My supernatural power and marvelous deeds—drawing water and carrying firewood." The Zen Buddhist using the koan seeks through serious contemplation on seemingly nonsensical statements to arrive at his own understanding of life. Zen Buddhists believe that by concerted effort a person will arrive at his or her own glimpse of enlightenment through a sudden intuition which will shed once and for all the complexities and strivings that keep people in turmoil.

Is That So?

The Zen Master Hakuin was praised by his neighbors as one living a pure life.

A beautiful Japanese girl whose parents owned a food store lived near him. Suddenly, without any warning, her parents discovered she was with child.

This made her parents angry. She would not confess who the man was, but after much harassment at last named Hakuin.

In great anger the parents went to the master. "Is that so?" was all he would say.

After the child was born it was brought to Hakuin.

By this time he had lost his reputation, which did not trouble him, but he took very good care of the child. He obtained milk from his neighbors and everything else the little one needed.

A year later the girl-mother could stand it no longer. She told her parents the truth—that the real father of the child was a young man who worked in the fish market.

The mother and father of the girl at once went to Hakuin to ask his forgiveness, to apologize at length, and to get the child back again.

Hakuin was willing. In yielding the child, all he said was: "Is that so?"

—*Paul Reps,* Zen Flesh, Zen Bones *(Tokyo: Charles E. Tuttle Co., 1975), 22.*

Let's Talk about It . . .

1. In this situation, what was the "ordinary" that brought wisdom?
2. Why do you think Hakuin responded with only "Is that so?"
3. What lesson did you learn from the girl's parents? From Hakuin? From the girl?

Growing and Blooming

Buddhism in North America

Buddhism in North America is strongly tied to the various forms of Buddhism in Asia. Beyond these, we are beginning to see the development of a western form of Buddhism. North American Buddhists trace their roots back to two main sources: (1) The Theravada tradition of Sri Lanka and Southeast Asia (chiefly Thailand and Burma), and (2) Mahayana Buddhism of China, Japan, and Tibet.

Theravada Buddhism, the more conservative school, had a very limited existence in North America prior to 1965. The repeal of the Asian Exclusion Act and the influx of refugees from Vietnam dramatically increased the presence of Theravada Buddhism in North America. Nevertheless, it is still limited primarily to non-English-speaking Asian Americans.

From the Mahayana tradition, Buddhism came to the United States with Chinese immigrations between 1854 and 1883. Today, most Chinese Buddhist centers are located in Honolulu, San Francisco, and New York City.

In 1868, large numbers of Japanese laborers began to arrive in Hawaii. Their immigration continued until 1907, when it was limited. Buddhism began in the countryside and then, as the plantations declined, it moved to Honolulu. Japanese Buddhism came to the mainland of North America only a short time later as Japanese began to settle in California. The first Buddhist temple in the United States was built at Hilo, Hawaii, in 1889.

First to bring Zen Buddhism to North America were students of Imakita Kosen, a nineteenth-century Zen Buddhist in Japan who was renowned for taking western thought and culture seriously. In 1893, Soyen Shaku, a student of Kosen, spoke at the World Parliament of Religions in Chicago. However, his presentation did not have the impact of other speakers from Asia, and he soon returned to Japan. The work of two other students of Kosen had more lasting effects. Daisetz Teitaro Suzuki was a scholar who taught American audiences through his books. Sokatsu Shaku brought six disciples with him to California in 1906. In time this group gradually returned to Japan without leaving an organization behind. One of this group, however, Shigetsu Sasaki, returned to New York in 1928. His settlement marks the beginning of a continuous Zen Buddhist history in North America.

The Zen school of Mahayana Buddhism is one of the fastest growing groups of Buddhism found in the United States. The Zen Center of San Francisco is just one of many dynamic Zen Buddhist organizations. The center conducts a Sunday program of early-morning meditation, instruction by the abbot, group discussion over tea, and a vegetarian meal. This Zen Center also maintains Green Gulch Farm, which offers people an opportunity to engage in more intensive Zen practice. To help in the support of the center, the farm owns and operates Tassajara Breads, renowned for its baked goods and cook books.

Scriptures

Like Hinduism, Buddhism encompasses a vast collection of sacred texts gathered from the centuries. The scriptures of Mahayana Buddhism were written in Sanskrit, and those of Theravada Buddhism in the Pali language. For both, the texts are traditionally divided into three sections called the **Three Baskets** (or *Tipitaka* in the Theravada version). The Sutta Pitaka ("Basket of Discourses") is a collection of material attributed to the Buddha and his close disciples. The Vinaya Pitaka ("Basket of Discipline") consist of rules for the training of monks and information on the Buddha. The Abhidhamma ("Basket of Higher Teachings") is more metaphysical, dealing with the nature of reality. Other texts are held sacred by Buddhists, but the ones most highly reverenced are the originals.

Three Baskets
Buddhism's most sacred books, including the discourses of the Buddha

From the Tipitaka . . .

Buddha spoke thus once to his disciples: . . . If men speak evil of you, this must you think: "Our heart shall not waver; and we will abide in compassion, in loving kindness, without resentment. We will think of the man who speaks ill of us with thoughts of love, and in our thoughts of love shall we dwell. And from that abode of love we will fill the whole world with far-reaching, wide-spreading, boundless love."

Moreover, if robbers should attack you and cut you in pieces with a two-handed saw, limb by limb, and one of you should feel hate, such a one is not a follower of my gospel.

—Majjhima–nikaya, Sutta Pitaka, Tipitaka.

Let's Talk about It. . .

1. What is the message of this passage?

2. In what other tradition(s) have you encountered a similar message?

3. Do you think that the message of this passage is realistic? Why or why not?

4. Does one need to be Buddhist to benefit from this message? Why or why not?

Many varieties of Mahayana Buddhism exist, such as Pure Land and Hua-yen, which produced the meditation schools Ch'an and Zen. Though these schools recognize many of the same scriptural works, each has works of its own, with a single work that usually stands apart from the rest. Of all the works that comprise the scriptures of Mahayana Buddhism, the Saddharma-pundarika (Lotus Sutra) has had the most far-reaching influence. It has been called "the gospel of Mahayana Buddhism." The Lotus Sutra makes two important points:

1. All people can attain Buddhahood.

2. The "eternal cosmic" Buddha gives people the grace (help) necessary to attain salvation, or Buddhahood.

> *I am the Tathagata [Buddha], the Worshipful, the All-wise, the Perfectly Enlightened in Conduct, the Well-departed, the Understander of the World, the Peerless Leader, the Controller, the Teacher of Gods and Men, the Buddha, the World-honored One. Those who have not yet been saved, I cause to be saved; those who have not yet been set free, to be set free; those who have not yet been comforted, to be comforted; those who have not yet obtained Nirvana, to obtain Nirvana. I know the present world and the world to come as they really are. I am the All-knowing, the All-seeing, the Knower of the Way, the Opener of the Way, the Preacher of the Way. Come to me . . .*
>
> —*Lotus Sutra 5.*

The Buddhist Journey

The Buddha never spoke of God. It is probably not because he did not believe in a god or the gods. It is more likely that in his Middle Path, he focused on enlightenment. Any concern about the gods would have distracted him from the path.

Karma

Buddhists believe in karma, which means "action and its fruits" or "the result of what we have thought." In this view, "for every event that occurs, there will follow another event whose existence was caused by the first, and this second event will be pleasant or unpleasant [depending on whether] its cause was skillful or unskillful." A *skillful event* is an action that does not cause pain. The performer of a skillful event looks upon himself or herself as connected to other people. An *unskillful event* describes an action that causes pain; the force behind this action is craving—craving for continued existence, material wealth, power, or sensual pleasures. The performer of an unskillful event has failed to recognize the interconnectedness of all things. Karma causes suffering, relative happiness, and ultimate happiness (**nirvana**—release from suffering).

Samsāra

Buddhists also believe in **samsāra**, which means the "repeated births and deaths caused by karma." In this view, people are reborn to learn—to evolve. The present life is the fruit of past lives; karma shapes the circumstances of a person's rebirth. Karma determines whether a person will exist as a (1) deity, (2) human being, (3) animal, (4) hungry ghost, (5) demon, or (6) a resident of hell. The second state is regarded as especially desirable, since humans have the opportunity to hear and understand Buddhist teachings.

Buddhists believe that observance of the Four Noble Truths ensures a good rebirth—entry into a good state of existence.

nirvana
release from suffering; ultimate happiness, the state of enlightenment

samsāra
the repeated births and deaths caused by karma

The Four Noble Truths

The Buddha was very concerned with the world's suffering. He devoted himself to helping people liberate themselves from suffering (attain nirvana). Thus, the teaching of the Buddha is remarkably simple. It begins with the Middle Way and the **Four Noble Truths**. As the peerless physician and supreme surgeon, the Buddha devised this four-part formula. The Four Noble Truths exist so that people can heal themselves, to ultimately attain nirvana.

Four Noble Truths
Siddhartha Gautama's foundational concepts on suffering, desire, and the path to nirvana

1. Unhappiness exists. There is suffering.

This is apparent in many ways: the trauma of birth, sickness, fear of death, to be forced to be with what one dislikes or to be separated from what one loves. The Buddha specified that there are three kinds of suffering: (1) suffering rooted in pain, (2) suffering rooted in a conditioned state, and (3) suffering rooted in change.

Understanding of the second kind of suffering (suffering rooted in a conditioned state) requires an explanation of the term *conditioned state*. Conditioned state means "temporariness." All people exist in a conditioned state. Each person is made up of five forces: (1) matter, (2) sensations, (3) consciousness, (4) perceptions, and (5) volitions (acts of will). These forces are constantly changing, so people are constantly changing. Human beings make the mistake of believing the constantly changing "self" to be real and permanent. The reality is that the person is process, is continually becoming. Recognition that everything is subject to change causes dissatisfaction (suffering).

2. The cause of this sorrow and suffering is desire.

We want to fill our egos. We might want selflessness, but the craving (desire) for the pleasures of life comes back. Craving brings short-term satisfaction; for this reason, people cannot stop craving (desiring). They continually desire to enjoy (sensual pleasure), to become somebody (existence), or to want something that is always beyond reach. As long as there is desire, there will be suffering, because of the mental stress in the acquiring of the object of desire or in the disappointment due to the elusiveness of the object of desire.

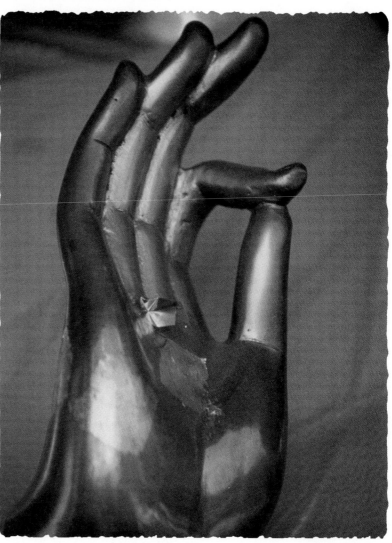

Let us live happily, though we call nothing our own. Let us be like God, feeding on love.
—*Dhammapada*

3. There is a cure for the sorrow and suffering of life.

We must let go of our desires—the end to suffering is non-attachment. Separation from the five forces that make up a person brings suffering to an end. Overcoming the cravings and sufferings of life will lead to nirvana.

Eightfold Path
Siddhartha Gautama's path that leads to the cessation of suffering

4. The way to do this is to follow the Eightfold Path.

This is the path of

- Wisdom (prajna)—right views, right intent
- Morality (sila)—right speech, right conduct, right livelihood
- Mental discipline (samadhi)—right effort, right mindfulness, right concentration

> *Relatives and friends and well-wishers rejoice at the arrival of [someone] who had been long absent and has returned home safely from afar. Likewise, meritorious deeds will receive the good person upon . . . arrival in the next world, as relatives welcome a dear one on his [or her] return.*
>
> —*Dhammapada (Verses of Righteousness), 219–220.*

The Eightfold Path

Before beginning the Eightfold Path, one must practice a certain preliminary: Right association.

> *Robert Ingersoll once remarked that had he been God he would have made health contagious instead of disease; to which an Indian contemporary responded: "When shall we come to recognize that health is as contagious as disease, virtue as contagious as vice, cheerfulness as contagious as moroseness?" One of the three things for which we should give thanks every day, according to Shankara, is the company of the holy; for as bees cannot make honey unless together, human beings cannot make progress on the Way unless they are supported by a field of confidence and concern that Truthwinners generate. The Buddha agrees. We should associate with Truthwinners, converse with them, serve them, observe their ways, and imbibe by osmosis their spirit of love and compassion.*
>
> —*Huston Smith,* The World's Religions, *revised edition, 105.*

Another way to say this is: hang around the right people. Having begun with this preliminary, one then proceeds to the eight steps:

1. **Right views.** We must believe it will work. Just as an elephant will not walk on the path unless it believes the path will support it, says the Buddha, so too must we believe that the eightfold path will work.

2. **Right intent.** The first step, right views, says our mind must be in the right place; the second step says our heart must also be in the right place. One must be single-hearted in seeking escape from suffering and achieving the goal of nirvana.

3. **Right speech.** One must never lie or speak uselessly. One must never speak badly of others. Notice how you are untruthful or uncharitable in speech. Then make changes. Speak truthfully. Speak charitably.

4. **Right conduct.** Notice how your conduct is not right. What is your motive in acting? This step includes prohibitions against killing, stealing, and engaging in illicit sex. Consuming intoxicants is also prohibited, since it interferes with right views and often leads to conduct that is not right.

5. **Right livelihood.** One must have the right occupation—one which supports following the Way. The ideal is to be a monk. For others, there must at least be an occupation that supports right living. Earning a living is a means, not an end in itself. Prohibitions include trafficking in weapons or alcoholic drink, the killing of animals, and prostitution.

6. **Right effort.** Make persistent, patient progress. Just as a hiker must take one careful step at a time climbing a mountain, so too must we be determined in our effort to reach nirvana.

7. **Right mindfulness.** A person must engage in continuous self-examination in order to overcome ignorance. Continue to lift the mind above physical desires. Try to see the larger perspective.

8. **Right concentration.** This is the kind of meditation which leads to enlightenment. From here on, the Buddha essentially followed the raja yoga of Hinduism. In this step, one achieves nirvana.

Nirvana

Ideally, all Buddhists seek nirvana, the state of enlightenment. Anyone who is enlightened may be called a *buddha*. The Buddha taught that it is possible to reach nirvana within a single lifetime. It is not necessary to be reincarnated indefinitely; at most, perhaps it would take two or three lifetimes. When a person attains nirvana, he or she loses the boundaries of a finite individual self. Attaining nirvana allows him or her to cease existing as an individual consciousness. It is believed to be impossible to describe to those who have not attained it what nirvana is like.

The Goal—Enlightenment

It is said that when Buddha attained enlightenment, all he wanted to do was to show the rest of us the nature of mind and share completely what he had realized. But he also saw, with the sorrow of infinite compassion, how difficult it would be for us to understand.

For even though we have the same inner nature as Buddha, we have not recognized it because it is so enclosed and wrapped up in our individual ordinary minds. Imagine an empty vase. The space inside is exactly the same as the space outside.

Only the fragile walls of the vase separate one from the other. Our buddha mind is enclosed within the walls of our ordinary mind. But when we become enlightened, it is as if that vase shatters into pieces. The space "inside" merges instantly into the space "outside." They become one: There and then we realize they were never separate or different; they were always the same.

—*Sogyal Rinpoche*, The Tibetan Book of Living and Dying.

Let's Talk about It. . .

1. How would you describe enlightenment?
2. Is there anything in other religions to which you would compare enlightenment? Nirvana?

Reaping the Fruit

Sikhism

History

The word *Sikh* comes from the Sanskrit *sisya*, which means "disciple." A Sikh is a person who follows the teachings of the Ten Gurus and recognizes the authority of the Guru Granth Sahib. The Ten Gurus refers to the ten greatest teachers in **Sikhism**: Nanak Dev, Angad Dev, Amar Das, Ram Das, Anjan Dev, Hargobind, Har Rai, Har Kishan, Tegh Bahadur, and Gobind Singh. The Guru Granth Sahib, or Adi Granth, which means "Eternal Living Guru," refers to the core scriptures of Sikhism. For Sikhs, the Adi Granth contains the living essence of the Ten Gurus and is considered "the only true guru."

In essence, the history of Sikhism is the story of Guru Nanak Dev and his nine successors. In the early sixteenth century, the northern part of India was the scene of bitter conflict. In 1526, Muslims gained control of the area, particularly the region called the Punjab (an area encompassing parts of eastern Pakistan and northwestern India). On April 15, 1469, Guru Nanak Dev, the founder of Sikhism, was born of Hindu parents in Talwandi, Punjab.

Sikhism

a reform of Hinduism with Islamic elements; the religion of disciples who follow the Ten Gurus

At an early age, Nanak showed an interest in religious matters, asking a broad range of questions about God and life. He studied at both Hindu and Muslim schools and counted children from both religions as his friends. As a young man, Nanak herded the family cattle; this occupation gave him an opportunity to converse with Hindu and Muslim mystics living in a nearby forest. He spent long hours meditating with these men and asking them questions. Nanak later married Sulakhani, the daughter of a local merchant; they had two sons. Guru Nanak enjoyed his life, but found that neither Hinduism nor Islam met his needs.

Early one morning, Nanak went to the Bain river to bathe. While there, he had a vision of God in which he was told to go out into the world and teach the repetition of the name of God, the practice of charity, meditation, and worship, and the keeping of ritual purity through absolution. When he returned, his family and friends saw "a divine light in his eyes"; they described his face as "resplendent." Shortly thereafter he quit his accounting job and gave his possessions to the poor. Then, at age thirty, he left his family to tell people to rejoice in God's name. He was accompanied on his travels by a childhood friend, Mardana, who played the rabab, a stringed instrument.

Nanak declared, "There is no Hindu, no Muslim." He taught a religious belief which combined aspects of many religions, primarily Hinduism and Islam, the religions with which he was most familiar. From Hinduism, he taught karma, reincarnation, and the ultimate illusion (māyā) of reality. From Islam, he taught one creator God, whom he called the True Name. The canopy over the scriptures of Sikhism displays the symbol *Ek Oankar*, which means "There is one God." Nanak wished to avoid both the names *Allah* and *Vishnu*.

California became an early center for Sikhs emigrating to the United States.

Nanak adopted a unique garb, combining elements of Hinduism and Islam. One of its features is the turban, which makes Sikhs readily identifiable. He and Mardana traveled throughout Asia preaching God's word. They often communicated the message in the form of a musical composition. At nearly every stop, Nanak established study houses (manjis) where his followers meditated and sang hymns.

Stories of Guru Nanak

Honest Food

At Saidpur, Punjab, Guru Nanak stayed with Lalo, a low-caste carpenter. At the same time, Malik Bhago, the town's wealthy leader, was having a feast for religious leaders and other notables. Guru Nanak was invited, but declined to attend. This angered Malik Bhago who summoned Guru Nanak to appear before him. When Malik Bhago demanded an explanation, Guru Nanak asked both Malik and Lalo to prepare a meal for him.

Guru Nanak held food from Malik's house in one hand and food from Lalo's in the other. And he squeezed both foods at the same time. Malik's food dripped blood, and Lalo's dripped milk. This great miracle had a profound effect on Malik Bhago: "He was put to shame and realized that his riches had been amassed by exploiting the poor, while what Lalo offered was the milk of hard-earned honest work."

Reward and Punishment

At another town, one of Guru Nanak's students became involved with a prostitute. This man began rendezvousing with the prostitute instead of visiting Guru Nanak. On one occasion, the man's friend, who visited Guru Nanak daily, cut himself on a thorn. A few days later, the man seeing the prostitute found a gold coin. This prompted the injured man to tell Guru Nanak everything. The Guru responded: "Your friend was destined to come across a treasure, but due to his evil ways, it has been reduced to a single coin. While on the account of your past karma you were to have been impaled with a stake. By having reformed yourself, you have been let off with the mere prick of a thorn."

Let's Talk about It . . .

1. What is the message of each of these stories?
2. Are there any similar stories or teachings in other religions you have studied?

At the end of his life, Nanak returned to his wife and sons. As death approached, Guru Nanak's Hindu followers said, "We will cremate you," and his Muslim followers said, "We will bury you." Guru Nanak addressed both groups: "You place flowers on either side, Hindus on my right, Muslims on my left. Those whose flowers remain fresh tomorrow will have their way." He then instructed them to cover him with a sheet. On September 22, 1539, Guru Nanak "merged with the eternal light of the Creator." When his followers lifted the sheet, they found that all of the flowers were fresh.

After his death, Nanak was succeeded by nine more gurus. The fourth of these, Ram Das, began the Golden Temple of Amrisar, which is the present headquarters of the world Sikh community. The fifth guru completed the temple and gave Sikhism its holy book, the Granth Sahib. This book contains hymns of Sikh gurus as well as those of Hindu and Muslim saints. The sixth guru abandoned vegetarianism and encouraged strong bodies; he eventually established a Sikh army. The tenth guru is second in importance to Nanak in Sikhism. Guru Gobind Singh completed the writings of the Granth Sahib and further formed Sikhs into a community. He engaged the Sikhs in an unsuccessful struggle with Muslim Mogul rulers. After his death in 1708, the Granth Sahib itself became the guru.

Following Gobind's death, the Sikhs were persecuted by Muslim Mogul rulers until 1799 when, under the leadership of Ranjit Singh, the Sikhs laid claim to a large part of northwest India. After Ranjit's death, however, this Sikh kingdom disintegrated into anarchy. The British moved into the area, the Sikhs were defeated in the wars which followed, and the British annexed the Punjab. The Sikhs were not to recover until the twentieth century when they were given control of their holy places. In 1947, western Punjab became Pakistani and eastern Punjab became part of India. Riots followed, especially in the Pakistani section, and two and one-half million Sikhs migrated to India. In 1990, there were about sixteen million Sikhs in India, about 1.9 percent of the population.

Sikhism in North America

It is possible that some unnamed East Indian visitors to Salem, Massachusetts, in 1790 were Sikhs. The first known Sikhs traversed Canada in 1897. Apparently they had been in England celebrating Queen Victoria's silver anniversary and were taken home across Canada, where they were impressed by the prairies. In 1903, a few Sikhs came to Canada, and by 1904, Sikhs living in British Columbia numbered 204. Several more thousand came within the next four years. Because of immigration restrictions, the population shifted to the United States. By 1915, there were seven thousand East Indians living in the United States, most of them Sikhs and mostly living in California. Sikh communities in the United States and in Canada now have at least a million members.

The first U.S. **guruwara** (Sikh house of worship) opened in 1908 in Vancouver, Washington. The second was opened in 1912 in Stockton, California. In 1969, the largest Sikh temple in the world was built at Yuba City, California. Today there are guruwaras all across the country. The Sikh Council of North America is located in Richmond Hill, New York. Since 1970, the Sikh Council of North America has sought to forge communication links between Sikh organizations and temples throughout the United States and Canada. The council continues to publish a wide variety of Sikh periodicals.

guruwara
Sikh house of worship

Beliefs of Sikhism

Sikhs believe in a personal God. The attributes of God are described in their morning prayer, Japji.

There is one God;

He is the Supreme Truth.

He, the Creator, is without fear and without hate . . . .

He, the omnipresent, pervades the Universe.

He is not born; nor does he die to be born again.

By his grace shall you worship.

For Sikhs, God is the eternal creator, the source of all worlds. Sikhs look to gurus to help them have limited experiences of God. While the goal of Sikhism is union with God, a complete knowledge of God is impossible. In the words of Guru Nanak, "Only one who is as great as He, can know Him fully." Sikhs call the Supreme Being *Wahi Guru*, which means "hail guru." The name has also been interpreted as "wonderful Enlightener and wonderful Lord." *Allah*, *Mahakal*, *Pritam*, *Rahim*, *Ram*, and *Yar* are other Sikh names for God.

God is both above the universe and in it. The God who is above the universe is abstract and existed in the very beginning; God in this sense is called *Nirgun*. According to Guru Nanak, there was nothing other than chaos, clouds, darkness, and mists for millions of years. Guru Nanak described this state of precreation in these words: "There was darkness for countless years. There was neither earth nor sky; there was only His Will. There was neither day nor night, neither sun nor moon. He [God] was in deep meditation. There was nothing except Himself."

Then God created the universe. God within the universe is called *Sargun* (quality-ful). In these words, Guru Nanak explained God's will to create: "You created all Your Universe to please Yourself, to enjoy the spectacle, the reality, which is the light of Your own Reality-Self." The Divine Will maintains order throughout the universe. People can experience true happiness only if they submit to God's will. "Your Will be done" is one of the basic principles of Sikhism. According to the gurus, God desires that people merge their will with His will. This merging of wills helps to preserve cosmic order and to bring an end to suffering. The qualities associated with God are beauty, charity, goodness, justice, love, mercy, peace, truth, and wisdom. Sikhs believe that people can absorb these qualities by meditating on them.

The concept of truth is central to Sikhism. Truth is several things: the Almighty; virtue; holy, pure and sacred; correct and proper; and eternal happiness or bliss. From the Sikh perspective, there are three dispensers of truth: God, Satguru (true guru), and Holy Congregation.

Sikhs believe that God dwells in the human being. For this reason, they call the body the Temple of God. According to the Adi Granth, "Whatever is found in the Universe is found in the body, whoever searches it shall find it." The Universe is the macrocosm, and the body is the microcosm (of the universe). Sikhs believe in karma—that a person is punished or rewarded on the basis of his or her deeds. On more than one occasion, Guru Nanak spoke about karma: "According to one's action, one gets near to or distant from God." Only God can neutralize karma, but the person must practice love, prayer, and repentance.

In the Sikh view, the body will mix with the soil after death, but the soul will continue. The righteous either merge with God or prepare for another life, a noble life. The unrighteous, however, remain forever in the cycle of birth and death—reincarnation. Either they will enter a non-human form or begin a life fraught with difficulty.

> The Earth is a garden,
>
> the Lord its gardener,
>
> Cherishing all, none neglected.
>
> —Taken from the Adi Granth (Majh Ashtpadi 1, M.3, page 118).

Practices of Sikhism

Sikhs take a vow not to cut their hair as well as not to smoke or drink alcoholic beverages. It was Guru Gobind Singh who militarized the Sikhs and formed them into the martial fraternity Khalsa, the Community of the Pure. Members of the community vow to keep the five Ks: to wear long hair (*kesh*), a comb in the hair (*kangha*), a steel bracelet on the right wrist (*kara*), soldier's shorts (*kachha*), and a sword (*kirpan*). The Khalsa is open to men and women and is a tradition which persists to the present day.

Nanak emphasized the importance of the guru as necessary to lead people to God; Sikhs place great trust in the abilities of a guru. The guru, or satguru, is "just a shade below God." A guru helps a Sikh attain **moksha** (release from suffering—birth, death, rebirth). The chief task of the guru is to make persons aware of the treasure within themselves and then help them to unlock the jewel box. "The guru's word has the sage's wisdom, the guru's word is full of learning, for, though it be the guru's word, God himself speaks therein." The guru keeps a person on the path leading to moksha. Guru Nanak spelled out what one should look for in a guru: "Take him as a guru who shows the path of truth, who tells you of the one of whom nothing is known, who tells you of the divine word."

Gurus do not perform ceremonies; gurus guide. There are no priests in Sikhism. Guru Nanak stressed that every Sikh should be his or her own priest. Sikhs reject Hindu worship, rituals, and yoga. Not only do they reject the caste system, they accept equality for women. Throughout the year Sikhs observe gurupurabs. A **gurupurab** honors the birth, death, guruship, or martyrdom of the great Sikh gurus. Nearly forty gurupurabs are listed on the Sikh calendar. Though Guru Nanak was born on April 15, 1469, it is on November 10 that Sikhs celebrate his birth.

moksha
for Sikhs, release from suffering—birth, death, rebirth

gurupurab
a Sikh celebration honoring the birth, death, guruship, or martyrdom of one of the great Sikh gurus

Why the Innocent Suffer

Upon completion of his fourth and last journey, Guru Nanak once again stopped at Saidpur, Punjab, which was in the path of an invading Mogul army. On this occasion, Mardana asked Guru Nanak the question: "Why are so many innocent people put to death along with the few who are guilty?" Guru Nanak told Mardana to sit beneath a banyan tree and wait for an answer. As Mardana sat, he was bitten by an ant. In anger he stomped on every ant in sight. Guru Nanak returned and said, "You know now Mardana, why do the innocent suffer along with the guilty?"

Let's Talk about It...

1. Why do the innocent suffer?
2. Do you agree with Guru Nanak's explanation? Why or why not?

Scriptures of Sikhism

The scriptures of Sikhism are called *Gurbani*, which means "guru's word." From the Sikh perspective, God revealed the *bani* (the truth) through the guru. The Sikhs have an expression that emphasizes the intimate connection between bani and guru: "The bani is the Guru and the Guru is the bani." In the Guru Granth Sahib or Adi Granth, the core scriptures of Sikhism, every chapter begins with the words, "The One God—by the grace of Guru, worship." The Adi Granth contains some nine thousand hymns, which are divided into thirty-one ragas (musical modes). Guru Arjan, who looked upon the Adi Granth as a universal scripture, composed many of these hymns. This passage from the Adi Granth is an example of the scripture.

> *Hindus bathe in holy waters for His sake; Muslims make the pilgrimage to Mecca. The Hindus perform pūjā; others bow their heads in namaz. There are those who read the Vedas and others—Christians, Jews, Muslims—who read the Semitic scriptures. Some wear blue, some white robes, some call themselves Muslims, others Hindus. Some aspire to bahishat (Muslim heaven), some to swarga (Hindu heaven). Says Nanak, "Whoever realizes the will of the Lord, he will find out the Lord's secrets."*
>
> —*Adi Granth, Ramkali, M.5, page 885.*

A Calendar

Winter

Swami Vivekananda Jayanti (January 26). On this day, many Hindus celebrate the birth of Swami Vivekananda. His appearance at the first World's Parliament of Religions (1893) sparked interest in Vedanta throughout the United States.

Parinnirvana Day (February 15). On this day, Buddhists living in the countries of northern Asia celebrate the Buddha's death. Mahayana Buddhists mark this occasion by reading and discussing portions of the Mahparinirvana Sutra, which contains accounts of the Buddha's death.

Maha Shivaratri (March 2) is the day Hindus honor the God Shiva. They spend the entire night fasting and worshiping, in hope of drawing closer to him. Some Hindus honor their gurus on this day by bringing them gifts.

Sri Ramakrishna Jayanti (March 6) is the day on which many Hindus celebrate the birth of Sri Ramakrishna, who was the teacher of Swami Vivekananda.

Holi (March 18). On this day, Hindus celebrate the life of Sri Krishna. They throw colored powder or spray colored water, which signifies the many colors of the spring season.

Spring

Wesak (April 8) is the day Buddhists living in the countries of northern Asia mark the anniversary of the Buddha's birth.

Ramnavami (beginning April 11) is a nine-day Hindu festival which focuses on the life of Rāma. Hindus spend the first day telling stories about Rāma.

Baisakhi (April 13). For Sikhs, this day marks the beginning of the New Year.

Hanuman Jayanti (April 17) is the day Hindus celebrate the birth of Hanuman, the monkey who became the faithful servant of Rāma. Many Hindus believe that Hanuman protects his followers from evil spirits. Some spend the day constructing charms to ward off evil.

Visakha (May 16). On this date, many Buddhists celebrate three events: the birth, the enlightenment, and the death of the Buddha. Theravada Buddhists give money to Buddhist monks on this day. Some imitate the Buddha's compassion by releasing captive, caged animals.

Summer

Narali Purnima, or **Rakhi** (August 13). On this occasion, the Hindus of India celebrate the end of the monsoon (a period of torrential rains). People honor the water god Varuna by tossing coconuts into the sea.

Krishna Janmashtami (August 21) is a Hindu festival which focuses on the life of Krishna. Hindus come together and tell stories about Krishna.

Ganeś Chaturthi (August 31). This Hindu festival honors Ganeśa. The god Ganeśa is the bringer of good luck and the remover of obstacles.

Autumn

Navaratra (September 27–October 5). This nine-day Hindu festival honors Durgā, the Divine Mother. Hindus pay tribute to her by fasting and praying.

Dashara, Vijaya Dashami (October 6). On this date, Hindus celebrate Durgā's victory over evil. They also commemorate Rāma's defeat of the demon king Rāvana, which is recorded in the epic *Ramayana*. Many people send greeting cards to one another.

Diwali (October 25) Diwali, which means "cluster of lights," is a popular Hindu festival. It recalls the coronation of Sri Rāma as well as the legacy of King Vikarāma. People mark the occasion by decorating with strings of lights, and giving presents.

Guru Nanak's Birthday (November 10). Though Guru Nanak, the founder of Sikhism, was born on April 15, 1469, it is on November 10 that Sikhs commemorate his birth.

Bodhi Day (December 8). On this day, Buddhists living in the countries of northern Asia celebrate the Buddha's enlightenment.

D i s c o v e r i n g

1. Be able to identify the meaning of each of the words in the vocabulary list.

2. Name and explain the four human wants according to Hinduism.

3. What is ātman? Does the concept relate to a concept in any other religion?

4. Explain the goal of Hinduism.

5. Explain to a classmate the four yoga of Hinduism.

6. What is morality for a Hindu? How does it relate to the law of karma?

7. Explain the Buddha's Middle Path.

8. Name the Buddha's Four Noble Truths.

9. Discuss with a classmate each of The Four Noble Truths.

10. Name and explain the two main divisions of Buddhism.

11. Point out characteristics of Sikhism which are from Hinduism and Islam.

12. What is the role of a guru?

E x p l o r i n g

1. Illustrate each of the four wants of humans by stating a contemporary example in your culture.

2. Compare the four yoga of Hinduism with examples from another religious tradition, preferably your own. How do you see, for example, jnāna yoga, a stress on knowledge, emphasized in the other religious tradition? Do this for all four yoga.

3. In a small group, discuss the merits of reincarnation. Why do you think that people are so intrigued by reincarnation? If you believed in reincarnation, what would this do to your self-concept? To your view of life's purpose? To your commitment to living life? To your concept of the future? Apply the perspective of reincarnation to several aspects of a worldview.

4. In a small group, discuss and compare the merits of morality that is directed primarily at the self and a morality that is directed outwards toward the world.

5. Select a typical teenage activity—such as playing on a basketball team or a soccer team, or playing a musical instrument—and apply to the activity the steps of the Eightfold Path. For example, what is the importance of *right association* for a basketball player? How important is *right views*? Do this for each step of the Eightfold Path. This would be a good small-group activity.

Integrating

1. What is your personal experience of what Hinduism regards as the four human wants? Have you experienced these yourself? In what context?

2. Which of the four yoga of Hinduism would be most helpful to you in your practice of religion? How does this yoga relate to your personality type?

3. Which steps of the Eightfold Path of Buddhism might help you in achieving your goals? Are there any you are particularly good at? Are there some you need to emphasize more?

4. What aspects of eastern thought reinforce or give new insight to your own religious perspective?

5. Some scholars say that Guru Nanak purposely drew together elements of both Hinduism and Islam in the hopes of bringing peace to his own people. Do you think that combining elements of religions among people who have differences would be a helpful way to bring peace and harmony? Or do you think it is better that each group maintain their own religion but try to grow in respect for each other? How can religion serve such noble ideals as building world peace, giving all people their rights, and achieving social justice?

Words to Know

ātman	ISKCON	samnyāsin
avatār	jnāna yoga	samsāra
bhakti yoga	karma	samskāras
Brahmā	karma yoga	satori
Buddha	Mahayana Buddhism	Shiva
Buddhism	mantra	Siddhartha Gautama
caste system	māyā	Sikhism
Eightfold Path	moksha	smriti scriptures
Four Noble Truths	nirvana	śriti scriptures
god-consciousness	path of desire	Theravada Buddhism
guru	path of renunciation	vedanta
gurupurab	raja yoga	Vedas
guruwara	reincarnation	Vishnu
Hinduism	rishis	yoga
		Zen Buddhism

Epilogue

After reading this epilogue, you will be able to
- Identify characteristics of recent developments in religious expression
- Critique the value of these new developments
- Formulate your own worldview

We arrive now at the end of an astonishing survey of religions in North America. At one time it was believed that with the development of the physical and social sciences and technology, all of the mysteries confronting humanity would be resolved. Religion would gradually fade away and become obsolete. The evidence at the turn of the millennium indicates quite the contrary! Apparently the responses offered by science and technology do not satisfy the hunger of human beings for responses to life's ultimate questions. The observation was made in the first chapter that the United States is home to an estimated two thousand religions. Present trends suggest that this number will grow as people continue to seek answers which give meaning to life.

Religion is far from becoming obsolete. The pluralistic and relatively tolerant culture of North America provides an environment in which the world's religions can proliferate. This environment, together with the demands of new problems, issues, and contemporary life, encourages the revitalization of religion and new forms of expression. We have seen how Native American religions, as well as other of the world's great religions, have taken on new forms of expression in North America. Sometimes religious bodies separate and form an entirely new religion or a new expression within a particular religious family. We've seen that some of these religious bodies later merge. Some religious movements transcend denominations and are found in several denominations and religions. It seems that some religious ideas and forms go underground in history, or lie dormant for centuries, and then emerge later in a slightly different form or combined with another ancient idea or practice.

In the latter half of the twentieth century, new forms of religious belief and practice have been added to the traditional religions already present in North America. During the 1960s, religious faith once expressed in a church, mosque, or synagogue was lived in the streets in the form of social protest. In the 1970s, people turned more inward to pursue personal faith journeys. The 1980s saw a more public expression of religion in the form of debates on the role of religion in society and on significant ethical issues. In the 1990s, religion took on more mystical forms as many people sought self-perfection and contact with other realms or spirits through various media. Some groups prepared for and celebrated the third millennium. This flurry of activity may level off as the third millennium settles in within a decade or two, but the opposite may also prove true.

Before some concluding observations, we will briefly survey new religious expression at the end of the second millennium.

New Religious Expressions

Neo-paganism

Neo-paganism, or **witchcraft**, is generally known as **Wicca** or **the Craft**. It is a movement based on pre-Christian European religions. Neo-paganism encompasses a wide variety of beliefs and practices. The modern-day movement can perhaps be traced to Gerald Gardner, an Englishman who brought together various folk and occult practices surfacing in the nineteenth century into a religion he called *Wicca*. In the 1920s, Gardner began teaching his ideas in Britain. One of his students, Alexander Sanders, developed his own version of Gardner's teachings. Then Janet and Stewart Farrar, students of Sanders, developed their version of witchcraft. These three forms of Wicca—Gardnerian, Alexandrian, and Farrarian—began to filter to the United States in the 1960s.

Once in the United States, Wicca took on new forms. It blended with other pagan traditions and the emerging feminist movement. Some philosophers tried to explain ritual and magic by using computer and technological ideas. The movement also sparked the revival of other ancient pagan traditions distinct from Wicca. By the late twentieth century, there was a wide variety of neo-pagan groups in the United States. The number of practitioners of Wicca is unknown. Estimates range from several tens of thousands to hundreds of thousands.

Most established religions consider the beliefs and practices of neo-paganism and all its forms to be more or less contrary to the beliefs and practices of the more traditional religious groups. However, a central concept which would be agreed upon by most witches and acknowledged in some fashion by most religions is, "Do what you will but harm no one." In 1974, the Council of American Witches met in Minnesota and published thirteen tenets of their belief system (see the list). Those who wish to identify with the Wiccan witchcraft movement must accept all thirteen principles.

neo-paganism, witchcraft, Wicca, the Craft

various strands of folk and occult practices and nature religions; modern form of paganism rooted in pre-Christian European religions

The Tenets of the Council of American Witches, 1974

1. We practice rites to attune ourselves with the natural rhythm of life forces marked by the phases of the Moon and the seasonal Quarters and Cross-quarters.

2. We recognize that our intelligence gives us a unique responsibility toward our environment. We seek to live in harmony with Nature, in ecological balance offering fulfillment to life and consciousness within an evolutionary concept.

3. We acknowledge a depth of power far greater than is apparent to the average person. Because it is greater than ordinary, it is sometimes called "supernatural," but we see it as lying within that which is naturally potential to all.

4. We conceive of the Creative Power in the Universe as manifesting through polarity as masculine and feminine and that this same Creative Power lives in all people and functions through the interaction of the masculine and feminine. We value sexuality as pleasure, as the symbol and embodiment of Life, and as one of the sources of energies used in magical practice and religious worship.

5. We recognize both outer worlds and inner, or psychological worlds—sometimes known as the *Spiritual World*, the *Collective Unconscious*, the *Inner Planes*, etc.—and we see in the interaction of these two dimensions the basis for paranormal phenomena and magical exercises. We neglect neither dimension for the other, seeing both as necessary for our fulfillment.

6. We do not recognize any authoritarian hierarchy, but do honor those who teach, respect those who share their greater knowledge and wisdom, and acknowledge those who have courageously given of themselves in leadership.

7. We see religion, magic, and wisdom-in-living as being united in the way one views the world and lives within it—a worldview and philosophy-of-life which we identify as *Witchcraft*, the *Wiccan Way*.

8. Calling oneself *Witch* does not make a Witch—but neither does hereditary itself, or the collecting of titles, degrees, and initiations. A witch seeks to control the forces within him/herself that make life possible in order to live wisely and well, without harm to others, and in harmony with Nature.

9. We acknowledge that it is the affirmation and fulfillment of life, in a continuation of evolution and development of consciousness, that gives meaning to the Universe we know and to our personal role within it.

10. Our only animosity toward Christianity, or toward any other religion or philosophy-of-life, is to the extent that its institutions have claimed to be "the one true right and only way" and have sought to deny freedom to others and to suppress other ways of religious practices and beliefs.

11. As American Witches, we are not threatened by debates on the history of the Craft, the origins of various terms, or the legitimacy of various aspects of different traditions. We are concerned with our present and our future.

12. We do not accept the concept of "absolute evil," nor do we worship any entity known as *Satan* or *the Devil* as defined by Christian Tradition. We do not seek power through the suffering of others, nor do we accept the concept that personal benefits can be derived only by denial to another.

13. We seek within Nature for that which is contributory to our health and well-being.

Let's Talk about It . . .

1. Which of the above tenets are contrary to your beliefs?

2. Which tenets seem to you to be compatible with the beliefs of major religions?

Within the whole spectrum of neo-paganism there are no central creeds or scriptures. Practitioners borrow freely from each other and from various religious and philosophical traditions. In general, three tendencies can be identified within neo-paganism:

1. There is an emphasis on the worship of the feminine principle in divinity. Thus goddess worship is included.

2. As mentioned above, practitioners do not seek to do harm. Neo-paganism is closely associated with care for the environment and with feminist concerns.

3. Stress is placed on developing an ability to work magic. Magic is used for defensive or good purposes. Those who would seek to work evil (black magic) are shunned by mainstream practitioners.

There are eight principle celebrations, called Sabbats. They are:

• Imbolg on February 2

• Spring Equinox, March 21

• Bealtaine, April 30

• Midsummer, June 22

• Lughnasadh, July 31

• Autumn Equinox, September 21

• Samhain, October 31

• Yule, December 22

There are many other rituals as well, including rituals for birth, marriage, and death. Rituals involve the creation of a sacred space by casting a circle and performing the ritual within the circle. The ritual may take place anywhere. Food and drink are typically shared during the ritual. Practitioners use thirteen different "tools" in carrying out a ritual. The four most common tools are the wand, the cup, the pentacle, and the dagger, representing fire, water, earth, and air. These four tools also correspond to the will, emotions, body, and intellect of a human being. The one who casts the circle represents a fifth element, that of the spirit.

Neo-paganism is not—and does not want to be—organized with a central organization. The highest level of organization is the **coven** which is a local group. Witches may also be independent. Practitioners may be either male or female, although there are more female witches than male.

Both witchcraft and Satanism are part of the **occult**. *Occult* means "hidden." Thus, information about these beliefs and practices is difficult to obtain, since such information is considered reserved for a few. It would be a mistake, however, to associate these two groups any more than this. Practitioners of witchcraft claim they have nothing to do with Satanism and wish to maintain that distance. Unfortunately, practitioners of Satanism do not push that distinction as forcefully.

coven
a local group of witches

occult
hidden beliefs and practices associated with neo-paganism and Satanism

Satanism

Satanism

the worship of Satan
and the doing of evil

Satanism is the exact antithesis of everything we have studied so far. All religious systems we have presented in this text worship God in some positive sense and seek to do good. Satanism is the worship of Satan and the doing of evil. It pursues self-indulgence to the ultimate degree. Its central creed might be stated as: "Do what you will."

Traces of Satanism and Satanic activity can be found dating back to the Middle Ages. The Satanic movement of the twentieth century is attributed to Aleister Crowley, an acknowledged murderer and criminal in Britain, who lived in the early part of the twentieth century and wrote *The Book of the Law*. His philosophy is expressed later in the century through the writing and ideas of Anton LaVey, a one-time animal trainer and carnival organist. LaVey wrote *The Satanic Bible*, *The Satanic Rituals*, and *The Compleat Witch*, in which he espouses his philosophy.

LaVey founded the Church of Satan in San Francisco on Walpurgis-nacht, April 30, 1966. He shaved his head, put on a black robe, pronounced himself the *Black Pope*, and proclaimed 1966 as year one of the Satanic Age. Since that time, other churches of Satan have been founded, including the Temple of Set, Universal Church of Man, Thee Satanic Orthodox Church of Nethilum Rite, Thee Satanic Church and many others. The philosophies of these churches differ somewhat from one another. We will focus on the teachings of Anton LaVey.

In *The Satanic Bible*, LaVey presents nine Satanic statements. For example, No. 1 is: *Satan represents indulgence, instead of abstinence!* No. 4: *Satan represents kindness to those who deserve it, instead of love wasted on ingrates!* No. 5: *Satan represents vengeance, instead of turning the other cheek!* LaVey's philosophy promotes self-assertion, anti-establishmentarianism, and the gratification of one's physical and mental nature. Sex is considered natural and is encouraged as the biological instinct second only to self-preservation. Satan represents the source of all these values. There are three main categories of rituals:

- Sexual rituals to fulfill a desire

- Compassionate rituals to help another person

- Destructive rituals to annoy, anger, or display hatred

The Nine Satanic Statements

1. Satan represents indulgence, instead of abstinence!

2. Satan represents vital existence, instead of spiritual pipe dreams!

3. Satan represents undefiled wisdom, instead of hypocritical self-deceit.

4. Satan represents kindness to those who deserve it, instead of love wasted on ingrates!

5. Satan represents vengeance, instead of turning the other cheek!

6. Satan represents responsibility to the responsible, instead of concern for psychic vampires!

7. Satan represents man as just another animal, sometimes better, more often worse than those that walk on all fours, who, because of his "divine spiritual and intellectual development," has become the most vicious animal of all!

8. Satan represents all of the so-called sins, as they all lead to physical, mental, or emotional gratification!

9. Satan has been the best friend the church has ever had, as he has kept it in business all these years!

Let's Talk about It . . .

1. How do these statements compare (contrast) with your religious beliefs?

2. What type of lifestyle do you think flows from these statements?

Other rituals include *Shibboleth* which seeks to reduce fears by confronting them and *Das Tierdrama* which seeks to increase human sensory perception. The church celebrates three main holidays:

- The individual's birthday

- Walpurgisnacht (April 30)

- Halloween (October 31)

LaVey is preaching a realist philosophy; thus drugs are discouraged and are considered contrary to this view. The Church of Satan is opposed to all illegal acts which are contrary to laws established for the common good. Violence is expressly forbidden. Anyone violating church, state, or federal laws may be excommunicated. (Note there is a difference between performing a ritual to "display" hatred and actually doing an evil deed. Also, recall we are speaking here of LaVey's philosophy; this does not apply to all practitioners of Satanism.)

In the early 1970s, the church was organized into local chapters called *grottoes* which could be found in major cities of the United States. In the mid 1970s, this approach was abandoned, and the Church of Satan was reorganized as a secret society. It is estimated that in the 1970s there was a membership of about five thousand people. Membership numbers today are unknown.

It is important to note that Satanism exists on a wide spectrum. A very small percentage of people practice Satanism as a legitimate religion protected by law. But there are many, many other people involved in what they claim is "Satanism," and who are involved in all sorts of self-destructive and criminal activity. These people range from teenagers who read *The Satanic Bible* and dabble with Satanic rituals to adults who lure youth into groups for abusive activity to a large criminal element who use Satanic beliefs and practice. This is not Satanism as a religion.

During the 1980s, the United States and Canada experienced a "Satanic scare." All sorts of allegations were made about and against Satanists. It was postulated that there are all sorts of levels within Satanism and that it is a vast, secret, international organization. Satanists were accused of child abuse, ritualistic sacrifice, dismemberment, and cannibalism. Accusations were made that there is a connection between criminal Satanic activity and legitimately established churches of Satan and even major corporations. However, there is no empirical evidence to substantiate these claims. The extent of Satanism is largely unknown.

Nevertheless, lack of knowledge about Satanic activity in our world does not mean there is no danger. There are plenty of groups and unsavory individuals who will use Satanism, or any other means to manipulate, trap, endanger, and abuse other people, especially youth. For example, if a young person is lured into a group, they may be videotaped in sexual or criminal activity and then bribed to stay in the group. Thus the young person is trapped and finds it increasingly difficult to escape. Indeed, it is difficult to understand how the philosophy of Satanism could help one be successful in the third millennium.

Cults

The existence and dangers of cults came to public awareness in 1978 with the mass suicide of over 900 people who were members of the People's Temple in Jonestown, Guyana. Cults came under intense scrutiny again in March of 1997 when thirty-nine members of a small cult, Heaven's Gate, committed suicide in San Diego. Under the leadership of Marshall Herff Applewhite, who called himself *Do*, the group believed they were called to a higher level of existence and that the Hale-Bopp comet was a marker indicating the arrival of a space craft from the Level Above Human. They believed the time had come for group members to shed their "earthly containers."

In chapter one, a **cult** was defined as an organization characterized by mind control, charismatic leadership, deception, exclusivity, alienation, exploitation, and a totalitarian worldview. Not all cults are necessarily religious; other types of cults include political, psychological, or health cults. We are speaking here of destructive religious cults. Most cults claim some sort of religious affiliation; cults are considered destructive if they are somehow manipulative of members.

Who is vulnerable to cult recruitment techniques? Ultimately, anyone. If you think "it would never happen to me," then you are a very good candidate for cult recruitment because you are less likely to be cautious about protecting yourself.

People who join or are susceptible to cults include:

- Young people in a transition stage, especially those who move away from home, often living at college or in a totally new environment. They may become homesick and lonely, experience difficulties or a sudden change of plans, become disappointed or depressed. They are susceptible to a cult recruiter who gives companionship and promises to meet their specific need.

cult

an organization characterized by mind control, charismatic leadership, deception, exclusivity, alienation, exploitation, and a totali tarian worl dview

- Adults in transition stages, especially following times of loss resulting from such events as divorce, financial problems, and loss of a job. Elderly people may have financial resources but experience loneliness because of the loss of friends and family through death or infirmity.

- Independent people looking for ways to strike out on their own, do something different, rebel against family or traditional patterns.

- Highly idealistic people seeking transformation of the world to something better, an idealistic world, a utopia.

- Insecure people needing security, companionship, a family atmosphere.

- People disillusioned with their own religious upbringing or uneducated about the teachings of the world's religions.

Whatever one's situation, a cult recruiter will have the answer to what you are looking for. Often, involvement with a cult begins with a seemingly innocent invitation to a dinner or weekend get-away. Sometimes one is invited to a talk related to one's business or a special interest. The group's real identity is never clear. For example, it may sound like a group interested in serving humanity and making the world a better place in some way. The cult recruiter will be very warm and friendly, and he or she will seem extremely interested in the new recruit. The recruiter quickly learns the person's name and needs and begins to respond to those needs immediately.

Cults can present an inviting face to the unaware.

In the group, mind control techniques take over immediately. Included among these techniques are the following:

- Group pressure and "love-bombing," which discourages doubts and reinforces the need to belong through the use of child-like games, singing, hugging, touching, or flattery.

- Separation from other new recruits; this inhibits the individual's ability to question and verify new information. This separation may be accomplished through meditation, chant, and repetitious activity.

- Fear and guilt induced by eliciting confessions to produce intimacy and reveal fears and secrets. This process creates emotional vulnerability by implied or real threats.

- Sleep deprivation, which results from spiritual activities, necessary training, or urgent projects. This prevents giving the mind rest— and an opportunity to think.

- Inadequate nutrition sometimes disguised as a special diet to improve health or advance spirituality.

- Providing a mass of information in a very short period of time, not allowing the person time to process it. The information may appear to be very logical, but there are huge gaps in the logic. It is presented so rapidly that the new recruit cannot process it and thus concludes he or she simply doesn't understand it.

Listed here are the effects of cults upon members:

- Reduction of self-esteem. Members begin to see their lives as unimportant, to think that what they have learned so far in life is inadequate, and to believe that the group leaders have most, if not all, of the answers.

- Social control over the members. Members are required to attend long seminars, perform many mental exercises, and/or live in a controlled environment. (Note: cults are not necessarily composed of people who live together. Members may live in their own homes, but the group may still exert great control over their lives.)

- Members begin to think that their previous actions were unimportant or meaningless.

- The group induces new ways of acting. There may be a reward and punishment system for behavior.

- Loss of ability to form friendships outside of the group.

Some ways to protect yourself against the tactics of cults are:

- Be educated. Being aware of cults, their recruitment techniques and dangers, is the first line of defense

- Seek information. Ask questions. A person presenting a new idea ought to be able by which you can defend it logically and give you resources outside of the group by which you can check out his or her claims. You have the right to validate information through your own resources that you trust.

- When you are at those transition and vulnerable times in life, get in touch with people from your past. Connect with family, former teachers, and old friends. Share your problems with someone from the past, someone you trust.
- Realize that anyone, even you, is vulnerable.

Cults are generally deceptive about who they are, their intentions, and their techniques. Some, but not all, are elaborate money-making schemes that benefit a select few leaders. But it would be a mistake to think of cults as groups which are exclusively money making or into promiscuous sexual activity or drugs. Many are not. On the contrary, their responses to the ultimate questions of life often appear to be highly idealistic. They may expect a high moral standard from their members and seek the transformation and perfection of society. Unfortunately, in the process, they manipulate and undermine human dignity and freedom. Their goals remain, in the end, out of touch with reality.

New Age

New Age is an umbrella term embracing many late twentieth-century groups that espouse some type of transformative experience. Its major tenets are deeply rooted in western philosophy and are mixed with ideas from eastern thought. This mix was made possible especially after the United States rescinded the Asian Exclusion Act in 1965. While these groups do not have any sort of central organization, they do share some fundamental perspectives.

New Age
umbrella term embracing many late twentieth-century groups that espouse some type of transformative experience

The branch of philosophy called *metaphysics* is the background to New Age ideas. Metaphysics is the branch of philosophy that studies the nature of reality. Various nineteenth- and twentieth-century movements in this philosophical tradition contributed to the emergence of the New Age movement in the late twentieth century.

These include Swedenborgianism, a metaphysical tradition stemming from the ideas of Emanuel Swedenborg. Swedenborg was a leading Swedish scientist who abandoned science in his later life and followed religious pursuits. His most important idea is that this world is only a shadow of the real world. He proposed that there is a correspondence between this world and the spiritual world. Mesmerism stems from the work of Franz Anton Mesmer, a physician from Vienna who proposed that there is an underlying energy in the universe—"universal magnetic fluid." A third major component underlying the New Age movement is Transcendentalism, especially as it was developed by American philosopher and essayist Ralph Waldo Emerson. Transcendentalism emphasizes the transcendent (or divine) as ultimate reality. Emerson was the first to combine eastern ideas with this tradition.

Spiritualism, Christian Science, and New Thought were movements which tried to apply these metaphysical ideas. Spiritualism sought communication with the dead (the spirit world). Christian Science and New Thought tried to get in touch with the latent energy of the universe in order to achieve individual and social healing.

Theosophy, which emerged in the late nineteenth century, built on these ideas and proposed an overall vision of the structure of the universe. Part of this vision was that there are masters, or a "ruling spiritual elite," who control the universe. These masters continually call humanity to a higher level of living and, from time to time, send a leader to show human beings how to live. This led to the expectation of the arrival of a world teacher. The final two additions to this metaphysical tradition are the work of parapsychology and ideas from eastern religions.

As stated earlier, a fundamental goal of New Age practitioners is transformation; this means transformation of the individual and of society. Individuals see themselves as moving from an old, unsatisfactory, purposeless life to one filled with new energy, excitement, revitalized health, and new meaning. New Age practices are intended to facilitate this transformation. New Age practitioners also seek the transformation of society so there will be peace, harmony, an unpolluted environment, and strong economies. Some would say that this new age is already emerging.

Central beliefs of New Age people include the following:

- There will be one universal religion expressed in many different forms, but with the same basic faith.

- Transformation of individuals and of society is essential. Since transformation is so central to the New Age movement, reincarnation and karma become core beliefs. Transformation is facilitated through one's actions (karma) and the possibility of reincarnation.

- There is an underlying power, force, or energy which fuels transformation.

- "God" is a higher level of consciousness or awareness. It may be a principle which unifies all of the universe. Some New Agers are pantheists, believing that God and the universe are one and the same reality. One may also say that according to some New Agers, a person can become his or her own god.

- The great religious teachers of history have been teachers of many of these ideas. New Agers seek out gurus to teach New Age concepts and practices.

- There is need for a new world teacher who will usher in the New Age.

Practices of New Agers include meditation and other disciplines that facilitate transformation. Rebirthing, channeling, wearing a crystal, or participating in an intensive seminar are tools used for transformation. Most important among these is an alliance between the New Age and the holistic health movement. Transformation implies healing—healing of the body, mind, spirit, and relationships. The holistic health movement offers new and non-traditional ways to achieve healing, including special diets, psychological therapies, massage, and exercise. For most practitioners, these methods enable nature, the real healer as they see it, to assist the person being healed.

The merits of New Age beliefs and practices are questioned by many people. For example, emphasis on the spirit world as that which is really real can lead to a denial of earthly reality. Some New Age practices, especially healing methods, may be novel and interesting, but their healing value over the long term may not endure. This can lead, for example, to the rejection of surgery and medical drugs.

While certain aspects of the New Age movement may be questionable in value, much of the New Age is harmless. Other the other hand, some methods can be truly harmful, especially those that manipulate, control, and distort reality. The New Age movement largely exists and is supported through publishing enterprises which keep New Age beliefs and practices alive. As a new millennium settles in, New Age ideas may decline, but these ideas may transform into a new movement for the third millennium.

—The above information on the New Age is largely adapted from "Introductory Essay: An Overview of the New Age Movement," New Age Encyclopedia *(J. Gordon Melton, Gale Research Inc., 1990).*

The Great Invocation

This New Age prayer calls for the coming of a new avatār, a new world teacher.

From the point of Light within the Mind of God

Let light stream forth into the mind of men.

Let light descend on Earth.

From the point of Love within the Heart of God

Let Love stream forth into the hearts of men.

May Christ return to Earth.

From the center where the will of God is known

Let purpose guide the little wills of men.

The purpose which the Masters know and serve.

From the center which we call the race of man

Let the plan of Love and Light work out.

And may it seal the door where evil dwell.

Let Light and Love and Power restore the Plan to Earth.

Internet

Yes, the Internet. The arrival of the Internet facilitated communication about religion among millions of people. It now provides a forum for obscure or long-forgotten religions to express their ideas and be revitalized. Traditional religions can create their own Web page and provide their beliefs to an entirely new and larger audience. Non-traditional religions also have access to a larger audience and can more easily transmit their worldview. Persons on a spiritual quest have resources at their fingertips. Practitioners of all religions can more easily communicate with one another. Witches, for example, can work rituals together in cyberspace. The Internet is an entirely new means of communicating religious belief and may very well facilitate the emergence of new religious movements.

The Internet provides you, as a student of religion, with an incredible resource for information and contact with the world's religions and their practitioners. As with all resources, the information needs to be evaluated for its credibility. Anyone can put a page on the Internet and express an opinion. You need to consider the source and compare the information with other resources. Seek information from legitimately established authorities in the religion. Unfortunately, the Internet can also be a tool for unscrupulous individuals to trap, manipulate, and even control other individuals. Use the Internet for the information it provides, but be cautious.

A New Millennium

What a marvelous privilege it is to be alive at the turn of a millennium. In reality, it is just a change of numbers on the calendar, but that change carries with it a sense that something old is passing away and something new is about to happen. Just as a new year is often a time to say good-bye to the old and make new resolutions for the future, so the beginning years of a new millennium prompt us to reflect upon the past and move into the future with new goals, new hope, and a new vision. Your adult life will be lived in this new millennium. What will you make of this opportunity? How will you find your way?

The underlying thesis of this book is that a person's worldview is the principle means by which a person lives out his or her life. It is the lens through which an individual looks for answers to ultimate questions about human existence. These questions include one's ideas about and relationship with God, with other people, with the universe, and one's ideas about the purpose and meaning of life. A well-formed, well-grounded worldview will enable a person to successfully deal with the challenges of life and attain happiness and fulfillment. Religion is the institution in society which is the main carrier of these responses to the ultimate questions of life. From religion, we can learn perspectives that help us in the formation of our own worldview.

We hope that this journey through the *Religions in North America* has been a helpful enterprise for you. As you ponder your own views about life, we offer some final suggestions for living in the third millennium.

- **Begin with "home base."** Begin with your own religious tradition. Learn about its history, its beliefs, its values, its perspective on life. How does your study of other religions affirm, reinforce, and deepen your appreciation of your own religion? How can the ideas of other religions strengthen those same concepts already present in your own belief system?

- **Avoid syncretism.** Forming a worldview perspective is not simply an eclectic gathering of various ideas which sound good. A healthy worldview is grounded in solid principles and is integrated.

- **Be aware that this transition time of the new millennium generates many new ideas and practices.** Some of these ideas will be quite bizarre, manipulative, and dangerous. Some people may even be fearful and panic stricken. Keep things in perspective. While a new millennium is a significant moment in history, it is also likely not to bring cataclysmic events.

- **Ask questions. Be observant.** If an overly friendly person introduces you to an incredibly loving community with a leader who seems to have all answers to life's questions, and the group offers you an opportunity which goes beyond your wildest dreams, and the whole thing seems too good to be true, be careful. Be aware that there are very sophisticated methods used to trap people. Don't be trapped.

- **Check religious claims with reality.** Does this make sense? Does this seem possible? What do other people say? Will this really help you in your life? A healthy religious perspective should not distort reality. It should affirm reality and make life better. Further, a healthy religious perspective should never manipulate, control, or be a burden. It should not undermine human dignity or violate a person's conscience. It should be life-enhancing.

- **Finally, seek wisdom.** Huston Smith, a man who has spent his life studying the world's religions, has said, "If we take the world's enduring religions at their best, we discover the distilled wisdom of the human race." We need to realize that many millennia have preceded this one. Human beings have wrestled with the ultimate questions of life for a long time. A wise person will not ignore this treasury of experience and wisdom.

Discovering

1. Be able to explain each of the vocabulary words.

2. Name and state the central beliefs of each of the new religious movements at the end of the twentieth century.

3. Who is vulnerable to the tactics of cult recruiters? Explain the instances in life when a person is most vulnerable.

4. Describe the techniques used by cult recruiters to lure people into cults.

5. What are the effects of cults upon people?

6. How can you protect yourself against cults?

Exploring

1. Talk with someone who has experience with cults—either a former member or someone who has a family member in a cult. How does their experience compare with the information in this chapter?

2. Research the recent activities of cults. Find three articles about cults and report to the class on these articles.

3. In a small group, evaluate the claims of each of the movements discussed in this chapter. Do the claims seem plausible? Do you agree or disagree with the claims?

Integrating

As directed by your teacher, develop your own worldview perspective.

Words to Know

coven

cult

neo-paganism

occult

New Age

Satanism

Wicca

witchcraft, the Craft

Glossary

Act of Supremacy—declaration initiated by Henry VIII that the king of England was the supreme head on earth of the Church of England

Adventist—those churches who believe that the second coming of Christ is imminent

Allāh—Islamic name for the one God

Anabaptist tradition—movement of sixteenth-century reformers who believed in the baptism of believers and that infants should not be baptized

Anglican Communion—the worldwide fellowship of independent churches that stem from the Church of England

anointing of the sick—the Catholic sacrament that celebrates God's healing presence when a person is ill or dying

anti-semitism—hostility toward or discrimination against Jews as a racial or ethnic group or as a religion

apocalyptic—a kind of writing which uses many symbols and images to talk about the endtime, and often a present or coming event

Apocrypha—fifteen books or parts of the Old Testament considered canonical by some Christian groups and noncanonical by others

apostle—one of twelve members of Jesus' inner circle of followers

ark—the cabinet where the Torah scrolls are kept

Assemblies of God—full-gospel and Bible-based Pentecostal churches

ātman—Hindu understanding of the human person; the true self, the core of the person

atmospheric spirits—personified forces of nature

Augsburg Confession—the Lutheran formal profession of belief, doctrine, and practices formulated by Philip Melancthon, Luther's associate and theologian

avatār—in Hinduism, a manifestation of the divine; the earthly form or appearance of a diety

Avignon Papacy—the period of time, 1305–1377, when seven popes lived in Avignon in France rather than in Rome

Báb—a young Persian man, Siyyid [Mirza] 'Ali Muhammad, the originator of the Bahá'í faith

Bábí's—followers of the Báb of the Bahá'í faith

Bahá'í—follower of Bahá (glory) or follower of Bahá'ulláh (glory of God)

ban—excommunication from a Mennonite group

baptism—the rite or ceremony by which people enter into the Christian faith

baptism of believers—within the Anabaptist tradition, the baptism of adults

baptism of the Holy Spirit—Pentecostal understanding of the special gift of the Spirit with resulting speaking in tongues, interpretation of tongues, and healing

Baptists—members of non-creedal, free (members are not under the authority of a church) churches who practice baptism of adults

bar-mitzvah—initiation of thirteen-year-old Jewish boy into the community

bat-mitzvah—initiation of twelve-year-old Jewish girl into the community

Beatitudes—a list of attitudes and actions that Jesus taught as good; part of Jesus' Sermon on the Mount (Matthew 5, see also Luke 6) which serve as guidelines for Christian living; a kind of "prescription for happiness"

beliefs—those central concepts which a religion holds to be most important

bhakti yoga—a yoga discipline in Hinduism that emphasizes love and a relationship with the Ultimate Reality through prayer, ritual, and worship

Book of Common Prayer—the Church of England's collection of its church rituals

Book of Concord—the basic collection of Lutheran doctrinal writings and the definitive statement of Lutheran orthodoxy

Brahmā—the creator, the "grandfather" of Hindu gods; the dispenser of knowledge and wisdom

Buddha—one who has reached enlightenment

Buddhism—the way of life based on the teachings of Siddhartha Gautama; the Middle Path

Calvin, John—Second Father of the Reformation; systematic writer of Protestant theology and a major influence on the Reformed tradition

candidate— in the Catholic Church, a baptized person seeking membership in the church

canonization—the act by which an individual is named a saint in the Catholic Church

caste system—a series of social classes which have developed in Hindu India

catechumen—in the Catholic Church, an unbaptized person seeking membership in the church

catholic—universal, total, whole; sent on a mission to the entire human race

Catholicism—the branch of Christianity which acknowledges the leadership of the pope in Rome (Roman Catholicism)

charismatics—members of many Christian churches who accept Pentecostal beliefs and practices

chosen people—the Jewish people with a sense of a special mission in history: to bring God's word to the entire world

Christ of Faith— Christians' affirmations about Jesus as the Son of God become human and as the messiah, and his effect on their lives

Christian Science—the religious tradition which believes in healing people by spiritual means and in working for universal salvation from evil, including sin and death

Christianity—the religion founded on belief in Jesus, many denominations of which exist today

Christmas—the Christian feast celebrating the incarnation of the Son of God, the birth of Jesus; celebrated on December 25

Church of Jesus Christ of Latter-day Saints—the uniquely American church founded by Joseph Smith which claims to be the restoration of the original church of Jesus Christ; sometimes called the Morman Church

Church of the Nazarene—a holiness church with some Pentecostal roots and strong moral guides

circuit riders—traveling Methodist preachers who carried the tenets of the religion through many parts of the developing United States

Communion—the sharing of bread and juice or wine as part of a Christian church service, commemorating or reenacting Jesus' last supper with his friends before he died; Communion in some churches is also called the Lord's Supper and, in some churches, the Eucharist

confirmation—the second sacrament of initiation, believed to confer the fullness of the gifts of the Spirit; called *chrismation* in the Eastern Catholic churches; in some Protestestant denominations, a rite of mature affirmation of the faith rather than a sacrament

Congregationalist—Reformed tradition denomination(s) in which each congregation is self-governed

Conservative Judaism—a term used in the United States for Jewish worship that modifies the Law to meet modern needs while avoiding the more drastic changes of the Reform movement

consistory—part of the presbyteral form of government in the Reformed tradition, unique to each local church and made up of ministers, elders, and deacons

coven—a local group of witches

covenant—a sacred agreement, contract, testament between two parties

creed—a statement of a community's essential beliefs; most Christian churches have creeds, while some are non-creedal

cult—an organization characterized by mind control, charismatic leadership, deception, exclusivity, alienation, exploitation, and a totalitarian worldview

Dance Drum—drum used in the Drum religion; considered a living being

Decalogue—"ten words"; the Ten Commandments

denomination—a subset of a religion, a group within a larger religious branch

Diaspora or Dispersion—collective term for the dispersal of Jews to areas outside of Israel and for those Jews living outside of Israel

diocese—a jurisdictional division or geographical area of parishes or congregations, headed by a bishop

Divine Liturgy—the principal liturgical action of Eastern Orthodox Christians; an elaborate ceremony which engages all the human senses

doctrine—basic religious beliefs

Dordrecht Confession of Faith—a 1632 document systematizing beliefs of Mennonites

earth spirits—spirits who perpetuate animal life or inhabit natural places or inanimate objects

Easter—the Christian celebration of Jesus' resurrection from the dead; scheduled according to the lunar calendar in the spring

Eastern Catholic church—church originating in a national church in the East and in union with the Catholic Church centered in Rome

ecumenical—pertaining to openness among religions, especially strong among Christians in the latter half of the twentieth century

ecumenical council—a worldwide gathering of church leaders; since the Reformation, Catholic bishops in union with the pope have held their own councils, with other religions limited to observers

Edict of Milan—the decree of Constantine in 313 granting religious freedom in the Roman Empire

Eightfold Path—Siddhartha Gautama's path that leads to the cessation of suffering

encyclical—a letter from the pope addressing issues of major importance

English Baptists—seventeenth-century forerunners of the Baptist tradition in the United States

English Reformation—the Reformation in England, based on jurisdiction rather than theology

English tradition—the reformed Christian Church in England, dating from the time of Henry VIII and his ruling children

entire sanctification—for Holiness Christians, the point when the Holy Spirit erases any trace of sin from the person's life and fills the person with love

Episcopal Church of America—the Anglican Communion Church in the United States

ethics—how one should act; in a religion, determined by the response to fundamental questions dealing with the mysteries of life

Evangelical movement—the successor to the First Great Awakening, "gospel believers" who stressed faithfulness to the gospel—the message preached by Jesus

evangelicals—"believers in the gospel," self-description of early Protestant churches

excommunicate—formally exclude a person from a church community or organization

Exile—the seventy years during which Jewish leaders were sent to and remained in Babylon, following the conquest of Judah in 587 B.C.E.

Exodus—the escape of the Hebrews from Egypt, from slavery to freedom, under the leadership of Moses; the second book of the Torah or Pentateuch

filioque—a Latin word meaning "and the Son," added to the Nicene Creed in western Christianity and one reason for the controversy between Christianity in the East and in the West

five pillars of Islam—the five most important obligations or practices of Islam

Formative Period—the time of development, characterized by agriculture, domestication of animals, construction of houses and villages, production of pottery and woven baskets, and greater formulation of religious beliefs and practices

Four Noble Truths—Siddhartha Gautama's foundational concepts on suffering, desire, and the path to nirvana

Gemara—comments and rulings about the Mishnah which were collected and recorded

general atonement—General Baptist belief that salvation is possible for all people, not just for a select group

ghetto—a section of a city where Jews (or another minority group) were required to live

Ghost Dance—a Native American dance that lasted several days; performed to end the power of the whites and provide a period of prosperity

glossolalia—speaking in tongues; believed to be "initial, physical evidence" of baptism in the Spirit

god-consciousness—in Hinduism, a constant awareness of God's presence

godparent(s)—one person or two people chosen by an infant's parents to be witness(es) at the child's baptism and to assist them in raising the child in Christianity

grace—according to the Methodist tradition and many other Christian Churches, the undeserved, unmerited, and loving action of God in human existence through the ever-present Holy Spirit

Great Schism—the split of Christianity between the eastern and western branches

Great Spirit—Great Mystery, the supreme being

guardian spirits—typically animal spirits (or spirits disguised as animals) partial to a group or an individual

guru—teacher, guide

gurupurab—a Sikh celebration honoring the birth, death, guruship, or martyrdom of one of the great Sikh gurus

guruwara—Sikh house of worship

Ḥadīth—a collection of the teachings, sayings, and actions of the Prophet Muhammad

Ḥajj—the pilgrimage to Mecca which is to be performed once during life by every Muslim

Hanukkah—the feast commemorating the victory of the Maccabees over the oppressors of the Jewish people

Hasidic Judaism—devout form of Judaism with a strong mystical element

hero figure—cultural figure which unleashes creative energies, or forces, which improve people's lives; sometimes a trickster

hierarchical—having varying levels of authority united under a central authority

Hijra—the night flight by Muhammad and his followers on June 20, 622; the beginning of the Muslim calendar

Hinduism—an eastern worldview expressed in several religious traditions

Holiness movement—inward-looking Evangelicalism which emphasizes and cultivates personal holiness; the origin of Pentecostalism

Holocaust—the name given by Jews to the attempt by Nazi Germany under Hitler to exterminate the entire Jewish race; six million Jews were killed

holy orders—the sacrament that authorizes a man to work in the Catholic Church as a bishop, priest, or deacon

icon—a two-dimensional image of a saint or event in the life of Christ or Mary painted on wood in an ancient stylized way

iconostasis—a wooden screen on which are painted images of Jesus, Mary, John the Baptist, the saints, and the patron saint of the church, found in Eastern Orthodox churches

imām—Islamic leader able to interpret the Qur'ān infallibly; for Shī'is, a descendent of 'Alī and Fatima

incarnation—the divine "takes on flesh," the divine becomes human; in Christianity, the second person of the Trinity became human in the person of Jesus of Nazareth

indulgence—the remission by the church of the temporal punishment due to sin, forgiven by virtue of the merits of Jesus, Mary, and the saints

inerrancy—the belief that the Bible is free of error

infallibility—quality of a teaching by the pope and/or the bishops in union with him that is a matter of faith and morals and is declared free from error

ISKCON—International Society for Krishna Consciousness, founded in the U.S. in 1966

Islam—the religion preached by Muhammad; based on submission to God which leads to peace with God, people, and the environment

Jehovah's Witnesses—an Adventist group that believes the world is at present in transition between human rule and the reign of Christ

Jesus—the man born in Bethlehem about 6 to 4 B.C.E. who Christians believe is the Son of God become human and the messiah

Jesus of History—the historical person, Jesus of Nazareth

jnāna yoga—a yoga discipline in Hinduism that emphasizes intellectual reflection

justification—the first blessing, or work of grace; accepting Jesus as one's personal savior; being born again.

justification by faith—the principle espoused by St. Paul and Martin Luther that we are saved (justified) by God's free grace and our faith, rather than being saved by what we do to "earn" God's approval

Ka'ba—Arabian house of God, traditionally thought to have been built by Abraham and his son Ishmael; holy shrine of Islam

kachina—ancestral spirit mask; masked impersonator; "messenger of the gods"

karma—action or ritual work, with a "cause and effect" connotation

karma yoga— a yoga discipline in Hinduism that emphasizes work, which is done out of love for the Ultimate Reality

kiva—ceremonial structure

Knox, John—follower of Calvin and founder of Presbyterianism in Scotland

kosher—"proper" or "pure"; in Judaism, refers to the proper observance of stipulations regarding food

lector—reader of scripture at a religious service

limited atonement—the Calvinist belief that Jesus died only for the elect

Luther, Martin—the reformer who was the first strong guiding force behind the Reformation and the establisher of the Lutheran Church, the reformed Christian Church, especially in Germany and the Netherlands

Lutheran tradition—the first phase of the Reformation, flowing from the teaching of Martin Luther

Lutheranism—the way of thinking that subscribes to and follows Martin Luther's interpretation and reform of Christianity

Mahayana Buddhism—the larger branch of Buddhism, open to non-monks seeking enlightenment

mantra—a sound that appears as colored light in certain states of meditation, repeated in an attempt to awaken latent brain cells

mass—the eucharistic service in the Catholic Church

matrimony—for Catholics, the sacrament that celebrates the lifelong commitment of a man and woman in marriage

māyā—in Hinduism, cosmic illusion

medicine bundle—bundle with articles associated with the supernatural power received from a guardian spirit

medicine people—shamans, visionaries, spiritual guides, and physical healers

melachah—work of creative nature, work that controls one's environment

Mennonite—the Anabaptist denomination begun by Menno Simons in Holland in the sixteenth century

messiah—a person who brings about a national triumph over enemies and resulting importance of the nation in world affairs, or a spiritual renewal of the Jewish people (a messianic age of a new moral order)

Methodist Church—Protestant denomination which grew out of the methodical Bible-based discipline developed by John Wesley

Middle Path—Siddhartha Gautama's method of balance between excessive sensual pleasures and the severe asceticism of Hinduism

migratory hunters—Native American hunters in the period before European contact who pursued big game such as big-horn bison and woolly mammoths

millennialism—apocalypticism; the belief that Christ will soon bring this evil world to an end and replace it with a new order of happiness and goodness—a thousand-year reign (millennium) of Christ

Mishnah—the oral Torah of a legal nature, which was gathered together and written down

mitzvot—Hebrew word meaning "commandments"

moksha—in Hinduism, the release of the soul body from saṃsāra (reincarnation); for Sikhs, release from suffering—birth, death, rebirth

monotheism—belief in one God; religion based on that belief

mosque—place of worship for Muslims

mound builders—Native Americans who built huge burial and temple mounds, often in the shape of animals

Muhammad—founder and prophet of Islam

Muslims—followers of Islam

myth—a traditional story which unfolds a part of a people's worldview; a story with layers of meaning

nationalism—a sense of national consciousness over and above other nations and supranational groups; the division of the Holy Roman Empire into independent nations

Native American culture areas—divisions of Native Americans, primarily based on geography

nature—for Native Americans, a visible extension of the spirit world

neo-paganism, witchcraft, Wicca, the Craft—various strands of folk and occult practices and nature religions; modern form of paganism rooted in pre-Christian European religions

New Age—umbrella term embracing many late twentieth-century groups that espouse some type of transformative experience

New Testament—the Christian Scriptures; accounts of Jesus' life and teachings and the beginning of the Christian Church, letters from early Church leaders, and an apocalyptic book

Ninety-five Theses—Martin Luther's list of items for discussion regarding beliefs and practices of the Catholic Church

nirvana—release from suffering; ultimate happiness, the state of enlightenment

novena—a Catholic devotional prayer said for nine days; the prayer usually asks for the intercession of Mary or one of the saints

occult—hidden beliefs and practices associated with neo-paganism and Satanism

Old Testament—the name given to the Hebrew Bible by Christians; thirty-nine books sacred to Judaism and accepted by all Christians

oral Torah—the Talmud (the Mishnah and the Gemara); explains the written Torah

ordinance—a rite in Christianity that commemorates a practice of the early Church, for example, the Lord's Supper

original sin—the condition of and tendency toward sinfulness present in humans since the beginning of the human race

Orthodox Judaism—oldest tradition within Judaism; believes that God gave Moses both the written and the oral Torah atop Mount Sinai; keeps strict laws, including dietary laws

parable—a short story that highlights an attitude or principle; used by Jesus in his teaching

parish—local religious congregation, especially Catholic and Anglican

path of renunciation—in Hinduism, liberation, being, awareness, joy

path of desire—in Hinduism, pleasure, worldly success, and the need to fulfill human duty

patriarchs—male ancestors in the faith, the originators or founders of a religion; for Jews, Abraham, Isaac, and Jacob especially

Pentecost—in Judaism, Shavu'ot, also known as "Feast of Weeks"; for Christians, the religious feast recalling the descent of the Holy Spirit upon the followers of Jesus fifty days after Easter

Pentecostalism—Christian expression with a belief that persons who have been born again and sanctified should ask for baptism in the Spirit

Pesah or Passover—the eight-day Jewish festival commemorating the Exodus

peyote—a small, spineless cactus that grows in Texas and Mexico; has a sacramental use among some Native American groups

pogroms—sporadic persecutions of the Jews, especially those in Russia and Poland

polytheism—belief in many gods

pope—in the Catholic Church, the bishop of Rome, who has authority over the entire church

practical divinity—John Wesley's teaching that God wants people to be happy and holy; thus, faith and love must be put into practice

practices—actions and prayers which flow from a religion's beliefs

"Praying Indians"—Native Americans among the Algonquins who were converted to Christianity

predestination—election for service and salvation, as taught by John Calvin; God's predetermination of who will be saved and who will not

Presbyterian—Reformed tradition denomination in which each church is governed by presbyters or elders

presbytery—part of the presbyteral form of government in the Reformed tradition, made up of local consistories; gives advice and facilitates cooperation

Protestantism—the churches that separated from the Catholic Church in the sixteenth century as a result of the Reformation; the beliefs of these churches

Purim—the *Feast of Lots* commemorating deliverance of the Persian Jews by Esther

Puritans—English Protestants in a strict Calvinist model, some of whom immigrated to the thirteen colonies

Quakers, Friends—the Religious Society of Friends, a non-creedal religious group that attempts to live simply and meets for silent prayer

Qur'ān—the holy book of Islam; a record of the words that God gave to the angel Gabriel to deliver to Muhammad

raja yoga—a yoga discipline in Hinduism that emphasizes the practice of meditation which leads the practitioner deeper through each layer of the self

Ramaḍān—the month of fasting for Muslims

real presence—the belief of some Christian churches that the risen Jesus is actually present in the bread and wine of Communion

reconciliation—the Catholic sacrament that celebrates God's forgiveness and reintegrates the sinful person back into the life of the community

Reform movement—Jewish worship that modifies the Law to meet modern conditions

Reformation—the sixteenth-century movement that sought to reform the Catholic Church

Reformed tradition—the non-Lutheran churches that emerged during the Reformation

reincarnation—literally, "to reflesh"; born again and again in progressively higher life forms or higher levels in human life

religion—a major religious group with a belief system and a set of religious practices; includes a collection of specific influences that affects or alters behavior

religious order—a group of men or women who live in community, pray together, and generally share a common work, either within a monastary or among the people; more common in the Catholic Church and Orthodox Churches than in other Christian denominations

Renaissance—rebirth; usually refers to the rebirth of the spirit of the Classical Age during the late fifteenth and early sixteenth centuries

Restoration tradition—the product of the Restoration movement, a nineteenth-century American movement which sought to restore the New Testament basis of the Christian Church

rishis—ancient Indian sages; possessors of knowledge regarded as the "spiritual founders" of Hinduism

Rite of Christian Initiation of Adults—the process that prepares adults for baptism, confirmation, and Eucharist, and membership in the Catholic Church

rites—diverse liturgical traditions within the Catholic Church, for example, the Latin Rite or the Maronite Rite

Roman Curia—the central offices of the Catholic Church at the Vatican in Rome

Rosh Ha-shanah—Jewish new year holy days, the ten "Days of Awe"

sacrament—in some Christian groups, a reality imbued with the hidden presence of God; signifies Jesus' contact with the church and causes an encounter between Jesus and the church

Ṣalāt—the recitation of prayers five times daily required of Muslims

Salvation Army—a holiness Christian church with a military structure, an emphasis on moral living, and no sacraments

samnyāsin—in Hinduism, the final stage of life, beyond the attractions of this world, preparing for the next life

samsāra—in Buddhism, the repeated births and deaths caused by karma

samskāras—sacred life-cycle rites in Hinduism

sanctification—the Methodist doctrine that one can experience a blessing after justification which frees the person from all sinful desires; the second blessing, or work of grace; perfected by the Holy Spirit, thus sanctified

sand painting—a painting made with colored sand, often used in religious ceremonies, especially with healing rites

satori—in Buddhism, the sudden glimpse of enlightenment about life; bodhi

Satanism—the worship of Satan and the doing of evil

Ṣawm—the fasting during Ramaḍān for Muslims

scapegoat—a goat upon whose head was symbolically placed the sins of the people, after which the goat was sent to the wilderness; one who bears the blame for the sins or faults of another

schism—split within a religion over disputed beliefs or practices

Schleitheim Confession—document of 1527 expressing the central ideas of the Anabaptists

scientific prayer—the Christian Science process of turning human thought to the enlightening and saving power of God in order to bring about healing

sect—a group adhering to a distinctive doctrine or to a leader; a small group of people within a given religion who hold beliefs or practices which are considered unconventional

Seventh-day Adventists—a strict Adventist group which worships on Saturday and holds many beliefs similar to Baptists

Shabbat or Sabbath—in Judaism, the weekly celebration from dusk on Friday till darkness on Saturday

Shahāda—the profession of faith to which a Muslim witnesses

Sharī'ah—the sacred law of Islam, which covers every aspect of a community's life

Shavu'ot—the Feast of Weeks or Pentecost; the birthday of the Jewish religion

Shema—the Judaic confession of faith: "Hear, O Israel: The Lord is our God, the Lord alone." (Deuteronomy 6:4)

Shī'is—Muslims of the Shī'i school who believe that the immediate successor to Muhammad should be a member of his family

Shiva—the Hindu god commonly referred to as God the Destroyer

shunning—the practice of deliberately and habitually avoiding a Mennonite member who has seriously veered from the beliefs or practices of the group

Siddhartha Gautama—the Buddha, the enlightened one, the founder of Buddhism

Sikhism—a reform of Hinduism with Islamic elements; the religion of disciples who follow the Ten Gurus

Simchat Torah—the last day of the Sukkot festival which marks the end of the yearly reading of the Torah

sin—in Judaism, "missing the mark"; a failure to live as a responsible, caring member of society

sky beings—the sun (often closely associated with the supreme being), the moon, and the stars

smriti scriptures—in Hinduism, the words of the rishis, written down and remembered; include the Ramayana and Mahabharata, the Laws of Manu, the Puranas, and the Tantras

spirit world—the all-pervading world of the spirits which overlaps with the nonspirit, human world

spiritual beings—several types of non-corporeal beings

sponsor—a person chosen to help guide a candidate or catechumen through the process of the Rite of Christian Initiation of Adults

śruti scriptures—in Hinduism, the words of the Vedas, which the rishis heard

Sufis—Muslims of the Sufi school, who are often mystics

Sukkot—the Feast of Booths or Festival of Tabernacles, which recalls the wilderness travels of the people of Israel in the desert

Sun Dance—chief ceremony of the Plains nations; performed to gain supernatural power to fulfill a vow

Sunna—Muslim holy book, second in authority to the Qur'ān; contains the Ḥadīth

Sunnīs—Muslims of the Sunnī school who reverence the Ḥadīth as a supplement to the Qur'ān; the large group of orthodox or traditional Muslims

sūra—a chapter in the Qur'ān

sweat lodge—a ritual structure for the sweat bath, a purifying religious ceremony

synagogue—an assembly or a building for worship and instruction

syncretism—a collection; in religion, a collection of various beliefs not especially related to each other

synod—group of churches, within Lutheranism especially

Talmud—the Mishnah and Gemara, a commentary on the Jewish scriptures

Tanakh—the written Torah; the whole Hebrew Bible (Jewish scriptures)

ten lost tribes of Israel—the ten tribes of Israel destroyed or assimilated, perhaps through slavery, into Assyria, following 721 B.C.E.

testament—a covenant between God and humankind

testimony—for Quakers, the demonstration of a living truth, a bearing witness to a value

Theravada Buddhism—a conservative interpretation of Buddhism, emphasizing the search for nirvana apart from the world, as a monk

Three Baskets—Buddhism's most sacred books, including the discourses of the Buddha

Torah—the Pentateuch (first five books of the Bible), or scroll of the Pentateuch; the Hebrew Bible; the entire body of Jewish law and teaching

totems—inherited guardian spirits among Native Americans

tradition—for Catholics, the word of God entrusted to the apostles and handed on through their successors; scripture and tradition are seen as a single source of God's revelation

Trinity—the belief held by most Christians that God is one in essence but three in person—Father, Son, and Holy Spirit

ultimate questions—questions which address essential mysteries of life and ethical concerns, for example, "Does God exist?"

Unitarian tradition—a religious group that does not assent to the Trinity

Unitarian Universalist Association—in the U.S., the combination of Unitarian and Universalist churches, which do not hold to a belief in the Trinity and are not exclusively Christian

Unity tradition—a Christian tradition which originated in the late nineteenth century and which believes that people's acts, feelings, thoughts, and words exert power over their lives

vedanta—spiritual truth or spirtual wisdom of Hinduism

Vedas—four collections of religious material containing prayers, rituals, liturgy, hymns, and spells and charms of a popular nature

Vishnu—Hindu preserver god who protects and maintains the universe; for some, the source of life

vision quest—a regimen of fasting and meditation undertaken by Native Americans as preparation for a vision of the guardian spirit; usually takes place in a remote setting

wampum strings—beads strung together, often as a belt, and used as currency or as a means of keeping records or recording treaties

Westminster Confession—the standard of faith for Presbyterians in North America; sets doctrinal and ecclesiastical standards

worldview—from the German, *weltanschauungen*; it is an individual's or group's response to ultimate questions

written Torah—the whole Hebrew Bible (Jewish scriptures)

yarmulke—skullcap worn by Jewish men to show respect for God

yoga—a method of training designed to lead to integration or union; unites aspects of one's being so that one can unite with the divine; allows one to restrain the body and the mind

Yom Hasho'ah—the Holocaust Day of Remembrance

Yom Kippur—the Day of Atonement which concludes the ten days of Rosh Ha-Shanah

Zakāt—the required almsgiving in Islam

Zen Buddhism—a Japanese refinement of Mahayana Buddhism; emphasizes enlightenment

Zionist movement—search for and control of a homeland for the Jewish people, brought to reality in the mid-twentieth century

Zwingli, Ulrich—reformer whose teachings and leadership resulted in a break from the Lutheran tradition in Switzerland and parts of Germany

Index